A Field Guide to American Houses

New York
Alfred A. Knopf
1996

A Field Guide to American Houses

Virginia and Lee McAlester

with drawings
by Lauren Jarrett
and model house drawings
by Juan Rodriguez-Arnaiz

THIS IS A BORZOI BOOK
PUBLISHED BY ALFRED A. KNOPF, INC.

Library of Congress Cataloging in Publication Data
McAlester, Virginia Savage Talkington. [date]
A field guide to American houses.
Bibliography: p.
Includes index.
1. Architecture, Domestic—United States—Guide-books.
2. United States—Description and travel—Guide-books.
I. McAlester, A. Lee (Arcie Lee). [date]. II. Title.
NA7205.M35   1984   917.3 04927   82-48740
ISBN 0-394-51032-1
ISBN 0-394-73969-8 (pbk)
Manufactured in the United States of America

Published June 12, 1984

Reprinted Eleven Times

Thirteenth Printing, June 1996

to   Clement
Martine
Amy
Keven

Contents

How to Use This Book

Each chapter treats one of the major architectural fashions, or *styles*, that have been popular over our country's past. The chapters are arranged chronologically, with the earliest styles first. The opening page of each chapter features a large drawing showing the three or four most important *identifying features* which differentiate that style from others. The most common shapes, or *principal subtypes*, of each style are also pictured on the opening page, along with references to pages of photographs in the chapter that allow the reader to see quickly the common features in a range of examples from each particular style and subtype. Every chapter also includes drawings that show typical smaller details—for example, windows, doors, and roof-wall junctions—that cannot easily be seen in full-house photographs. Text supplementing the drawings and photographs discusses the *identifying features, principal subtypes, variants and details*, and *occurrence* of each style. Concluding *comments* provide a brief introduction to the origin and history of the style.

Confronted with an unfamiliar house to be identified, the reader may approach the problem three different ways. The simplest is to thumb through the many pages of house photographs, looking for examples similar to the unidentified house. Here one should pay particular attention to such large-scale features as roof form (gabled or hipped, low or steeply pitched?) and facade balance (symmetrical or asymmetrical?). When a similar photograph is located, the unknown example should be compared in smaller-scale features of architectural detailing: windows, doors, roof-wall junctions, porches, etc. The additional photographs and drawings provided in each chapter will aid in this process, which can be repeated until a final identification is made.

A second and more systematic approach is to turn to the Pictorial Key and Glossary on page 54. This illustrates a variety of different types of such common architectural features as windows, doors, and roofing materials, with a listing of the styles in which each type commonly occurs. Using the Key, the reader will find that a house with a red tile roof, for example, will most likely be found in either the Spanish Colonial, Mission, Spanish Eclectic, or Italian Renaissance styles. Photographs and drawings for these styles can then be compared with the unknown house as in the first approach.

A final approach is to become familiar with the relatively few historical precedents on which American house styles are based. These are reviewed in the introductory chapter on *Style*. With this background, one can learn to quickly determine if a house is of Modern, Medieval, Renaissance Classical, or Ancient Classical inspiration. With a bit of further practice, it becomes easy to distinguish between the half-dozen or so principal

American styles that have been based on each of these traditions. With this knowledge, style identification can become almost automatic. The book then becomes a useful back-up reference for identifying stylistic subtypes and subtleties.

Preface

This book grew from the authors' efforts to identify the houses found in typical American neighborhoods. Many excellent guides are available to detail the features of our country's monumental dwellings; other works deal with the everyday houses of specific towns and neighborhoods. What was lacking, we discovered, was a guide that related the architectural landmarks to their far more numerous cousins throughout the country—the common houses that make up most of our nation's built environment. Our book attempts to fill this gap by treating the entire spectrum of American domestic building, from the most modest folk houses to the grandest mansions but with a heavy emphasis on the familiar dwellings that lie between these extremes. It is intended not as a scholarly treatise on architectural history, but as a practical field manual for identifying and understanding the changing fashions, forms, and components of American houses. In treating this broad subject we have imposed certain limitations on the coverage. Because it emphasizes field identification, it concerns only the *exterior* appearance of houses. The important subjects of interior planning, design, and detailing are given only the most superficial treatment. The book also concentrates on *styled* houses built before 1940. Unstyled folk houses and post-1940 houses are included, but are treated in considerably less detail. The principal focus is on *single-family houses*, which may be either detached or, like attached urban houses, built with common walls. A few duplexes or triplexes built in the form of single-family buildings have been illustrated, but larger multi-unit dwellings are not included.

The book is organized chiefly by the chronology of changing architectural styles. In one sense these may be considered a merely ephemeral and somewhat superficial series of fashions. More fundamentally, however, they reflect the tastes and sensibilities of our forebears over three centuries of dynamic history. Looking still farther, most have deep roots in European history, whence they draw on Renaissance, Medieval, and Classical models for inspiration. An understanding of these stylistic traditions as they have repeatedly reappeared during our nation's history is, we believe, the most practical framework for identifying and understanding American houses.

A principal difficulty in stylistic analysis involves recognizing underlying similarities in style when buildings differ in size, shape, and degree of formality. Many Greek Revival houses, for example, bear little resemblance to Greek temples, but almost all show certain key features that can, with a bit of practice, be easily recognized. Such features are emphasized in schematic drawings placed on the opening pages of every chapter. Beneath are placed sketches of Principal Subtypes, usually based on roof form, to which the characteristic features of the style are most commonly applied. Photographs provide a variety of typical houses of each subtype as a further aid to recognizing a style in its many guises, while drawings illustrate typical architectural details.

The many photographs of typical houses are, we feel, the heart of the book. In choosing these and preparing their descriptive captions, we have attempted to follow certain guidelines for consistency. Most of the houses illustrated are still in existence; photographs of examples known to have been destroyed are included for only a few rare styles or subtypes. All houses are identified by the state and town (or county for rural houses) in which they are located; where possible, the year construction was completed, the last name of the first owner ("Johnson House"), and the architect are also noted. We have usually relied on secondary sources for this information and have not attempted the enormous task of documentation from original sources. Precise addresses have been omitted to protect the occupants, since most of the houses illustrated are privately owned and not open to the public. Where secondary documentation of the date of construction was lacking, as was the case for the bulk of the examples illustrated, we have estimated the dates, using the forms "late 19th century," "1920s," and "ca. 1905" to indicate increasing certainty of attribution. Familiar names of landmark houses (Biltmore, House of Seven Gables) are sometimes used instead of, or in addition to, the name of the original owner.

Most of the styles of American houses have been previously recognized and described, and we have thus drawn heavily on the works of others in preparing the book. Defining stylistic subtypes and characteristic details has, however, required much original research. To this end we have reviewed and analyzed photographs of more than a hundred thousand houses. In addition, we have traveled to almost every state to study and photograph the spectrum of American houses first hand. Even so, we can only claim to have scratched the surface of stylistic analysis. Most styles, we discovered, provided problems enough to occupy the energies of architectural historians for many years. We very much hope that our preliminary efforts will lead to such refinement and correction.

We have been aided by many people in the preparation of the book. Two have been involved in almost every aspect. Lorraine Weiss was our research assistant for eighteen months, concentrating on gathering and cataloging photographs. After Lorraine left to pursue her graduate studies, Millyanne Tumlinson helped obtain the remaining photographs, typed the final manuscript, and aided in coping with a myriad of details. Mae Kazan carefully typed early drafts of much of the manuscript. Lauren Jarrett executed the bulk of the artwork, painstakingly translating our notes, sketches, and photographs into finished drawings. Juan Rodriguez-Arnaiz skillfully prepared the sample house drawings that introduce each chapter. We are particularly indebted to our editor, Jane Garrett, and to the publisher's art director, Betty Anderson, for patient encouragement and support throughout the entire project. Anthea Lingeman designed the book, bringing unity and clarity to our rough ideas. John Woodside and Virginia Tan coped with organizing and keeping track of the myriad parts and pieces of the book; John with the text and Virginia with the art. In addition, John dealt with the complexities of architectural vocabulary and Virginia produced all the maps. Andy Hughes gathered the gargantuan efforts of all and guided the book through production.

The assembly of photographs, both for study and for inclusion in the book, has involved help from numerous individuals. Here our greatest debt is to Doug Tomlinson, whom we consider to be one of our country's most talented architectural photographers. We had admired Doug's work for years and were flattered when he agreed first to advise us on film and equipment and then to instruct us in the subtleties of photographing houses. Finally, he prepared the publication prints from our negatives, which helped mask our unsuccessful attempts to meet his high standards.

In planning travel for study and photography we have leaned heavily on the following Advisors or Trustees of the National Trust for Historic Preservation, who generously guided us to the most promising byways, towns, and neighborhoods in their vicinity: Charles C. Arensberg, J. Glenn Beall, Jr., Janice Biggers, Brice M. Clagett, Edward Clements, Robertson E. Collins, Hope Howell Cooper, Rosemary Straub Davison, L. Y. Dean III, Richard S. DeCamp, Bernd Foerster, Robert C. Giebner, Harlan H. Griswold, Billie Harrington, Helen Harvey, Royster Lyle, Jr., Hyman Myers, Osmund R. Overby, Ruth Price, Robert Puckett, Betty Sherrill, J. B. Smith, James C. Thomas, Gwyn C. Turner, Sue Turner, Helen Vanmeter, Rufus A. Ward, Jr., Emily Warren, Parker Westbrook, and George S. Wislocki. We are particularly indebted to Ed Clements of Salisbury, North Carolina, Harlan and Dorothy Griswold of Woodbury, Connecticut, and Robert A. Puckett of Wichita, Kansas, for extraordinary generosity and help in our travels.

The acquisition of photographs made by others was a lengthy job in which many have aided, both in person and by mail. Two superb professionals, Carleton Knight III of Washington, D.C., and Thomas Hahn of New London, Connecticut, allowed us to look through their collections and then made available numerous photographs at minimum cost. In addition, the following photographers have generously contributed specific prints that we requested: Allison Abraham, Stephen W. Baldwin, R. Bruhn, Van Jones Martin, Thomas R. Martinson, Wayne McCall, Hans Padelt, William Plymat, Jr., Daniel D. Reiff, Curt Smith, Roger B. Smith, C. Eric Stoehr, Eric Sutherland, Philip Trager, Nemo Warr, Marion Warren, John A. Wenrich, and Mark C. Zeek. We are also grateful to persons at the following institutions for their assistance in obtaining photographs, which often went far beyond the ordinary demands of their duties: Alabama State Historic Commission—Cathy Donaldson, F. Lawrence Oaks, Mary Lou Price; Arkansas Historic Preservation Program—Jacalyn Carfagno, Donna Duvall; Arlington County [Virginia] Department of Libraries; Association for the Preservation of Tennessee Antiquities, Nashville Chapter; Atlanta Historical Society—Elsbeth L. Eltzroth; Belle Meade Mansion [Tennessee]—John E. Hilboldt; Biltmore House [North Carolina]— William A. V. Cecil, Stephen P. Miller; Bowdoin College Library—Dianne M. Gutscher; Buffalo and Erie County Historical Society—Bob Green, Clyde E. Helfter, Marty King; Cambridge Historical Commission; Capra Press; Catskill Center—Thomas H. Miner; City of Biloxi, Mississippi—Julia Guice; City of Mason City, Iowa, Community Development Department; City of Mobile Planning Commission; City of New Bedford, Massachusetts—Antone G. Souza, Jr.; Colorado Historical Society—Judith Kremsdorf Golden, Kaaren K. Patterson; Commission of Fine Arts—Jeff Carson, Sue Kohler; Connecticut Historical Commission—John Herzan, Judith Paine, John W. Shannahan; Cuyahoga County [Ohio] Archives—Franklin Piccirillo, Roderick Boyd Porter, Donald Sherman, Dave Thum; Dallas Historical Society—John Crain, Peggy Riddle; Dallas Public Library—Katherine P. Jagoe; Delaware Division of Historical and Cultural Affairs—Dean E. Nelson; Detroit Public Library—Alice C. Dalligan; Florida Department of State—Dan G. Deibler, L. Ross Morrell; Free Library of Philadelphia—Robert Looney; Galveston [Texas] Historic Foundation—Peter Brink, Gwen Marcus; Genesee Valley [New York] Council on the Arts—Richard C. Quick; Georgia Parks and Historic Sites Division—Kacy Ginn; Greater Portland [Maine] Landmarks, Inc.; Greene and Greene Library—Betty Ulner; Historic American Buildings Survey—Carter Christensen, Alicia Stamm; Historic Landmarks Foundation of Indiana—Tina Connor; Historic Pittsford [New York]—Patricia Place; Historic Preservation League [Dallas]—Tom Black; Historic Salisbury [North Carolina] Foundation, Inc.; Historic Savannah Foundation; Housing & Home Finance Agency, Office of Public Affairs; Idaho State Historical Society—Jennifer Eastman Attebery; Indiana Division of Historic Preservation—Nancy J. Long; Indiana Historical Society Library—Tim Peterson; Iowa Division of Historic Preservation; Iowa State Historical Department—Phyllis Stiefel; Kansas City Landmarks Commission—Jane F. Flynn; Kansas State Historical Society; Kentucky Department of Parks; Kentucky Heritage Commission—Robert M. Polsgrove, Anne Thompson; Kentucky Historical Society Library—Mary E. Winter; Kirksville [Missouri] College of Osteopathy & Surgery; Landmark Society of Western New York—Billie Harrington, Kathy Houk, Denise Phillips-Dickinson; Lexington-Fayette County [Kentucky] Historic Commission—Richard S. DeCamp, Bettie L. Kerr, Walter Langsan; Library of Congress—Mary Ison; Louisiana State Museum—Amy Husten; Louisville Landmarks Commission—Ann Hassett, Marty Poynter Hedgepeth; *The Louisville Times*—Bernice Franklin; Madison County Historical Society; Maine Historic Preservation Commission; Manufactured Housing Institution—Patrick Dichiro; Marshall [Michigan] Historical Society—Carol B. Lovett; Maryland Historical Society—Paula Velthuys, Laurie A. Baty; Massachusetts Historical Commission—Candace Jenkins; Michigan Department of State, History Division—Martha Bigelow; Minnesota Historical Society—Tracey Baker, Charles W. Nelson; Mississippi Department of Archives and History—Pamela Guren; Missouri Historical Society—Judy Cianpoli; Montana Historical Society—Dr. Robert Archibald; Museum of the City of New York—Cathy Butsko, Nancy Kessler Post; National Association of Home Builders—Mrs. Doris Campbell, Mrs. Margery Clark; National Trust for Historic Preservation—Tamara Coombs, Alice Morgan; Nebraska State Historical Society—John E. Carter, Penny Chatfield; New Hampshire Historic Preservation Office—Christine Chase; New Haven Preservation Trust; New Jersey Department of Environmental Protection—Terry Karschner, Betty Wilson; Nevada Division of Historic Preservation and Archeology—Mimi Rodden; New Mexico Historic Preservation Bureau—Ellen Threinen; New York Landmarks Commission—Andrew Dolkart, Marion Cleaver; New York Life Insurance Company—Pamela Dunn Lehrer; New York State Historic Association—Miss Bielaski, Ron Burch, Kathy Stocking; New York State Parks and Recreation—Kathleen LaFrank; North Carolina Department of Cultural Resources, Survey and Planning Branch, Division of Archives and History—Mary Dunston, Rene Early, Drucilla Haley, David Hood, Kim Walton; Ober Park Associates, Inc., Pittsburgh, Pennsylvania; Ohio Historical Society—Edward R. Lentz, Arlene J. Peterson; Oregon Historical Society—Susan Seyl; Oregon Parks and Recreation Division—Karla Owens; Paper Vision Press; Pennsylvania Historical and Museum Commission—Barbara Philpott; Preservation of Historic Winchester [Virginia], Inc.; Rhode Island Department of Community Affairs—Frederick C. Williamson; Ruggles House Society [Maine]—Mrs. Edward Browning, Jr., Mrs. E.

Vaughan Cleaves; Russell House Museum [Connecticut]; Smithsonian Institution National Anthropological Archives, Bureau of Ethnology Collection; Society for the Preservation of New England Antiquities—Mrs. Elinor Reichlin; South Carolina Department of Archives and History—Bob Dalton, Janet Lamb, Elizabeth Mallin, Martha Walker; South Carolina Department of Parks, Recreation and Tourism; State of Alabama Bureau of Publicity and Information; State of Albama Department of Archives and History; State Historical Society of Missouri—Leona S. Morris, Jo Ann Tuckwood; State Historical Society of Wisconsin—Donald N. Anderson; State University of New York College of Arts and Sciences at Genessee Library; State University of New York at Fredonia Library—Joanne L. Schweik; State of Utah—A. Kent Powell; Sumter County [Alabama] Preservation Society; Syracuse University; Technische Universitat München [Germany]—Verena Gaems; Tennessee Department of Conservation—Sue Gamble; Texas Historic Commission—Truett Latimer, Joe Williams; Texas Parks and Wildlife Department—Bill Reaves; Transylvania University Library—Kathleen C. Bryson, Robert Sheridan; Tulane University Library, Southeastern Architectural Archive; Mark Twain Memorial [Connecticut]—Wynn Lee; United States Department of Housing and Urban Development; University of Chicago Library, Department of Special Collections; University of Iowa Press—John E. Simmons; University of Louisville Photographic Archives—James C. Anderson, David Horvath; University of New Mexico Press; Utah Division of State History—Shelley Merrill; Utah State Historical Society Historic Preservation Office; Virginia Historic Landmarks Commission—Valerie S. Payne; Westchester County [New York] Historical Society—Karen Mory Kennedy; The Western Reserve Historical Society; West Virginia Department of Culture and History—Rodney S. Collins; Wichita-Sedgwick County [Kansas] Historical Museum Association—Robert A. Puckett; The King William Association [San Antonio, Texas]; Wyoming Recreation Commission—Mark Junge.

The following individuals kindly provided photographs from their personal collections or other assistance: Jean Block, M. Wayland Brown, Mary V. Burkholder, Mr. and Mrs. Paul Crews, Mary Wallace Crocker, Michael S. Gant, David Gebhard, Robert C. Giebner, Josephine Evans Harpham, Peirce Lewis, Lenore E. Locke, Janet Needham McCaffrey, Robin McCaffrey, Tom Nutt-Powell, George Pearl, Dorothy Harris Savage, William D. Shipman, James Sodeman, Lee S. Tabor, Milo H. Thompson, Richard L. Turner, and William Van Saun.

Finally, we wish to thank Terry Morton and Diane Maddex of the Preservation Press, National Trust for Historic Preservation for encouragement in the first stages of the book. Diane, in particular, gave us a careful critique of some early chapters, suggested the inclusion of the Native American dwellings and, later, gave guidance in obtaining photographs.

A Field Guide to American Houses

Looking at
American Houses

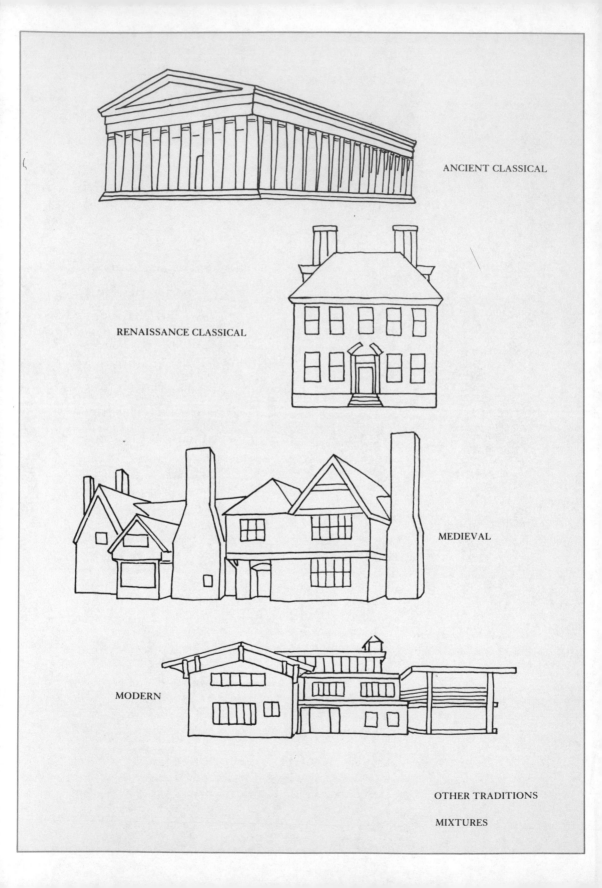

ANCIENT CLASSICAL

RENAISSANCE CLASSICAL

MEDIEVAL

MODERN

OTHER TRADITIONS

MIXTURES

Style

Domestic buildings are of two principal sorts: folk houses and styled houses. Folk houses are those designed without a conscious attempt to mimic current fashion. Many are built by their occupants or by non-professional builders, and all are relatively simple houses meant to provide basic shelter, with little concern for presenting a stylish face to the world. Most surviving American houses are not folk houses but are styled; that is, they were built with at least some attempt at being fashionable. As such, they show the influence of shapes, materials, detailing, or other features that make up an architectural style that was currently in vogue. The bulk of this book is organized by the changing chronology of these American architectural fashions or styles, for they provide the most effective framework for identifying and understanding American houses.

The majority of styled American houses are loosely modeled on one of four principal architectural traditions: Ancient Classical, Renaissance Classical, Medieval, or Modern. The earliest, the Ancient Classical tradition, is based upon the monuments of early Greece and Rome. The closely related Renaissance Classical tradition stems from a revival of interest in classicism during the Renaissance, which began in Italy in the 15th century. The two classical traditions, Ancient and Renaissance, share many of the same architectural details.

The third tradition, the Medieval, separated the Ancient Classical and the Renaissance Classical in time. The Medieval tradition includes architecture based on the formal Gothic style used for church buildings during the Middle Ages, as well as that based upon the simpler domestic buildings of the same era. Most of the Medieval architecture that has influenced American houses originated in England and France.

The fourth tradition, the Modern movement, began in the late 19th century and continues to the present. It is based primarily on the lack of applied ornamentation and a resulting external simplicity or "honesty," as well as on spatial variations made possible by new construction techniques.

Other traditions that have influenced American houses are mostly of Spanish origin. Both the simple structures built during the Spanish Colonial era in the United States and the more elaborate architecture of Spain and Latin America have inspired American domestic buildings. In addition, Oriental and Egyptian models have occasionally provided patterns for American house design.

As we shall see in the following pages, each of these traditions has produced several different styles of American houses as they have been interpreted and re-interpreted during different building eras. Stylistic mixtures are also common in American domestic architecture. These have been created both by those who knowingly sought the unusual, as well as by those who unwittingly combined historical precedents.

ANCIENT CLASSICAL STYLES

The monumental architecture of Greece from about the 9th to the 4th century B.C., and that of Rome from the 1st century B.C. to the 5th century A.D., provide the models for those styles based upon Ancient Classical traditions. An entry or full-facade porch supported by large columns, frequently two-story, or "colossal," columns, is the feature most commonly associated with American houses patterned after Ancient Classical buildings. The columns are most often in one of the classical orders, but simple squared and octagonal interpretations are also found. The houses usually have symmetrical facades and, most commonly, a low-pitched roof.

Three styles of American houses are based on Ancient Classical precedents. The first is the Early Classical Revival style (1780–1830). These are loosely based upon Roman models and are simple side-gabled or hipped roof houses with full-height entry porches, usually with a classical pediment above.

The next Ancient Classical style is the Greek Revival (1820–60). Greek Revival houses normally have a very wide band of trim beneath the eaves, mimicking the entablature of Greek temples. Many have full-facade or full-height entry porches with large columns, but some have only a small entry porch and others have no porch or columns. Both side-gabled and hipped roofs are common. In some regions, many of the houses built in this style are oriented so that the gable end becomes the front facade; these most closely resemble their prototype Greek temples.

The third Ancient Classical style is the Neoclassical (1895–1940). These are normally two-story houses with prominent full-height columns. The columns usually have very elaborate capitals of either Roman or Greek inspiration. The forms of Neoclassical houses are varied, and secondary details characteristic of the later Renaissance Classical movement are often used.

RENAISSANCE CLASSICAL STYLES

The Renaissance Classical styles are based upon buildings built during the revival of interest in Ancient Classical models which began in Italy in the early 15th century and gradually worked its way northward to France, where it arrived in the mid-16th century, and to England, where it had little influence until the early 17th century. From England the Renaissance traveled still later to America, where it profoundly influenced 18th-century building in the English colonies. Each country developed somewhat different interpretations of Renaissance Classical ideals and each of these has inspired several later American styles. All, however, share certain features: they usually have balanced, symmetrical facades and typically have such decorative details as pedimented (crowned) doors and windows, dentils, quoins, and pilasters. Two-story columns are rare in American interpretations, although colonnaded, one-story entrance porches are frequent.

In America, the Italian version of the Renaissance tradition inspired both the Italianate (1840–85) and Italian Renaissance (1890–1935) styles. Arches and cornice-line brackets are the two elements that most consistently mark American houses as having Italian Renaissance roots.

The French Renaissance tradition inspired the Second Empire (1855–85) and the

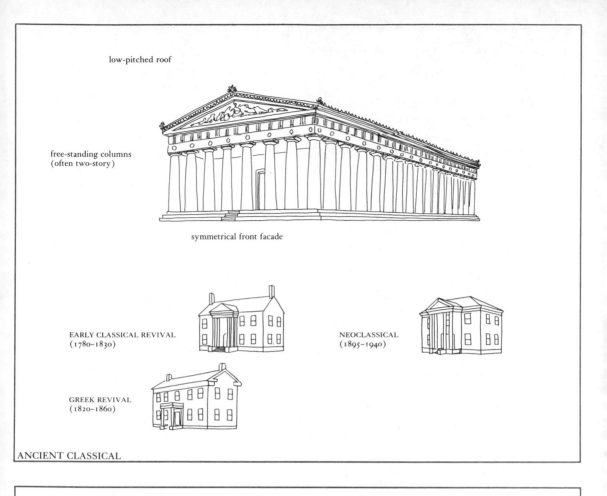

low-pitched roof

free-standing columns
(often two-story)

symmetrical front facade

EARLY CLASSICAL REVIVAL
(1780–1830)

NEOCLASSICAL
(1895–1940)

GREEK REVIVAL
(1820–1860)

ANCIENT CLASSICAL

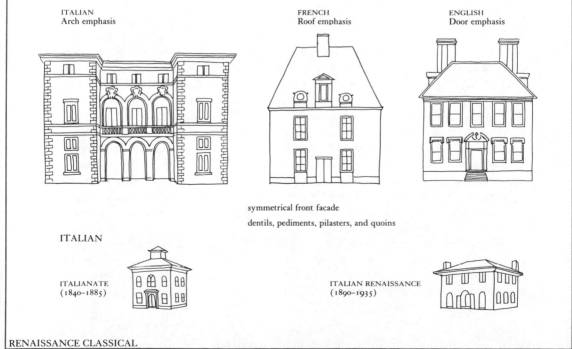

ITALIAN
Arch emphasis

FRENCH
Roof emphasis

ENGLISH
Door emphasis

symmetrical front facade

dentils, pediments, pilasters, and quoins

ITALIAN

ITALIANATE
(1840–1885)

ITALIAN RENAISSANCE
(1890–1935)

RENAISSANCE CLASSICAL

Beaux Arts (1885–1930) styles as well as some subtypes of the French Eclectic (1915–45) style. A steeply pitched hipped roof, or dual-pitched mansard roof, is a characteristic feature of many of these French Renaissance–inspired houses.

The English version of the Renaissance tradition was exported to the American colonies as the Georgian (1700–80) and Adam (1780–1820) styles. Note that these are original Renaissance buildings directly inspired by the earlier Italian Renaissance. Other American houses based on Renaissance traditions are later revivals of these same influences. These are included in the long-lived Colonial Revival style (1880–1955), which draws heavily on American Georgian and Adam precedents. All of these English-inspired Renaissance houses are united by an emphasis on elaborated front door surrounds. These usually have side pilasters supporting an entablature or pediment (Georgian) or a fanlight above the door (Adam).

MEDIEVAL STYLES

Medieval architecture is that built during the Middle Ages, the era from the end of the Ancient Classical period until the beginning of the Renaissance (roughly encompassing the 6th to the 15th centuries A.D.). Throughout most of this period, the primary focus of European, styled architecture was on ecclesiastical buildings—churches, cathedrals, and abbeys. The dominant style for these was Romanesque.from the end of the 9th century until the 12th century and Gothic from the mid-12th century until the beginning of the Renaissance. The Romanesque, modified from the Roman Ancient Classical tradition, is characterized by the extensive use of rounded arches. It has inspired only one American domestic style, the Richardsonian Romanesque (1880–1900). Gothic buildings are easily identified by their characteristic pointed arches, used over doors and windows and in interior vaulting. These inspired the Gothic Revival style (1840–80) and, in addition, influenced the Stick style (1860–ca. 1890).

Large-scale domestic architecture during most of the Middle Ages took the form of fortified castles. These have inspired relatively few American houses, although castellated parapets are sometimes used on Gothic Revival and Tudor houses. More modest European domestic buildings from Medieval times usually had roofs covered with thatch; such roofs had to be very steeply pitched in order to shed water properly. During much of the Middle Ages, chimneys were not yet in common use; attics under the steep roofs were left open so that smoke could escape through small openings in the roof. The chimney was a crucial invention, for it allowed second stories and attics to be floored to provide additional living space. Postmedieval houses with prominent chimneys typically have steeply pitched roofs, asymmetrical facades, and, frequently, wall surfaces elaborated either by exposed half-timbered construction or by protective clay tiles hung upon such construction. They also frequently have an overhanging second story that adds structural stability to the timber framing. Such houses were imported directly to the New World as the Postmedieval English style (1600–1700) built by the earliest English colonists. They also provided the inspiration for many informal examples of the later Tudor style (1890–1940).

When Renaissance influence began to spread to France and England from Italy, it first took the form of classical detailing being applied to houses of Medieval form. In France, this era produced many of the great chateaux that provided the inspiration for the American Chateauesque style (1880–1910). In England, such mixed Medieval-Re-

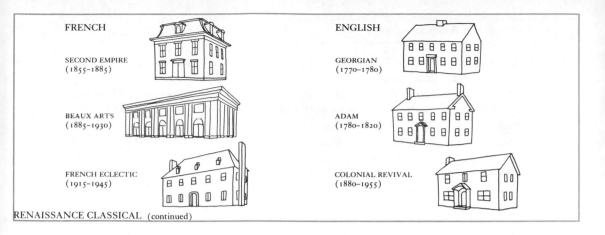

FRENCH

SECOND EMPIRE
(1855–1885)

BEAUX ARTS
(1885–1930)

FRENCH ECLECTIC
(1915–1945)

ENGLISH

GEORGIAN
(1770–1780)

ADAM
(1780–1820)

COLONIAL REVIVAL
(1880–1955)

RENAISSANCE CLASSICAL (continued)

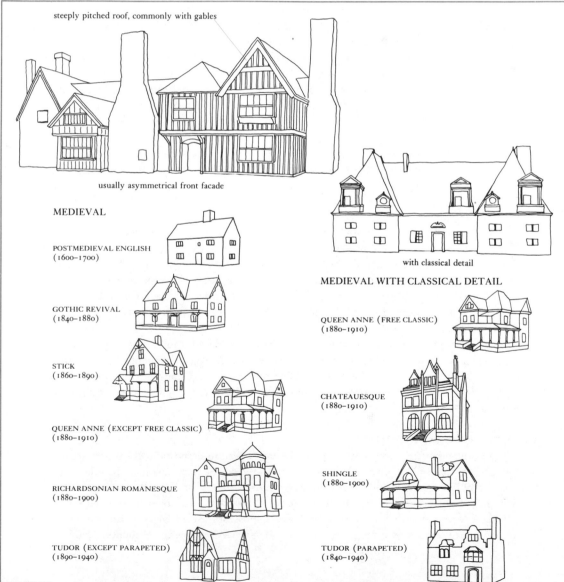

steeply pitched roof, commonly with gables

usually asymmetrical front facade

MEDIEVAL

POSTMEDIEVAL ENGLISH
(1600–1700)

GOTHIC REVIVAL
(1840–1880)

STICK
(1860–1890)

QUEEN ANNE (EXCEPT FREE CLASSIC)
(1880–1910)

RICHARDSONIAN ROMANESQUE
(1880–1900)

TUDOR (EXCEPT PARAPETED)
(1890–1940)

with classical detail

MEDIEVAL WITH CLASSICAL DETAIL

QUEEN ANNE (FREE CLASSIC)
(1880–1910)

CHATEAUESQUE
(1880–1910)

SHINGLE
(1880–1900)

TUDOR (PARAPETED)
(1840–1940)

MEDIEVAL

naissance buildings inspired the more formal examples of the American Tudor style, as well as some examples of the Queen Anne style.

English architects during the latter half of the 19th century, tiring of two hundred years of buildings dominated by classical influences, began to turn back to their Medieval heritage for inspiration. The result, the English Queen Anne movement, was quickly followed by the related American Queen Anne style (1880–1910), which used Medieval forms both with and without the addition of classical detailing. The Shingle style (1880–1900), which was also inspired by the English Queen Anne movement, introduced simplified exterior surfaces and open interior planning, and thus foreshadowed the Modern phase of architectural styling.

MODERN STYLES

The Modern movement in domestic architecture developed in two stages during the years from 1900 to 1940. The first phase, the Arts and Crafts movement, deliberately turned its back on historical precedent for decoration and design. Ornamentation was not eliminated but merely "modernized" to remove most traces of its historic origins. Low-pitched roofs with wide eave overhangs were favored. Although there were many variations within the movement, it led to two distinctive styles of American houses. The first was the Prairie style (1900–20), which began in Chicago under the leadership of Frank Lloyd Wright, who designed many houses in the style during the period from 1900 to 1913. These elegantly simplified buildings by Wright and his followers were to have a profound influence on the beginnings of modernism both here and in Europe. The second style inspired by the Arts and Crafts movement is the Craftsman style (1905–30), begun in southern California in about 1903 by the Greene brothers. It emphasizes exposed structural members and wood joinery and, like the Prairie style, eschews formal historic precedents.

The second phase of the Modern movement began after World War I as a full-scale reaction against all previous architectural tradition. The emphasis in this phase was on design that was clearly of the Machine Age, with standardization of parts, absence of all non-functional decoration, and structural "honesty" as hallmarks. Houses were to become "machines for living." Flat roofs and smooth wall surfaces were favored. Both the Modernistic style (1920–40) and the International style (1925–present) are products of this more austere modernism.

The Modern movement continued to evolve in the decades following 1940 as new stylistic outgrowths of the Arts and Crafts and the Machine Age movements arose. These were to dominate American domestic building during the 1950s and '60s before beginning to be replaced, in the 1970s, by a return to stylistic adaptations loosely based on classical or Medieval prototypes.

OTHER STYLISTIC TRADITIONS

Many of the other traditions that have influenced American domestic architecture are of Spanish or Spanish Colonial origin. In the New World, Spanish colonists blended the adobe building traditions of the Native Americans with similar Spanish housing traditions originally brought to Spain from North Africa. Both the Spanish Colonial style (1600–1850) and the Pueblo Revival style (1910–present) use adobe construction techniques which show this mixing of Spanish and Native American precedents. Spanish

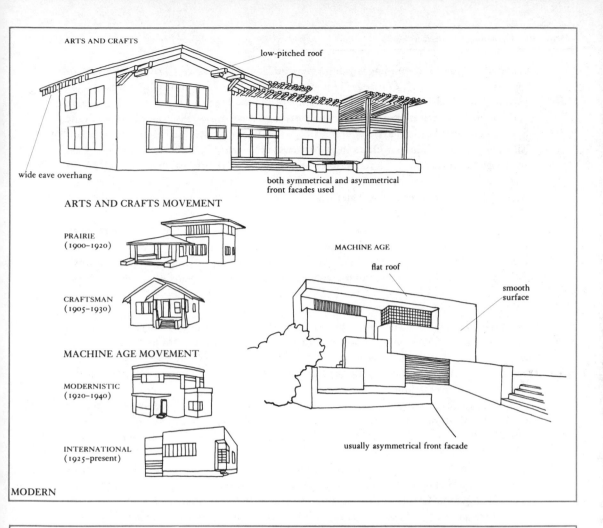

ARTS AND CRAFTS

low-pitched roof

wide eave overhang

both symmetrical and asymmetrical
front facades used

ARTS AND CRAFTS MOVEMENT

PRAIRIE
(1900–1920)

CRAFTSMAN
(1905–1930)

MACHINE AGE MOVEMENT

MODERNISTIC
(1920–1940)

INTERNATIONAL
(1925–present)

MACHINE AGE

flat roof

smooth
surface

usually asymmetrical front facade

MODERN

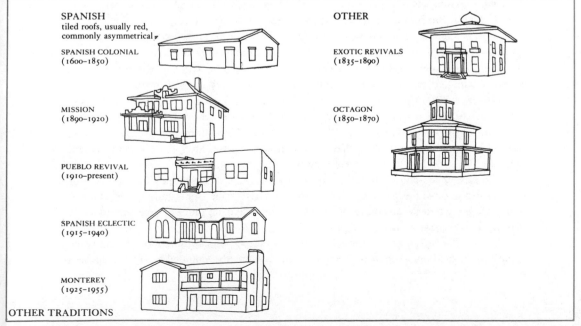

SPANISH
tiled roofs, usually red,
commonly asymmetrical

SPANISH COLONIAL
(1600–1850)

MISSION
(1890–1920)

PUEBLO REVIVAL
(1910–present)

SPANISH ECLECTIC
(1915–1940)

MONTEREY
(1925–1955)

OTHER

EXOTIC REVIVALS
(1835–1890)

OCTAGON
(1850–1870)

OTHER TRADITIONS

Colonial ecclesiastical buildings of the American Southwest provided the inspiration for the Mission style (1890–1920). This was followed by the Spanish Eclectic style (1915–40), which broadened the precedents to include the entire spectrum of Spanish and Spanish-American architecture, thus making it an unusually varied style. Some Spanish Eclectic houses have elaborate decorative detailing patterned after formal Spanish Renaissance buildings. Others show Moorish and Islamic influences, while still others are based upon rural Spanish folk houses with little or no decorative detailing. The most recent style in the Spanish tradition is the Monterey style (1925–55), which is loosely based on certain houses of the American Southwest that show a mixing of Spanish and English Colonial influences.

Other architectural traditions have influenced several minor styles of American houses. Oriental, Egyptian, and Swiss Chalet prototypes inspired the Exotic Revivals (1835–ca. 1890), while the Octagon style (1850–70) developed from one man's enthusiastic sponsorship of houses designed with unorthodox ground plans of octagonal shape.

STYLISTIC MIXTURES

Most American houses have been built in one of the many architectural styles outlined in the preceding sections. Some, however, do not fit neatly into one of these stylistic categories but, instead, have characteristics of two or more styles. Such houses may have been originally built as stylistic mixtures or may have resulted from later attempts to alter the style through remodeling.

Prior to about 1840, American architectural styles were rather widely separated by time or by location; that is, only one fashion usually prevailed in a region over a long interval of time. Most early stylistic mixtures occurred during the transitional periods when these persistent fashions were changing. Thus, some transitional houses in the English colonies share Georgian and Adam features, while others blend Adam with Greek Revival detailing. Similarly, Dutch, French, and Spanish Colonial buildings began to show Adam or Greek Revival detailing as Anglo influence increased with the expansion of the country. These originally built combinations of styles increased after about 1840 when pattern books, particularly A. J. Downing's influential *Cottage Residences, Rural Architecture and Landscape Gardening*, published in 1842, presented several choices of fashionable building styles. Downing, for example, advocated both Gothic and Italianate modes of design. As might be expected, some readers and builders avoided the choice by combining features of both. Another popular mixture of the romantic era added Italianate detailing to the previously dominant Greek Revival form.

Houses of the Victorian era seldom show such dramatically obvious mixtures of style. Most Victorian styles are closely interrelated and draw heavily on Medieval precedents for inspiration. Thus they naturally tend to blend into one another. Steeply pitched roofs and textured wall surfaces are common to most. Stick-style structural members are found on many Queen Anne houses; Richardsonian arches occur on Shingle-style houses, wood-shingled walls may dominate on either Queen Anne or Shingle houses, and so on. Thus the separation of the Victorian styles sometimes becomes a matter of degree, whereas the dominant Greek-Gothic-Italianate modes of the preceding romantic era were unmistakably different.

During the early years of the eclectic era, experimental combinations of styles were common. From about 1890 to 1915, styles as different as the Colonial Revival, Neoclassi-

MIXTURES: ROMANTIC AND VICTORIAN

1. Cleveland, Ohio; mid-19th century. Otis House. A mixture of Gothic and Italianate design. The shape of the house with its low-pitched hipped roof, symmetrical facade, and centered gable is Italianate, as is the bracketed cornice. The pointed arches over upper-story windows and the flattened arches of the front porch and lower-story windows are Gothic.

2. Canton, Mississippi; mid-19th century. A mixture of Greek Revival, Gothic, and Italianate influences. The doors and porch with classical columns are borrowed from Greek Revival. The bracketed cornice is Italianate, and the flattened arch and jigsaw-cut wood detailing of the upstairs porch show Gothic Revival influences.

3. New Albany, Indiana; 1866. McCord House. This mixture of Gothic and Italianate design is a reversal of Figure 1. The house form with its gabled roof and steeply pitched, front-facing gables shows Gothic influence. The bracketed cornice and the windows with heavy rounded crowns are Italianate.

4. Rolla, Missouri; late 19th century. Romanesque and Shingle elements combined with square Prairie-style porch supports.

5. Richmond, Virginia; late 19th century. A mixture of Queen Anne (patterned masonry subtype), Romanesque, and Exotic influences.

Style 13

cal, Prairie, Tudor, Mission, and Craftsman were being built simultaneously. Many architects and builders experimented with fanciful combinations of these styles, sometimes adding a touch of Victorian detailing as well. Some early eclectic neighborhoods contain whole streets of such marvelously experimental stylistic combinations. These innovative houses were, however, far less common than more correct stylistic interpretations, even in the early eclectic years, and by 1915 they had all but disappeared. Thus began the era of the Period House, an interval in which stylistic combinations became rare. This lasted until the late 1930s, when architects and builders began to experiment with restrained mixtures of Tudor, Colonial Revival, and Mediterranean influences.

A second and far more common category of stylistic mixture results not from original design, but from later alteration of an existing house. Most houses more than a few years old have had at least some exterior alterations, and it is important to be able to recognize these changes in order to identify a house's original style and appearance.

Most exterior alterations are undertaken for one or more of the following purposes:

- To update the appearance of the house
- To add additional living space to the house
- To minimize exterior maintenance of the house

Each of these changes tends to produce somewhat different exterior appearances.

The most common means of updating the appearance of a house is to add, remove, or alter a porch. The most frequent porch alteration, because it is the simplest, is to replace the original porch roof supports. For example, many a Queen Anne house had its spindlework supports replaced by heavy masonry piers during the early years of this century when the Prairie style was in vogue. The massive piers of Prairie and Craftsman houses, in turn, have often been replaced by narrow wooden or metal posts which dramatically alter the appearance of the house. Entire new porches are also commonly added to houses that originally had none, or as replacements for porches of quite different character. Many Queen Anne houses, for example, now sport elaborate Neoclassical porches added in the early 1900s. Equally startling are those houses which have had the original porches removed without replacement.

Following porches, the most commonly altered facade elements are doors, windows, and wall materials, changed in an attempt to mimic current fashion. Most of these updating changes in facade details, including porches, are easily recognized with a little practice, for the new additions appear out of context with the overall shape, form, and materials of the remainder of the house.

Still more fundamental changes occur when a smaller earlier house is incorporated into a larger later house of a different style. All housewatchers have had the experience of visiting, for example, an Italianate museum house that the guide insists was built in 1798. Upon close questioning it transpires that a log house was built on the site in 1798 and that in 1855 the original owner's granddaughter's husband came into some money, leading to a remodeling (we would say "rebuilding"). For purposes of identification, such houses can be considered to have been built in 1855; the fact that an earlier house is buried within is of historical significance but does not affect the exterior appearance. When the rebuilding is less complete, however, traces of the earlier house may be revealed by a careful look at roof, walls, and—especially—the roof-wall junctions, which quite often provide the best clues to large-scale stylistic updating.

MIXTURES: ECLECTIC

1. Emporia, Kansas; early 20th century. A mixture showing a Prairie-influenced wide roof-overhang combined with a Shingle-style front gambrel and a rusticated stone arch borrowed from the Richardsonian Romanesque.

2. Dallas, Texas; 1928. Wade House. Here a Tudor front-facing gable with half-timbering is mixed with Italian Renaissance roof tiles and arched windows.

3. Cleveland, Ohio; 1910. Mather House; Charles Schweinfurth, architect. A mixture of Tudor (windows, lintels, and chimneys) and Colonial Revival details (roofline balustrade, low-pitched hipped roof).

4. Louisville, Kentucky; early 20th century. This example combines the side-gabled Craftsman form with Italian Renaissance tiled roofing and arched entries.

5. Louisville, Kentucky; early 20th century. This house combines elements of several stylistic traditions (Prairie, Craftsman, Mediterranean, and Germanic).

The second principal reason for exterior alteration is to add living space to an existing house. This is usually accomplished in one of two ways: either by adding an entire
extension or wing to the existing house or, at less expense, by converting a house's
under-utilized areas (attic, basement, porch, or garage) into living space. In the first in-
stance, extensive additions can be undertaken in the style of the original house and, depending on the skill of the architect involved, leave the original lines of the house undi-
minished or, occasionally, enhanced. Lyndhurst in Tarrytown, New York, is an
outstanding example of this (page 208). Carefully done additions and alterations that use
the same materials and style as the existing house can be very difficult to detect. More
commonly, additions differ in some fundamental way—form, materials, or details—from
the original house and are easily recognized.

Converting existing spaces to living areas does not usually affect the exterior appearance of the house when it involves only a basement or attached garage (although the
method of handling the garage door opening is important). An attic remodeling usually
involves the addition of dormers or skylights but otherwise leaves the facade intact. The
decision to gain space by enclosing all or part of a front or side porch, on the other hand,
can drastically change the character of a house. Rarely can such alterations be done in a
manner which maintains the stylistic integrity of the facade.

The third principal reason for altering house exteriors is to minimize maintenance.
The need regularly to paint wooden walls, caulk drafty windows, and repair leaky roofs
can cause a house owner to make drastic changes that are designed to decrease this rou-
tine maintenance. Some of these maintenance-minimizing alterations even promise to do
away with these problems "forever." Owners tired of painting wooden walls frequently
add a layer of pre-finished siding (aluminum, asbestos, etc.). In addition to hiding the
texture of the original walls, such siding usually obscures such details as window and
door surrounds, cornices, and moldings and thus quite dramatically changes a house's appearance. It also may hasten the deterioration of the wooden walls it covers; fortunately it
can often be removed without serious damage. For those tired of caulking, patching, and
painting older wooden windows, replacing them with pre-finished metal windows can be
tempting. Such changes significantly alter the house's appearance. Original slate, tile, tin,
or wood-shingle roofs are commonly replaced with composition roofing materials. Sometimes these materials closely resemble the original roof but more often, like changes of
wall materials or windows, they fundamentally alter the nature of the facade.

Most maintenance-minimizing alterations do not completely obscure a house's stylistic origins but are apparent as inappropriate changes in external appearance. If the
changes are extensive, however—for example, siding added and windows and roofs replaced—the original character of the house may be undiscernible.

ALTERATIONS: STYLISH UPDATES

1. Cooperstown, New York; early 19th century (roof, late 19th century). Lakelands. A Federal house with a Victorian roof added (the porch is likely an intermediate addition). Cover the roof to see the symmetrical house; uncover it to see how completely the roof form changes the feel of the house.

2. Granbury, Texas; late 19th century (porch, early 20th century). A Queen Anne house (note hipped roof with cross gable and tower) behind an added Neoclassical porch.

3. Cooperstown, New York; mid-19th century (addition, late 19th century). Holt House. A Second Empire house (on the right) has had a major half-timbered Queen Anne addition to the left.

4. Dallas, Texas; 1914. Arrington House. A relatively unaltered Prairie-style example. Both figures 5 and 6 below originally resembled this house, although without the porte cochere to the side.

5. Dallas, Texas; early 20th century (remodeling ca. 1975). This remodeling of a house similar to Figure 4 removed the porch and added a small broken pediment to the door, which is poorly scaled and out of character with the form and roof of the house.

6. Dallas, Texas; early 20th century (remodeling 1982; Teddy Taylor, designer). This remodeling of a house similar to Figure 4, although obscuring the earlier Prairie character, picks up on the Mediterranean tiled roof by adding a Palladian entry motif. The changed brick pattern shows the line of the original porch roof. When painted, the brickwork will appear uniform and only very careful observation would reveal the modifications.

1

4   5

8

ALTERATIONS: MAINTENANCE

St. Genevieve, Missouri; ca. 1920. In a development of several dozen almost identical Craftsman houses built in the 1920s, only the example shown in Figure 1 remains essentially unaltered. The photographs show a series of modifications typical of those that obscure the original stylistic details of many older American houses.   1. In the unaltered example, note the wood shingles in the gable, narrow bands of wood siding, triangular knee braces at the cornice, original porch supports, and original window surrounds, sash, and mullions.   2. This example is original except for the addition of asbestos shingles covering the wood shingles and siding.   3. Another type of added siding, this time with metal awnings.   4. In addition to new siding and awnings, the original wood porch supports and railing have been replaced by iron, the triangular knee braces sheathed, and shutters added.   5. These alterations are similar to those in Figure 4, but without the shutters and awnings.   6. Here the windows have been changed, two types of siding added, the triangular knee braces removed, the porch supports changed, and a rear side porch added.   7. In this example, siding has been added and the front porch screened.   8. The entire porch area has been enclosed and two types of siding added.   9. Here most of the front porch has been enclosed for additional interior space, the triple window on the right has been reduced to one, and siding has been added.

2

3

6

7

9

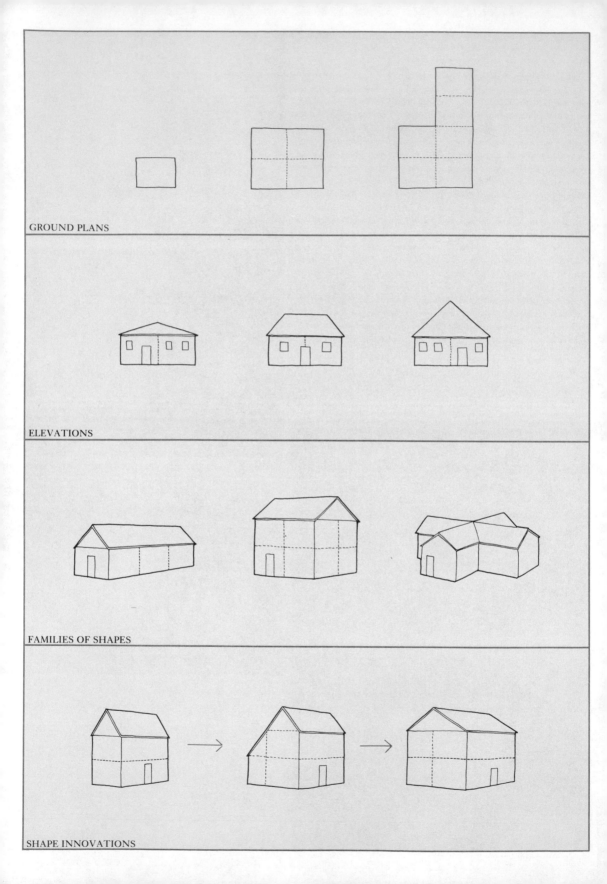

GROUND PLANS

ELEVATIONS

FAMILIES OF SHAPES

SHAPE INNOVATIONS

Form

The Shapes of American Houses

The chronology of changing architectural fashions or styles provides the fundamental framework for identifying American houses. A second basic feature of houses is form or shape. House form is not endlessly varied. Instead, a few fundamental shapes, and relatively minor variations on them, tend to be used again and again through a range of changing architectural styles.

House shape is best analyzed by dividing the three-dimensional house into two separate two-dimensional components. The first is the ground plan, the pattern made by the exterior walls when viewed from directly above. The second two-dimensional component is elevation, the pattern made by wall, roof, and details when viewed, as they normally are, from ground level. In theory, ground plans and elevations can be varied to form an infinite number of house shapes. In practice, there are only a relatively few common variants of both plan and elevation. These combine to make several fundamental families of house shapes that dominate American domestic architecture.

Certain uncomplicated house shapes have been continuously used since the first colonists arrived. On the other hand, several technological changes over the past three hundred years have permitted greater flexibility and freedom of design and have led to important innovations in house shape.

GROUND PLANS

A ground plan shows the shape of a house as if one were viewing it from directly above with the roof and the upper floors (if any) removed to leave only the ground-floor walls. The shape of the ground plan can usually be broken down into a pattern of smaller, room-sized modules or structural units. The simplest folk houses have only a single such room-sized unit. As larger houses were required, folk builders developed techniques for combining two or more units into multi-unit plans. These room-sized structural units may or may not correspond exactly to the placement of interior walls to form actual rooms. In general, the earlier and more modest the house, the more likely it is that each principal room will correspond to a structural unit (although even in the simplest houses, one or more units are commonly partitioned into smaller rooms). Since in this book we are concerned with the external appearance of houses, these differences in internal room arrangement can be discounted. The important point is that ground plans are almost always made up of rather simple combinations of room-sized units. The basic house sizes and shapes defined by these combinations have persisted in all but the largest and most pretentious houses from early colonial times to the present day.

In the simplest case, square or rectangular room-sized units are combined into larger squares or rectangles known as simple plans. These are of two principal types: (1) linear plans, made up of units aligned into single rows one unit wide or deep, and (2) massed plans, which have both a width and depth of more than one unit. The rectangles and squares of simple plans can, in turn, be combined to make compound plans, the most frequent of which resemble in shape the letters L, T, or U. Many other compound arrangements are also possible; some of the most frequent are shown in the illustrations. Note that simple plans with minor wall projections may resemble compound plans but can usually be distinguished by whether or not the projections from the principal mass of the house are room-sized or smaller.

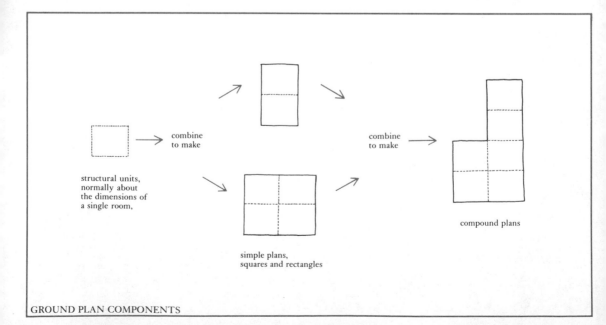

structural units,
normally about
the dimensions of
a single room,

combine
to make

simple plans,
squares and rectangles

combine
to make

compound plans

GROUND PLAN COMPONENTS

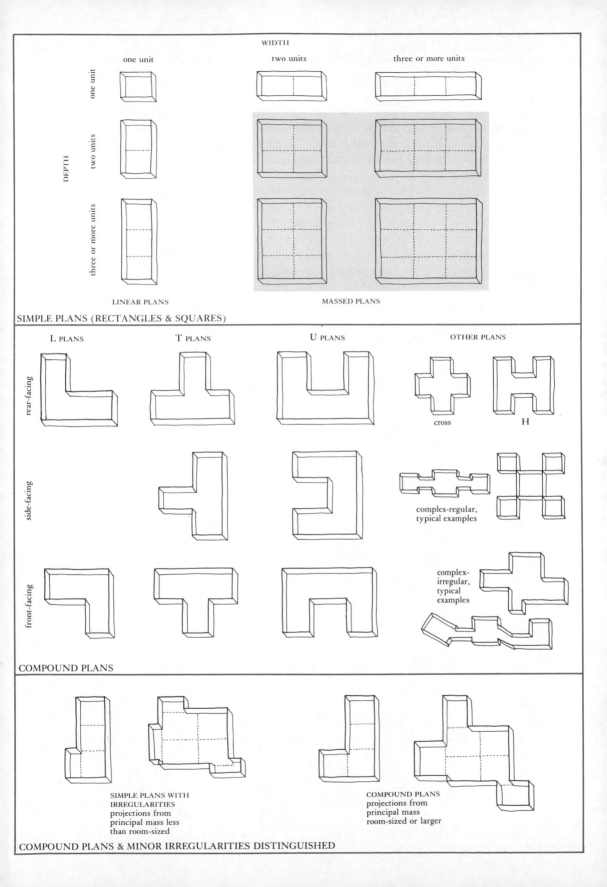

WIDTH

one unit — two units — three or more units

DEPTH

one unit

two units

three or more units

LINEAR PLANS — MASSED PLANS

SIMPLE PLANS (RECTANGLES & SQUARES)

L PLANS — T PLANS — U PLANS — OTHER PLANS

rear-facing

cross — H

side-facing

complex-regular, typical examples

front-facing

complex-irregular, typical examples

COMPOUND PLANS

SIMPLE PLANS WITH IRREGULARITIES projections from principal mass less than room-sized

COMPOUND PLANS projections from principal mass room-sized or larger

COMPOUND PLANS & MINOR IRREGULARITIES DISTINGUISHED

ELEVATIONS

Elevations show the shapes of houses as viewed normally from the ground at eye level. Elevations are generally straight-on views that show the appearance of a single wall with its overlying roof and architectural details. Four such elevation views—one each of the front, the sides, and the rear walls—are required to describe fully all details of shape. On the other hand, the general form of a house can normally be understood from just the front elevation (also called the principal elevation or facade) and the ground plan which, together, define the basic three-dimensional shape of the house.

The most fundamental factor in analyzing elevations is wall height. American houses are normally either one or two stories high. Less common are heights of one and one-half, two and one-half, and three stories (a half-story has less than full-height external walls; the remaining headroom is developed from attic space beneath the roof line). Houses more than three stories high are rare except in densely populated urban settings where narrow town houses sometimes have four or more stories.

Most simple-plan houses have facades either one, two, or three structural units in width. Each width normally has a characteristic pattern of symmetry in the arrangement of door and window details. These patterns frequently allow identification of the width of the underlying ground plan. Two asymmetrical ranks of window and door openings normally occur on one-unit widths; three symmetrical or four asymmetrical ranks on two-unit widths; and five symmetrical ranks on three-unit widths. In symmetrical three-ranked facades the two principal front rooms behind the facade are normally of unequal size, the entrance door opening into the larger of the two. Less commonly the door opens into a narrow entrance hallway or vestibule. The middle unit of three-unit widths is normally a central hallway and may also be somewhat narrower than the two flanking units. The presence of five, rather than three, ranks of window openings normally distinguishes this plan from symmetrical two-unit plans.

Elevations reveal not only wall height, width, and symmetry, but also the varying relative proportions of roof and wall. If the roof is flat or of low pitch, the wall will dominate the facade. Conversely, steeply pitched roofs dramatically dominate their underlying walls. Roofs of normal pitch show about equal dominance of roof and wall.

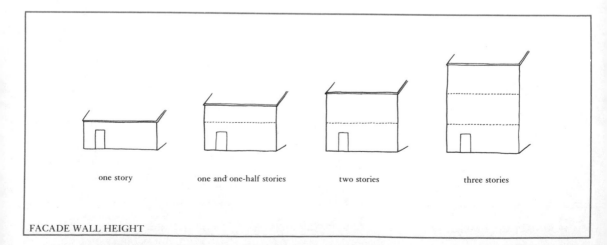

one story   one and one-half stories   two stories   three stories

FACADE WALL HEIGHT

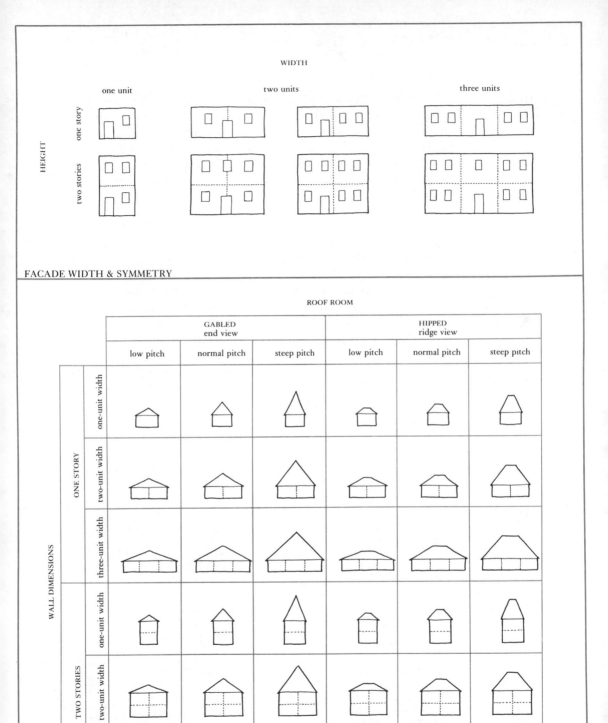

WIDTH

one unit · two units · three units

HEIGHT

one story

two stories

FACADE WIDTH & SYMMETRY

ROOF ROOM

		GABLED end view			HIPPED ridge view		
		low pitch	normal pitch	steep pitch	low pitch	normal pitch	steep pitch
ONE STORY	one-unit width						
	two-unit width						
	three-unit width						
TWO STORIES	one-unit width						
	two-unit width						
	three-unit width						

WALL DIMENSIONS

ROOF-WALL PROPORTIONS

FAMILIES OF SHAPES

Ground plan and elevation combine to make several persistent and recurring patterns or families of shapes that are characteristic of most American houses. Much of the history of American domestic architecture involves the varying patterns of details—roofs, doors, windows, chimneys, porches, and decoration—applied to these relatively few basic shapes. Note that several simple-plan families have such distinctive shapes that they have familiar names (saltbox, shotgun, town house, etc.). Others have less common names (I-house, massed side-gable, etc.) but all are easily recognized with a little practice. The principal compound-plan families are also easily recognized, but they show more variation in details of shape. Wings of varying ground plan and elevation can be combined to form many variants of the basic L, T, and U plans.

Most of the fundamental styles of American houses display several of these shape patterns. In a few styles, however, a single family tends to dominate. Thus, Georgian houses are principally box-house or saltbox shapes, Adam mostly box-house, the Stick style usually gable-front, the Prairie usually four-square, and so on. In many styles, shape families provide useful criteria for defining one or more of the principal subtypes within the style. The distinctive town-house shape, in particular, makes up a characteristic urban subtype in several styles.

The principal use of shape families in house identification applies not to styled houses but to folk houses. Such houses generally lack the architectural detailing that characterizes and differentiates styled buildings. In these, shape becomes a principal criterion for distinguishing types.

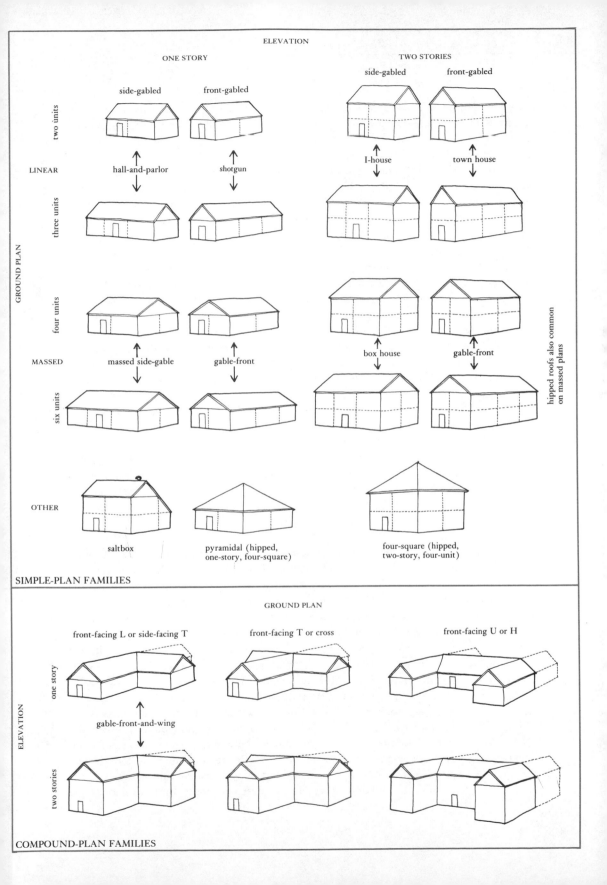

ELEVATION

ONE STORY

TWO STORIES

side-gabled   front-gabled

two units

side-gabled   front-gabled

LINEAR

hall-and-parlor   shotgun

I-house   town house

three units

GROUND PLAN

four units

MASSED

massed side-gable   gable-front

box house   gable-front

six units

hipped roofs also common on massed plans

OTHER

saltbox   pyramidal (hipped, one-story, four-square)   four-square (hipped, two-story, four-unit)

SIMPLE-PLAN FAMILIES

GROUND PLAN

front-facing L or side-facing T   front-facing T or cross   front-facing U or H

ELEVATION

one story

gable-front-and-wing

two stories

COMPOUND-PLAN FAMILIES

SHAPE INNOVATIONS

Several important technological advances have influenced the shapes of American houses over the three-and-one-half centuries that have passed since the earliest European colonization.

MASSED PLANS—The first advance was the introduction of massed plans into the English colonies during the 18th century. All but a rare handful of 17th-century English colonial houses were of linear plan (one room deep) with high, steeply pitched roofs. These traditional roofs were of ancient origin and were designed to be covered with thatch, which sheds water only if the surface to which it is applied slopes very steeply. Such steep roofs became impossibly high when applied to large massed plans; as a result, most modest English dwellings were of linear plan. The rigors of the New World climate soon led to the abandonment of thatch as a roof covering in favor of more durable wooden planks or shingles. At the same time, the long severe winters of the northern colonies made additional interior space desirable. During the period from about 1700 to 1750, many houses were built, or were expanded, to a one-and-one-half-unit depth. The roofs on these, although now usually shingled, retained the steep framing of Medieval origin. The increased depth was accommodated either by a lower-pitched shed roof over the half-unit extension (most common in one-story houses) or by a rearward continuation of the main roof slope to give a saltbox shape (most common in two-story houses). This shape limited the rearward extension to the relatively shallow depth covered by the downward projection of the steeply pitched roof line. It also truncated the rearward extension at the second-floor level, which could be used only for storage rather than as living space. These disadvantages were overcome through the development of lower-pitched roof framing, which could span a full two-unit depth without excessive height. This transition was virtually completed by 1750; since that time, massed-plan houses have been a dominant feature of American architecture. Note, however, that linear plans, descended from the earlier tradition, have also persisted, particularly in rural and folk building.

HEATING—Two separate technological innovations during the 19th century had profound effects on house shape. The first relates to improvements in heating. Massive fireplaces for burning wood or coal were the principal heating devices until the 1830s, when the first practical cast-iron stoves were introduced. These were vented to the exterior either through metal stovepipes or through small masonry flues. Both of these were far easier to install than massive fireplaces and thus permitted the wider use of larger—and less regular—house plans. Compound plans, in particular, now became more common. Still further improvement came with the introduction of central furnaces that burned wood or coal. These came into common use in the colder northern sections of the country after about 1880. In this system, heat is transferred from the furnace to individual rooms by means of heated water, steam, or air; only a single masonry flue is required to serve the furnace. This development further accelerated the trend toward compound and irregular plans. Yet with each of these heating innovations, the earlier systems were not completely abandoned. Many 19th- and 20th-century houses retain one or more fireplaces, along with stoves or coal-burning furnaces, as a sort of nostalgic interior ornament without essential function. In addition, stoves (now most commonly burning natural gas

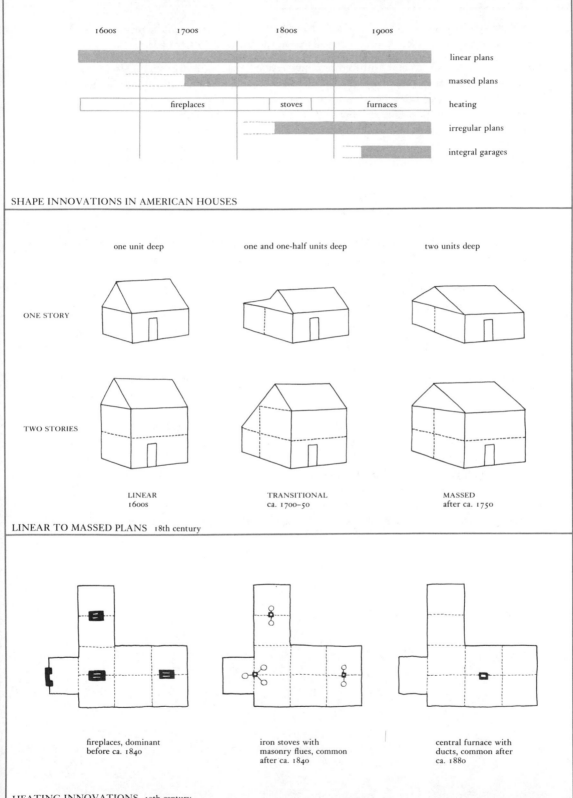

1600s   1700s   1800s   1900s

linear plans

massed plans

fireplaces   stoves   furnaces   heating

irregular plans

integral garages

SHAPE INNOVATIONS IN AMERICAN HOUSES

one unit deep   one and one-half units deep   two units deep

ONE STORY

TWO STORIES

LINEAR
1600s

TRANSITIONAL
ca. 1700–50

MASSED
after ca. 1750

LINEAR TO MASSED PLANS 18th century

fireplaces, dominant
before ca. 1840

iron stoves with
masonry flues, common
after ca. 1840

central furnace with
ducts, common after
ca. 1880

HEATING INNOVATIONS 19th century

rather than wood or coal) and fireplaces have continuously remained the principal means of heating many modest houses, particularly in the milder southern part of the country.

IRREGULAR PLANS—A second 19th-century innovation affecting house shape was balloon-frame construction (see page 37). This relatively rapid and inexpensive method of wooden framing was developed in the Chicago area during the 1830s. In earlier wooden framing systems (post-and-girt; braced-frame), as well as in solid masonry construction, outside corners are particularly difficult to fashion. Masonry is especially susceptible to erosion and failure at corner junctions and usually requires carefully shaped stones—or strengthened brick-bonding patterns—to make secure and permanent corners. Similarly, the heavy timbers of post-and-girt or braced frames require complex, hand-hewn corner joints and braces to give them rigidity. For these reasons, unnecessary outside corners were traditionally avoided in all but the most pretentious houses built with these wall systems. In contrast, corners in balloon (and later, platform) framing are readily constructed with only a few two-inch boards and wire nails. Balloon framing thus freed house shapes from their traditional plane-walled patterns by allowing for easily constructed irregular plans with many extensions and re-entrants. Since the mid-19th century, such irregular wall forms have been commonly superimposed upon both simple and compound plans as balloon framing became the standard construction technique.

INTEGRAL GARAGES—One other technological innovation that affected house shape relates not to building techniques but to transportation: the rise of the automobile as the principal means of personal travel in the 20th century. When automobiles first became common in the decade between 1910 and 1920 they were universally housed, as had been carriages and horses before, in detached, external garages. Such garages have persisted to the present day, but since the 1920s there has been an accelerating trend to house automobiles within portions of, or extensions to, the main house. This trend has dramatically affected the overall size and shape of many houses constructed between 1920 and 1950, and of almost all constructed since 1950. The illustration shows graphically the changing average amount of space devoted to automobile storage (within a standard six-unit plan of 1,000-square-foot area) during the period from 1930 to 1960. Whether placed within the principal mass of the house, as shown, or added as attached units, these automobile shelters have affected the style and form of many 20th-century house facades.

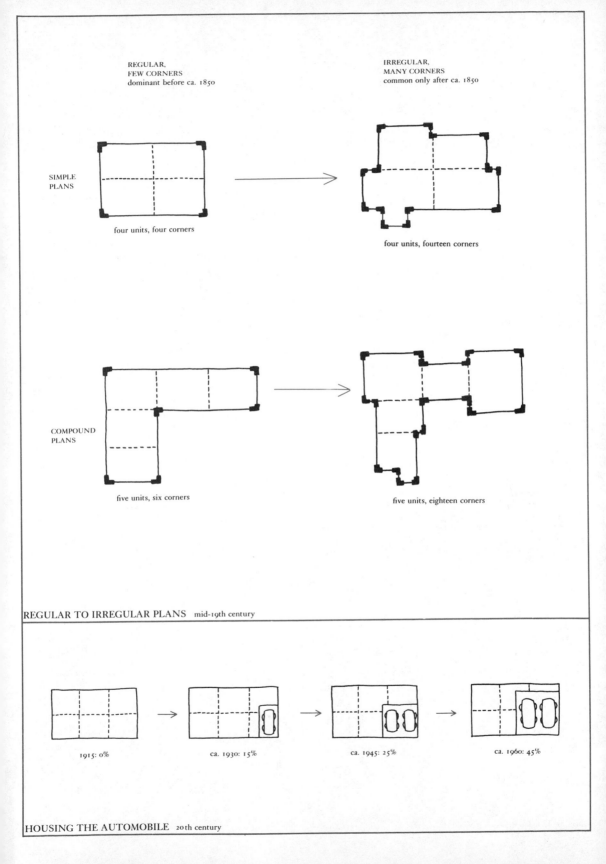

REGULAR,
FEW CORNERS
dominant before ca. 1850

IRREGULAR,
MANY CORNERS
common only after ca. 1850

SIMPLE
PLANS

four units, four corners

four units, fourteen corners

COMPOUND
PLANS

five units, six corners

five units, eighteen corners

REGULAR TO IRREGULAR PLANS   mid-19th century

1915: 0%

ca. 1930: 15%

ca. 1945: 25%

ca. 1960: 45%

HOUSING THE AUTOMOBILE   20th century

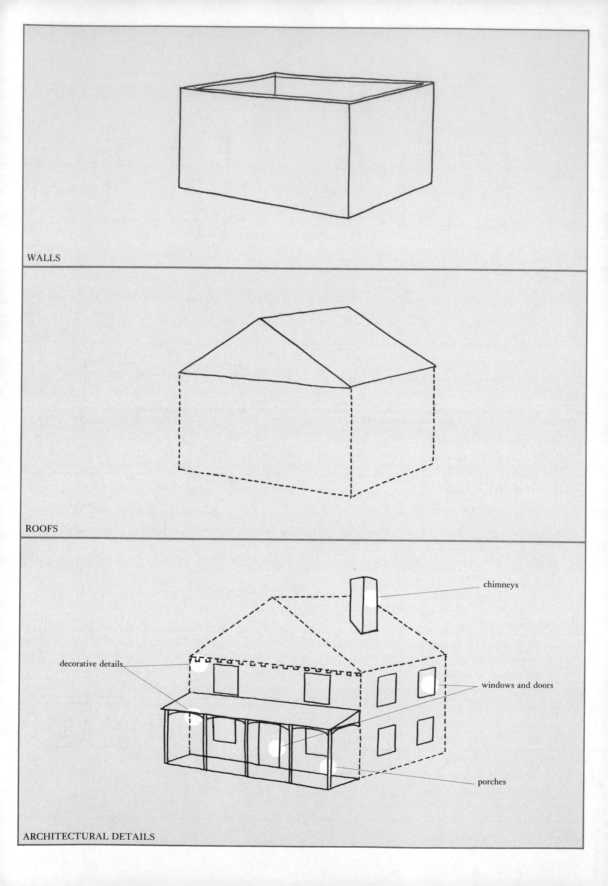

WALLS

ROOFS

ARCHITECTURAL DETAILS

chimneys

decorative details

windows and doors

porches

Structure

In addition to style (fashion) and form (shape), there is a third and somewhat more technical element that is useful for identifying and understanding American houses. This is structure, which can be defined as the several individual components of houses that give them their characteristic forms and styles.

All houses are composed of three basic structural units. First come walls, the vertical units that serve both to screen the interior spaces and to support the second basic unit, the roof, which shields the interior spaces from weather and completes the enclosure. In very simple houses—for example, tipis or modern A-frames—roof and wall may be a single unit. Far more commonly, each is made of different materials combined into separate structural systems. The most important materials and systems used for walls and roofs in American houses are described in the pages that follow. A house made up only of walls and a roof, with an entrance opening in the walls, can be a fully functional shelter. Many simple folk houses have little more. Most American houses, however, have added architectural details to the basic walls and roof, including some or all of the following components: windows, to provide light and ventilation to the interior; doors, to permit the entranceway to be closed against the weather; chimneys, to confine and eliminate smoke from interior fires; porches, partially exposed areas having roofs but lacking one or more walls; and, finally, decorative details, which function to enrich the external appearance of the house.

WALLS

The walls of houses have two separate and distinct functions; first, they provide support for the roof and for any upper floors that may be present; second, they screen the house interior from weather and intrusion. In some types of wall structure—for example, those made up entirely of stone or brick—the same materials serve both functions. In others the functions are separated: one material provides the structural support and another the screening. The most familiar example is the wood-frame house, in which vertical wooden members provide structural support while an exterior covering, or cladding, screens the interior. This first section describes the principal structural support systems used for walls of American houses. The principal cladding materials used with these wall structures are treated below.

WALL FOUNDATIONS—Walls of very modest houses are sometimes built directly on the ground with little or no underlying foundation. Such walls rest on the surface soil, which makes a very poor base for most types of construction. Wooden walls tend to rot when in direct contact with damp earth, while masonry tends to be undercut by rainwater erosion of the soil beneath. For these reasons, most house walls are set upon foundations designed to protect them by raising them above the underlying soil. Simplest are wooden walls set upon wooden posts of some rot-resistant variety such as oak, cedar, or bois d'arc. (Sometimes the posts are, themselves, set directly on the ground surface, but more commonly with this and all other foundation systems, the soil is removed to a depth ranging from several inches to several feet and the base of the foundation is "buried" to provide firmer support.) Columns of brick or stone masonry known as masonry piers provide a similar supporting system for wooden walls, without the danger of rotting. On the other hand, failure of mortar joints can lead to equally serious problems that can be avoided by the use of monolithic piers, sometimes of metal but usually of concrete reinforced by steel rods.

The strong basal timbers of wooden walls can be supported by separated posts or piers; masonry walls, on the other hand, require continuous underlying support. In earlier masonry houses, soil has typically been excavated beneath the proposed wall and the first courses of stone or brick laid on the firm base of the trench. For additional stability, this underlying masonry wall is usually wider and of heavier materials than is the masonry of the overlying walls. When a basement is desired, some or all of the space between the exterior walls is excavated and the foundation walls constructed around the margins of the pit. Similar masonry wall foundations are also common beneath wooden walls, particularly in larger houses or in smaller houses requiring a basement. Foundation walls of masonry, like masonry piers, are subject to erosion and failure of the mortar joints and thus require periodic repair. This problem is avoided by monolithic concrete walls made of concrete beams poured in place and reinforced with internal steel rods. Such foundations first became common in the late 19th century; by the mid-20th century they had generally replaced wooden and masonry foundations beneath all types of wall construction. Note that in all the foundation systems mentioned so far, the internal floors and walls are supported by piers of wood, masonry, concrete, or metal even when the external walls have a continuous masonry or concrete foundation. One additional foundation system, developed in this century, eliminates these internal piers. In such concrete slab foundations, a relatively thin sheet of monolithic poured concrete underlies the entire house. This system completely eliminates floor framing and support at the first-floor level, and has become increasingly common since the 1950s.

WOODEN STRUCTURAL SYSTEMS—Most American houses (probably well over 90 percent) use pieces of wood to support the upper floors and roof. Simplest are walls of horizontal logs, either left round or hewn square, which serve to provide both structural support and, when the cracks between the logs are filled with clay or other materials, weather screening as well. The principal structural support of a log wall is provided by the notched corners, where adjacent logs are in close contact. Several systems of log corner notching have been developed to strengthen this crucial junction. Simplest to construct but least rigid is the saddle joint; progressively more rigid are square, V-notched, and half-dovetail joints; while complex full-dovetail joints provide the strongest structure of all (see also the treatment of log houses on pages 82–3).

Far more common than horizontal log walls are those in which spaced vertical members provide structural support. Earliest is the Medieval post-and-girt system, imported

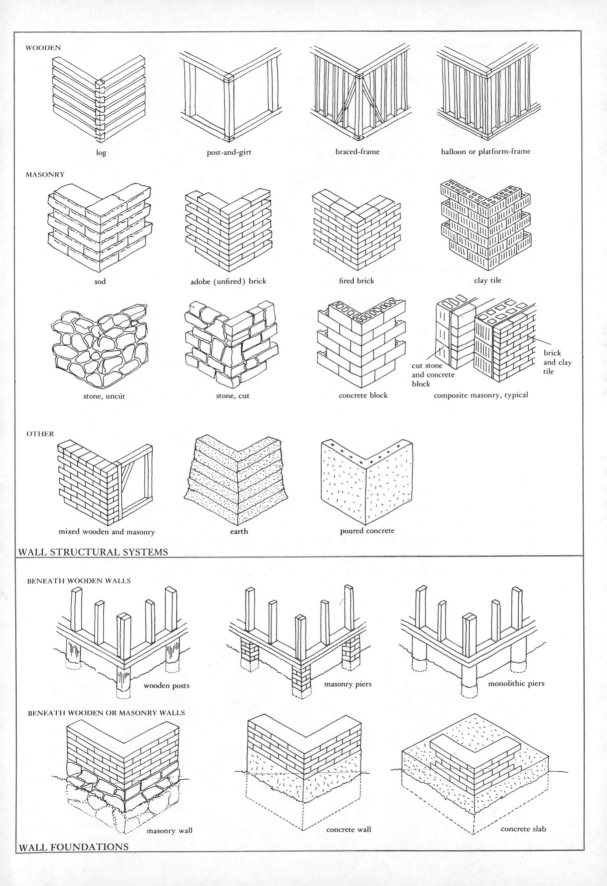

WOODEN

log   post-and-girt   braced-frame   balloon or platform-frame

MASONRY

sod   adobe (unfired) brick   fired brick   clay tile

stone, uncut   stone, cut   concrete block   composite masonry, typical

cut stone and concrete block

brick and clay tile

OTHER

mixed wooden and masonry   earth   poured concrete

WALL STRUCTURAL SYSTEMS

BENEATH WOODEN WALLS

wooden posts   masonry piers   monolithic piers

BENEATH WOODEN OR MASONRY WALLS

masonry wall   concrete wall   concrete slab

WALL FOUNDATIONS

from England and France by the first colonists. In this system, upper loads are borne by heavy corner posts and widely spaced intervening posts; heavy cross timbers carry upper floors which are unsupported by the thin internal walls below. Typically, all structural joints in post-and-girt houses are laboriously hewn into interlocking shapes and held fast by wooden pegs. Post-and-girt houses dominated the English and French colonies and persisted until well after the American Revolution. In the early 19th century, however, the increasing abundance of commercially sawed lumber, together with the development of relatively inexpensive wire nails, led to a modification of the traditional post-and-girt system known as braced-frame construction. This system still employs heavy corner posts connected by heavy horizontal timbers, generally with hewn joints. But within this heavy skeleton, loads are carried not by widely spaced and equally massive intervening posts and cross members, but by light, closely spaced vertical studs nailed between the horizontal timbers. Internal walls constructed entirely of light studs also now become strong bearing walls which help support the floors and roof above. This system takes its name from diagonal corner braces used to give lateral stability to the wooden framework. Note, however, that such braces are by no means unique to the system, but are common in all types of wooden framing.

By the early 19th century, braced frames were replacing post-and-girt construction throughout the former English colonies of the Atlantic seaboard; in this region braced-frame houses persisted well into the 20th century. Westward migration from these states also made this a common mode of construction throughout the country during the 19th century. By the time of the Civil War, however, another still more simplified method of frame construction was coming to dominance in the rapidly developing midwestern states. This was the balloon-frame system, begun in Chicago in the 1830s. This system eliminated altogether the tedious hewn joints and massive timbers of braced-frame and post-and-girt construction, for balloon-frame houses are supported entirely by closely spaced two-inch boards of varying widths (two-by-two, two-by-four, two-by-six, two-by-twelve, etc.) joined only by nails. Corner posts and principal horizontal members are made of two or more two-inch boards nailed together. As in braced-frame houses, the principal supporting members are the closely spaced two-by-four or two-by-six vertical studs of both the exterior and key interior walls. This system allowed both cheaper and more rapid construction by eliminating the need for skilled hand-hewing of the principal

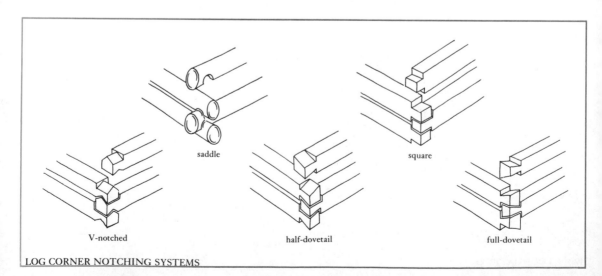

saddle

square

V-notched

half-dovetail

full-dovetail

LOG CORNER NOTCHING SYSTEMS

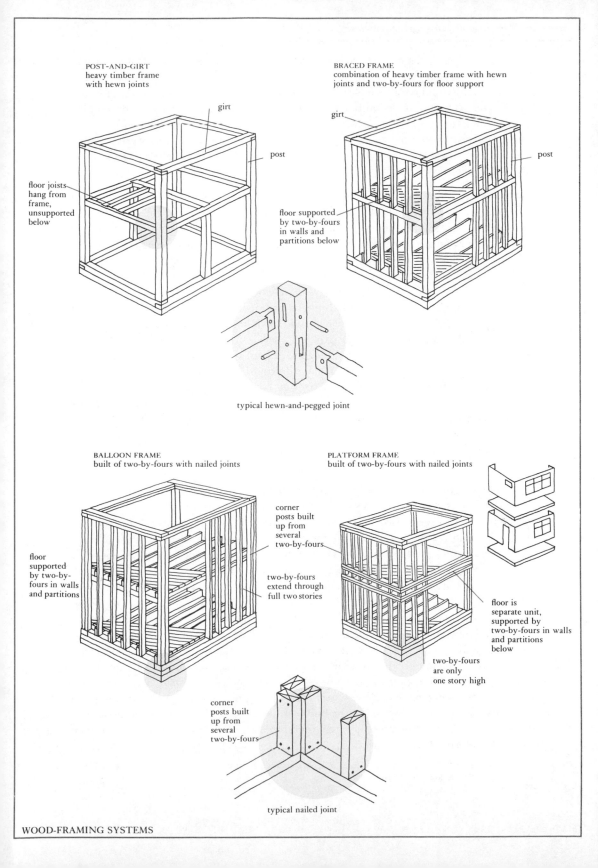

POST-AND-GIRT
heavy timber frame
with hewn joints

girt

post

floor joists
hang from
frame,
unsupported
below

BRACED FRAME
combination of heavy timber frame with hewn
joints and two-by-fours for floor support

girt

post

floor supported
by two-by-fours
in walls and
partitions below

typical hewn-and-pegged joint

BALLOON FRAME
built of two-by-fours with nailed joints

floor
supported
by two-by-
fours in walls
and partitions

PLATFORM FRAME
built of two-by-fours with nailed joints

corner
posts built
up from
several
two-by-fours

two-by-fours
extend through
full two stories

floor is
separate unit,
supported by
two-by-fours in walls
and partitions
below

two-by-fours
are only
one story high

corner
posts built
up from
several
two-by-fours

typical nailed joint

WOOD-FRAMING SYSTEMS

wall timbers. With slight modification it remains the dominant method of American house construction today. The most common modification, known as platform framing, relates primarily to the wall studs and flooring. In balloon-frame construction, the studs are continuous from foundation to roof and the floors are hung upon the studs. In platform framing the floors are constructed as independent units, like thin, flat platforms; the shorter wall studs are then erected upon these platforms to support the overlying platform or roof. This system is both simpler and more rigid than balloon framing, which it has largely replaced through this century.

MASONRY STRUCTURAL SYSTEMS—Although wooden framing has always dominated American house construction, European immigrants to the New World brought with them an intimate knowledge of masonry techniques as well. Indeed, in colonial times, just as today, masonry houses far outnumbered those made of wood throughout most of western Europe. (For this reason first-time visitors from Europe are always surprised to find the United States to be a land of wooden houses). Although making up only a few percent of American houses, those with masonry walls show almost all variations of masonry building technique. Spanish colonists brought traditions of building in uncut stone and unfired adobe brick. The English, French, and Dutch had elaborate techniques of building with harder, fired brick and cut stone, as well as more modest folk traditions of building with sod (blocks of earth held together by grass roots) and uncut stone. These traditions tended to dominate certain regions during the colonial period; most persisted through the 19th century and a few survive even today. Within the last fifty years, 20th-century technology has added two more masonry materials to the traditional repertoire: hollow, fired clay tiles and hollow concrete blocks. These new materials are as strong as fired brick or stone, but are both lighter and cheaper. They have thus come to dominate 20th-century masonry construction, either alone or combined with an exterior layer of brick or stone to make composite masonry walls.

OTHER STRUCTURAL SYSTEMS—Only a very small fraction of one percent of American houses rely on structural systems other than wood or masonry. A few houses, mostly built in colonial times, used both wood and masonry in combination for structural walls.* Typically, end-chimney bearing walls were of masonry, the other walls of post-and-girt frames. In another variation, favored in the French colonies, the first-floor walls were of masonry and the overlying floor was post-and-girt.

Wooden and masonry walls are both composite, that is, they are made up of many small units linked together to make a wall system. Walls can also be of massive or monolithic construction, where only one or, at most, a very few units make up the entire wall. The simplest such walls are made of earth, either mixed with water to make mud and then built up in layers, or pressed into layers while only slightly damp (rammed earth). Such walls are found in both European and Native American folk houses, but are rare in post-colonial America. Somewhat more common are monolithic walls of poured concrete, usually reinforced with iron or steel rods. Such walls can either be poured in place or pre-cast and then transported to the building site. They are common in 20th-century commercial buildings but are only rarely found in houses, most of which date from the late 19th and early 20th centuries.

* Note that many houses have exterior wall *claddings* of both wood and masonry. Houses with true structural walls of both materials are, however, extremely rare.

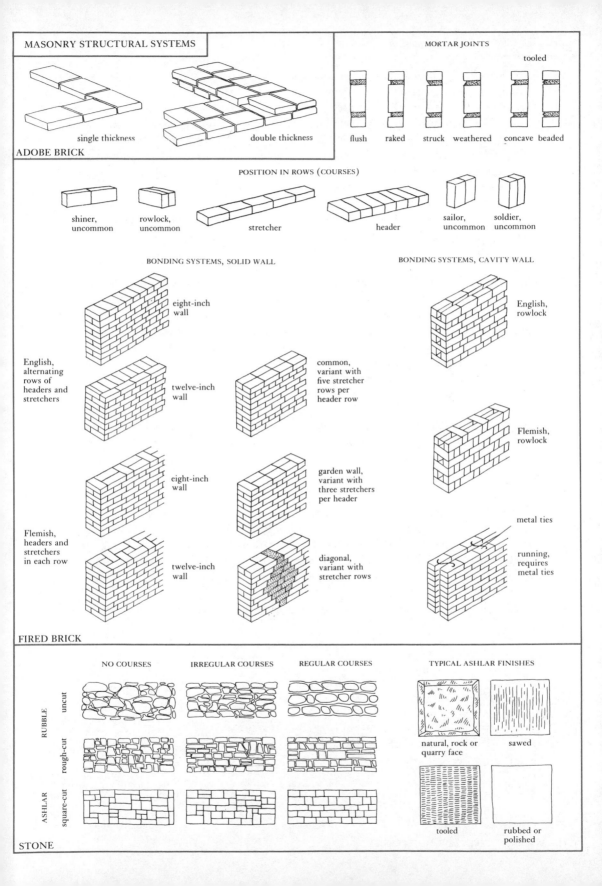

MASONRY STRUCTURAL SYSTEMS

MORTAR JOINTS

tooled

single thickness   double thickness

flush   raked   struck   weathered   concave   beaded

ADOBE BRICK

POSITION IN ROWS (COURSES)

shiner, uncommon   rowlock, uncommon   stretcher   header   sailor, uncommon   soldier, uncommon

BONDING SYSTEMS, SOLID WALL   BONDING SYSTEMS, CAVITY WALL

eight-inch wall   English, rowlock

English, alternating rows of headers and stretchers   twelve-inch wall   common, variant with five stretcher rows per header row

Flemish, rowlock

eight-inch wall   garden wall, variant with three stretchers per header

metal ties

Flemish, headers and stretchers in each row   twelve-inch wall   diagonal, variant with stretcher rows   running, requires metal ties

FIRED BRICK

NO COURSES   IRREGULAR COURSES   REGULAR COURSES   TYPICAL ASHLAR FINISHES

RUBBLE   uncut

natural, rock or quarry face   sawed

rough-cut

ASHLAR   square-cut

tooled   rubbed or polished

STONE

WALL CLADDING—Relatively few systems of wall structure are immediately evident from looking at the exteriors of houses. In masonry walls the structural units of stone or brick *may* be exposed, but equally commonly they are covered with a protective and decorative layer of stucco which masks the underlying structure. As a further complication, wood-frame buildings are often covered with an external layer of brick or stone, which gives them a superficial resemblance to masonry construction. These cladding materials can, however, provide clues to the underlying structure, which is almost always evident on close examination of foundations, basements, and attics.

All wood-frame houses *must* have external cladding. Traditionally the cladding is also of wood, either boards or shingles; since these materials are rarely applied to masonry walls, they indicate an underlying wooden frame. It is usually difficult to tell the exact system of wood framing unless some of the cladding is removed (although, again, a careful examination of wall openings, foundations and attics may reveal the underlying framing). Such modern cladding materials as plywood or fiberboard panels, metal or plastic strips, or asbestos, asphalt, metal, or shingles are also seldom applied to masonry walls, and thus indicate an underlying wood frame. As noted earlier, brick or stone veneers may be difficult to distinguish from solid masonry, except that veneers are far more common; thus the first suspicion should be that *any* house showing external masonry—particularly if constructed in this century—has a veneered wooden frame. An additional clue is that most brick veneers use only a running (stretcher) bond, since no headers are necessary to lock together the multiple rows required in a solid brick wall. Stucco walls can be the most enigmatic of all, for stucco finishes are commonly applied to both wood-frame and masonry buildings. Simple tapping to see if the walls sound hollow will sometimes distinguish between underlying wood or masonry. Likewise, areas of thin or failing stucco may reveal the structure beneath.

HALF-TIMBERING (FILLED WOOD FRAMES)—American wood-frame houses normally have cladding added to the exterior of the frame as a continuous covering that conceals the underlying structure. European framed houses of post-and-girt construction have, since Medieval times, commonly used another system of wall enclosure in which the spaces between the heavy supporting timbers are *filled* rather than covered. Such fillings normally leave the sides of the supporting timbers exposed and are known as half-timbered construction. The most frequent filling material is clay (daub) which is usually applied over a lath of short wooden sticks or woven basketwork (wattle). Brick or stone are also commonly used as filling materials; these are generally covered with stucco and thus

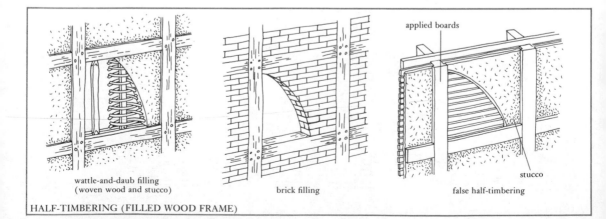

wattle-and-daub filling
(woven wood and stucco)

brick filling

applied boards

stucco

false half-timbering

HALF-TIMBERING (FILLED WOOD FRAME)

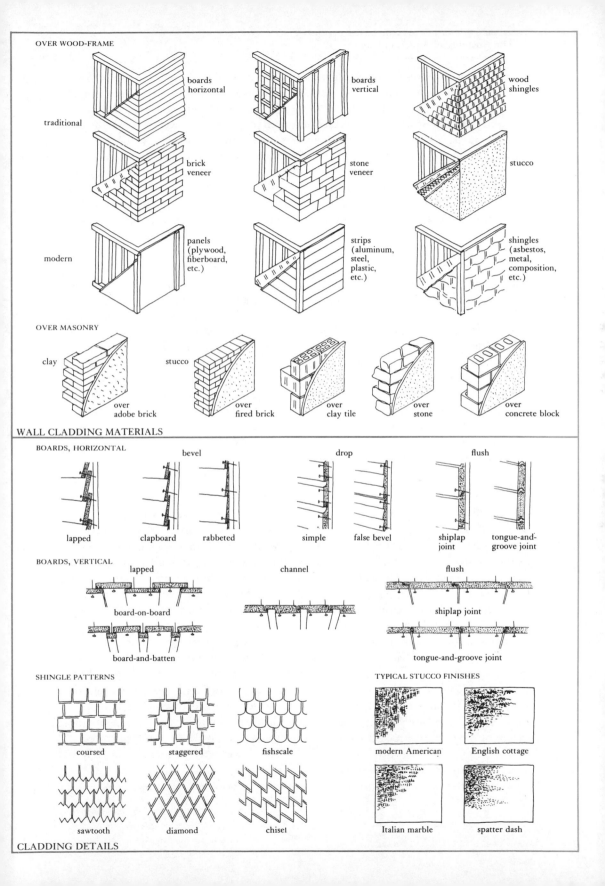

OVER WOOD-FRAME

traditional

boards horizontal

boards vertical

wood shingles

brick veneer

stone veneer

stucco

modern

panels (plywood, fiberboard, etc.)

strips (aluminum, steel, plastic, etc.)

shingles (asbestos, metal, composition, etc.)

OVER MASONRY

clay

over adobe brick

stucco

over fired brick

over clay tile

over stone

over concrete block

WALL CLADDING MATERIALS

BOARDS, HORIZONTAL

bevel

drop

flush

lapped

clapboard

rabbeted

simple

false bevel

shiplap joint

tongue-and-groove joint

BOARDS, VERTICAL

lapped

channel

flush

board-on-board

board-and-batten

shiplap joint

tongue-and-groove joint

SHINGLE PATTERNS

coursed

staggered

fishscale

sawtooth

diamond

chisel

TYPICAL STUCCO FINISHES

modern American

English cottage

Italian marble

spatter dash

CLADDING DETAILS

closely resemble wattle and daub fillings. Early colonists in America first built half-timbered houses, but the rigorous New World climate made it difficult to keep the exposed fillings uncracked and weather-tight. As a result, half-timbering was generally abandoned for wooden claddings or full stuccoing, both of which completely covered the underlying frame. Some surviving English and French colonial houses of post-and-girt construction retain the filled frames of Medieval tradition; in most, the filled frame was either originally—or very early in the house's history—covered by continuous external cladding of wood or stucco. (Some of these have, in this century, been overzealously restored to an exposed, half-timbered exterior.) The half-timbered tradition, although unsuited to the American climate, has persisted as an applied surface decoration (false half-timbering) on 19th- and 20th-century houses that mimic the earlier technique.

ROOFS

Roofs, the second principal structural component of houses, occur in three fundamental shapes: the first is gabled—that is, with two sloping planes supported at their ends by triangular, upward extensions of two walls known as gables. In gabled roofs, the junction of roof and wall occurs not in a single horizontal plane, but at varying levels and angles from the horizontal. In the other two roof shapes, hipped and flat, the roof meets the walls in a single horizontal plane. In hipped roofs, four sloping surfaces form the roof, while only a single horizontal or slightly sloping surface occurs in flat roofs. Each of these three principal shapes has several subtypes. These patterns of roof shape are among the most dominant features in determining the external appearances of houses. Thus they provide the basis for many of the stylistic subtypes defined throughout this book. After shape, the most apparent roof feature is pitch—the angle the sloping roof planes make with the horizontal. Both gabled and hipped roofs show marked changes in character as they pass from low pitches (under 30°) through "normal" pitches (30°–45°) to steep pitches (over 45°).

Roof framing—Roofs in all but a very small number of American houses are supported by wooden frameworks, for wood combines suitable strength and relatively light weight (as does metal, which is rarely used for this purpose in houses), thus making possible the long spanning members required for roof support. Two principal roof-framing systems have been used in American houses.* The earlier employed heavy principal rafters with hewn joints as the principal supporting members. Lighter members (either common rafters or common purlins) were placed between the principal rafters to provide a base for attaching the roofing material. This system is analogous to post-and-girt wall framing and, indeed, is found on most early post-and-girt—as well as masonry—houses. With the rise of lighter braced, balloon, and platform wall framing it was discovered that light, closely spaced common rafters, joined by nails, provided adequate roof support without the need for intervening heavy timbers. Such common rafter roof-framing systems are almost universal in American houses built after the mid-19th century.

Principal rafters of heavy timber require little additional bracing to support the weight of the overlying roof, particularly if the roof is steeply pitched and spans a relatively narrow space below. Rafters of lighter weight, lower pitch, or longer span require underlying supporting systems of joists or trusses.

* A third system uses horizontal logs rather than a wooden framework and is employed in many Spanish Colonial houses; see page 131.

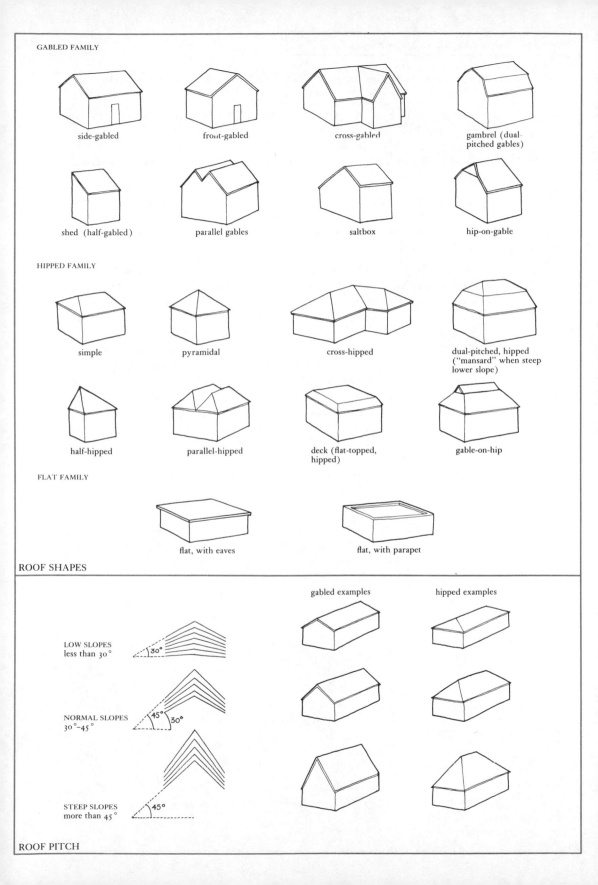

GABLED FAMILY

side-gabled front-gabled cross-gabled gambrel (dual-pitched gables)

shed (half-gabled) parallel gables saltbox hip-on-gable

HIPPED FAMILY

simple pyramidal cross-hipped dual-pitched, hipped ("mansard" when steep lower slope)

half-hipped parallel-hipped deck (flat-topped, hipped) gable-on-hip

FLAT FAMILY

flat, with eaves flat, with parapet

ROOF SHAPES

gabled examples hipped examples

LOW SLOPES less than 30° 30°

NORMAL SLOPES 30°–45° 45° 30°

STEEP SLOPES more than 45° 45°

ROOF PITCH

Simple gabled roofs always require the least complex underlying framing; the additional roof planes of gambreled or hipped roofs demand additional framing members.

ROOF-WALL JUNCTIONS—The lines of junction between roof and wall are crucial features of house design, both esthetically and structurally, for they join differing roof and wall materials in a junction that must be watertight to protect the underlying structure from damaging moisture. There are various systems of attaching roof to wall (and for enclosing this important junction).

DORMERS—Finally, roof slopes may be interrupted by dormers, subunits resembling miniature houses with their own walls, roofs, and windows. These are added to provide space, light, and ventilation to the attic, thus making it a functional part of the house. Dormers are most easily characterized by their roof shapes.

ROOFING MATERIALS—Resting upon the wooden framework is the watertight covering, which adds texture and color to the sloping roof planes and thus has a dominant effect on the external appearance of a house. Four principal kinds of materials are used for roofing.

The first are organic coverings. Of these, thatch, closely packed bundles of reeds or straw, is the most common roofing for folk houses throughout the world. Although thatch is commonly used on modest European dwellings, it was quickly abandoned by American colonists because it was particularly vulnerable to the high winds, driving rains, and severe winters of the New World. Long boards of split wood were sometimes substituted for thatch in early colonial houses but these, too, were rather quickly abandoned for roofs of wooden shingles—thin wedge-shaped rectangles that were either rough-split or sawed from oak, cedar, or other durable woods. Shingles could be closely aligned and generously overlapped to give an impervious and weather-resistant roof;

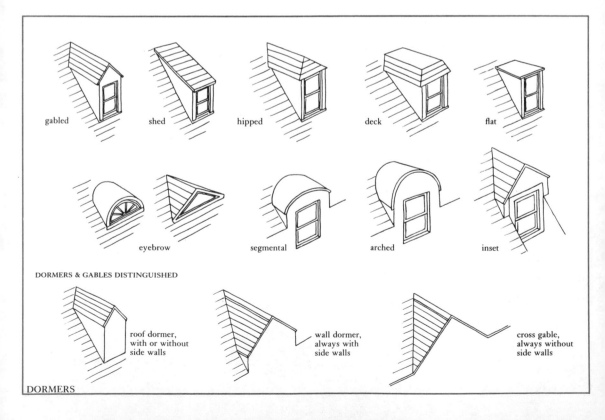

gabled   shed   hipped   deck   flat

eyebrow   segmental   arched   inset

DORMERS & GABLES DISTINGUISHED

roof dormer, with or without side walls

wall dormer, always with side walls

cross gable, always without side walls

DORMERS

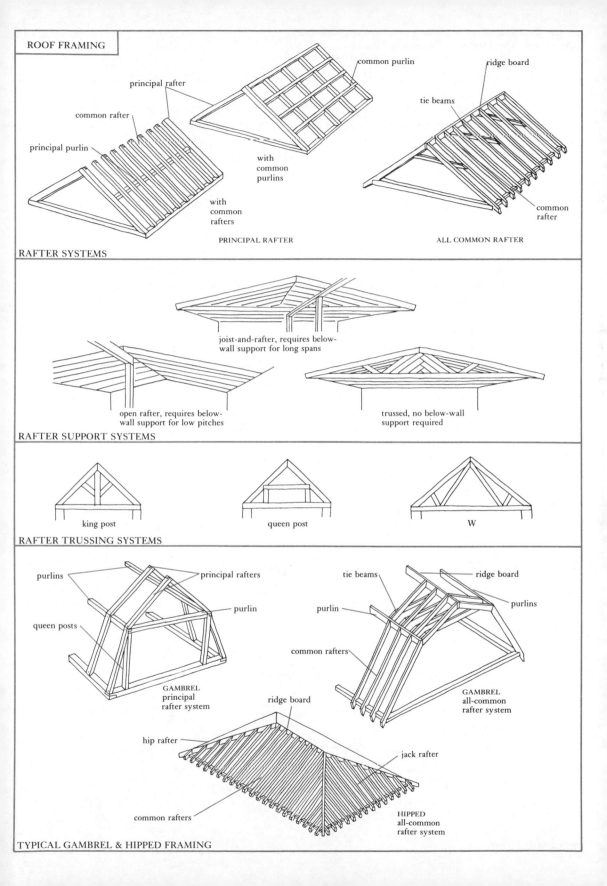

ROOF FRAMING

principal rafter

common rafter

principal purlin

with common rafters

common purlin

with common purlins

PRINCIPAL RAFTER

ridge board

tie beams

common rafter

ALL COMMON RAFTER

RAFTER SYSTEMS

joist-and-rafter, requires below-wall support for long spans

open rafter, requires below-wall support for low pitches

trussed, no below-wall support required

RAFTER SUPPORT SYSTEMS

king post

queen post

W

RAFTER TRUSSING SYSTEMS

purlins

principal rafters

purlin

queen posts

GAMBREL principal rafter system

tie beams

ridge board

purlins

purlin

common rafters

GAMBREL all-common rafter system

ridge board

hip rafter

jack rafter

common rafters

HIPPED all-common rafter system

TYPICAL GAMBREL & HIPPED FRAMING

since colonial times, wooden shingles have remained a dominant roofing material of American houses.

Roofs of mineral materials also have a long history. Simplest are roofs of earth, or of earth bound by grass roots to make sod; both are common on folk dwellings everywhere. Both the earliest New World colonists and 19th-century settlers in the treeless western half of the country commonly used earth or sod roofs on temporary dwellings. They are also used for the roofs of permanent Spanish-influenced dwellings in the American Southwest. Roofs of thin, flat pieces of natural stone, tightly overlapped as with wooden shingles, were common in the larger dwellings of Medieval and Postmedieval Europe. An abundance of wood for making shingles—and a relative scarcity of quality slate, the most easily split and durable type of stone—made such roofs uncommon in this country until the late 19th century, when they began to be used in houses that simulated earlier European traditions. A third type of mineral roof, composed of thin, shaped units of baked clay tiles, was developed in classical times and has since remained a continuous feature in European architecture. Several systems of interlocking tile units have been developed through this long history. Most of these systems have been employed on monumental New World houses since colonial times but, like slate roofs, they have been common only since the late 19th century. In the 20th century, tiles made from concrete and other composite ceramic materials have been developed which simulate clay tile. (Note also that metal and composition roofs are often shaped and colored to resemble ceramic tile.)

Metal roofs also have a long history, for sheets of lead or copper have been used as roofing since classical times. A few landmark colonial houses of the New World used such roofs, but metal became a common roofing material only in the early 19th century when sheet iron (usually coated with zinc, tin, or lead to prevent rust) first became relatively inexpensive and plentiful. Usually metal roofs are applied as large sheets joined with standing seams, which help prevent leaks. Later in the 19th century, stronger corrugated panels of iron became common for roofing of commercial and modest domestic

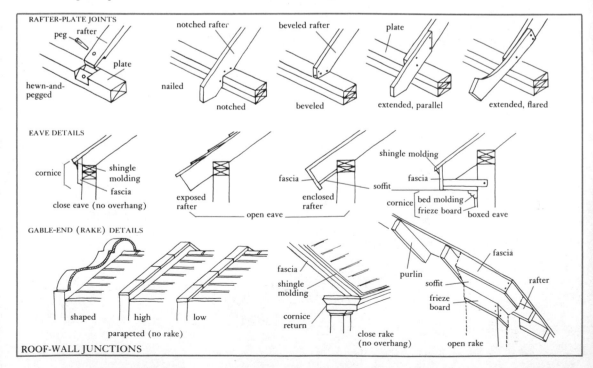

ROOF-WALL JUNCTIONS

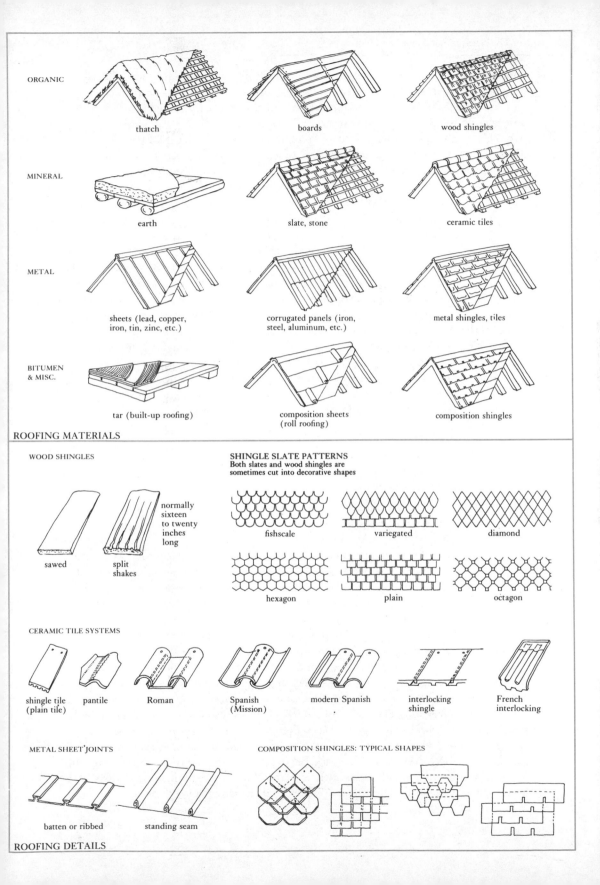

ORGANIC

thatch

boards

wood shingles

MINERAL

earth

slate, stone

ceramic tiles

METAL

sheets (lead, copper, iron, tin, zinc, etc.)

corrugated panels (iron, steel, aluminum, etc.)

metal shingles, tiles

BITUMEN & MISC.

tar (built-up roofing)

composition sheets (roll roofing)

composition shingles

ROOFING MATERIALS

WOOD SHINGLES

sawed

split shakes

normally sixteen to twenty inches long

SHINGLE SLATE PATTERNS
Both slates and wood shingles are sometimes cut into decorative shapes

fishscale

variegated

diamond

hexagon

plain

octagon

CERAMIC TILE SYSTEMS

shingle tile (plain tile)

pantile

Roman

Spanish (Mission)

modern Spanish

interlocking shingle

French interlocking

METAL SHEET JOINTS

batten or ribbed

standing seam

COMPOSITION SHINGLES: TYPICAL SHAPES

ROOFING DETAILS

buildings. Their rigidity gives such panels the advantage of requiring less underlying support than do most roofing materials. In the 20th century, panels of corrugated aluminum are sometimes used for the same reason. Other metal roofs are made up of smaller units shaped to resemble shingles or ceramic tiles.

The fourth type of roofing is based on bitumen, natural semi-solid petroleum residues such as tar and asphalt. Since colonial times natural tar deposits have been used—along with tar-impregnated sheets of cloth, felt, or paper—to make built-up roofs. Unlike roofs made up of smaller units, which must be pitched upward to prevent water from entering the joints between units, monolithic roofs of tar (or earth) can remain impervious when almost flat (many flat-roofed Spanish Colonial houses of the Los Angeles area had built-up tar roofs, the material coming from nearby natural tar pits). Although most common on commercial buildings, built-up roofs have also been a standard technique of house roofing since the mid-19th century. Tar normally has to be heated to make it liquid enough to spread on built-up roofs. It also must be protected from the sun's rays, which make it hard and brittle, by gravel or other material. By the late 19th century, techniques had been developed to convert tar or asphalt into "cold" roofing by impregnating sheets or shingles of felt, paper, or cloth with bitumen. Such composition roofs had the advantage of being easy to apply, relatively inexpensive, and fire-resistant. They have become the dominant roofing (or re-roofing) material for American houses in the 20th century. Other materials, in addition to petroleum-based bitumen, have also been used for making composition shingles. In particular, shingles of asbestos fibers bound together by concrete were widely used in the early decades of the 20th century.

ARCHITECTURAL DETAILS

In addition to walls and roofs, many kinds of architectural details contribute to the external appearance of houses. The most important of these are windows and doors; chimneys; porches; and decorative details.

WINDOWS AND DOORS—Windows are wall openings that provide light and ventilation for the house interior. The word itself derives from "wind-holes," early openings that served principally to supply draft, and emit smoke, from internal fires. Early windows were without glass, which was a rare and expensive luxury until the 17th century. When ventilation wasn't required, the openings were covered with fabric or skins or by solid wooden sashes or shutters. Many schemes have been devised for opening and closing such shutters, and later glazed sashes; most have been in continuous use since at least Medieval times.

To admit light through the closed window, frames covered with translucent oiled cloth or paper came to be used instead of solid shutters in prosperous Medieval houses. Many such windows were used in colonial America, but glass glazing was also becoming widespread in England, Holland, and France at about the time of the first New World colonization. These 17th-century window sashes were glazed with many small panes of glass, usually either square or diamond-shaped, held in a wooden or metal frame by narrow strips of soft lead. Throughout the 18th and early 19th centuries, window sashes came to be glazed with panes of increasing size, as glass-making techniques improved and costs decreased. By the mid-19th century, panes large enough to glaze sashes in only one or, at the most, two units became widely available. Since then, multi-paned sashes have been used only because of historical precedent rather than technological necessity.

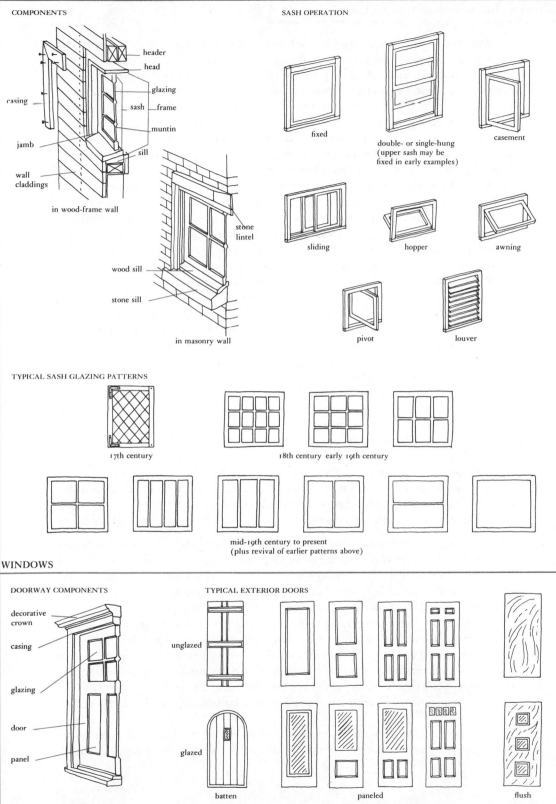

COMPONENTS

header
head
glazing
casing
sash
frame
glazing
muntin
jamb
sill
wall claddings

in wood-frame wall

stone lintel
wood sill
stone sill

in masonry wall

SASH OPERATION

fixed

double- or single-hung
(upper sash may be
fixed in early examples)

casement

sliding

hopper

awning

pivot

louver

TYPICAL SASH GLAZING PATTERNS

17th century

18th century   early 19th century

mid-19th century to present
(plus revival of earlier patterns above)

WINDOWS

DOORWAY COMPONENTS

decorative crown
casing
glazing
door
panel

TYPICAL EXTERIOR DOORS

unglazed

glazed

batten

paneled

flush

DOORS

Although some 17th-century window frames and sashes were of iron, windows with wooden frames, sashes, and glazing bars (muntins) became almost universal in the 18th and early 19th centuries. Beginning in the mid-19th century, industrialization made available mass-produced metal windows. These remained relatively rare until the 1930s; since then they have progressively increased in use and are now the dominant type of window in American houses.

Windows are an architectural luxury lacking in some modest folk houses. At least one exterior doorway is essential, however, to permit entrance and exit of the occupants. Originally the doorway served also as the principal "wind-hole" for regulating light and ventilation (hence the phrase: "Never again darken my doorway"). Doors for closing off the doorway are almost universally made of wood in American houses. Because single pieces of wood are never large enough to cover a full door opening, doors are always composite—that is, made up of many small pieces of wood. In the earliest and simplest form of the door, vertical planks are held together with horizontal strips called battens, which are nailed or screwed to the surface of the larger planks.

By the 18th century, more elaborate doors were becoming common. These paneled doors consisted of an exterior framework of relatively thick planks, carefully joined and interlocked, which supported thinner internal planks (or panels). Such doors combine the virtues of strength, light weight, and decorative appearance; they remain the most common type of door in American houses, although they have come to be increasingly replaced in this century by the flush door. Flush doors appear to be single, flat pieces of wood but are, in fact, of veneered construction. They are made up of large, thin sheets of wood that are first peeled from a log with a razor-sharp knife, then glued together to make a strong, composite unit (this same process also produces plywood panels, which have replaced wooden planks for many construction uses in this century). In more modest flush doors, single thin sheets of veneer are applied to the exterior of a solid or hollow framework of joined planks to make a sort of sandwich structure.

It is usually desirable for external doorways, when closed, to admit light into entrance rooms or hallways. Thus many doors are partially glazed with fixed glass panes, which are found in all the principal types—batten, paneled, and flush. Note also that additional glazing is often provided around the door in the form of side or overhead lights.

CHIMNEYS—Chimneys are hollow columns of masonry that provide a restricted exit for the smoke and fumes of internal cooking and heating fires. Houses have sheltered fires since the dawn of human civilization, yet chimneys are a relatively recent innovation, having only become widespread in modest English houses at about the time of the first American colonization. This innovation was brought to the New World, where chimneys became a standard feature of American houses. The simplest chimneys are constructed of wooden frameworks covered with a hardened coating of clay. Such chimneys require constant repair and become a serious fire hazard if the coating fails. Thus they are usually replaced by solid masonry chimneys as quickly as circumstances permit. Both brick and stone masonry are widely used in chimney construction, but brick is the preferred material since the regular shape decreases the chance of joint failures, and thus hidden chimney fires.

Although internal fires for heating and cooking are all but universal in American houses, chimneys are not. The first cause of their decline was the development of practi-

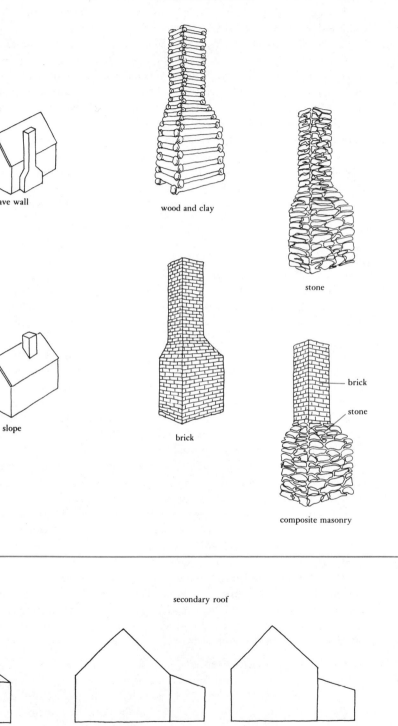

PLACEMENT

exterior

gable wall

eave wall

interior

end

slope

ridge

TYPICAL CONSTRUCTION

wood and clay

stone

brick

composite masonry

brick

stone

CHIMNEYS

principal roof

secondary roof

extended

dropped

PORCH ROOF CONSTRUCTION

cal iron stoves and ranges. Stoves made of iron plates were known in Medieval Europe and were introduced in the United States by Benjamin Franklin in the 18th century. These sheet-iron stoves were, however, leaky and inefficient; the widespread adoption of iron stoves and ranges did not begin until the 1830s when relatively cheap and airtight units of cast iron were introduced. These required only a metal pipe to vent smoke and fumes to the outside and led to widespread abandonment of large masonry chimneys. In modest houses the stoves were often vented only by metal pipes extended through roof or wall. More commonly, massive fireplaces were replaced with narrow masonry flues, to which the metal stovepipes were connected. These led to small chimneys and provided a safer, fireproof escape for the hot concentrated fumes of stove and range.

A second cause of the decline of external chimneys has been the widespread adoption of natural gas and electricity for heating and cooking in the 20th century. These, too, require only metal pipes for external venting and thus the once essential chimney and fireplace have become only nostalgic luxuries in most 20th-century houses.

PORCHES—In British usage the word "porch" means sheltered entranceway, either partially open or enclosed on all sides to make a small room. Porches in the American sense—that is, roofed but incompletely walled living areas—are rare in Europe, where such spaces are known by other names: *verandah* or *piazza* (Britain), *galerie* (France), *portale* (Spain), or *loggia* (Italy). The origin and inspiration of the far more common *porch* of American houses has been much debated. It was clearly adopted because of the oppressive heat and frequent thundershower deluges of the New World summers, but its exact sources remain uncertain.

Porches are normally constructed in either of two ways: one or more external walls can be omitted under the principal house roof to give an inset porch; or, an additional roof can be added onto the principal roof to give a smaller porch roof which is relatively independent of the main roof. Both types are common in American houses. Roofs are normally supported by the external house walls; when some of these are deleted to make a porch, columns or other roof-supporting devices are required. In addition, when porches occur much above ground level, a railing or low wall, usually with an open framework to admit breezes, is required for safety. These supporting members and enclosures can be of wood, masonry, or metal and provide rich opportunities for decorative embellishment of the house facade.

Even in colonial times, porches were becoming common in the New World: both French and English colonists in the warmer, southern colonies commonly added verandahs or galeries to their houses. The use of large porches expanded until, by the late 19th and early 20th centuries, they had become an almost universal, and quite distinctive, feature of American domestic architecture. These showed an enormous variety of size, shape, and placement; many houses had several porches, or extended porches covering several walls. By the mid-20th century, this trend was completely reversed. Changing fashions—and the development of air-conditioning for summer cooling—have all but eliminated this once dominant feature of the American house facade.

DECORATIVE DETAILS—Architectural details such as windows, doors, chimneys, and porches all serve important practical functions. One other category of detail has no such obvious use but is, instead, added principally to enhance the beauty of the house exterior. Such decorative details are of two main types: in the first, the principal coverings of the house exterior—the wall cladding or roofing—are decoratively elaborated. Shaped shingles or patterned masonry are examples of this kind of decorative detail. Still more common is the second type of decorative elaboration, in which neither the roof nor walls but rather some smaller functional detail is elaborated with decorative trim. Door and window openings are commonly embellished in this way; door surrounds are particularly favored since they are closely observed by all who enter the house. Indeed, certain eras of American house building are largely characterized by their distinctive elaborated door surrounds. Windows are commonly embellished by decorative surrounds or crowns, by shaped window openings, or, most commonly, by differing shapes and sizes of glass panes. Roof-wall junctions are another favored site for the addition of decorative detail: elaborate moldings or trim, commonly matched to those of doors and windows, are frequently added beneath eaves and rakes. Chimneys, too, provide decorative opportunities; decorative shapes and patterns in brick, stone, or stucco are common. Finally, as noted above, porches provide a wealth of decorative opportunity; roof-support columns and protective balustrades have been elaborated in a nearly endless variety of decorative patterns.

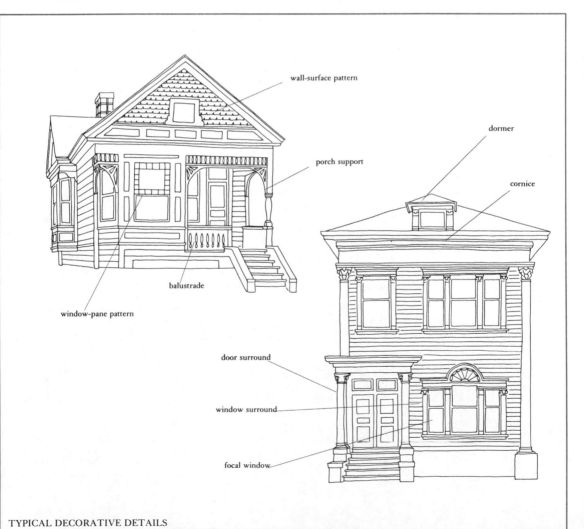

TYPICAL DECORATIVE DETAILS

Pictorial Key

Walls

IF YOU SEE		TRY THESE FIRST
logs		Pre-Railroad Folk
half-timbering		Tudor, Craftsman, Queen Anne, French Eclectic, Prairie
adobe		Pueblo Revival, Spanish Colonial
rough-faced stone		Richardsonian Romanesque, Shingle (first story only)
smooth stone		Beaux Arts, Chateauesque, Italian Renaissance
stucco		Tudor, Mission, Spanish Eclectic, Prairie, Modernistic, International, Italian Renaissance, French Colonial, occasionally in most other styles
patterned wood shingles		Queen Anne, Shingle, Folk Victorian
plain wood shingles		Shingle, Craftsman, Colonial Revival, Postmedieval English
patterned stick-work on walls		Stick, Queen Anne, Exotic Revival (Swiss)
rusticated stone (joints exaggerated)		Beaux Arts, Italian Renaissance
wall surface material extends up into gable without break		Gothic Revival, Tudor, Postmedieval English
second-story overhang		Colonial Revival, Tudor, Postmedieval English

Roof form

IF YOU SEE			TRY THESE FIRST
side-gabled	steep pitch		Tudor, Gothic Revival, Stick, Queen Anne, French Colonial, Postmedieval English
	moderate or varied pitch		Colonial Revival, Georgian, Adam, Early Classical Revival, Folk Victorian, Neoclassical, Shingle, National Folk, Pre-Railroad Folk
	low pitch		Craftsman, Spanish Eclectic, Italianate, Monterey, Greek Revival, Dutch Colonial, Spanish Colonial, Adam
front-gabled (also tri-gabled)	steep pitch		Gothic Revival, Stick, Queen Anne, less commonly Tudor
	moderate or varied pitch		National Folk, Shingle, Folk Victorian, Neoclassical, less commonly Colonial Revival
	low pitch		Greek Revival, Italianate, Craftsman, less commonly Spanish Eclectic

Roof form

IF YOU SEE		TRY THESE FIRST
cross-gabled (or gable front and wings)	steep pitch	Tudor, Queen Anne, Stick, Gothic Revival
	moderate or varied pitch	Shingle, National Folk, Early Classical Revival
	low pitch	Craftsman, Spanish Eclectic, Greek Revival, Monterey
centered gable or	steep pitch	Gothic Revival
	moderate or varied pitch	**Colonial Revival, Georgian, Adam**
	low pitch	**Italianate, Italian Renaissance, Beaux Arts**
gambrel		Dutch Colonial, Shingle, Colonial Revival, Georgian
hipped (with ridge)	steep pitch	French Eclectic, Chateauesque, French Colonial
	moderate or varied pitch	Colonial Revival, Georgian, Adam, Early Classical Revival, Folk Victorian, Mission, Neoclassical
	low pitch	Italianate, Adam, Greek Revival, Italian Renaissance, Spanish Eclectic, Prairie
hipped (pyramidal)	steep pitch	Chateauesque, French Eclectic
	moderate or varied pitch	National Folk, Colonial Revival, Neoclassical, Folk Victorian, Mission
	low pitch	Prairie, Italianate
mansard		Second Empire, Beaux Arts, Richardsonian Romanesque
hipped with cross gables		Queen Anne, Richardsonian Romanesque, Shingle
flat	symmetrical	Beaux arts, Italian Renaissance, Adam (rare), town house subtypes
	asymmetrical	International, Modernistic, Pueblo Revival, Spanish Eclectic, Spanish Colonial, town house subtypes
pent or visor		Georgian, Colonial Revival, Mission

Roof-wall junction

IF YOU SEE	TRY THESE FIRST
parapet on flat roof (wall extends up beyond roof edge)	Beaux Arts, Italian Renaissance, Pueblo Revival, Spanish Eclectic, Mission, Modernistic, International, Spanish Colonial
parapet on gabled roof	Tudor, Queen Anne, Richardsonian Romanesque, Mission, French Colonial
no eaves (little or no overhang)	International, Modernistic, Spanish Eclectic, Postmedieval English
slight eave overhang, boxed with modillions, dentils, or other classical moldings	Colonial Revival, Neoclassical, Beaux Arts, Adam, Georgian, French Eclectic, Early Classical Revival, Chateauesque, Italian Renaissance
slight eave overhang, open, not boxed	Stick, Gothic Revival
slight eave overhang with brackets	Second Empire, Folk Victorian, Italianate

55

Roof-wall junction

IF YOU SEE		TRY THESE FIRST
slight eave overhang with wide band of trim below		Greek Revival
wide eave overhang, boxed without brackets		Prairie
wide eave overhang, boxed with brackets		Italianate, Italian Renaissance, Prairie, occasionally Mission
wide eave overhang, open, not boxed		Craftsman, Mission

Dormers

IF YOU SEE		TRY THESE FIRST
hipped		Prairie, French Eclectic, Shingle
gabled		Craftsman, Colonial Revival, Adam, Georgian, Shingle, Queen Anne, Stick, Gothic Revival, Tudor, Chateauesque, French Eclectic
shed		Dutch Colonial, Craftsman, Colonial Revival
arched top		French Eclectic, Second Empire, Beaux Arts
round or oval		French Eclectic, Beaux Arts
pedimented		Colonial Revival, Georgian, Adam
wall dormers		Gothic Revival, Chateauesque, Richardsonian Romanesque, Mission
eyebrow		Shingle, Richardsonian Romanesque

shaped		Mission, Queen Anne, Tudor

Other roof elaborations

IF YOU SEE		TRY THESE FIRST
towers, square		Italianate, Stick, Second Empire, occasionally Queen Anne, Mission, Italian Renaissance
towers, round		Queen Anne, Richardsonian Romanesque, Chateauesque, Shingle, French Eclectic, occasionally Spanish Eclectic
roof-top cupolas		Italianate, Octagon, Second Empire, Greek Revival
decorated verge boards		Tudor, Gothic Revival, Queen Anne
trusses in gables		Craftsman, Stick, Gothic Revival, Queen Anne, Tudor
false beams at gable end		Craftsman, Prairie
flared eaves		French Eclectic, French Colonial, Prairie, Stick, Dutch Colonial, Craftsman
multi-level eaves		Tudor, Shingle, French Eclectic, others occasionally
tile roof	rounded tiles, usually red	Spanish Eclectic, Mission, Italian Renaissance, Prairie
	flat pantiles	Tudor, occasionally Neoclassical, Colonial Revival, Italian Renaissance
exposed rafters		Craftsman, Stick, Mission, occasionally Prairie or Gothic Revival

Other roof elaborations

IF YOU SEE		TRY THIS FIRST
pinnacles		Chateauesque, Richardsonian Romanesque
castellations		Gothic Revival, Tudor
roof-top or roof-line balustrade		Neoclassical, Colonial Revival, Adam, Georgian, Beaux Arts, Early Classical Revival, Italian Renaissance
metal roof cresting		Queen Anne, Chateauesque

Arched doors, windows, porches

IF YOU SEE		TRY THIS FIRST
segmental		Georgian, Adam, Colonial Revival, Italianate
round		Italian Renaissance, Italianate, Richardsonian Romanesque, Spanish Eclectic, less common in Adam, Colonial Revival, Beaux Arts, Mission, Tudor
Syrian		Richardsonian Romanesque, Shingle
pointed (Gothic)		Gothic Revival
Tudor (flattened Gothic)		Tudor, Gothic Revival
baskethandle (elliptical)		Chateauesque, Beaux Arts, Italianate
ogee		Exotic Revivals, Chateauesque

Doors

IF YOU SEE		TRY THIS FIRST
transom lights		Georgian, Colonial Revival, Pre-Railroad Folk
round fanlight or elliptical fanlight with sidelights		Adam, Colonial Revival, Early Classical Revival, Neoclassical
rectangular transom and side lights		Greek Revival, Neoclassical
six- to eight-panel door		Adam, Georgian, Colonial Revival, Early Classical Revival
board-and-batten door		Postmedieval English, Spanish Colonial, Tudor, Spanish Eclectic, Pueblo
pilasters to sides of door (may have pediment)		Georgian, Adam, Early Classical Revival, Greek Revival, Italianate, Second Empire, Colonial Revival, Neoclassical, Chateauesque, Beaux Arts, Italian Renaissance, French Eclectic
pediment / broken pediment		Colonial Revival, Georgian, Neoclassical, Italian Renaissance, Beaux Arts, Italianate, Greek Revival (triangular only)

Windows

IF YOU SEE		TRY THIS FIRST
casement		Prairie, Tudor, Spanish Eclectic, Postmedieval English, Dutch Colonial, Modernistic, International (metal only)
Palladian		Adam, Queen Anne (free classic), Shingle, Colonial Revival, Neoclassical

Windows

IF YOU SEE		TRY THESE FIRST
pediment	unbroken	Colonial Revival, Georgian, Adam, Italianate, Beaux Arts, Italian Renaissance, Neoclassical
	broken	Colonial Revival, Neoclassical, occasionally Georgian, Queen Anne
oriel		Gothic Revival, Tudor, Chateauesque
label mold		Gothic Revival, Chateauesque, occasionally Tudor, French Eclectic
hood mold		Italianate
ribbon (three or more contiguous windows)		Prairie, Craftsman, Modernistic, International, all post-1900 Eclectic styles may have such windows, but usually on side wings, not on main house block
		Shingle, Richardsonian Romanesque
large pane surrounded by smaller panes		Queen Anne
blank lower pane with patterned pane above		Queen Anne, most Eclectic styles
paired window		Italianate or later style
attic story		Greek Revival, Beaux Arts, Italian Renaissance
bracketed tops		Italianate, Second Empire, Gothic Revival, Stick

Chimneys

IF YOU SEE		TRY THESE FIRST
dominant decorated chimneys		Tudor, Queen Anne, Postmedieval English, French Eclectic (towered)

Porch supports

IF YOU SEE		TRY THESE FIRST
classical columns, two-story (colossal)		Neoclassical, Greek Revival, Early Classical Revival, Beaux Arts
classical columns, one-story		Italianate, Greek Revival, Early Classical Revival, Neoclassical, Beaux Arts, Adam, Colonial Revival, Queen Anne (free classic), Italian Renaissance
columns with cushion capital		Richardsonian Romanesque
chamfered (corners shaved off at 45° angles)		Italianate, Gothic Revival, Second Empire, Stick
turned spindles		Queen Anne (except free classic), Folk Victorian
heavy squared piers		Prairie, Mission, Craftsman
piers with slanted sides		Craftsman, Prairie, Mission
rough hewn		Pueblo, Pre-Railroad Folk

Porches

IF YOU SEE		TRY THESE FIRST
entry		Can occur on most styles

Porches

IF YOU SEE		TRY THESE FIRST
full-height entry (commonly with pediment)		Early Classical Revival, Greek Revival, Neoclassical, Folk Victorian (two-tier)
full-facade		Greek Revival, Neoclassical, Folk Victorian (two-tier)
full-width, one-story		Prairie, Craftsman, Colonial Revival, Folk Victorian, Italianate, Gothic Revival, Dutch Colonial, Italian Renaissance, Queen Anne, Shingle, Stick, French Colonial, Second Empire, Octagon, Greek Revival, Mission
partial (often inset in L)		Gothic Revival, Italianate, Second Empire, Stick, Queen Anne, Richardsonian Romanesque, Folk Victorian, Monterey (upper-story), Craftsman
wrap		Queen Anne, occasionally in other styles
three or more sides		Greek Revival, French Colonial, Folk Victorian

Other decorative details

IF YOU SEE		TRY THESE FIRST
quoins		Georgian, Adam, Italianate, Colonial Revival, French Eclectic, Beaux Arts, Italian Renaissance, Second Empire
belt course		Georgian, Adam, Italianate, Colonial Revival, French Eclectic, Beaux Arts, Italian Renaissance, Second Empire
Garlands, floral ornament		Beaux Arts, Adam, Colonial Revival
pilasters		Georgian, Adam, Italianate, Colonial Revival, French Eclectic, Beaux Arts, Italian Renaissance, Greek Revival, Neoclassical

Pictorial Glossary

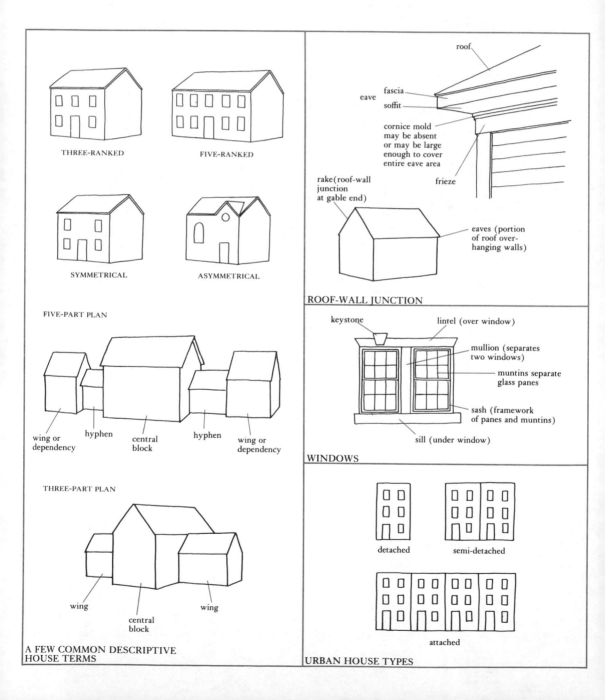

THREE-RANKED

FIVE-RANKED

SYMMETRICAL

ASYMMETRICAL

FIVE-PART PLAN

wing or dependency

hyphen

central block

hyphen

wing or dependency

THREE-PART PLAN

wing

central block

wing

A FEW COMMON DESCRIPTIVE HOUSE TERMS

roof

eave

fascia

soffit

cornice mold may be absent or may be large enough to cover entire eave area

rake (roof-wall junction at gable end)

frieze

eaves (portion of roof over-hanging walls)

ROOF-WALL JUNCTION

keystone

lintel (over window)

mullion (separates two windows)

muntins separate glass panes

sash (framework of panes and muntins)

sill (under window)

WINDOWS

detached

semi-detached

attached

URBAN HOUSE TYPES

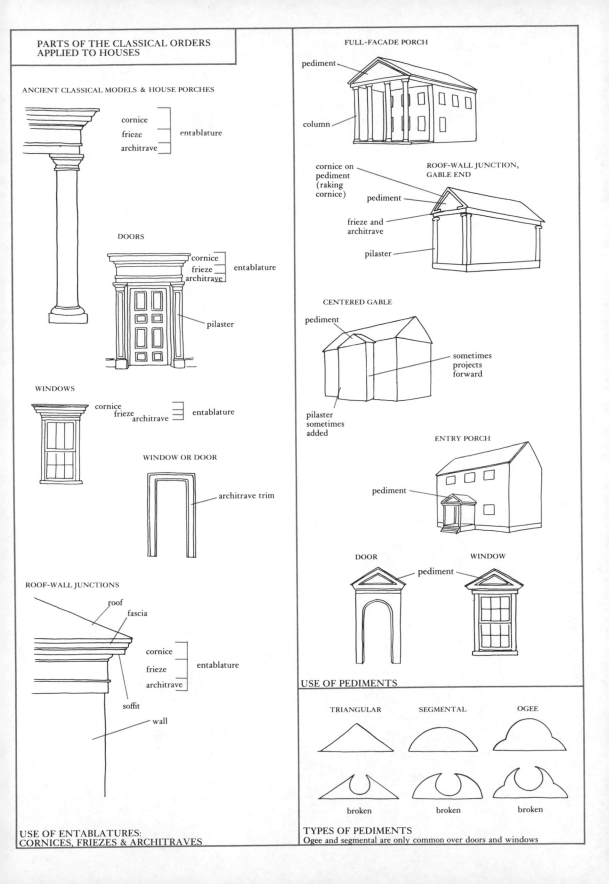

PARTS OF THE CLASSICAL ORDERS
APPLIED TO HOUSES

ANCIENT CLASSICAL MODELS & HOUSE PORCHES

cornice
frieze
architrave
entablature

DOORS

cornice
frieze
architrave
entablature

pilaster

WINDOWS

cornice
frieze
architrave
entablature

WINDOW OR DOOR

architrave trim

ROOF-WALL JUNCTIONS

roof
fascia
cornice
frieze
architrave
entablature
soffit
wall

USE OF ENTABLATURES:
CORNICES, FRIEZES & ARCHITRAVES

FULL-FACADE PORCH

pediment

column

ROOF-WALL JUNCTION,
GABLE END

cornice on
pediment
(raking
cornice)
pediment
frieze and
architrave
pilaster

CENTERED GABLE

pediment
sometimes
projects
forward
pilaster
sometimes
added

ENTRY PORCH

pediment

DOOR   WINDOW

pediment

USE OF PEDIMENTS

TRIANGULAR   SEGMENTAL   OGEE

broken   broken   broken

TYPES OF PEDIMENTS
Ogee and segmental are only common over doors and windows

Folk Houses

Most American houses are built in one of the many architectural fashions, or styles, that have been popular over our country's long history. These changing fashions, which are the subject of the succeeding sections of this book, either incorporate earlier architectural images (for example Classical porch columns or Medieval half-timbering) or consciously eschew the past to create modern styles with their own fashionable images. There is, however, another and less familiar type of dwelling that lacks this concern for architectural taste. These folk houses are built to provide basic shelter with little regard for changing fashion. Early folk houses were constructed of materials found near the building site—rock, clay, logs, and timbers—and prepared by the builders themselves, rather than in distant mills, kilns, or factories. These builders, usually the future occupants of the house, were often aided by part-time local craftsmen. Unlike fashionable styles, folk building traditions, handed down from generation to generation, show relatively little change with time; they are, however, more strongly influenced by *geography* than are architectural styles. The local availability of building materials, as well as the building traditions imported by the earliest settlers of an area, can lead to strong contrasts in the structure and form of folk houses from region to region.

Our country's first folk dwellings were, of course, those built by the Native American inhabitants. Early European explorers found them using a remarkable variety of complex building techniques that had developed over many millennia. The European colonists, in turn, imported their own folk building techniques, but adapted these to the same local materials used by the Natives—wood in the heavily forested eastern half of the country and stone or clay in the more arid West. These European folk traditions persisted, with minor modification, from the earliest colonies of the 17th century until the spread of the railroads in the mid-19th century. Rail transportation made inexpensive building materials—principally lumber from large mills located in timber-rich areas—readily available over much of the nation. This, in turn, led to a change in folk building traditions, as local materials—logs, heavy timbers, and crude masonry—were replaced by light and inexpensive sawn lumber in most folk dwellings. In spite of this change in building materials, many traditional folk *shapes* persisted into the 20th century, when they were joined, and eventually replaced, by still other forms of National Folk housing.

ROUND-PLAN, WOOD-FRAME FAMILY

RECTANGULAR-PLAN, WOOD-FRAME FAMILY

EARTH-WALL FAMILY

Native American

The most truly American folk houses are those that were built by the native inhabitants before Europeans discovered and occupied the North American continent. Native peoples have occupied North America for thousands of years, and during that long interval many diverse building traditions arose and evolved. The first Europeans thus found cultures with widely differing patterns of dwelling construction. These are known primarily from written descriptions, drawings, and early photographs, for most tribes have long abandoned their traditional dwellings in favor of European-influenced houses. Modern reconstructions with varying degrees of authenticity are, however, found in museum villages scattered throughout the country and these provide a glimpse of the complex building traditions of our native forebears. In addition, a few traditional dwellings survive in isolated areas of the American West, where a handful of native cultures have persisted relatively intact to the present day.

The first Europeans found native buildings constructed with both wood-frame and masonry techniques. The wood-frame structures were particularly remarkable since they were fashioned not with the Europeans' iron axes, saws, and other implements but only with simple stone tools. These wood-frame houses were of two general sorts. Round-plan houses, such as the familiar tipi, were relatively small and partially or fully portable. These tended to be associated with nomadic or semi-nomadic hunting cultures. Rectangular-plan houses, on the other hand, tended to be larger, permanent dwellings built by sedentary, usually agricultural, societies. Masonry houses, usually with earth-wall construction, were common in the more arid regions of the American West. These ranged from simple dugouts to the familiar multi-storied pueblos of some southwestern tribes.

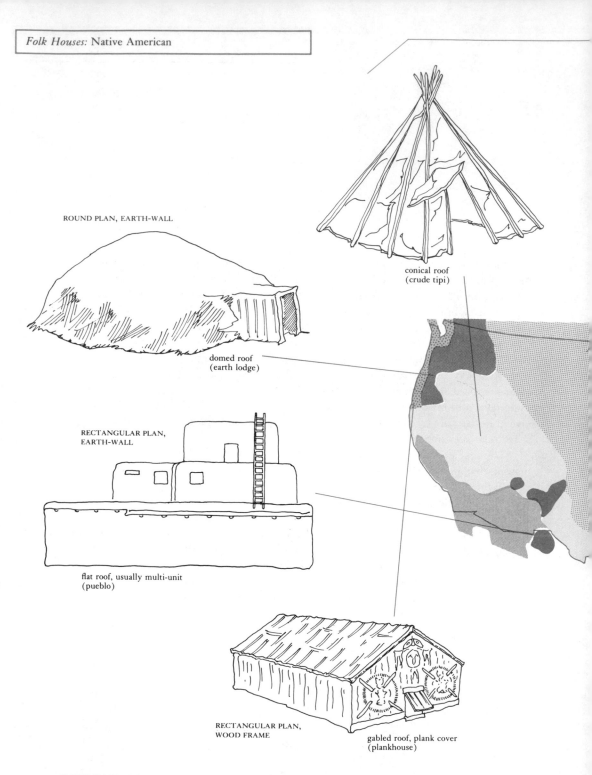

ROUND PLAN, EARTH-WALL

conical roof
(crude tipi)

domed roof
(earth lodge)

RECTANGULAR PLAN,
EARTH-WALL

flat roof, usually multi-unit
(pueblo)

RECTANGULAR PLAN,
WOOD FRAME

gabled roof, plank cover
(plankhouse)

DOMINANT NATIVE AMERICAN HOUSE TYPES
(adapted from Driver and Massey, 1957)

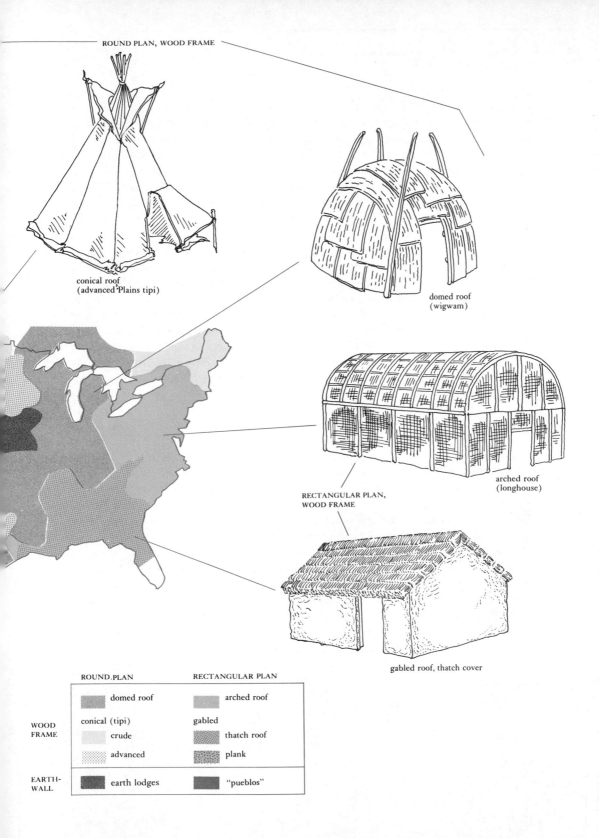

ROUND PLAN, WOOD FRAME

conical roof
(advanced Plains tipi)

domed roof
(wigwam)

arched roof
(longhouse)

RECTANGULAR PLAN,
WOOD FRAME

gabled roof, thatch cover

ROUND PLAN		RECTANGULAR PLAN	
WOOD FRAME	domed roof		arched roof
	conical (tipi)		gabled
	crude		thatch roof
	advanced		plank
EARTH-WALL	earth lodges		"pueblos"

ROUND-PLAN, WOOD-FRAME FAMILY

Wood-frame houses with rounded ground plans were generally constructed with a framework of relatively light poles or branches fastened together with leather cords. Various materials were then used to cover the framework and make it weatherproof. Among the most frequent were tanned animal skins, sheets of bark, which were sometimes sewn together to make larger mats, thatch (tied bundles of straw), and woven mats of vegetable fiber. The houses were built in two principal shapes: some were dome-shaped with rounded tops; others were conical with pointed tops. The dome shape dominated in the midwestern transition zone between woodlands and plains and tended to be larger and more permanent than dwellings of conical shape. Crude conical shelters of sticks and brush were commonly built on hunting expeditions and these were the principal shelters of some nomadic tribes. Such shelters were generally abandoned and rebuilt elsewhere as needed. From them probably evolved the tipi, a conical shelter that could be transported from place to place by being dragged behind domestic dogs or, after the beginning of European colonization, by captured wild horses. Simple tipis were the principal dwellings of many hunting tribes of the northern woodlands and arid Great Basin regions. These consisted of a number of straight poles joined at the top to form a cone and covered with many separate hides, mats, or pieces of bark, which were generally held down by having additional poles laid upon them. From this simple tipi evolved a still more efficient portable dwelling, the Plains tipi. This was covered not by separate units of hide, bark, or fiber, but by a tailored covering made by sewing together many carefully tanned buffalo hides. As a further improvement, two flaps, or ears, extending outward from the top of the cover, could be adjusted by attached poles to make a sort of controlled chimney that eliminated smoke from the interior (most round-plan dwellings have only a simple smoke hole at the top). Before the introduction of the horse, such tipis were probably used only during short seasons when the buffalo herds could be easily followed for hunting on foot. Most plains tribes then returned to villages where they practiced agriculture and lived in permanent wood-frame or earth-wall dwellings. This pattern changed after the introduction of the horse, which escaped from 16th-century Spanish expeditions to become wild on the vast grasslands of the American West. The plains tribes domesticated some of these wild horses and evolved a new culture based on year-round nomadic hunting of the buffalo, which was easily killed from horseback. Horses could also drag heavy tipi poles and covers from place to place. As a result, both the size and refinements of the Plains tipi increased during the centuries between the introduction of the horse and the first extensive European contacts with the plains tribes in the 19th century.

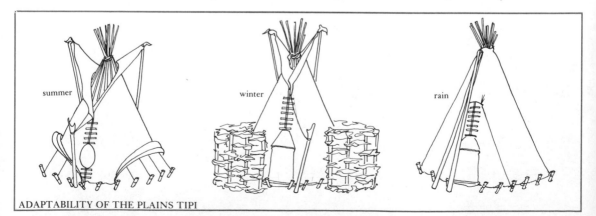

summer   winter   rain

ADAPTABILITY OF THE PLAINS TIPI

ROUND-PLAN, WOOD-FRAME FAMILY

1. Wisconsin(?); photo ca. 1890. Winnebago Tribe. Bark-covered, dome-shaped dwelling.

2. Uintah Valley, Utah; photo ca. 1875. Ute Tribe. Crude conical shelter.

3. Oklahoma(?); photo 1898. Wichita Tribe. Thatch-covered, dome-shaped dwelling. Note the wooden framework exposed at the top.

4. Idaho(?); photo ca. 1900. Umatilla Tribe. Tipi covered by woven mats and canvas cloth introduced by Europeans. Note the pole holding down the mats at right. Such tipis normally had many of these surface poles.

5. Kansas(?); photo ca. 1870. Kiowa Tribe. Plains tipi with fitted cover of tanned buffalo hides. Note the adjustable flaps at the top for controlling drafts to eliminate smoke from interior fires. The ends of the hide covering are joined by the horizontal wood pins above and below the entrance.

1

3

2

5

RECTANGULAR-PLAN, WOOD-FRAME FAMILY

Wood-frame houses of rectangular ground plan were generally large, permanent dwellings housing several related families. These were the first native houses encountered by European colonists along the Atlantic coast, for they were the principal dwelling type of the many woodlands tribes of the eastern United States. Regrettably, they are also among the most poorly known because the natives of that region were the first to be displaced and their villages and traditional cultures destroyed by European colonization. Two principal types of houses appear to have been present in the eastern woodlands. To the north occurred large arched-roof dwellings (longhouses) made of light wooden frames. These were usually covered with bark; woven mats, thatch, and hides were less common coverings. In construction, these houses resembled larger and more refined versions of the round-plan, domed dwellings found farther west. In the southern woodlands these arched-roof forms were replaced by gabled (or, less commonly, hipped) roofs covered with thatch. Unlike the northern longhouses, where the same material was generally used for both roof and walls, these southern rectangular houses had varying wall materials beneath the thatched roofs. Woven mats and hides were sometimes used, as was a sort of half-timbering in which a light wooden framework was laced with basketry and covered with clay. In the warmer regions thatched summer houses without enclosing walls were also common. All of these rectangular houses of the eastern woodlands were associated with agricultural traditions based on the cultivation of corn. Some anthropologists believe that the house form spread northward from Middle America where corn was first domesticated and where somewhat similar houses are found.

An entirely different tradition of rectangular, wood-frame building was found along the humid Pacific Coast from northernmost California to southern Alaska. There the natives built large dwellings with heavy timber frames having carefully fitted joints. The frames were covered with large softwood planks split with stone tools from the abundant local timber. These houses most commonly had gabled roofs, although shed roofs were used in the Puget Sound area. The more pretentious houses were sometimes adorned with decorative and ceremonial carvings, particularly the familiar totem pole. This building tradition is believed to be a relatively recent introduction from northeastern Asia, where similar native dwellings occur.

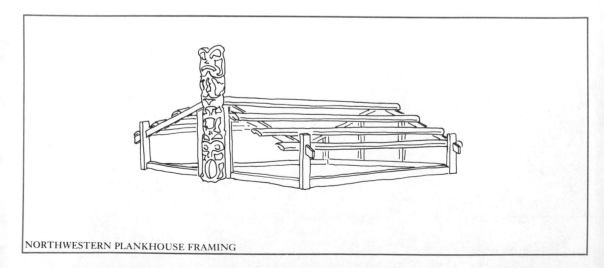

NORTHWESTERN PLANKHOUSE FRAMING

RECTANGULAR-PLAN, WOOD-FRAME FAMILY

1. Washington, District of Columbia (reconstruction); photo 1899. Abnaki-Passamaquoddy Tribe; northern New England. Bark-covered, arched-roof longhouse.

2. Fort Sill, Oklahoma, vicinity; photo ca. 1875. Caddo Tribe; displaced from Louisiana and eastern Texas. Thatch- and bark-roofed dwellings. Note the half-timbered walls on the enclosed buildings.

3. Fort Lauderdale, Florida; photo ca. 1917. Seminole Tribe. Thatch-roofed, open-sided dwellings.

4. Albert Bay, British Columbia, Canada; photo ca. 1889. Kwakiutl Tribe. Gabled, plank-walled houses. The siding behind the totem pole and the small building in the foreground were introduced by Europeans.

EARTH-WALL FAMILY

The third basic type of Native American dwelling used earth, rather than organic materials (hides, bark, straw), for covering the walls and roof. These earth-wall buildings ranged from crude dugouts to the magnificent multi-unit pueblos of the American Southwest. All use some system of wooden support for their earth-covered roofs—most commonly, heavy timbers spanned by smaller timbers and then covered with sticks, straw, or sod. The earth-covered walls were also sometimes supported by such a wooden framework. Alternatively, the walls were excavated below ground level or, as in the massive pueblos, built of sun-dried mud applied in successive layers (this is called puddled adobe; sun-dried adobe bricks were introduced by the Spaniards, although there is some archeological evidence for their use much earlier, along with complex stone masonry, by native peoples of the American Southwest). The most typical earth-wall dwelling was the round, partially excavated earth lodge, which generally housed several related families. These dwellings were usually supported by a carefully constructed wooden framework. An opening at the top permitted light to enter and smoke to escape. Sometimes the top opening was the only entrance, with descent inside by means of a log ladder; other earth lodges were entered by ground-level openings or tunnels. In the 18th and early 19th centuries these earth lodges were the dominant dwellings over much of the east-central plains and Columbia Plateau regions. They are also common among the native peoples of northeastern Asia and are thought to be among the earliest New World dwellings. There is some suggestion they were far more widespread before the introduction of the horse made possible year-round nomadic buffalo hunting over much of the West.

The most familiar of all Native American dwellings are the monumental pueblos of the Southwest, which are believed to have evolved from simple earth lodges (many incorporate round ceremonial chambers similar to lodges in shape and arrangement). The pueblos are multi-storied, communal structures made up of many rectangular rooms; exterior rooms are used for living quarters and interior rooms for food storage. The earthen roofs are supported by massive horizontal timbers placed on top of the thick adobe walls. Because of the difficulty of cutting the roof timbers to precise lengths with stone tools, the ends were normally allowed to project somewhat beyond the wall surface. This is the principal difference between these native buildings and related Spanish Colonial buildings built of adobe, which have otherwise similar roof-support systems (see page 131). Several of the New Mexico pueblos have been continuously occupied since pre-Columbian times and thus have the distinction of being the most authentic surviving Native American dwellings.

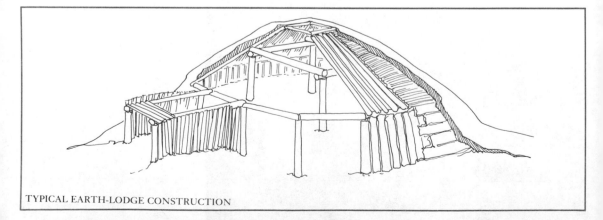

TYPICAL EARTH-LODGE CONSTRUCTION

EARTH-WALL FAMILY

1. Arizona?; photo ca. 1895. Navaho Tribe. Earth-walled dugout supported by conical frame of timbers (such Navaho dwellings are called hogans).

1. Loup Fork, Nebraska; photo 1871. Pawnee Tribe. Village made up of several earth lodges. Note the timber frame visible in the entrance tunnel and the bundles of tipi poles used on hunting expeditions.

3. Zuni Pueblo, New Mexico; photo 1879. Zuni Tribe. Close-up view of upper stories. Note roof-support timbers and access ladders.

4. Acoma Pueblo, New Mexico; photo 1899. Acoma Tribe. General view showing earth roofs in foreground.

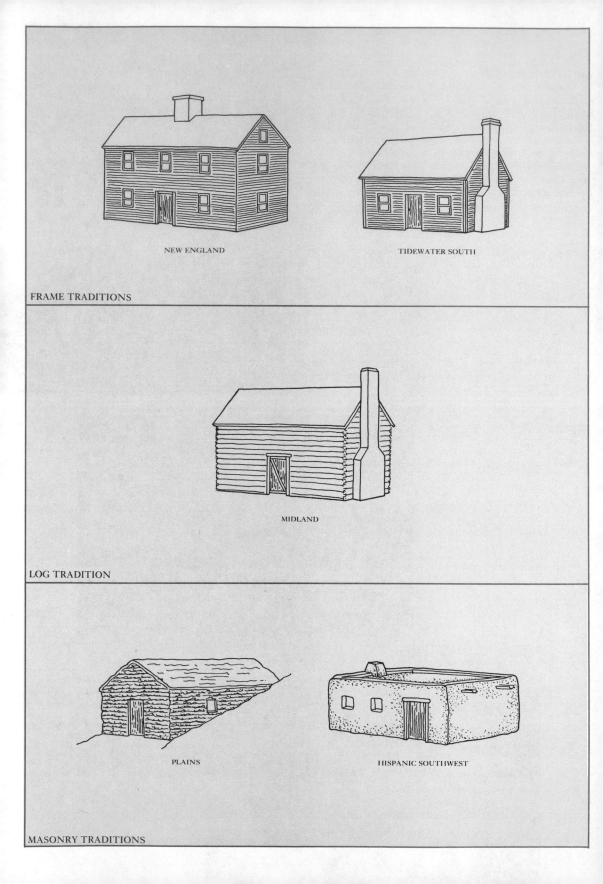

NEW ENGLAND

TIDEWATER SOUTH

FRAME TRADITIONS

MIDLAND

LOG TRADITION

PLAINS

HISPANIC SOUTHWEST

MASONRY TRADITIONS

Pre-Railroad

The first period of American folk architecture built by European colonists spanned the long interval between the earliest permanent settlements of the 17th century and the growth of the railroads as an efficient national transportation network in the last half of the 19th century. Throughout these two hundred years many modest dwellings were, of necessity, constructed of local materials without stylistic embellishment. Before the railroads, the only means of efficiently transporting bulky goods of relatively low value, such as lumber, brick, and quarried stone, was by water. Coastal towns and villages thus had access to a variety of domestic or imported construction materials, as did those inland farms and villages located near canals or the few dependably navigable rivers. Even modest houses in these areas tended to follow current architectural fashion and thus were generally styled, rather than folk, houses. Elsewhere the costs and difficulties of horse-and-wagon transport—the only alternative to boats and barges—restricted all but the most affluent to folk dwellings built with materials found on, or very near, the construction site. The eastern half of the country was covered with a seemingly endless supply of virgin forests; there, wooden folk building became the rule. The early English and French colonists were familiar with wooden building principally in the form of massive frameworks of hewn timber (post-and-girt construction) which, in the New World, were generally covered by thinner strips of wood to make a watertight exterior. These traditions dominated early folk building both in New England, where frame, massed-plan (more than one room deep) houses became the norm, and in the early settlements of the Tidewater South, where frame houses of linear plan (one room deep) dominated, probably because of the shorter and less confining southern winters. As settlement expanded to the West, a more distinctive tradition of wooden folk building evolved from a blending of the linear plans of the Tidewater South with techniques of construction using horizontal log walls brought to the middle colonies by immigrants from the heavily timbered areas of central and northern Europe. This Midland tradition of log building is the most familiar and well-studied aspect of American folk architecture. Still farther west, the vast woodlands gave way to grassy plains where timber was scarce. Large-scale settlement did not reach this area until well into the 19th century, but in the relatively brief interval before the arrival of the railroads a new folk tradition developed in this region: as a result of the shortage of wood, folk houses were constructed of primitive masonry. In a few areas the skills and materials were available to construct rough stone dwellings. More commonly, houses were made of sod—earth held together by fibrous grass roots. Still other masonry traditions developed in the southwestern United States,

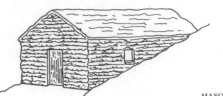

MASONRY CONSTRUCTION DOMINANT

PLAINS
(dugout, sod)

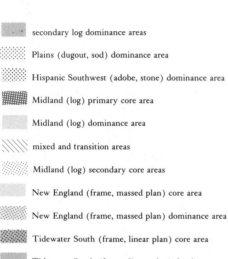

secondary log dominance areas

Plains (dugout, sod) dominance area

Hispanic Southwest (adobe, stone) dominance area

Midland (log) primary core area

Midland (log) dominance area

mixed and transition areas

Midland (log) secondary core areas

New England (frame, massed plan) core area

New England (frame, massed plan) dominance area

Tidewater South (frame, linear plan) core area

Tidewater South (frame, linear plan) dominance area

HISPANIC SOUTHWEST
(adobe, stone)

PRE-RAILROAD FOLK TRADITIONS to ca. 1850–1890 (locally to ca. 1920)

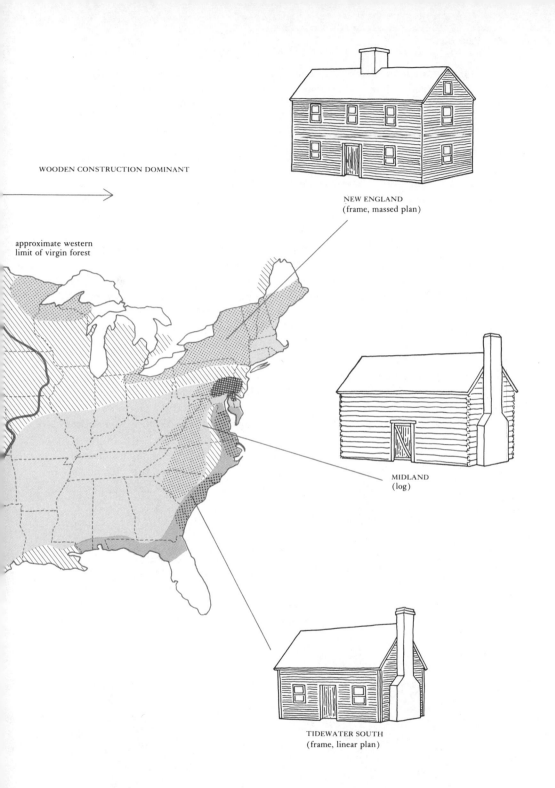

WOODEN CONSTRUCTION DOMINANT

NEW ENGLAND
(frame, massed plan)

approximate western
limit of virgin forest

MIDLAND
(log)

TIDEWATER SOUTH
(frame, linear plan)

which was part of Spain or Mexico throughout most of the pre-railroad era. In this Hispanic Southwest, Spanish folk traditions of building with sun-dried adobe bricks or with
rough stonework were dominant.

NEW ENGLAND TRADITION

The first New England colonists of the 17th century built primarily linear-plan houses
having heavy timber frames covered with boards or shingles. These were commonly of
the two-story, I-house form, although single-story, hall-and-parlor houses were also
built. Both were among the commonest folk forms in 17th-century England. In the early
18th century, these plans were expanded to the rear to give increased interior space; this
resulted in the one-and-one-half-room-deep saltbox and Cape Cod forms, which were
better adapted to the severe and confining New England winters. From these evolved, by
the mid-18th century, massed-plan houses that were to dominate New England building
throughout the following century. These houses at first had two-room widths and central
chimneys, as had their saltbox and I-house precursors. By the time of the Revolution,
center-hall plans with paired end chimneys were common. One more change came in the
early 19th century when the Greek Revival style made accentuated front gables fashionable. This trend ultimately led to simple gable-front folk houses, which became increasingly common after about 1825.

This full sequence of change in building traditions took place only in those parts of
New England that were settled first—coastal Massachusetts, Connecticut, and Rhode Island. There, most surviving examples reflect the early affluence of the region in the pre-
dominance of Postmedieval, Georgian, or Adam stylistic detailing. As New Englanders
spread northward and westward from this core area in the late 18th and 19th centuries,
they tended to build less pretentious folk houses in the same forms as the more fashionable houses then being built farther east. Saltboxes and I-houses thus occur only in the

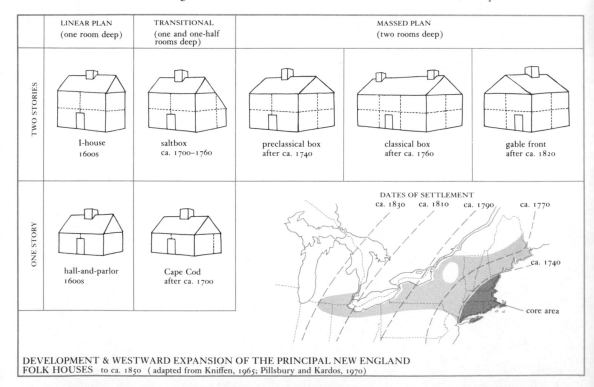

**DEVELOPMENT & WESTWARD EXPANSION OF THE PRINCIPAL NEW ENGLAND
FOLK HOUSES** to ca. 1850 (adapted from Kniffen, 1965; Pillsbury and Kardos, 1970)

NEW ENGLAND TRADITION

1. Newbury, Massachusetts; 1696. Jackman House (restoration). Rare northern hall-and-parlor without stylistic detailing.

2. Melrose, Massachusetts; 1703. Upham House (restoration). Early saltbox without stylistic detailing.

3. Halifax, Massachusetts; 1730. Standish House. Cape Cod with modest Georgian doorway.

4. Meriden, Connecticut; late 18th century. Redfield House. Preclassical box house (note central chimney) with modest Georgian doorway.

5. New Harmony, Indiana; 1815 (photo, 1903). Schnee House. Gable front without stylistic detailing. This example was built by German immigrants; similar forms were spread throughout the midwest by settlers from New England.

coastal region; box-houses occur farther afield; and gable-front houses are the most wide-spread of all. An exception was the 19th-century revival of one-story forms having both the linear-plan, hall-and-parlor shape as well as the deeper Cape Cod plan. These smaller houses were well suited for initial settlement in remote areas; they were replaced or ad-joined by two-story forms as prosperity increased.

Settlers from New England first moved westward along the Mohawk corridor of central New York. From there they dominated the Western Reserve area around Lake Erie and spread beyond into the upper Midwest, where their building traditions became diluted by others from farther south. New England folk houses are scattered today throughout this large area, but intact survivors are quite rare. Because they were rela-tively large and substantially built, many of these houses had original stylistic details that took them beyond the folk threshold. Even when built as pure folk forms, they have usually been modified beyond recognition by later stylistic alterations. The New England tradition is, however, reflected in large gable-front-and-wing folk houses that became common throughout the Northeast after the expansion of the railroads.

TIDEWATER SOUTH TRADITION

Like their countrymen to the north, the earliest English colonists of the coastal South built primarily linear-plan, hall-and-parlor houses or I-houses. In contrast to the north-ern colonies, however, a tradition of building with brick masonry was established early in

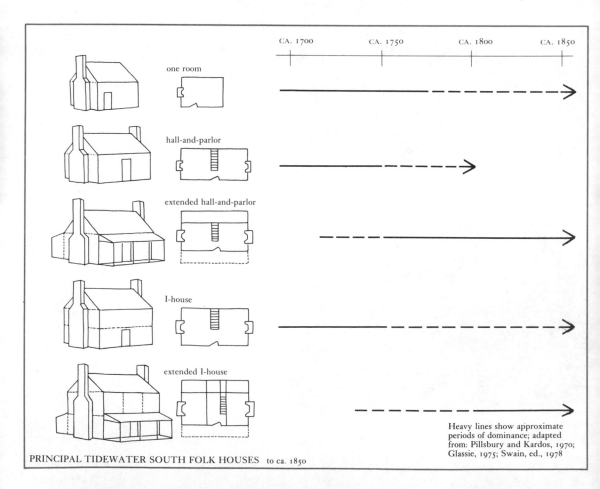

one room

hall-and-parlor

extended hall-and-parlor

I-house

extended I-house

CA. 1700   CA. 1750   CA. 1800   CA. 1850

Heavy lines show approximate periods of dominance; adapted from: Pillsbury and Kardos, 1970; Glassie, 1975; Swain, ed., 1978

PRINCIPAL TIDEWATER SOUTH FOLK HOUSES   to ca. 1850

TIDEWATER SOUTH TRADITION

1. Rocky Mount, North Carolina, vicinity; late 18th century(?). Wilkins House. Rare surviving example of early single-room frame house.

2. Guilford, Virginia; ca. 1820. Clayton House. A late example of the traditional British hall-and-parlor plan, without a porch. The hipped roof of a later rear wing is barely visible; the dormer windows are probably also a later addition.

3. Newlin, North Carolina; ca. 1830. Allen House. Hall-and-parlor plan, with added shed porch. The metal roofing and door are also later modifications; the original chimney has been removed.

4. Perquimans County, North Carolina; ca. 1825. Winslow House. Typical extended hall-and-parlor plan. The rear flue and decorative shutters are later additions.

5. Wrendale vicinity, North Carolina; 1789. Early I-house with added shed porch and rearward extension and later metal roof.

6. Ingold, North Carolina, vicinity; 1840. Johnson House. Typical extended I-house; note the additional shed extension at the rear.

1

2

3

4

5

6

the South. The exact reason for this is unclear, although an abundance of brick clay in the region and differing English backgrounds of many of the southern colonists are probably responsible. Because of the expense of masonry construction, most of these brick houses were built with Postmedieval, Georgian, or Adam stylistic detailing and thus were not folk houses. Massive timber-frame construction, like that in the northern colonies, was also used in the South and these early wood-frame houses were more commonly modest folk dwellings; unfortunately very few 17th- or 18th-century examples survive intact. Instead, these early southern folk houses are known primarily from their modified descendants built in the first half of the 19th century, many of which survive.

Because of the milder winters of the southern colonies, there was less emphasis on enlarging the early linear plans to create more interior space. One-story houses are far more common than in the North and true massed plans (more than one room deep) are rare. Instead, one-story shed extensions were typically added to the rear of both one- and two-story, linear-plan houses as more space was needed. By the late 18th century, another innovation was becoming universal in the southern folk house. This was the full-width, shed-roofed front porch, which provided a cool shelter in summer from the scorching sun and frequent sudden thunderstorms. Tidewater hall-and-parlor and I-house forms were the prototypes for similar pre-railroad shapes executed with log walls; these became far more widely distributed as a part of the Midland folk tradition. These Tidewater forms also persisted into the railroad era and were the dominant folk architecture throughout the rural South until well into the 20th century.

MIDLAND TRADITION

This third principal folk building tradition, like those of New England and the Tidewater South, originated with early colonization along the Atlantic seaboard. It began in the middle colonies (Pennsylvania, New Jersey, Delaware, and Maryland), where Germanic immigrants from heavily wooded areas of central and northern Europe introduced techniques of building with logs hewn square and then placed horizontally, one on top of the other, to make a solid wooden wall. This massive structure was held together by various systems of carefully interlocking or notching the squared timbers where they joined at the corners of the buildings (see page 36). Such construction contrasted sharply with the frame buildings of the adjacent English colonies to the north and south, where open frameworks of hewn timbers were covered by lighter planks or shingles to make them weatherproof. This framing technique used far less wood than did solid log walls and was originally inspired by the relative scarcity of timber in westernmost Europe, where the virgin forests had largely been cleared by the late Middle Ages.

The early Germanic settlers in the core area of Pennsylvania and adjacent colonies built large log houses with an almost square, three-room plan and a central chimney (the Continental log house). This pattern persisted as settlement spread westward from the core area to central Pennsylvania and then southward along the forelands and valleys in front of the Appalachian Mountain barrier which loomed to the west. In this secondary core area (see map) the Germanic settlers were joined by Scotch-Irish and English pioneers who quickly adopted the log building techniques, which were much simpler than constructing complex hewn frameworks to be covered with laboriously split planks or shingles. These settlers from the British Isles, however, modified the shape of the three-room Continental House into the familiar one room deep linear plan with external chim-

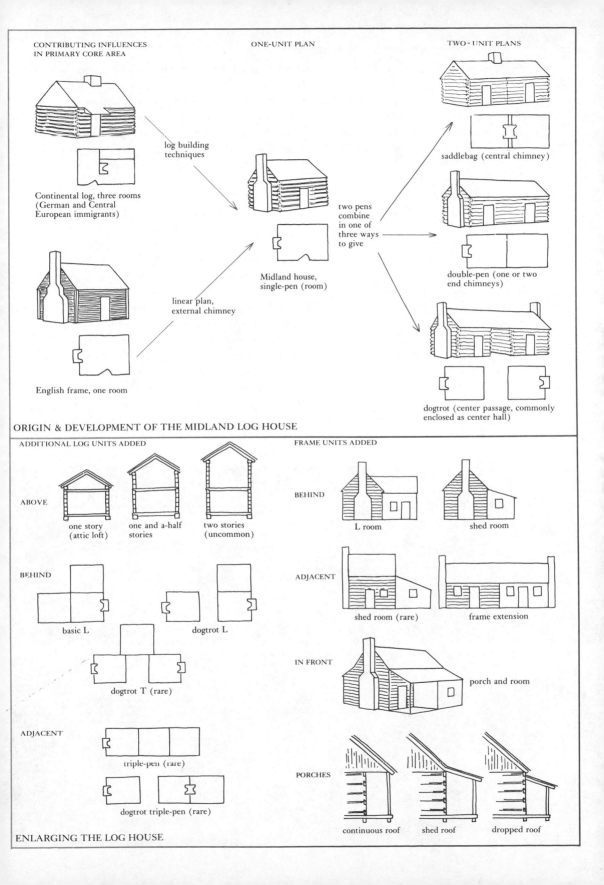

CONTRIBUTING INFLUENCES
IN PRIMARY CORE AREA

ONE-UNIT PLAN

TWO - UNIT PLANS

log building
techniques

Continental log, three rooms
(German and Central
European immigrants)

linear plan,
external chimney

English frame, one room

Midland house,
single-pen (room)

two pens
combine
in one of
three ways
to give

saddlebag (central chimney)

double-pen (one or two
end chimneys)

dogtrot (center passage, commonly
enclosed as center hall)

ORIGIN & DEVELOPMENT OF THE MIDLAND LOG HOUSE

ADDITIONAL LOG UNITS ADDED

ABOVE

one story
(attic loft)

one and a-half
stories

two stories
(uncommon)

BEHIND

basic L

dogtrot L

dogtrot T (rare)

ADJACENT

triple-pen (rare)

dogtrot triple-pen (rare)

FRAME UNITS ADDED

BEHIND

L room

shed room

ADJACENT

shed room (rare)

frame extension

IN FRONT

porch and room

PORCHES

continuous roof

shed roof

dropped roof

ENLARGING THE LOG HOUSE

ney that dominated in the Tidewater South. Thus was born the Midland log house, a tradition that was carried across the Appalachians by frontiersmen to become the dominant Pre-Railroad Folk housing over much of the heavily wooded eastern half of the country. Because of their strong, massive walls, many early log houses survive relatively intact, particularly in out-of-the-way rural areas. For this reason, Midland log houses are the most familiar and thoroughly studied Pre-Railroad Folk dwellings.

A principal problem of log-wall houses is the difficulty of expanding them as additional space is required. Because the strength of the structure depends on the four corner joints, log houses are generally made up of room-sized square or rectangular units called "pens." The simplest log houses have only a single unit, usually with a loft area above used for sleeping. Two-unit plans, joined in various ways, are very common; three-unit and two-story forms were also developed. Framed additions and porches were commonly added to log houses as local sawmills provided nearby sources of cut lumber. Similarly, many log houses were later covered with weatherboards, both to provide an additional seal and to make them appear more up-to-date. The tradition of building with horizontal log walls persisted in many areas long after cut lumber was locally available. Usually a framework of roughly squared and notched logs was constructed to be originally covered with either shingles or weatherboard. These second-generation log houses can sometimes be distinguished from those originally built with exposed log walls by imprecise squaring of the logs, which resulted in relatively large, irregular gaps between timbers.

A distinction is usually made between log *houses*, such as those discussed so far, which have walls of square-hewn logs joined by carefully hewn corner notching, and log *cabins*, in which the timbers are left round and are joined at the corners by overlapping saddle notches. Such walls are difficult to chink—that is, to fill the spaces between the

3   4

7   8

MIDLAND TRADITION

1. Summers, Missouri, vicinity; photo 1880. Typical single-pen (one room). Note the absence of windows and the stick chimney, which is lined on the inside with clay. Ladders were usually kept handy so that chimney fires could be easily reached. A later frame extension is visible to the rear.

2. Springfield, West Virginia. Urban single-pen (one room) with upper half-story and window openings fitted with early, small-paned sashes. The original roof was probably shingled.

3. Duchesne County, Utah. Primitive log cabin (rounded logs and saddle notching) typical of those built in wooded areas of the western mountains.

4. Hale County, Alabama. Dogtrot (note central passage) with later roof and rough-sawn siding added over log walls.

5. Mercer County, Kentucky; photo ca. 1900. Typical saddlebag. Note the difference in corner notching on the two units. The right-hand pen was probably added later, around the chimney of the pen to the left.

6. Versailles, Kentucky, vicinity; late 18th century. Crittenden House. Early double-pen with primitive corner notching. The original roof would have been shingled.

7. Boundary County, Idaho. Typical log house of the western mountains.

8. Jessamine County, Kentucky; late 18th century. Peyton House. Dogtrot with upper half-story. Note the recessed doorway added to the central passage.

9. Warrensville, North Carolina, vicinity. Gentry House. Double-pen with upper half-story and typical Tidewater porch.

10. Louisiana, Missouri; ca. 1830. Stark House. Restored example of unusual double-pen with units of differing size.

rounded logs with clay or other material to make them weatherproof. For this reason they were generally used only for temporary shelters in the woodlands of the eastern United States. In wooded areas of the western mountains, however, folk traditions of building with rounded logs became established in the 19th century and persist to the present day in isolated areas.

PLAINS TRADITION

Folk building traditions based on wood-frame or log construction dominated the pre-railroad era in the heavily timbered eastern half of the country. As settlement spread into the treeless plains of the West in the mid-19th century, new building techniques had to be developed (see map). Only the most arid western regions lacked wood altogether. Over much of the plains, rivers and streams were bordered by at least small trees that provided short timbers for roof support and other essential construction details. Walls and roofs made entirely of wood were, however, rare and expensive luxuries on the plains before the expansion of the western railroad network in the late 19th century. Like their Native American predecessors, early settlers on the plains generally solved the shortage of wood by building with crude masonry. Many of these settlers were undoubtedly familiar with brick construction but, although suitable brick clays were widely distributed in the West, the fuel required to fire the bricks was not. Brick buildings were thus confined to areas near rail or water transport. In some regions local stone could be gathered or quarried without elaborate equipment; in these areas crude stone dwellings were common. Much of the best agricultural land of the plains was covered with thick soils that prevented access to the underlying rock for use as building stone. In these regions, which included most of Kansas, Nebraska, and the Dakotas as well as eastern Colorado, Wyoming, and Montana, pioneer settlers developed techniques of building with sod. In sod construction the uppermost few inches of soil, along with the interlocking roots of the tough plains grasses, were cut into brick-like units with a special plow. These were then laid like bricks to make thick earthen walls that provided excellent insulation from both summer heat and winter cold. The exact origins of this building tradition are obscure. Some writers suggest that the earliest settlers borrowed it from the somewhat similar earth lodges of local native tribes. Others point out that similar construction is used for simple folk dwellings in some treeless parts of Britain. Whatever their sources, folk houses made of sod quickly became the standard plains dwelling and were built at all levels of refinement, from simple dugouts to elaborate two-story mansions.

A principal difficulty with early sod dwellings was the roof. Lacking wood shingles as a roof covering, roofs were typically also made of sod blocks set on a framework of wooden poles, sticks, and brush. Such roofs were notoriously unpleasant in wet weather, as they normally leaked and dripped muddy water into the interior for several days after a rain. A high priority for plains dwellers thus became watertight roofing. Roofs were supported by wooden planks, when available, on which sod was placed for insulation. As affluence increased, fully framed roofs covered with shingles were sometimes added. Most sod houses of the plains have long disappeared, but a few with these improved roofs are still in use as comfortable, energy-efficient dwellings.

HISPANIC SOUTHWEST TRADITION

The houses of the Hispanic Southwest are treated in the chapter on the Spanish Colonial style, which also outlines Hispanic building techniques of the region.

PLAINS TRADITION

1. Custer County, Montana. Typical plains half-dugout. Partial walls of rounded logs with primitive notching were commonly used when nearby stream valleys provided sufficient timber. Note the earth roof.

2. Jackson County, Oklahoma; 1888. Perryman House. Partly restored plains half-dugout with partial walls of primitive stonework laid without mortar. Such stonework was common in the eastern and southern plains where exposures of bedrock are frequent.

3. Custer County, Nebraska; photo 1887. Barnes House. Plains half-dugout with partial walls of sod blocks. Note the sod roof.

4. Pennington County, South Dakota. Sod house with improved roof and framed rear addition. The house was still in use in 1936 when the photo was made.

5. Custer County, Nebraska; photo 1886. Reeder House. Typical plains sod house with sod roof. Timbers support the sod blocks above the windows.

6. Custer County, Nebraska; 1884. Haumont House. Elaborate two-story sod house which survived into the 1970s.

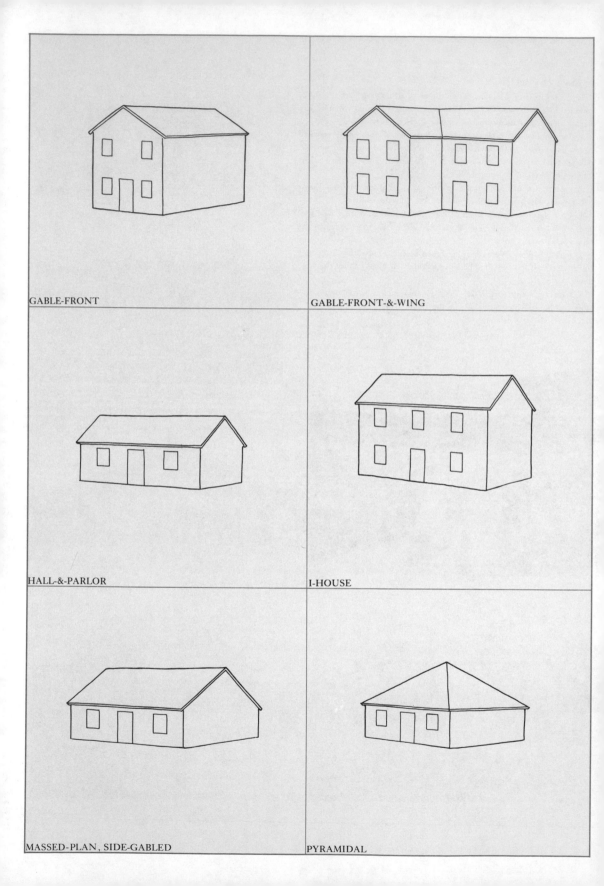

GABLE-FRONT

GABLE-FRONT-&-WING

HALL-&-PARLOR

I-HOUSE

MASSED-PLAN, SIDE-GABLED

PYRAMIDAL

The nature of American folk housing changed dramatically as railroads mushroomed across the continent in the decades from 1850 to 1890. Modest dwellings built far from water transport were no longer restricted to local materials. Instead, bulky items used for construction, particularly lumber from distant sawmills in heavily forested areas, could now be moved rapidly and cheaply over long distances. As a result, large lumberyards quickly became standard fixtures in the thousands of new towns which sprouted as trade centers along the railroad routes. Soon folk houses built with logs, sod, or heavy hewn frames were being abandoned for wooden dwellings constructed with light balloon or braced framing covered by wood sheathing. The railroads thus changed the traditional building materials and construction techniques of folk dwellings over much of the nation. By the turn of the century, pre-railroad building traditions survived only in isolated areas, far from the nearest rail service.

The railroad-inspired era of national folk housing did not completely erase the earlier traditions, however, for many of the previous folk shapes persisted even though now built by different techniques. These, along with some new shape innovations, make up six distinctive families of house shapes that dominated American folk building through the first half of the 20th century. Only recently have these generally been abandoned for still other forms of folk dwellings (see pages 496–99).

After the expansion of the railroads, gable-front houses remained common in the northeastern region formerly dominated by the New England folk tradition, as did similar massed plans with an added extension known as gable-front-and-wing houses. In much of the remaining eastern half of the country, hall-and-parlor and I-house shapes, both descended from the Tidewater South tradition by way of the Midland log adaptations, remained the dominant folk dwellings. All of these later folk forms, however, tend to show much less geographic restriction than did their pre-railroad predecessors, for as

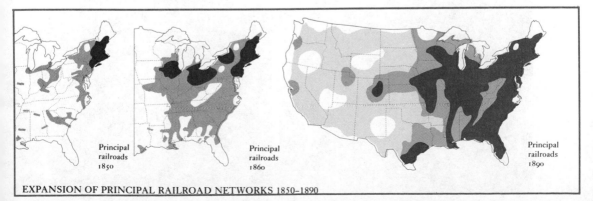

Principal
railroads
1850

Principal
railroads
1860

Principal
railroads
1890

EXPANSION OF PRINCIPAL RAILROAD NETWORKS 1850–1890

transportation and communication improved, each shape became distributed beyond its area of traditional dominance. Light framing techniques also led to new folk forms which grew in popularity through the early decades of this century. These were generally massed-plan houses that were now relatively simple to construct because light wooden roof framing could easily be adapted to span two-room depths. Such houses, when of rectangular shape, normally had side-gabled roofs and are called massed-plan, side-gabled folk houses. More nearly square plans typically had pyramidal (equilateral hipped) roofs.

GABLE-FRONT FAMILY

The Greek Revival movement, which dominated American styled houses during the period from 1830 to 1850, commonly used the front-gabled shape to echo the pedimented facade of typical Greek temples. This form was particularly common in New England and the adjacent northeast region where simple gable-front folk houses also became popular during the pre-railroad era. This shape persisted with the expansion of the eastern railroad network in the 1850s and became a dominant folk form until well into the 20th century. Gable-front houses were particularly suited for narrow urban lots in the rapidly expanding cities of the northeast. There, many late 19th- and early 20th-century neighborhoods are dominated by both styled and simple folk examples built in this form. Most are narrow, two-story houses with relatively steep roof pitches. A related one-story urban form first became common in expanding southern cities in the late 19th century. This is the shotgun house, narrow gable-front dwellings one room wide that dominated many modest southern neighborhoods built from about 1880 to 1930. Some are elaborately styled but most are simple folk houses. The origin of these southern shotgun houses has been much debated. Some scholars note that similar forms are common in the West Indies and trace them from Africa to early Haitian influences in New Orleans, whence they became popular with Black freedmen migrating to southern urban centers following the Civil War. A less complex theory is that they are simply the familiar one-room-deep, hall-and-parlor plan of the rural South turned sideways to accommodate narrow urban lots.

An additional wave of interest in the gable-front shape grew from styled houses of the early 20th-century Craftsman movement, which were typically built in this form. Many modest folk houses without stylistic detailing were inspired by such Craftsman houses in the decades from 1910 to 1930. These are usually one-story, double-width forms with low-pitched roofs; they are most common in rural areas and occur throughout the country.

5   6

GABLE-FRONT FAMILY

1. Cuba, New York; late 19th century. Typical urban two-story example. The spindlework porch detailing and patterned shingles in the gable are borrowed from the contemporary Queen Anne style.

2. Buffalo, New York; ca. 1907. An urban one-and-one-half-story example with modest Queen Anne detailing. The door and windows are later additions.

3. Cleveland, Ohio; late 19th century. Urban example executed in masonry.

4. Carteret County, North Carolina; 1864. Thomas House. Early example showing Greek Revival influence in the pedimented gable and double porch, which was common in the coastal Carolinas. Metal doors and storm windows are later additions.

5. Biloxi, Mississippi; ca. 1905. Typical shotgun house of the urban south. This example has integral porch and modest Queen Anne detailing.

6. Louisville, Kentucky; ca. 1910. Shotgun with Greek Revival–like entry porch.

7. Gibson County, Indiana; ca. 1935. Late example inspired by the Cape Cod shape of the Colonial Revival movement.

8. Thomaston, Louisiana; ca. 1938. Typical example inspired by similarly shaped Craftsman houses.

1

2

3   4

7   8

GABLE-FRONT-AND-WING FAMILY

While two-story gable-front houses dominated urban folk building in the northeast, a related shape, also descended from styled Greek Revival houses, became common in rural areas. In this form, an additional side-gabled wing was added at right angles to the gable-front plan to give a compound, gable-front-and-wing shape. A shed-roofed porch was typically placed within the L made by the two wings. Because these were relatively large and complex houses, most built in the pre-railroad era had Greek Revival detailing and were not folk houses. With the coming of the railroads, however, abundant lumber and balloon framing led to an expansion of unstyled folk houses with this form. Some grew in stages as two-story, front-gabled wings were added to simple hall-and-parlor and I-house plans. These were typically stepped in shape—that is, the roof ridge of the gable-front portion was higher than the adjacent wing. More commonly, the entire structure was built as a unit with a roof ridge of uniform height.

Two-story houses of gable-front-and-wing plan became common only in the northeastern and midwestern states. In the South, however, traditional one-story, hall-and-parlor plans were frequently built with an added one-story, gable-front wing. These one-story, gable-front-and-wing houses had more flexible interior spaces than the typical southern hall-and-parlor plan, which they steadily replaced during the early decades of this century. These one-story forms also became common, along with larger two-story examples, in adjacent areas of the expanding Midwest and are the most widely distributed of the gable-front-and-wing family of shapes.

4   5

GABLE-FRONT-AND-WING FAMILY

1. Hartwick, New York; late 19th century, photo 1914. Gardner House. Stepped example. Note the small attic windows, common on Greek Revival houses, on the right-hand wing, which was probably built first, with the gable-front portion added later.

2. North Collins, New York; late 19th century. Stepped example.

3. Lawtons, New York, vicinity; late 19th century.

4. Belmont, New York; ca. 1900.

5. Fayetteville, Arkansas; ca. 1910.

6. Seaford, Delaware; ca. 1947. Temple House. Late example inspired by the Minimal Traditional style of the 1940's.

7. Chicago, Illinois; ca. 1950. Late example inspired by the Ranch style of the 1950s.

HALL-AND-PARLOR FAMILY

Simple side-gabled, hall-and-parlor houses (two rooms wide and one room deep) are a traditional British folk form which, when expanded by a front porch and rearward addition, became the dominant pre-railroad folk housing over much of the southeastern United States. Hall-and-parlor houses were first executed with heavy timber framing in the Tidewater South and then with hewn log walls over the vast Midland region. After the expansion of the railroad network this form, now executed with light framed walls, remained the dominant folk housing over much of the rural Southeast until well into the 20th century. This folk form is thus a persistent survivor which has shown relatively little change since colonial times. The principal variations in extended hall-and-parlor houses involve differing chimney placements, porch sizes, porch roof shapes, and differing patterns of rearward extensions for enlarging the interior space.

HALL-AND-PARLOR FAMILY

1. Gadsden County, Florida; late 19th century. Note the open shuttered window without a glass sash and the discontinuous siding on the rearward extension, added after the main house was built. Early hall-and-parlor houses had separate front doors leading to the two principal rooms, a pattern that survives in this example and those in figures 4, 5, and 8.

2. Carteret County, North Carolina; ca. 1898. The gabled entry porch is probably a later addition.

3. Smithfield, North Carolina; ca. 1910.

4. Smithfield, North Carolina; ca. 1910. Note the central chimney and ornamental front gable. A full rear wing replaced the traditional shed-roofed rearward extension on many later examples.

5. McAlester, Oklahoma; ca. 1890. Note the vertical, board-and-batten siding, which is less expensive than horizontal weatherboarding and is commonly seen on modest folk houses.

6. Salisbury, North Carolina; ca. 1900. Note the central chimney and double rearward extension.

7. Crocketville, South Carolina; ca. 1890. Front-porch rooms were often added to increase interior space.

8. New Roads, Louisiana, vicinity; late 19th century. Early example expanded by adding a room to the right of the original house. The metal roof, now covering both, is a later addition.

9. Lexington, Kentucky; ca. 1870. Dolan House. A one-and-one-half-story example on its way to becoming an I-house.

1

5

3

7

6

9

I-HOUSE FAMILY

Like the one-story, hall-and-parlor plan, two-story I-houses (two rooms wide and one room deep) are traditional British folk forms that were common in pre-railroad America, particularly in the Tidewater South. Similar forms occurred in the Midland area of log construction but were uncommon, probably because of the difficulty of constructing two-story walls made of solid, hewn logs. With the arrival of the railroads, however, I-houses again became a popular folk form over much of the eastern half of the country. They were particularly favored as modest folk dwellings in the midwestern states where the relatively long and confining winters made large houses more of a necessity than farther south. Post-railroad southern examples are also common, but these were usually the more pretentious houses of affluent local gentry. For this reason, many of these later southern I-houses have added stylistic detailing to make them appear fashionable. Like their hall-and-parlor relatives, post-railroad I-houses were elaborated with varying patterns of porches, chimneys, and rearward extensions.

1

4

5

I-HOUSE FAMILY

1. Mason County, West Virginia; late 19th century. Porchless central chimney examples, such as this, are most frequent in the midwestern states.

2. Clintonville, Kentucky; mid-19th century. An early post-railroad example. The windows and porch are later additions. Note the inside end chimneys and absence of side windows.

3. Helton, North Carolina, vicinity; ca. 1890. Blevins House. This example was expanded from a small log house, the walls of which are barely visible beneath the porch roof.

4. Salisbury, North Carolina; ca. 1898.

5. Cabarrus County, North Carolina; ca. 1900.

6. Perquimans County, North Carolina; mid-19th-century. Skinner House. An early example with Greek Revival detailing and large rear wing.

MASSED-PLAN, SIDE-GABLED FAMILY

Massed-plan (more than one room deep) folk houses were common in the pre-railroad era only in parts of the Northeast where the early New England building tradition developed roof-framing techniques for spanning large, two-room depths. With the expansion of the railroad this tradition evolved into the massed-plan versions of the gable-front and gable-front-and-wing families previously discussed. Light-weight lumber made widely available by the railroads permitted still simpler methods of light roof framing and these, in turn, led to other types of modest folk dwellings with two-room depths. These massed-plan houses, normally constructed with either side-gabled or pyramidal hipped roofs (see next section), had relatively large and flexible interior plans and thus slowly replaced the traditional one-room-deep hall-and-parlor and I-house forms.

Side-gabled folk houses with massed plans are usually one-story forms that vary principally in roof pitch and in the size and placement of porches. Earlier examples, particularly in the South, commonly had full-width, shed-roofed porches. From the front, these resemble their extended hall-and-parlor predecessors, but lack the latter's rearward extensions and resultant broken rear roof line. Examples from the 1930s and later commonly have only small entry porches, or no porch at all, probably in imitation of the then popular Cape Cod shape of the Colonial Revival style.

MASSED-PLAN, SIDE-GABLED FAMILY

1. Yanceyville, North Carolina, vicinity; ca. 1930.

2. Rolla, Missouri; ca. 1920. Example inspired by the contemporary Craftsman movement.

3. Abbeville, Louisiana, vicinity; late 19th century. The larger house to the right illustrates an early tradition of massed-plan, side-gabled folk building brought to Louisiana by French Canadian (Acadian) immigrants with a knowledge of long-span roof-framing techniques. Such Louisiana houses are known as Creole Cottages; they normally have the front wall moved back to make an integral porch under the steep roofline. Note how it dwarfs the traditional linear-plan hall-and-parlor to the left.

4. Irwinville, Georgia, vicinity; ca. 1920. Board-and-batten example similar to traditional hall-and-parlor plan, but with full, two-room depth. Note the lack of a broken rear roofline to cover a rearward extension.

5. Burlington, North Dakota, vicinity; ca. 1940.

6. New Madrid County, Missouri; 1940.

7. Austin, Minnesota; 1935.

3

4

6

7

PYRAMIDAL FAMILY

Massed-plan folk houses of rectangular shape are normally covered by side-gabled roofs. Those with more nearly square plans, in contrast, are commonly built with pyramidal (equilateral hipped) roofs, which require more complex roof framing but need fewer long-spanning rafters, and thus are less expensive to build. Such roofs appeared on modest folk houses earlier in the post-railroad era than did the side-gabled form. In the south, one-story, pyramidal houses became a popular replacement for the less spacious hall-and-parlor house during the early decades of the 20th century. One-story pyramidals are less common in the northern and midwestern states but are joined there by two-story examples, which similarly began to replace the traditional but less spacious rural I-houses of the region in the years from about 1905 to 1930. During the same period these two-story, pyramidal houses also became a popular urban house form throughout the country. Most urban examples were built with Colonial Revival, Neoclassical, Prairie, Tudor, or Craftsman stylistic detailing, but many also remained simple folk forms which lacked such fashionable details.

Like their side-gabled relatives, pyramidal folk houses differ principally in roof pitch and in the size and placement of porches.

1

4   5

PYRAMIDAL FAMILY

1. Stillwater, Oklahoma; ca. 1935.

2. Coffee County, Alabama; ca. 1905.

3. Greene County, Georgia; ca. 1900. Note the very steeply pitched roof. Such roofs are common on early southern examples; they may have been influenced by earlier roofs of similar shape built by French descendants in the Gulf Coast region.

4. Gwinnett County, Georgia; ca. 1920. Many one-story pyramidals have full or partial integral porches included under the principal roof.

5. Emporia, Kansas; ca. 1915. Such two-story pyramidals were a dominant urban form in the early decades of the century. Most urban examples had stylistic detailing but some, like this one, were unadorned folk houses. The metal storm windows are a later addition.

6. Cabarrus County, North Carolina; ca. 1900. An unusually large two-story example.

3

2

6

Colonial Houses

1600–1820

The early colonists arriving in the New World from Europe brought with them the prevailing architectural styles and building practices of their native countries. At first these were of late Medieval inspiration, for the new classicism of the Renaissance had not yet spread beneath the grandest palaces and mansions of their homelands. Indeed most Colonial dwellings built during the 1600s lacked even Medieval decorative detailing and might be classified as folk houses did they not so strongly reflect, in form and structure rather than stylistic detail, the distinctive building traditions of their countries of origin.

High-style Dutch, French, and Spanish dwellings remained rare in our area of the New World, for the Netherlands soon lost their colonies to England, and the centers of French and Spanish colonization were concentrated elsewhere. By contrast, the prospering English colonies of the eastern seaboard began in the early 1700s to import Renaissance-inspired Georgian fashion, which was to dominate these colonies for almost a century before being replaced, just as the American Revolution brought an end to British rule, by the closely related English Adam style.

It should be noted that Old World building practices persisted in each of these Colonial empires well beyond the end of European rule. The Dutch continued to settle and build traditional dwellings in the Hudson River area for over a hundred years after the formal loss of their colony to England. Likewise, French and Spanish influence lasted for many decades after their former territories became a part of the United States. Finally the Adam Style and a general taste for English fashion persisted in the English colonies for several decades after the Revolution.

Original examples of Colonial houses are relatively rare, but their forms and detailing are abundantly familiar because, beginning with the Centennial celebrations of 1876, they have been repeatedly copied in various stylistic "revivals." When faithfully done, these copies may be difficult to distinguish from originals. Two principal clues are of help here. First, each original style was built in a rather limited area of the country, whereas Revival copies are universal. For this reason, maps of the areas of original occurrence are provided for each Colonial style; outside these areas *any* example is sure to be a later copy. Secondly, Colonial houses were built before the era of industrialization and unaltered examples thus have, on close inspection, a characteristic "handmade" quality—in such details as doors, windows, brickwork, or siding—that is always lacking on Revival examples.

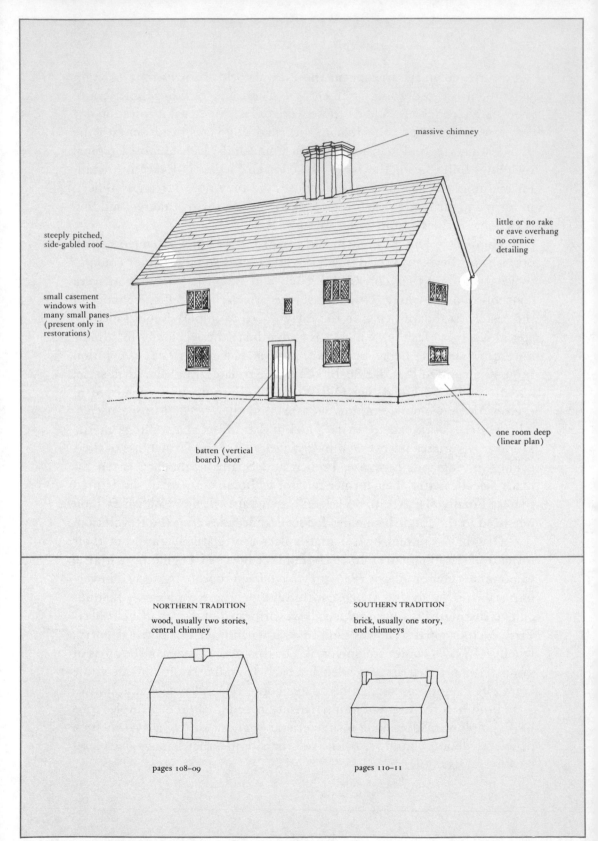

massive chimney

little or no rake
or eave overhang
no cornice
detailing

steeply pitched,
side-gabled roof

small casement
windows with
many small panes
(present only in
restorations)

one room deep
(linear plan)

batten (vertical
board) door

NORTHERN TRADITION

wood, usually two stories,
central chimney

SOUTHERN TRADITION

brick, usually one story,
end chimneys

pages 108–09

pages 110–11

Postmedieval English

IDENTIFYING FEATURES

Steeply pitched, side-gabled roof with little or no rake or eave overhang and no cornice detailing; massive central or end chimneys of brick or stone, often formed into decorative shapes; small windows, originally with narrow surrounds and fixed or casement sashes having many diamond-shaped panes (these were universally replaced by larger double-hung sashes during the 18th and 19th centuries; when the earlier type windows are present today, they are modern restorations); most were originally one room deep (linear plan) with batten (vertical board) doors.

PRINCIPAL SUBTYPES

Two distinct traditions became established in the 17th-century English colonies:

NORTHERN TRADITION—In the northern colonies wood-frame walls covered with weatherboard or wood shingles were the dominant mode of construction. These houses most commonly had two stories and a single large central chimney.

SOUTHERN TRADITION—Separated from the northern colonies by the Dutch in New York and New Jersey, the southern English colonies emphasized one-story forms with paired end chimneys. Most surviving examples have brick walls.

VARIANTS AND DETAILS

In Massachusetts and Connecticut a characteristic second-floor wall overhang is commonly present on the front facade; this is sometimes ornamented with decorative brackets or pendants. Similar wall overhangs at attic level are common beneath the end gables. Full-height cross gables were frequently used on the steeply pitched roofs to add space and light to the tall attic (few of these have escaped later roof modifications). In Rhode Island, stone end walls and chimneys were common on timber-frame houses; few of these stone-enders survive. In one-story southern examples, small dormers were sometimes used to provide attic light (many seen today are later additions).

Originally most Postmedieval houses were one room deep and symmetrical from front to back; later, lean-to rear projections were added to increase first-floor space. By around 1700 these rear additions were usually included under a single main roof in new construction, or under reframed and lowered roofs on earlier houses, to give the familiar saltbox roof form (see page 29). In all colonies, both timber-frame and masonry examples sometimes showed small, projecting wings or towers centered on the front or rear facades. In front, these typically served as entry areas, with a bedroom above; in the rear, they housed the stairway. When both were present, they gave the house a characteristic cross-shaped plan; few of these projections survive except in restorations.

OCCURRENCE

This was the only style in the English colonies from their founding (1607–20) to about 1700, when their population had grown to 220,000 and occupied the areas shown on the map. Only a few hundred houses remain of the many thousands built in this period. Most are in Massachusetts and Connecticut, where about a hundred are preserved as museum houses and at least that many more are in private hands. Fewer examples survive in Maryland, Virginia, and the middle colonies. After 1700, early Georgian houses with less steep roof slopes, smaller chimneys, large double-hung windows having one fixed and one movable sash, and classical door surrounds rapidly replaced this style throughout the English colonies. Postmedieval houses survived longest in the South, where scattered examples with Postmedieval details were built throughout the 18th century.

COMMENTS

These earliest English Colonial houses are New World adaptations of modest English domestic buildings which, in the decades immediately preceding colonization, had begun to undergo a transition from Medieval to Renaissance structural details. The steeply pitched roofs were a surviving Medieval development for thatch covering, which must be steep to shed water. In America the earliest roofs were also of thatch, but the ice, snow, thunderstorms, and high winds of the more severe New World climate soon made wooden shingles the preferred roofing material. The high pitch, now without function for relatively impervious shingle roofs, persisted for nearly a century. The roof pitch has been lowered in later alterations of most examples, including many restorations.

The chimney stack, replacing the open fire of Medieval vernacular houses, was the crucial Postmedieval improvement. Attic space, formerly unenclosed so that smoke could escape through roof openings, could be floored over to provide sleeping rooms. In the New World, large chimneys were used on all but the most modest 17th-century houses. In the northern colonies, central chimney placement was preferred, probably to conserve heat during the severe winters. In the southern colonies, the end chimneys may have helped to dissipate the heat of cooking fires during the oppressively hot summers.

Although only a few Postmedieval timber-frame houses survive in the southern colonies, they were probably far more common originally. With the growth of the southern plantation economy in the 18th century, many early wooden houses were converted to slave quarters or storage; most were ultimately abandoned and razed. As a result, the houses that survived were primarily early masonry examples. Most of these have also been lost due to indifference and neglect, some in only the past few decades.

The few surviving Postmedieval houses have generally been in continuous use for almost 300 years. During this long period they have been modified, improved, remodeled, and rebuilt, with the result that few reached this century in anything approaching their original form. Beginning about 1900, concern for our earliest colonial heritage led to modern restoration of many examples. When based on precise architectural and historical research, these restored houses closely approach the appearance of the 17th-century originals. When less carefully done, such restoration has produced bastard buildings with combinations of features that never existed.

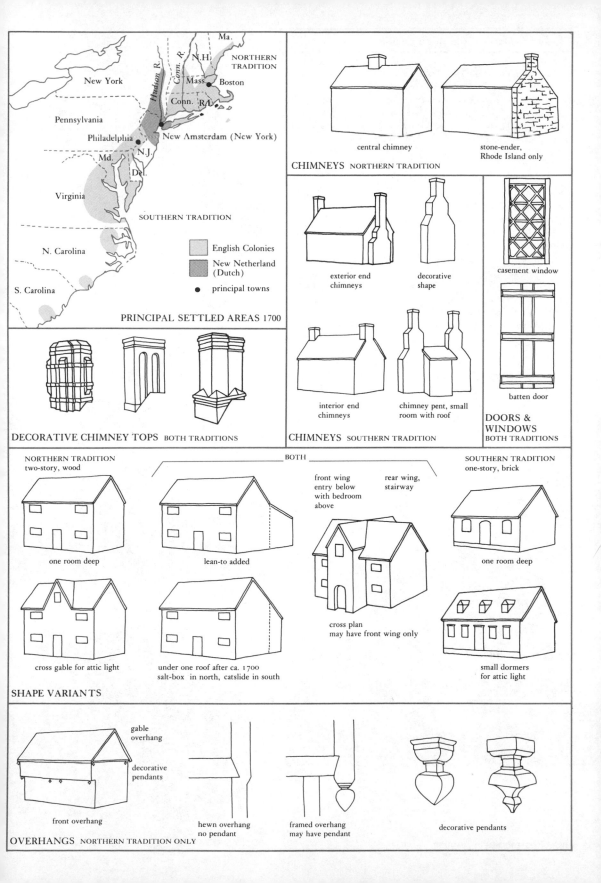

PRINCIPAL SETTLED AREAS 1700

New York
Pennsylvania
Philadelphia
Virginia
N. Carolina
S. Carolina
Hudson R.
Conn. R.
N.H.
Ma.
Mass.
Boston
Conn.
R.I.
New Amsterdam (New York)
N.J.
Md.
Del.
NORTHERN TRADITION
SOUTHERN TRADITION

English Colonies
New Netherland (Dutch)
principal towns

CHIMNEYS NORTHERN TRADITION

central chimney

stone-ender, Rhode Island only

exterior end chimneys

decorative shape

interior end chimneys

chimney pent, small room with roof

CHIMNEYS SOUTHERN TRADITION

casement window

batten door

DOORS & WINDOWS
BOTH TRADITIONS

DECORATIVE CHIMNEY TOPS BOTH TRADITIONS

NORTHERN TRADITION
two-story, wood

BOTH

SOUTHERN TRADITION
one-story, brick

one room deep

lean-to added

front wing entry below with bedroom above

rear wing, stairway

one room deep

cross gable for attic light

under one roof after ca. 1700
salt-box in north, catslide in south

cross plan
may have front wing only

small dormers for attic light

SHAPE VARIANTS

gable overhang

decorative pendants

front overhang

hewn overhang
no pendant

framed overhang
may have pendant

decorative pendants

OVERHANGS NORTHERN TRADITION ONLY

NORTHERN TRADITION

1. Medfield, Massachusetts; late 17th century. Peak House (restoration). One of the few surviving northern one-story examples.

2. Watertown, Massachusetts; 1694–1701. Browne House (restoration).

3. Topsfield, Massachusetts; 1683. Parson Capen House (restoration). The original windows were probably smaller casements.

4. Lincoln, Rhode Island; ca. 1687. Arnold House (restoration). A typical Rhode Island stone-ender.

5. Saugus, Massachusetts; ca. 1686. Boardman House. The saltbox rearward extension was added before 1696; the double-hung sash windows were probably added in the 18th century.

6. Salem, Massachusetts; ca. 1668. Turner House (The House of the Seven Gables, restoration). The original windows were probably smaller casements.

7., 8. Saugus, Massachusetts; ca. 1680. Appleton House (Ironworks House, restoration). Figure 7, taken about 1900, shows the house after 200 years of modifications. Figure 8 shows a later restoration to its probable 17-century cross-plan form.

9. Salem, Massachusetts, ca. 1698, Hunt House. An early photo; the house was demolished in 1863. The double-hung sash windows are probably an 18th-century addition.

2   3

5   6

9

SOUTHERN TRADITION

1. Virginia Beach, Virginia, vicinity; mid-18th century, Hudgins House. A rare survivor of the once common wood-frame hall-and-parlor folk houses in the tidewater South. This example has high-style Post-medieval chimneys which may remain from a partially destroyed earlier brick house.

2. Norfolk, Virginia, vicinity; mid-17th century. Thoroughgood House. In a later restoration the dormers have been removed and the windows replaced with leaded casements.

3. Hollywood, Maryland, vicinity; ca. 1660 (left two-thirds only). Resurrection Manor. The double-hung sash windows were probably added when the house was expanded from two or three rooms in the 18th century.

4. Virginia Beach, Virginia; late 17th century. Keeling House. The windows and cornice line dentils are probably 18th-century additions.

5. Newport News, Virginia, vicinity; early 18th century (as modified). Jones House. An earlier one-story house (note the trace of the original steep roof) altered to a two-story cross-plan in the 18th century. The windows are modern.

6. Salisbury, North Carolina, vicinity; chimney late 18th century. Long House. A late example of a composite Postmedieval chimney (the house is a much modified restoration). Most such chimneys date from the late 17th and early 18th centuries when houses two rooms deep first replaced the earlier southern linear plans. The space between the two principal chimneys was commonly enclosed and covered by a shed roof to make a small interior room or closet.

7., 8. Surry County, Virginia; mid-17th century. Bacon's Castle. Although somewhat altered, this is the only high-style house surviving from the 17th century. Note the cross form, shaped parapets, and multiple chimney stacks. Figure 7 shows the front facade and Figure 8 the rear.

1

3

5

6

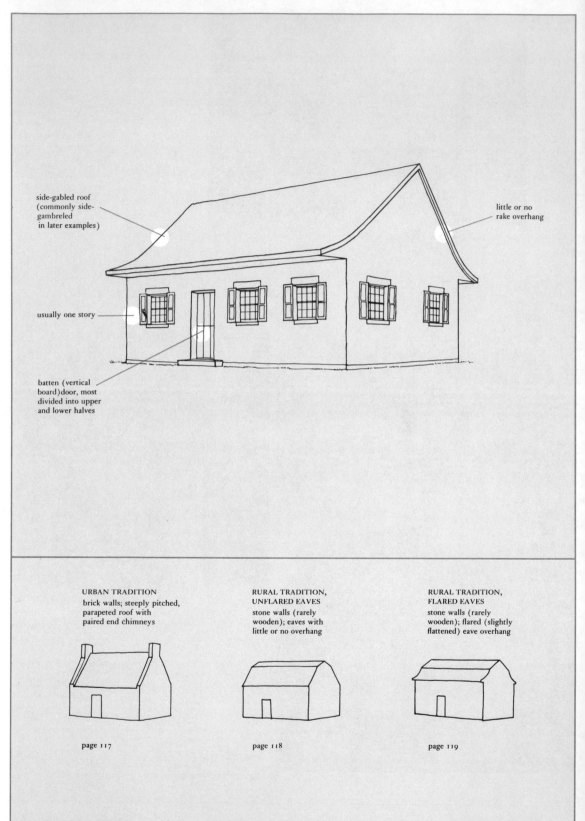

side-gabled roof (commonly side-gambreled in later examples)

little or no rake overhang

usually one story

batten (vertical board) door, most divided into upper and lower halves

URBAN TRADITION
brick walls; steeply pitched, parapeted roof with paired end chimneys

page 117

RURAL TRADITION, UNFLARED EAVES
stone walls (rarely wooden); eaves with little or no overhang

page 118

RURAL TRADITION, FLARED EAVES
stone walls (rarely wooden); flared (slightly flattened) eave overhang

page 119

PRINCIPAL SUBTYPES

Dutch Colonial

1625–ca. 1840

IDENTIFYING FEATURES

One story (less commonly one and one-half stories, rarely two stories) with side-gabled or side-gambreled roof having little or no rake (side) overhang; most originally with entrance doors divided into separately opening upper and lower halves (in about half the surviving examples, these have been replaced by later single-unit doors).

PRINCIPAL SUBTYPES

New World colonists from the Netherlands constructed three distinctive types of houses:

URBAN TRADITION—Among the earliest were brick urban houses of Medieval inspiration having steeply pitched and parapeted gable roofs and paired end chimneys. This type dominated the 17th-century Dutch trading settlements that grew at each end of the region's principal navigation route, the Hudson River: New Amsterdam (later New York) to the south and several outposts in the Albany area to the north. These towns became increasingly Anglicized in the 18th century with the result that few Dutch urban houses were built after about 1730.[1]

RURAL TRADITION, UNFLARED EAVES—Dutch building traditions persisted far longer in rural areas. Brick, the preferred Dutch building material, was replaced by coursed stone in most rural houses. The shaping and finish of the stonework became increasingly refined as colonial inhabitants grew more affluent during the 18th century. Early rural examples had side-gabled roofs and little or no eave overhang. After about 1750 gambrel roofs became common in this type.

RURAL TRADITION, FLARED EAVES—This tradition is similar to the rural subtype described just above, but has flared, overhanging eaves, which became common on both gable- and gambrel-roofed examples after about 1750 in the southern Hudson River area (see map).

VARIANTS AND DETAILS

As in the adjacent English colonies, the pitch of rural Dutch roofs decreased during the early 18th century as wood shingles replaced thatch, tile, and slate as the preferred roofing material. Steeply pitched, Medieval-style roofs survive on only a few rural Dutch

---

[1] A handful of urban-style houses were built in rural settings in the Albany region. These had the entrance on the long, non-gabled wall; in contrast, houses built in towns had the entrance in the narrow, gabled end, which always faced the street to conserve space on narrow urban lots. Ironically, only these "rural" urban houses have survived, those of the larger towns having been destroyed by three centuries of urban growth.

houses, all built before about 1720. (The dating of roofs and architectural details in rural Dutch houses is unusually difficult because early stone walls were typically incorporated into expansions and modifications throughout the 18th and 19th centuries. For this reason, most houses of supposed early date show later features, particularly roof, door, and window details.) In many rural examples the stone walls do not extend into the side gables, which are instead constructed of either brick or, more commonly, of shingle- or weatherboard-covered wooden framing. After about 1750, distinctively shaped gambrel roofs with short, flattened upper slopes became common, along with gable roofs of normal pitch which continued to be built. In the southernmost areas of Dutch influence, around present-day New York City and adjacent New Jersey, distinctive flared eaves were usual on both gable and gambrel roofs after about 1750. Where the Dutch colonists were in close contact with English building traditions, particularly on western Long Island, timber-frame rural houses with weatherboard or shingle siding replaced the more usual stone construction. Most existing Dutch Colonial houses have double-hung sash windows which may be original or replacements of earlier types. Like their English counterparts, 17th-century Dutch houses apparently had leaded casement windows. In the English colonies these were supplanted by wooden, double-hung windows with one movable sash early in the 18th century. The Dutch, however, apparently used outward-swinging wooden casements, sometimes hung in side-by-side pairs, during an early 18th-century transitional period between leaded casements and wooden double-hung sashes. Few of these early casement windows, either leaded or wooden, survive. The Dutch double door was probably developed to keep out livestock (with the bottom section closed) while allowing in light and air through the open top. This style of door is found in about half of the surviving houses. From the early 18th century, the treatment of the door surround commonly reflected the Georgian and subsequent Adam styles of the English colonies.

OCCURRENCE

Formal control by the Dutch of their New World colonies was remarkably brief. Dutch fur traders founded settlements near Albany in 1614 and at New Amsterdam (New York) in 1626. Centered in these areas, and along the Hudson River which connected them, Dutch colonization proceeded for only fifty years before expanding English colonies on either side led to English control in 1664. Thus New Netherland became New York and Dutch influence began to fade in the principal towns of the colony. All Dutch urban buildings have long vanished from New Amsterdam (the tip of Manhattan Island in what is now New York City) but a very few—probably less than a half-dozen—urban houses still survive in the Albany region. These are among the rarest of American domestic buildings; regrettably, several of the finest remaining examples have been lost during only the last few decades. In contrast, several hundred Dutch rural houses survive in various states of preservation and modification throughout the area of former Dutch influence. The English permitted feudal Dutch landholders, some of whom controlled enormous tracts along the Hudson, to retain their property. These landlords, in turn, continued to encourage rural immigration from Holland during the 18th century. As a result, most Dutch Colonial rural houses postdate by many years the era of Dutch ownership of the colony.

The building traditions brought by these Dutch immigrants survived, in isolated

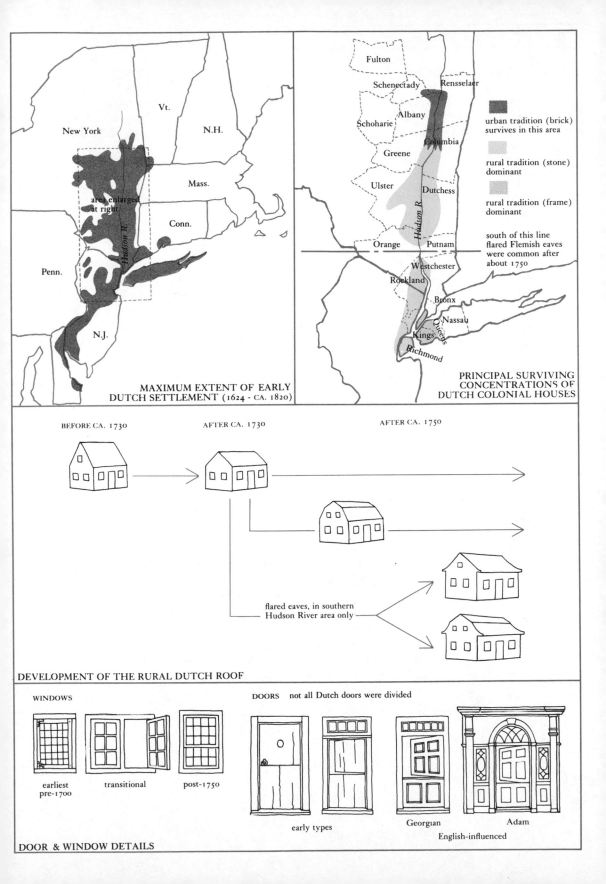

MAXIMUM EXTENT OF EARLY
DUTCH SETTLEMENT (1624 - CA. 1820)

New York

Vt.

N.H.

Mass.

Conn.

Hudson R.

area enlarged
at right

Penn.

N.J.

PRINCIPAL SURVIVING
CONCENTRATIONS OF
DUTCH COLONIAL HOUSES

Fulton

Schenectady

Rensselaer

Albany

Schoharie

Columbia

Greene

Ulster

Dutchess

Hudson R.

Orange

Putnam

Westchester

Rockland

Bronx

Nassau

Kings

Queens

Richmond

urban tradition (brick)
survives in this area

rural tradition (stone)
dominant

rural tradition (frame)
dominant

south of this line
flared Flemish eaves
were common after
about 1750

DEVELOPMENT OF THE RURAL DUTCH ROOF

BEFORE CA. 1730

AFTER CA. 1730

AFTER CA. 1750

flared eaves, in southern
Hudson River area only

DOOR & WINDOW DETAILS

WINDOWS

earliest
pre-1700

transitional

post-1750

DOORS   not all Dutch doors were divided

early types

Georgian

Adam

English-influenced

examples, into the early decades of the 19th century. Today, concentrations of Dutch rural houses are found principally in Bergen County (New Jersey), adjacent Rockland County (New York), and farther up the Hudson, in Ulster and Dutchess counties (New York). A handful of formerly rural houses are preserved within the bounds of present New York City, particularly in Queens County and Staten Island. Scattered examples are found throughout the area of former Dutch influence (see maps).

COMMENTS

Dutch Colonial houses of the urban type are quite similar to their Old World counterparts built in the prosperous mercantile cities of 17th-century Holland. In sharp contrast, the origins of the American Dutch rural house are uncertain and have attracted much speculation. The earliest were simple stone-walled, gable-roofed folk houses. Similar houses are found in the rural building traditions of Flanders (which includes the coastal regions of modern Belgium and immediately adjacent France) but are rare in the Netherlands, which generally lacks both stone and abundant timber for building (hence the Dutch emphasis on brick construction). Most rural Dutch immigrants, however, were persecuted Protestants from Flanders, from France, and elsewhere, who sought refuge first in Holland and then in her New World colony. With them most probably came the tradition of stone folk building. The principal controversy thus centers not on the stone walls of the rural Dutch Colonial house, but on its distinctive roof features: the unusual gambrel and, especially, the flared eaves, both of which became common after about 1750. The gambrel is perhaps the easiest to explain, since gambrels of somewhat different shape were also becoming common, as a means of increasing both roof span and useful attic space, throughout the English colonies at the same time. More difficulty attaches to the origin of the flared eaves. These have been considered to be: (1) a distinctive New World innovation, or (2) an adaptation of a French-Flemish tradition of protecting plastered walls under steeply sloping, thatched roofs by adding a more gently sloping extension of tiles at the eaves. Pending actual research on the question, the latter explanation appears more likely, particularly since many French-influenced colonial buildings show similar eaves (see the next chapter, on French Colonial houses).

Dutch rural houses, with their substantial stone walls, were less easily expanded than were their wooden English counterparts. Although there are many examples of early Dutch stone walls being incorporated into later, and larger, houses, these thrifty colonists generally favored another method of house expansion. When a house became too small, a larger version was built immediately beside the smaller, which then became a kitchen or bedroom wing of the new dwelling. Dutch Colonial houses thus often show a linear sequence of two or three (rarely more) units built at different times. Although the smallest unit is normally the oldest, this is not invariably the case, for small kitchen or bedroom wings were also added to larger houses long after they were built.

URBAN TRADITION

1. Schenectady, New York; early 18th century. Yates House. The only surviving example in an urban setting with the entrance in the narrow gable end. Note the dagger-shaped wrought-iron anchors for roof and wall beams, a characteristic feature of urban Dutch houses. This example has wood-frame side walls. The windows and classical doorway are later additions.

2. East Greenbush, New York; 1723. Bries House. Typical urban house built in rural setting, with entrance on long, nongabled wall. The windows and porch are later additions.

3. Kinderhook, New York; 1737. Van Alen House (restoration). Urban house in rural setting expanded by adding an adjacent unit in typical Dutch fashion.

4. Cohoes, New York; mid-18th century. Van Schaick House. A transitional example with urban-style brickwork and newly fashionable gambrel roof. The porch is a late-19th-century addition.

1

2   3

4

RURAL TRADITION, UNFLARED EAVES

1. Rotterdam, New York; early 18th century. Mabie House. One of the few surviving rural Dutch houses that preserve the steep Medieval roof pitch. The walls are of whitewashed stone; the frame extension to the right is a later addition.

2. Hurley, New York; mid-18th century. Restoration.

3. New Paltz, New York; early 18th century. Bevier House. The original house (left-hand portion) was expanded by early additions. The gable-end entrance is unusual.

4. Coeymans, New York; ca. 1761 (altered ca. 1790). Coeymans House. An early example expanded and altered by the early addition of a fashionable gambrel roof.

5. Ulster County, New York; mid-18th century. Ten Broeck House. Note the expansion by adding two units to the portion to the left with casement windows, which is the earliest. The middle unit was added in 1751 and the right-hand unit in 1765.

1

3

2

4

5

RURAL TRADITION, FLARED EAVES

1. Old Tappan, New Jersey; ca. 1751. Haring House. Note the more carefully finished stonework on the front facade.

2. Dumont, New Jersey; ca. 1760 (smaller portion in foreground), ca. 1810 (larger portion). Zabriskie House. Note the absence of flared eaves on the small early portion. The wide-end overhang of the gambrel roof is a 19th-century development.

3. Brooklyn, New York; ca. 1676. Schenck House. A very early wood-frame example preserving the steep Medieval roof pitch. The dormers, porch, and flared eaves are 18th-century modifications.

4. Mahwah vicinity, New Jersey; late 18th century. Van Horn House.

5. Closter, New Jersey; ca. 1800. Durie House. The dormers and porch supports are later additions, as is the smaller frame wing added in 1854.

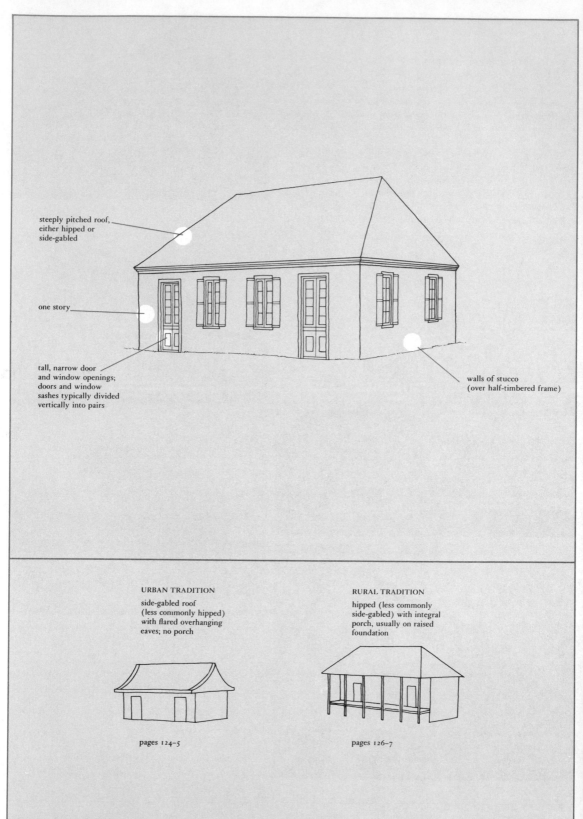

steeply pitched roof, either hipped or side-gabled

one story

tall, narrow door and window openings; doors and window sashes typically divided vertically into pairs

walls of stucco (over half-timbered frame)

URBAN TRADITION

side-gabled roof (less commonly hipped) with flared overhanging eaves; no porch

pages 124–5

RURAL TRADITION

hipped (less commonly side-gabled) with integral porch, usually on raised foundation

pages 126–7

PRINCIPAL SUBTYPES

French Colonial

1700–1830; to ca. 1860 in New Orleans

IDENTIFYING FEATURES

One story with many narrow door and window openings having paired shutters (these openings originally had paired French doors and paired casement windows which have commonly been altered to single doors and double-hung sash windows); steeply pitched roof, either hipped or side-gabled; walls of stucco, usually over a half-timbered frame.

PRINCIPAL SUBTYPES

French Colonial houses are of two basic types:

URBAN TRADITION—In New Orleans there remain many French urban cottages which lack porches and are built right up to the adjacent sidewalk. These normally have side-gabled (sometimes hipped) roofs and flared eaves that overhang the front facade.

RURAL TRADITION—More familiar than the urban cottages of New Orleans are French rural houses with extensive porches supported by slender wooden columns under the main roof line. These usually have steeply pitched, hipped roofs and are commonly raised on high masonry foundations, the porch area above being supported by massive masonry columns.

VARIANTS AND DETAILS

As in their 17th-century English and Dutch counterparts, early French Colonial houses had very high, steeply pitched roofs, following the Medieval tradition of constructing thatched roofs at a very steep pitch in order to shed water. Early French examples usually had a characteristic pavilion roof form, which is steeply hipped with the side roof planes sloping even more steeply than the front and back planes. Very few of these survive. The addition of wide porches around such houses, a mild-climate tradition that probably originated in the West Indies, was accomplished by extending the hipped roof out over the porch but at a gentler pitch, giving it a distinctive, dual-pitched form. As this tradition developed, such roofs were even used occasionally on urban houses without porches. Somewhat later, simple hipped roofs, lower and with uniform slopes on all sides, came to dominate. Original side-gabled roofs are uncommon in rural houses, although many early hipped forms have been modified to this shape. In New Orleans, side-gabled roofs were dominant on urban cottages built after about 1830, probably to reduce roof drainage to narrow passageways between the closely spaced cottages of the expanding city. These later urban cottages also typically have extended and flared eaves, a characteristic that they share with Flemish-inspired Dutch Colonial houses of New York and New Jersey. In all roof forms, tall and narrow gabled dormers were sometimes used to provide attic light.

Most French Colonial houses originally had paired French doors, with small glass panes set above wooden panels. The doors sometimes had a line of transom lights above; in later examples these were often supplanted by an Adam fanlight. Originally the doors were framed by a simple, narrow surround. Vertical board shutters hung on strap hinges covered the doors and transom (but not the fanlight, if present). The interior surface of the shutter was sometimes paneled; the shutters usually swung outward and the doors inward. In later examples, Adam or Greek Revival door surrounds are common. Early French windows were paired wooden casements which swung inward. These were generally glazed with small panes of glass and were covered by vertical board shutters which had horizontal battens on the interior and swung outward on iron strap hinges. The window surround was narrow and simple. In later examples these French-style casements were supplanted by English double-hung sashes.

OCCURRENCE

In the 18th century, France occupied much of eastern North America by means of military outposts and settlements scattered along the principal waterways, particularly the St. Lawrence, Great Lakes, and Mississippi valleys (see map). After Jefferson's purchase of Louisiana in 1803, French building traditions began to fade, although they persisted in New Orleans for half a century more and survive today in French Canada. In the United States, only a few concentrations of French-influenced buildings remain from this vast empire. All of these are in Louisiana and adjacent Mississippi save one, the little-known French Colonial houses of St. Genevieve, Missouri (see map). Several hundred houses, all of the rural type, survive in these areas; a handful of others are scattered elsewhere. Most date from the late 18th and early 19th centuries. The early outskirts of New Orleans had many similar rural houses but only a few survived the later growth of the city. Until at least the 1860s, however, French-style urban cottages were built in the Creole suburbs of New Orleans, to the north and east of the original town, or Vieux Carré.

More than half of the country's surviving French Colonial houses are found in these New Orleans neighborhoods, but are seldom seen by visitors to that city. Only a handful remain in the Vieux Carré, which was all but destroyed by fires in 1788 and 1791. As the commercial center of town, the Vieux Carré was rebuilt during the early 19th century largely with mixed-use structures having shops on the first floor and living quarters above. Many of these survive and show strong French influences, especially in the door and window treatments, but most were altered as the city grew during the later 19th century. For example, small and delicate wrought-iron balconies were originally common under full-length upper windows (Figure 5, page 124). The expansion of cast-iron technology in the mid-1800s led to the replacement of many by elaborate systems of iron porches extending over the sidewalks and around the building at each upper level (Figure 6, page 124). These provided outdoor living areas for residents of the upper floors, but they also dramatically altered the facades. Paradoxically, it is these American-made additions, almost unknown in France, that have come to characterize French New Orleans.

With the growth of the city as a principal United States seaport after the Louisiana

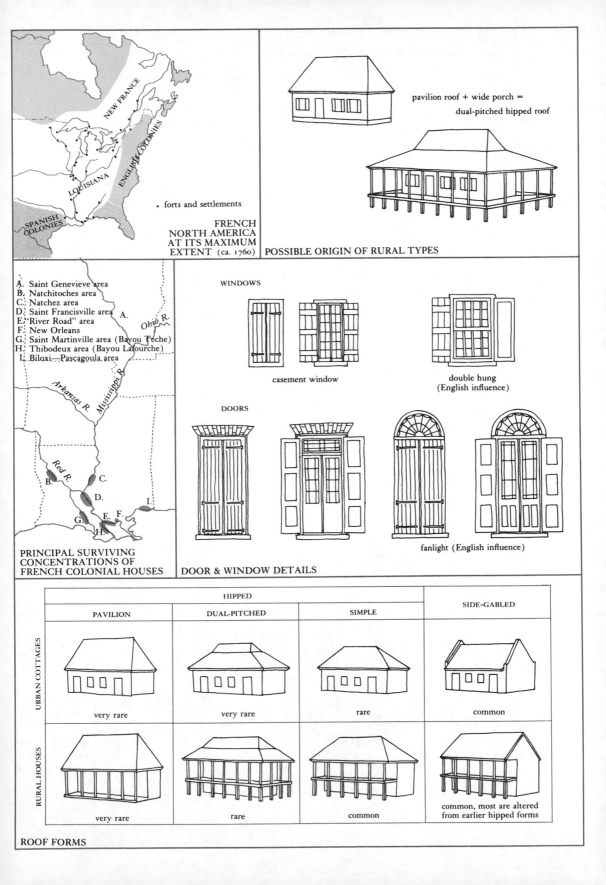

FRENCH
NORTH AMERICA
AT ITS MAXIMUM
EXTENT (ca. 1760)

· forts and settlements

POSSIBLE ORIGIN OF RURAL TYPES

pavilion roof + wide porch =

dual-pitched hipped roof

A. Saint Genevieve area
B. Natchitoches area
C. Natchez area
D. Saint Francisville area
E. "River Road" area
F. New Orleans
G. Saint Martinville area (Bayou Teche)
H. Thibodeux area (Bayou Lafourche)
I. Biloxi—Pascagoula area

PRINCIPAL SURVIVING
CONCENTRATIONS OF
FRENCH COLONIAL HOUSES

DOOR & WINDOW DETAILS

WINDOWS

casement window

double hung
(English influence)

DOORS

fanlight (English influence)

ROOF FORMS

	HIPPED			SIDE-GABLED
	PAVILION	DUAL-PITCHED	SIMPLE	
URBAN COTTAGES	very rare	very rare	rare	common
RURAL HOUSES	very rare	rare	common	common, most are altered from earlier hipped forms

Purchase, a flood of American immigrants built principally upriver (southwest) of the Vieux Carré. At the same time, the more slowly expanding French population built new suburbs in the opposite or downriver direction. Most of the city's surviving French houses are urban cottages built in these neighborhoods from 1810 to about 1860.

COMMENTS

English houses are usually directed inward; they have few external entrances and emphasize internal halls and stairways for access to the rooms. French houses, on the other hand, typically look outward; each room is likely to have its own exterior doorway and the stairways are commonly on exterior porches, rather than within the main body of the house. Hallways are also normally absent, the interior rooms opening instead directly into each other. These traditions are reflected in the many exterior doors and in the external stairways of French Colonial houses. Even small urban cottages, usually built in a square four-room plan, have at least four external doors, two of which lead from the two front rooms directly onto the adjacent sidewalk.

Most French Colonial houses were constructed, at least in part, with half-timbered walls. Earliest, and most primitive, was post-in-ground construction, with closely spaced vertical timbers buried in the ground and filled in between with clay mixed with such binding materials as hair or straw. Later, typical timber framing, using a sill set on a foundation, was adopted; often such walls had soft brick infilling. Both the post-in-ground and framed types were originally covered with stucco or, in later examples, weatherboarding, to protect the timbers and infilling. In raised rural houses the foundation is commonly of stuccoed brick, which supports the half-timbered walls of the main floor above.

The several hundred surviving French Colonial houses are among the rarest and least appreciated American buildings. While comparable English houses of the eastern seaboard have long been revered landmarks, only a few French examples are similarly esteemed. Recent preservation efforts in New Orleans have renewed interest in its urban cottages, but unique rural houses are still being lost through indifference and neglect.

5

6

URBAN TRADITION

1. New Orleans, Louisiana; 1820. Dolliole House. Hipped-roof example of unusual shape. The roof is covered with the original flat tiles; note the projecting tiles at the eaves and the four doorways.

2. New Orleans, Louisiana; mid-19th century. Late hipped-roof example with wood-frame walls and modest Italianate detailing.

3. New Orleans, Louisiana; 1824. Gaillard House.

4. New Orleans, Louisiana; ca. 1850. Mansion House. Late wood-frame example with Greek Revival doorway. The three-ranked facade is unusual.

5. New Orleans, Louisiana; ca. 1806. Font-Juncadella Building. A well-preserved example of a typical early-19th-century French shop-residence of the Vieux Carré. Note the delicate wrought-iron balcony railing.

6. New Orleans, Louisiana; 1836. Gardette House. Large Vieux Carré town house with elaborate cast-iron porches added in the mid-19th century.

7. New Orleans, Louisiana; ca. 1828. Boutin House. Early parapeted example with Adam doorway and pilasters. The Victorian eave brackets and trim are later additions.

RURAL TRADITION

1., 2. Ste. Genevieve, Missouri; late 18th century. Bolduc House (restoration). Figure 1 shows the side and rear of the house before restoration. Figure 2 shows the rear of the house as restored with a dual-pitched hipped roof and exposed wall timbers.

3. Ste. Genevieve, Missouri; late 18th century. Amoureaux House. This example has been much modified over the years. The roof framing suggests that the original roof was of pavilion-shaped hipped form without porches.

4. Hahnville, Louisiana, vicinity; early 19th century. Lehman House. A modest example built without the usual Louisiana high basement. The dormer and metal roof are later additions.

5. New Orleans, Louisiana; 1820. Olivier House. Large example with dual-pitched hipped roof. Note the brick columns supporting the wood porch above and the outside stairway. Originally a plantation house beyond the city, this example survived the urban growth around it until 1950, when it was demolished.

6. St. Martinville, Louisiana, vicinity; late 18th century. Houssaye House (Acadian House, restoration). An early example, probably built originally with side-gabled roof as shown.

7. Hahnville, Louisiana, vicinity; early 19th century. Fortier House (Homeplace Plantation). The front stairway replaces an earlier one beneath the right corner of the porch. The metal roof is a later addition.

8. New Roads, Louisiana, vicinity; early 19th century. Riche House. The elaborate stairway probably replaces an earlier one beneath the porch, like that in Figure 5. Note the partial side porches.

1

4

7

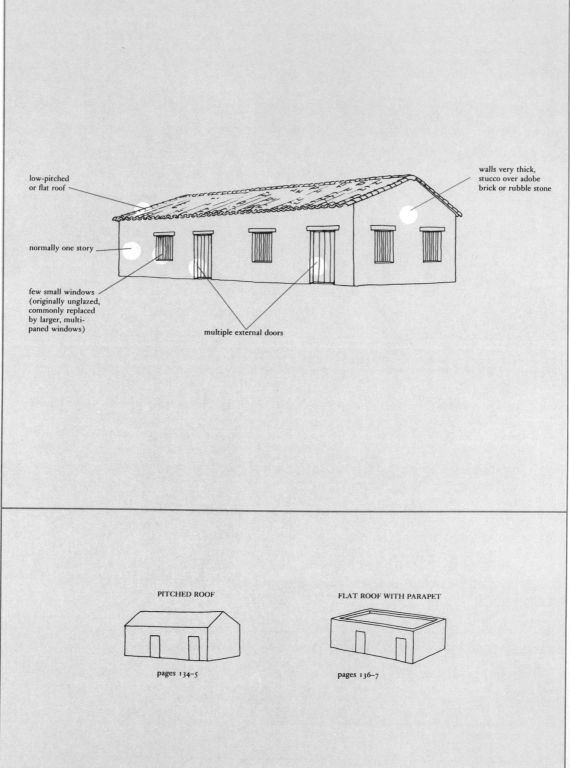

low-pitched
or flat roof

normally one story

few small windows
(originally unglazed,
commonly replaced
by larger, multi-
paned windows)

multiple external doors

walls very thick,
stucco over adobe
brick or rubble stone

PITCHED ROOF

pages 134–5

FLAT ROOF WITH PARAPET

pages 136–7

PRINCIPAL SUBTYPES

Spanish Colonial

IDENTIFYING FEATURES

One story (less commonly two stories) with low-pitched or flat roof; thick masonry walls of adobe brick or rubble stone (usually covered with protective stucco); originally with multiple external doorways and few small window openings lacking glass (bars or grilles of wood or wrought iron covered the exterior openings, which were closed from the interior by solid wooden shutters; except in reconstructions, most such early windows have been altered to accommodate double-hung, glazed sashes and trim).

PRINCIPAL SUBTYPES

Spanish Colonial houses are of solid masonry construction[1] but show two fundamentally different roof types which are found both in Spain and in her New World colonies:

PITCHED ROOF—The first basic type includes pitched-roof houses with traditional European roof framing. These, in turn, are of three kinds: The first consists of steeply pitched, usually side-gabled forms in which the wooden framing supports a covering of thatch; in the United States, this tradition survives principally in Hispanic folk houses with steeply pitched, shingled roofs. In the second and most familiar type, the roofs are low-pitched with a covering of half-cylindrical tiles. These tile roofs are usually of shed- or side-gabled form, less commonly hipped. A third variant, originally found in the Los Angeles area but now very rare, consists of an almost flat, tar-covered shed roof with overhanging eaves.

FLAT ROOF WITH PARAPET—The second basic type consists of flat-roofed houses without traditional European roof framing. Instead, massive horizontal timbers are embedded in parapeted masonry walls to support an extremely heavy roof of earth or mortar. Cylindrical rainspouts of wood, tin, or tile project through the parapet along one or more walls to provide drainage. This type, introduced into Spain from North Africa by the Moors, was also developed independently by several groups of Native Americans, and was well established in Mexico and the southwestern United States when the Spaniards arrived.

From early Spanish Colonial times, each of the two basic roof types has tended to dominate in different parts of Mexico and adjacent Hispanic areas of the United States (see map). The reasons for this pattern are uncertain; the flat, earthen roof would appear to be more suitable for very hot and dry regions, yet each type dominates through a range

---

[1] Inspired by Native American traditions, folk houses with crude, half-timbered walls and thatched roofs are also common in Spanish America. Known as *jacal* or *palisado* construction, the walls consist of vertical posts set in the ground to provide support for a framework of twigs covered with clay. An example appears to the right of the masonry house in Figure 3, page 136.

of climates. Most probably the building traditions of the original colonial settlers, interacting with those of the local natives, determined the patterns.

VARIANTS AND DETAILS

The earliest houses in areas of the United States that were formerly Spanish territories showed few decorative or stylistic details when compared with more imposing Spanish or Mexican prototypes. Built in remote and impoverished colonial outposts, these houses were simple by necessity. Only with the opening of trade with the United States in the 1830s did increased prosperity come to these regions; along with the new wealth came Anglo immigrants with their own building traditions. First came wooden decorative details, principally in the Greek Revival style, and glazed, double-hung sash windows. In areas with the pitched-roof tradition, shingled roofs were introduced. In other areas, flat-roofed houses became modified by the addition of framed, shingled roofs above the parapeted walls. These innovations quickly became fashionable with both Anglo and Hispanic residents, who superimposed them upon the traditional adobe construction. Such Anglo-Spanish-Greek Revival houses, in two-story variants with cantilevered second-floor porches, have come to be called Monterey style, after the colonial capital of California where many survive (figures 5, 6, 7, page 135). In New Mexico, western Texas, and Arizona, related flat-roofed, single-story forms, usually with a protective topping of fired brick crowning the roof parapet, are known as Territorial style houses (figures 5, 6, page 136). The spread of the western railroads in the 1880s provided ready access to quantities of milled lumber and led to the final decline of Hispanic building styles as adobe construction was abandoned for wood-frame houses in all but a few remote pockets of surviving tradition.

PORCHES—Spanish domestic buildings commonly have long, narrow porches (the *corredor* or *portale*) that open onto internal courtyards and function as sheltered passageways between rooms, which usually lacked internal connecting doorways. In more pretentious Spanish and Mexican prototypes, the porches often took the form of colonnaded arcades with elaborate masonry arches supporting the roof. In more modest examples, which include all that survive in the United States, porch roofs were supported by hewn logs, usually capped by distinctive carved brackets. In pitched-roof houses these columns supported either extensions of the main roof or separate shed roofs abutting the main walls. In flat-roofed houses, porches were normally recessed into the main structure, with the principal adobe walls supporting the ends of the porch roof timbers. Upon these were built a lower and somewhat thinner version of the main earthen roof. Because they faced internal courtyards, traditional porches are seldom evident on the external facades. With the arrival of Anglo influence, however, front-facade porches became fashionable. Particularly characteristic were cantilevered second-floor porches on two-story houses. These usually show delicate wooden balustrades and were probably inspired, at least in part, by the cantilevered balconies common on the upper floors of traditional Spanish town houses. Anglo influence also led to the traditional massive roof supports' being abandoned for more delicate wooden columns of vernacular Greek Revival inspiration.

OCCURRENCE

Most of what is now the southwestern United States was Spanish from the 17th century until 1821, when Mexico gained its independence; it remained part of Mexico until ceded

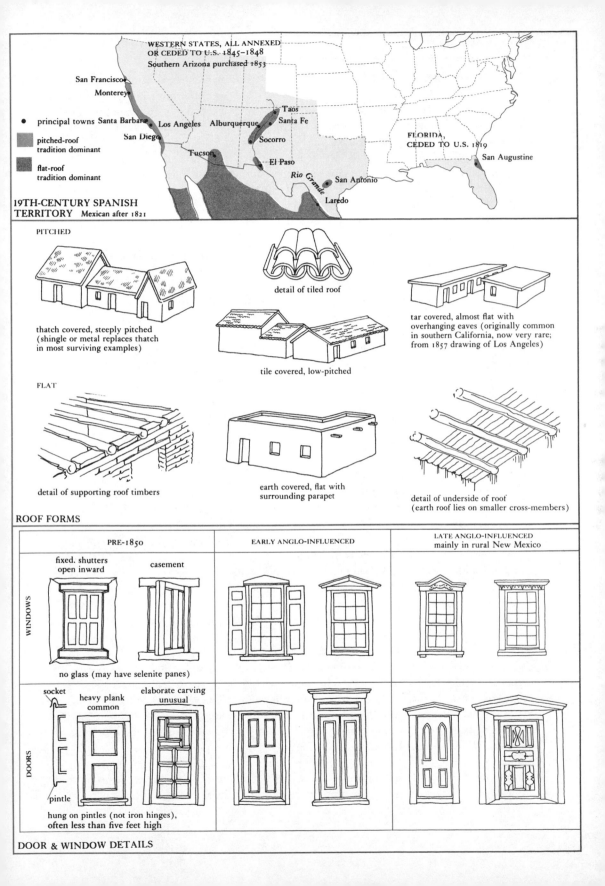

WESTERN STATES, ALL ANNEXED
OR CEDED TO U.S. 1845–1848
Southern Arizona purchased 1853

- • principal towns Santa Barbara
- pitched-roof tradition dominant
- flat-roof tradition dominant

San Francisco
Monterey
Santa Barbara
Los Angeles
San Diego
Tucson
Alburquerque
Socorro
Taos
Santa Fe
El Paso
Rio Grande
San Antonio
Laredo
FLORIDA, CEDED TO U.S. 1819
San Augustine

19TH-CENTURY SPANISH TERRITORY Mexican after 1821

PITCHED

thatch covered, steeply pitched
(shingle or metal replaces thatch
in most surviving examples)

detail of tiled roof

tile covered, low-pitched

tar covered, almost flat with
overhanging eaves (originally common
in southern California, now very rare;
from 1857 drawing of Los Angeles)

FLAT

detail of supporting roof timbers

earth covered, flat with
surrounding parapet

detail of underside of roof
(earth roof lies on smaller cross-members)

ROOF FORMS

	PRE-1850	EARLY ANGLO-INFLUENCED	LATE ANGLO-INFLUENCED mainly in rural New Mexico
WINDOWS	fixed. shutters open inward / casement / no glass (may have selenite panes)		
DOORS	socket / heavy plank common / elaborate carving unusual / pintle / hung on pintles (not iron hinges), often less than five feet high		

DOOR & WINDOW DETAILS

to the United States in the late 1840s following the Mexican War. Spanish Texas gained independence from Mexico in 1836 and was a separate country until annexed to the United States in 1845. Florida was Spanish from 1565 until ceded to the United States in 1821, with a brief interruption of British rule from 1763 to 1783. (A similarly brief interval of Spanish control of French Louisiana, from 1762 until 1800, resulted in a few Spanish public buildings but little change in the local French housing traditions). This vast territory was a sparsely settled frontier region during the Spanish and Mexican periods. Forts and missions to convert the Native Americans were established at many places, but few led to permanent settlements with substantial domestic architecture: St. Augustine in Florida; around San Antonio, Texas; scattered along the length of the Rio Grande from southern Texas to northern New Mexico; around Tucson, Arizona; and along the California coast from San Diego northward to around San Francisco (see map). Today significant concentrations remain only in St. Augustine, Tuscon, Santa Fe, San Diego, Santa Barbara, Monterey; and a few rural communities in Texas and New Mexico. Almost all surviving examples show Anglo-influenced modifications from the mid- and late 19th century. Many have also suffered from 20th-century renovation and overly zealous restoration, this particularly for those in modern urban centers; relatively unaltered examples from the 19th century survive principally in rural areas, from which they are fast disappearing through neglect and decay.

COMMENTS

Unlike their English counterparts, larger Spanish Colonial domestic buildings were not usually conceived as multi-roomed wholes but grew, instead, as series of independent rooms. Modest households had but a single room. As affluence increased, one-room units were added to make extended dwellings whose size was limited only by the wealth of the builder. Typically, the first two or three rooms were joined end-to-end to make a linear row; units were then added single file but at right angles to make an L or U. In the largest houses, the rooms made rectangular masses, enclosing an inner courtyard (the *patio* or *placita*). In smaller houses, masonry walls, rather than rooms, usually completed the enclosure of similar courtyards. Traditionally, few internal openings existed between rooms; each was entered through its own door opening onto the courtyard. Long, narrow porches commonly provided sheltered passageways between rooms. The external facades of extended houses were usually austere, revealing only small windows and a single entrance door or gateway.

Spanish Colonial buildings are unusually durable when executed in stone. Although the wooden roof framing quickly decays if neglected, walls often survive many decades, even centuries, of abandonment. Spanish mission buildings in Texas, Arizona, and California, some constructed in the 17th and early 18th centuries, have mostly been reconstructed in this century upon such remaining wall segments. In sharp contrast, adobe walls are unusually susceptible to deterioration; if the roofs are not continually repaired, rainwater literally melts them into a formless mass of mud. As a general rule, adobe buildings abandoned for more than twenty-five years are beyond repair. Because most Spanish Colonial houses had adobe walls, the only survivors are those that have had continuous care. Regrettably, many of the most authentic examples were abandoned just during the past thirty years in favor of frame dwellings. This is particularly true in rural New Mexico, where irreplaceable examples have been, and are being, lost.

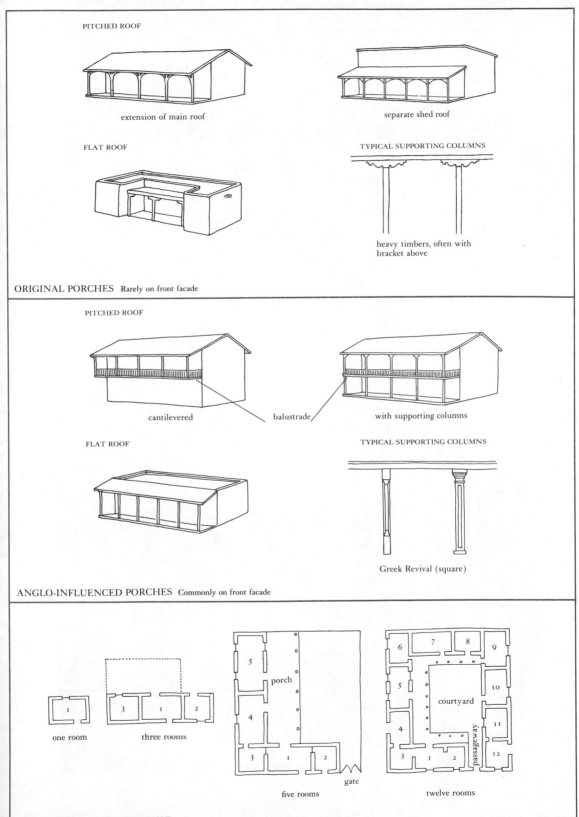

PITCHED ROOF

extension of main roof

separate shed roof

FLAT ROOF

TYPICAL SUPPORTING COLUMNS

heavy timbers, often with
bracket above

ORIGINAL PORCHES Rarely on front facade

PITCHED ROOF

cantilevered

balustrade

with supporting columns

FLAT ROOF

TYPICAL SUPPORTING COLUMNS

Greek Revival (square)

ANGLO-INFLUENCED PORCHES Commonly on front facade

one room

three rooms

5

porch

4

3   1   2

gate

five rooms

6   7   8   9

5

courtyard

10

4

passageway

11

3   1   2   12

twelve rooms

PLAN OF THE SPANISH HOUSE

PITCHED ROOF

1. Salinas vicinity, California; early 19th century. Sherwood House. Courtyard view of a little-altered rural survivor of modest scale. The wide rake overhang of the gable is unusual.

2. San Diego, California; 1829. Estudillo House (restoration). Exterior view of a part of an extended, U-shaped example that survives relatively intact. Note the intersecting shed roofs.

3. Santa Barbara, California; ca. 1830. Lugo House (restoration). A small example restored as a part of a 20th-century building complex. The original door and windows would have been unglazed.

4. Templeton vicinity, California; early 19th century. Blackburn House. Courtyard view of a little-altered rural survivor. Note the intersecting roof planes.

5. Rio Grande City vicinity, Texas; 19th century. A modest rural two-story example with a Monterey-style cantilevered porch. Note the absence of windows.

6. San Juan Bautista, California; 1841. Castro House. A very large example of the Monterey style. Note the adobe bricks exposed beneath the falling stucco. The house has been restored since the photograph was taken.

7. Monterey, California; ca. 1824 (expanded 1846). Amesti House. Early Monterey style that survives with little alteration. The house has had additional restoration since the photograph was taken.

3

5

7

FLAT ROOF WITH PARAPET

1. Ranchos de Taos, New Mexico; early 19th century. Courtyard view; note the recessed porch with simple, bracketed roof supports. The Anglo door and windows are probably later additions.

2. Tucson, Arizona; ca. 1875. Verdugo House. In this example the original flat roof, revealed by the rainspouts, has been covered by a later pitched roof. The doors and windows are probably also later additions.

3. San Ygnacio, Texas; ca. 1851 (later additions). Treviño House. Extended example built from right to left in three progressively larger units (defined by the doors and rainspouts). Note the stone walls and adjacent "*jacal*" folk house with crude half-timbering and thatch roof.

4. San Pablo, Colorado; mid-19th century. An extended example with Anglo doors and windows.

5. Santa Fe, New Mexico; 1851. Tully House. A Territorial example with the exterior surviving as originally built.

6. Santa Fe, New Mexico; early 19th century (later additions). Borrego House (restoration). A Territorial example modified from an earlier house by the addition of front porch, brick coping along the parapet, and Anglo window crowns.

1

4

6

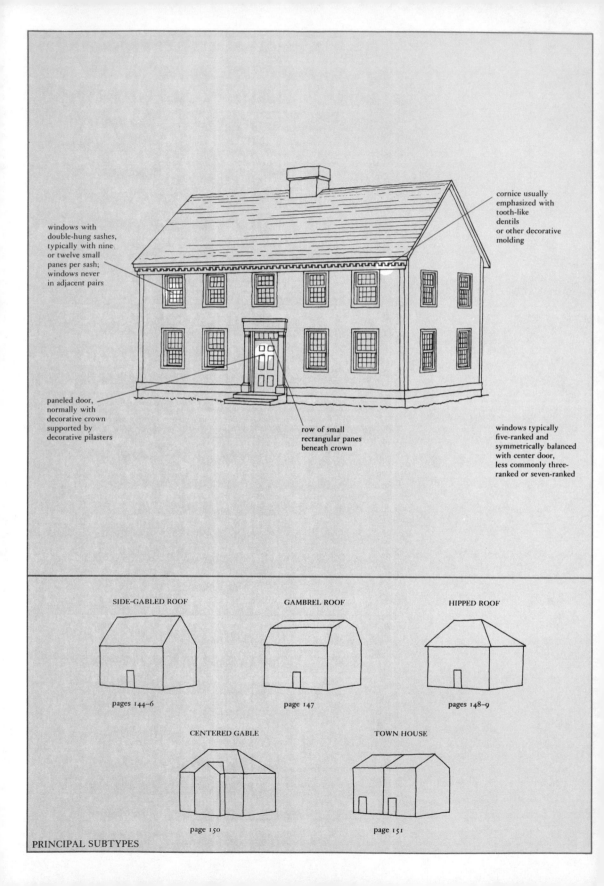

windows with double-hung sashes, typically with nine or twelve small panes per sash; windows never in adjacent pairs

cornice usually emphasized with tooth-like dentils or other decorative molding

paneled door, normally with decorative crown supported by decorative pilasters

row of small rectangular panes beneath crown

windows typically five-ranked and symmetrically balanced with center door, less commonly three-ranked or seven-ranked

SIDE-GABLED ROOF

pages 144–6

GAMBREL ROOF

page 147

HIPPED ROOF

pages 148–9

CENTERED GABLE

page 150

TOWN HOUSE

page 151

PRINCIPAL SUBTYPES

Georgian

1700–1780; locally to ca. 1830

IDENTIFYING FEATURES

Paneled front door, usually centered and capped by an elaborate decorative crown (entablature) supported by decorative pilasters (flattened columns); usually with a row of small rectangular panes of glass beneath the crown, either within the door or in a transom just above; cornice usually emphasized by decorative moldings, most commonly with tooth-like dentils; windows with double-hung sashes having many small panes (most commonly nine or twelve panes per sash) separated by thick wooden muntins; windows aligned horizontally and vertically in symmetrical rows, never in adjacent pairs, usually five-ranked on front facade, less commonly three- or seven-ranked.

PRINCIPAL SUBTYPES

The Georgian house is usually a simple one- or two-story box, two rooms deep, with doors and windows in strict symmetry. Five principal subtypes can be distinguished:

SIDE-GABLED ROOF—About 40 percent of surviving Georgian houses are of this type, which is the most common in the northern and middle colonies, but also occurs in the southern colonies.

GAMBREL ROOF—This roof form is found primarily in the northern colonies where it is characteristic of about 25 percent of surviving Georgian houses. Few gambrels survive in the middle or southern colonies, although restoration research in Williamsburg indicates they may have formerly been common on one-story southern examples. The shape is an adaptation of the gable form which provides more attic space for storage or sleeping.

HIPPED ROOF—About 25 percent of surviving Georgian houses have hipped roofs (some are dual-pitched hipped). This is the most common type in the southern colonies, but is not unusual in the middle and northern colonies, where it occurs principally on high-style landmark examples.

CENTERED GABLE—Less than 10 percent of surviving Georgian houses have a gable (pediment) centered on the front facade. The facade beneath the gable may either remain in the same plane as the rest of the wall or be extended slightly forward for emphasis as a pavilion. This subtype became common only after 1750, and is found in high-style examples in all the former colonies.

TOWN HOUSE—The earliest surviving urban houses with narrow front facades and linear plans date from the Georgian period. These were originally built in all the pre-Revolutionary urban centers of the Atlantic Coast (see map), but only a few examples remain today, principally in Philadelphia and Boston, and in Alexandria, Virginia.

VARIANTS AND DETAILS

The structure and detailing of Georgian houses show distinct regional variations:

NORTHERN COLONIES—Wood-frame construction with shingle or clapboard walls and central chimneys dominated, as in the preceding Postmedieval English houses of the region.

MIDDLE COLONIES—Brick or stone construction dominated here. Some examples have details not found elsewhere, notably the pent roof separating the first and second floors, and the hooded front door, in which elements of the decorative crown project forward to form a small roof over the entryway.

SOUTHERN COLONIES—Brick was the dominant building material in surviving southern examples. End chimneys continued to be common, as in Postmedieval English houses. Shapes were more varied in the South than elsewhere; dependencies were sometimes in separate connecting wings or detached from the main house in separate buildings. Some southern examples are raised off the ground on high foundations. On southern brick examples doors were sometimes accentuated only by changes in the surrounding brick pattern, rather than by an enframement of wooden pilasters and crown.

POST-1750, ALL COLONIES—After 1750, a few well-documented examples have the entire door enframement extended forward to form an entrance porch. Most such porches are, however, post-Georgian innovations. Dormers and decorative quoins became common after 1750 in all colonies. In later brick examples the separation between floors is usually marked by a change in the masonry pattern (belt course). Still more elaborate detailing appears in some high-style examples after 1750. Among these are two-story pilasters, centered gables, and roof balustrades. A cupola projecting above the roof, while common on Georgian public buildings, is found on only a handful of surviving houses. Door and window detailing is discussed in the following chapter, on the closely related Adam style.

OCCURRENCE

Georgian was the dominant style of the English colonies from 1700 to about 1780, when the population had grown to almost three million and covered the area shown on the map. In this area many thousands of Georgian houses survive today. Most have been lost from those colonial cities, such as Boston, New York, and Philadelphia, that grew rapidly in the 19th and 20th centuries. In sharp contrast are other colonial seaports (all the larger 18th-century towns had direct water communication with England; only villages occurred inland) that declined sharply in importance with the expansion of railroads in the 19th century. Examples are Portsmouth, New Hampshire; Newport, Rhode Island; New Castle, Delaware; Annapolis, Maryland; New Bern, North Carolina; and Charleston, South Carolina. Having had relatively little population growth since colonial times, these towns today preserve much of their Georgian heritage. In addition to the Georgian houses preserved in such coastal towns, many village and rural residences survive, particularly in New England. Landmark plantation houses are the principal southern survivors. With the end of the Revolution and independence (1781–83), the country began to develop new building styles (Adam and Early Classical Revival) based on changing European fashions. Although scattered Georgian houses were built for many decades after independence, even these usually showed some details of the newer styles.

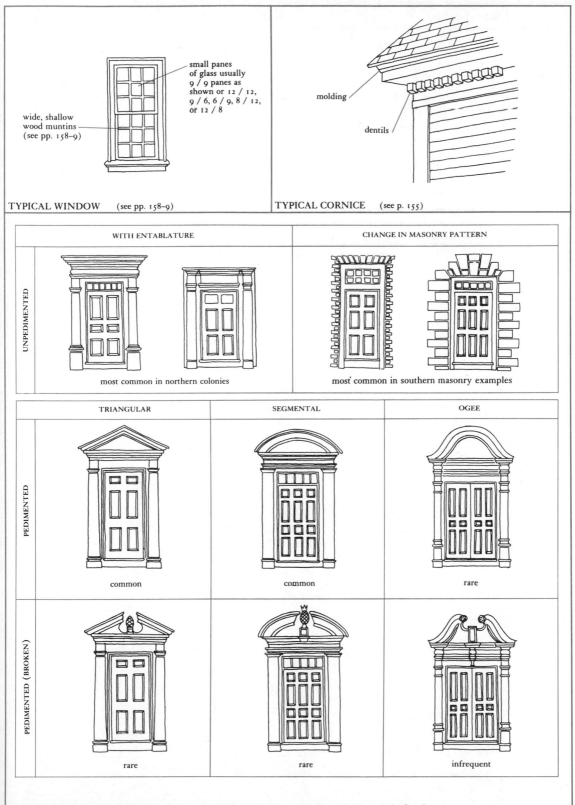

TYPICAL WINDOW (see pp. 158–9)

small panes
of glass usually
9 / 9 panes as
shown or 12 / 12,
9 / 6, 6 / 9, 8 / 12,
or 12 / 8

wide, shallow
wood muntins
(see pp. 158–9)

TYPICAL CORNICE (see p. 155)

molding

dentils

WITH ENTABLATURE

CHANGE IN MASONRY PATTERN

UNPEDIMENTED

most common in northern colonies

most common in southern masonry examples

PEDIMENTED

TRIANGULAR

SEGMENTAL

OGEE

common

common

rare

PEDIMENTED (BROKEN)

rare

rare

infrequent

DOOR SURROUND VARIANTS Similar entablatures, pediments, and broken pediments may be found atop
Georgian windows (see pp. 158–9) and on Colonial Revival houses, both as door surrounds and window crowns

COMMENTS

Georgian is among the most long-lived styles of American building, having dominated the English colonies for most of the 18th century. The style grew from the Italian Renaissance, which emphasized classical details and reached remote England only in the mid-16th century. There, Renaissance classicism first flourished during the period 1650–1750 under such master architects as Inigo Jones, Christopher Wren, and James Gibbs. The style did not, however, begin to replace Postmedieval traditions in the American colonies until about 1700, when an expanding and increasingly prosperous population began to seek more fashionable buildings. It was brought to the New World principally through architectural building manuals known as pattern books. These ranged from expensive treatises stressing Italian models—the same books from which Jones, Wren, and Gibbs received much of their inspiration—to inexpensive carpenters' handbooks showing how to construct fashionable doorways, cornices, windows, and mantels.

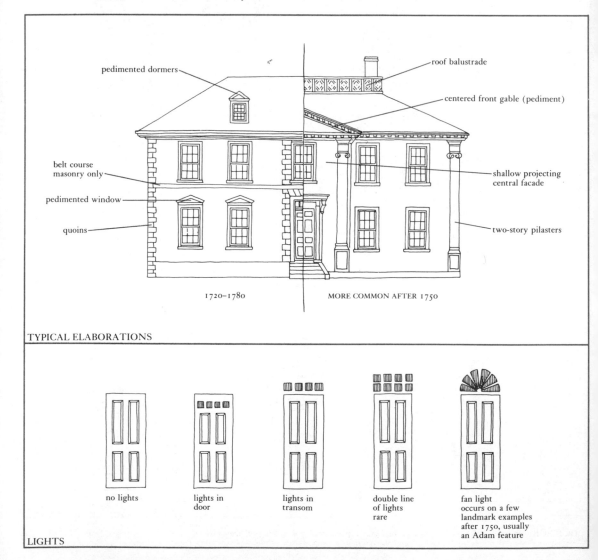

pedimented dormers

roof balustrade

centered front gable (pediment)

belt course masonry only

pedimented window

quoins

shallow projecting central facade

two-story pilasters

1720–1780

MORE COMMON AFTER 1750

TYPICAL ELABORATIONS

no lights

lights in door

lights in transom

double line of lights rare

fan light occurs on a few landmark examples after 1750, usually an Adam feature

LIGHTS

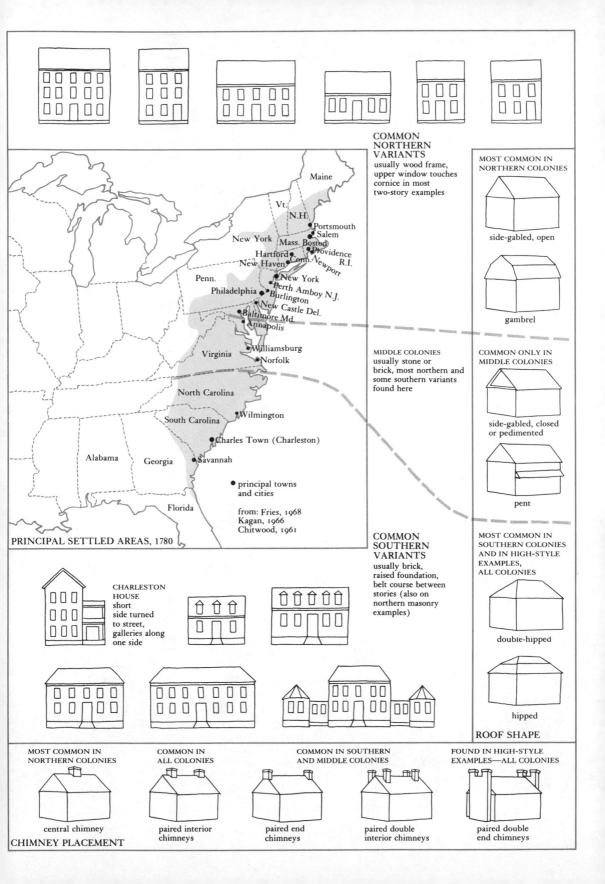

COMMON NORTHERN VARIANTS usually wood frame, upper window touches cornice in most two-story examples

MOST COMMON IN NORTHERN COLONIES

side-gabled, open

gambrel

Maine

Vt.

N.H.

Portsmouth
Salem
New York Mass. Boston
Hartford Providence
Conn. Newport R.I.
New Haven
New York
Perth Amboy N.J.
Philadelphia Burlington
New Castle Del.
Baltimore Md
Annapolis

Penn.

Virginia Williamsburg
Norfolk

North Carolina

South Carolina Wilmington

Charles Town (Charleston)

Alabama Georgia Savannah

• principal towns and cities

Florida

from: Fries, 1968
Kagan, 1966
Chitwood, 1961

PRINCIPAL SETTLED AREAS, 1780

MIDDLE COLONIES usually stone or brick, most northern and some southern variants found here

COMMON ONLY IN MIDDLE COLONIES

side-gabled, closed or pedimented

pent

COMMON SOUTHERN VARIANTS usually brick, raised foundation, belt course between stories (also on northern masonry examples)

MOST COMMON IN SOUTHERN COLONIES AND IN HIGH-STYLE EXAMPLES, ALL COLONIES

double-hipped

hipped

CHARLESTON HOUSE short side turned to street, galleries along one side

ROOF SHAPE

CHIMNEY PLACEMENT

MOST COMMON IN NORTHERN COLONIES — central chimney

COMMON IN ALL COLONIES — paired interior chimneys

COMMON IN SOUTHERN AND MIDDLE COLONIES — paired end chimneys

paired double interior chimneys

FOUND IN HIGH-STYLE EXAMPLES—ALL COLONIES — paired double end chimneys

SIDE-GABLED ROOF

1. Deerfield, Massachusetts; 1749. Barnard House. Note the wide-board cladding and double door. The window screens are a later addition.

2. Providence, Rhode Island; ca. 1743. Hopkins House. Part of this house was built in 1707, with an expansion in ca. 1743; the door was added still later. Four-ranked examples such as this are sometimes called three-quarters houses.

3. Southport, Connecticut; late 18th century. Osborn House. A simple five-ranked, saltbox form with a central chimney.

4. Deerfield, Massachusetts; 1760. Williams House. Note the broken pediment over the door and the triangular pediments above the windows. The 6/6 window sashes are probably later additions.

5. Medford, Massachusetts; 1737. Royall House. Enlarged from a 17th-century brick house; an equally elaborate rear facade was added in 1747. Note the chimney stacks connected by a parapet and the unadorned side, the detailing being concentrated on the front facade.

6. Louisville, Kentucky; ca. 1790. Locust Grove. A post-Revolutionary example built in an outlying region.

7. Surry County, Virginia; 1652, rebuilt early 18th century. Warren House. This simple one-story example is a Georgian remodeling of a Post-medieval house. As is commonly the case in southern masonry examples, there is not an elaborated door surround but only a segmental arch in the brickwork above the paneled door.

8. Annapolis, Maryland; 1773. Brice House. A fine example of the five-part plan with "hyphens" connecting the main house and dependencies.

1

4

6

7

145

SIDE-GABLED ROOF (cont.)

9. Philadelphia, Pennsylvania; 1772. Deshler House. Note the arched dormer windows.

10. Philadelphia, Pennsylvania; 1768. Johnson House. Note the rubble-stone side walls and the more regular ashlar facade. The pent roof above the first floor is a common middle-colonies feature.

11. Philadelphia, Pennsylvania; ca. 1715. The hood over the front door and the cornice carried beneath the side gable are features found primarily in the middle colonies.

9   10

11

GAMBREL ROOF

1. Salem, Massachusetts; mid-18th century. Nathaniel Hawthorne Birthplace. This example was built around a smaller 17th-century house, a common practice. The 2/2 windows are later additions.

2. Newport, Rhode Island; ca. 1748. Nichols House (restoration).

3. Newport, Rhode Island; 1760. Robinson House. Originally a smaller two-story house built in 1725, this example was enlarged and a gambrel roof added in 1760; there have been few exterior changes since.

4. Woodbury, Connecticut; 1760. Bacon House. Note the slight overhang of the second story, a holdover from Postmedieval building practices.

5. Deerfield, Massachusetts; ca. 1725. Dwight House. Moved from Springfield, Massachusetts, this house has a fine door pediment and pedimented windows.

HIPPED ROOF

1. Rutland, Massachusetts; ca. 1750. Putnam House.

2. Newport, Rhode Island; 1759. Vernon House, attributed to Peter Harrison, architect. This example was rebuilt and enlarged in 1759 from an earlier house. Note the rusticated wall cladding (wood cut to look like stonework) and the balustrade around the flat roof deck. The 6/6 windows are probably later additions.

3. Richmond, Virginia, vicinity; ca. 1753. Wilton. This finely detailed example was moved in 1933.

4. Philadelphia, Pennsylvania; 1734. Logan House. Note the segmental arches in the brickwork over the door and windows, used in lieu of more elaborate wood crowns.

5. Clarksville, Virginia, vicinity; ca. 1765. Prestwould. Built of coursed stone ashlar with a seven-ranked facade. Both the front and side porches are later additions.

6. Charles City, Virginia, vicinity; 1734. Westover. An early high-style example with steeply pitched roof, double-paired interior end chimneys, belt course, and broken pediment door surround. This photo was taken before the modern addition of adjacent wings.

7. Lancaster County, Virginia; ca. 1754. Belle Isle. A three-ranked central block with lower wings forming a three-part plan. Two detached dependencies are not visible in the photo.

1

5

6

2

3, 4

7

CENTERED GABLE

1. Cambridge, Massachusetts; 1759. Longfellow House. The side porches were added in 1793, as likely were the 6/6 windows with slender muntins. Note that the centered gable crowns a shallow projection set 9 inches forward from the front facade of the house. Two-story pilasters are added for decorative effect.

2. Philadelphia, Pennsylvania; 1763–67. Cliveden. The front facade is of coursed ashlar; the stone urns on the roof are original.

3. Charleston vicinity, South Carolina; 1738–42. Drayton Hall. An unusually sophisticated early Georgian design that survives without alteration. The two-story recessed portico was inspired by the designs of Palladio; most American Georgian houses simply simulate such porticos with centered gables, as in the other photos on this page. See the Early Classical Revival style for similar but much later buildings inspired by Palladio.

4. Annapolis, Maryland; ca. 1774. Hammond House; William Buckland, architect. A high-style example in the Palladian five-part plan. The fanlight over the entrance was a feature found only occasionally in very late high-style Georgian houses; it became almost universal in the subsequent Adam style.

TOWN HOUSE

1. Philadelphia, Pennsylvania; mid-18th century. Note the pent roof, a typical middle-colonies feature.

2. Philadelphia, Pennsylvania; 1765. Powell House. A high-style late Georgian town house. Note the stone belt courses, keystone lintels, and door surround with fanlight.

3. Philadelphia, Pennsylvania; mid-18th to early 19th centuries. Elfreth's Alley. These twenty-nine adjoining brick houses have been continuously occupied and have had relatively little exterior alteration. They make up one of our few urban streetscapes surviving from the 18th century.

1

2

3

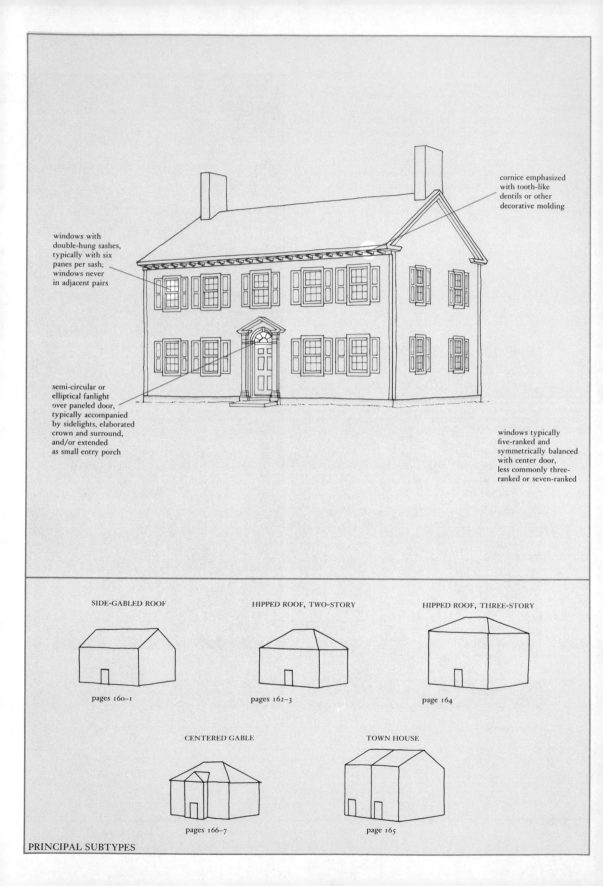

cornice emphasized
with tooth-like
dentils or other
decorative molding

windows with
double-hung sashes,
typically with six
panes per sash;
windows never
in adjacent pairs

semi-circular or
elliptical fanlight
over paneled door,
typically accompanied
by sidelights, elaborated
crown and surround,
and/or extended
as small entry porch

windows typically
five-ranked and
symmetrically balanced
with center door,
less commonly three-
ranked or seven-ranked

SIDE-GABLED ROOF

pages 160–1

HIPPED ROOF, TWO-STORY

pages 162–3

HIPPED ROOF, THREE-STORY

page 164

CENTERED GABLE

pages 166–7

TOWN HOUSE

page 165

PRINCIPAL SUBTYPES

Adam

IDENTIFYING FEATURES

Semi-circular or elliptical fanlight[1] over front door (with or without sidelights); fanlight often incorporated into more elaborate door surround, which may include a decorative crown or small entry porch; cornice usually emphasized by decorative moldings, most commonly with tooth-like dentils; windows with double-hung sashes usually having six panes per sash and separated by thin wooden supports (muntins); windows aligned horizontally and vertically in symmetrical rows, usually five-ranked on front facade, less commonly three-ranked or seven-ranked; windows never in adjacent pairs, although three-part Palladian-style windows are common.

PRINCIPAL SUBTYPES

The Adam house, like the preceding Georgian, is most commonly a simple box, two or more rooms deep, with doors and windows arranged in strict symmetry. More frequently than in Georgian houses, however, the box may be modified by projecting wings or attached dependencies; indeed, the style is perhaps best known for elaborate, but rather atypical, high-style examples having curved or polygonal projections to the side or rear. Five principal subtypes can be distinguished:

SIDE-GABLED ROOF—This is the most common Adam roof form, occurring in over 40 percent of surviving examples from all regions.

HIPPED ROOF, TWO-STORY—Hipped roofs of moderate to very low pitch (the latter may appear to be almost flat) are particularly common in New England, where they slightly outnumber side-gabled examples.

HIPPED ROOF, THREE-STORY—The three-story hipped roof Adam house is usually large and of landmark quality; it survives primarily in New England, with an unusually important concentration in the town of Salem, Massachusetts.

CENTERED GABLE—Less than 10 percent of surviving Adam houses have gables (pediments) centered on the front facade. The facade beneath the gable may either remain in the same plane as the rest of the wall or be extended slightly forward for emphasis as a pavilion.

TOWN HOUSE—Many Adam town houses survive; these include both attached row houses and narrow detached urban houses. Important concentrations remain in Boston; Philadelphia; Georgetown, District of Columbia; and Alexandria, Virginia. A few projects were built that treated individual houses as part of a larger unit, thus rendering the entire

[1] Fanlights are found in only a few high-style Georgian houses but become almost universal in the Adam house; they also occur in the closely related Early Classical Revival houses discussed in the next chapter.

facade as a total composition rather than a collection of individual elements. Regrettably, only a few parts and pieces of these ambitious schemes survive.

VARIANTS AND DETAILS

As with the Georgian and Postmedieval English styles, northern house builders continued to show a preference for frame construction with clapboard siding, and southern for brick construction. Stucco and stone occur infrequently in all regions. Smooth wooden siding was sometimes used for the front facade with weatherboards, or even bricks, used for the less conspicuous walls. Chimney placement is less predictable than in Georgian houses, probably as a result of interiors with more complex room arrangements. Nevertheless, central or interior chimneys still tend to dominate in the North, while end chimneys are most common in the South.

The exteriors of most Adam houses have few elaborations other than the fanlight and accentuated front door (which often includes an entry porch). Among the elaborations that sometimes occur are roof-line balustrades, particularly favored in the North; the use of a Palladian-style window in the second story over the main entrance; the use of flat or keystone lintels above the windows with prominent sills below. Elliptical, half-circular, or Palladian windows are sometimes used in side or front gables; dormers typically have arched windows; in brick examples, windows may be slightly recessed into arches built into the facade. A number of decorative details from the Georgian period continue to be found occasionally: quoins, two-story pilasters (which disappeared about 1800), belt courses (now sometimes in stone), and dentils. Typical Georgian dentils are usually supplanted by less blocky, more refined versions called modillions.

Houses of the Adam style are often characterized as having a lightness and delicacy in comparison with their close Georgian relatives. This generalization needs to be interpreted with care, however, for while the scale is smaller in many Adam *details* (moldings, columns, etc.), the scale of many *structural parts* (windows, ceiling heights, etc.) is enlarged.

In attached Adam town houses (row houses) such typical features as roof-line balustrades, Palladian windows, and entry porches are rare. Although the doorway remains the most important identifying feature, fanlights are a less consistent guide than in detached houses. Not only do fanlights occur in both late Georgian and early Greek Revival row houses, but they are often omitted in the simpler and earlier Adam examples. Front stair rails of iron were usual; iron balconies and curved front bays were particularly common in Boston.

The interiors of many Adam houses contain graceful decorative ornament, either carved in wood or cast in plaster, applied to mantels, walls, ceilings, and elsewhere. Less commonly, the external facade shows similar decorative detailing on door surrounds or entry porches, over windows, along the cornice, or in paneled wall insets. Typical decorative motifs include swags, garlands, urns, and classic geometric patterns (most commonly elliptical, circular, or fan-like shapes formed by fluted radiating lines).

ADAM AND GEORGIAN WINDOWS—Both Adam and Georgian houses have double-hung sash windows placed singly but in symmetrical rows. These windows have fixed upper sashes and movable lower sashes, the latter held open by metal pins (the familiar system of counterbalancing with weights had not yet been invented). Such windows first began to

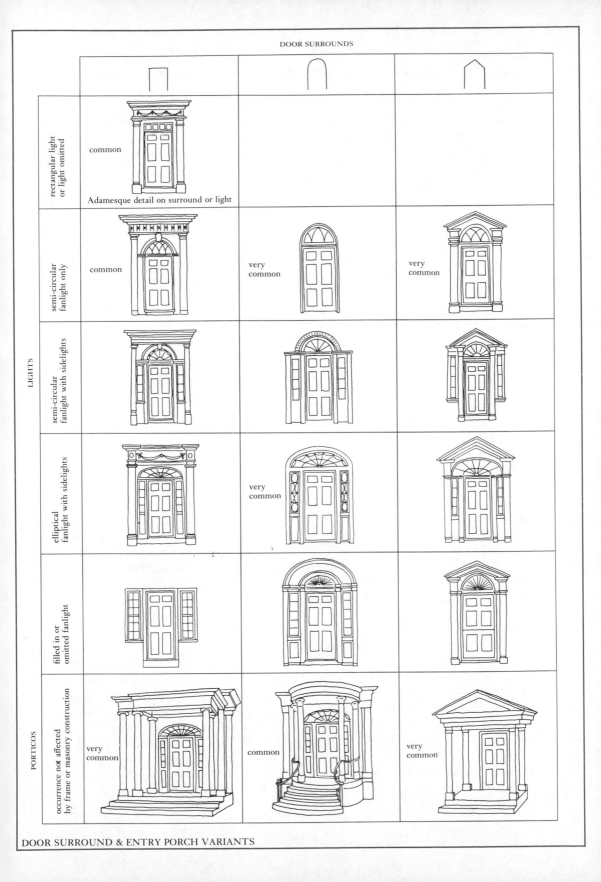

DOOR SURROUNDS

LIGHTS			
rectangular light or light omitted	common Adamesque detail on surround or light		
semi-circular fanlight only	common	very common	very common
semi-circular fanlight with sidelights			
elliptical fanlight with sidelights		very common	
filled in or omitted fanlight			
PORTICOS occurrence not affected by frame or masonry construction	very common	common	very common

DOOR SURROUND & ENTRY PORCH VARIANTS

be used in the English colonies in about 1700, and by 1720 had almost completely supplanted the earlier casement-style window (see page 107). Facilitating this transition was an increasing availability of larger panes of glass. Prior to the Revolution, the standard size of these panes was approximately 6 inches by 8 inches; afterward, the size increased to approximately 8 inches by 12 inches. Georgian houses thus generally have smaller windowpanes than do Adam houses. In Georgian houses these are most frequently arranged with 12 panes in each sash (12/12) in the Northern colonies and 9 panes (9/9) in the Southern colonies; 9/6, 6/9, 8/12 and other combinations are also found occasionally. Adam houses, with their larger panes, most commonly have 6/6 windows, although the earlier types also persist.

The wooden supporting moldings (or muntins) which hold the individual panes in place also differ in Georgian and Adam houses. In early Georgian houses these tend to be 1¼ inches wide and quite shallow; in later Georgian houses they remain shallow but are usually 1 inch wide; by Adam time they are more likely to be quite deep and narrower than 1 inch.

Both windowpanes and muntins are easily modified and thus many early houses now have 6/6, 1/1, 2/2, or other patterns of glazing. Occasionally the earlier windows will be left on rear or side walls where they reveal the original pattern. As a further complication, some houses were originally built with up-to-date windows on the front facades and with older, less fashionable (and probably less expensive) types on the rear.

Windows in Georgian and Adam wooden houses sometimes have elaborate decorative crowns placed above them. In Georgian houses these might be either a formal pediment, usually in one of the same patterns seen over front doors, or a decorative molding similar to those found on Georgian cornices. Adam windows more commonly have an elaborately decorated frieze above the window. These are sometimes topped by a cornice mold, but full-scale pediments are uncommon (pedimented or otherwise elaborated windows are most common on later, Colonial Revival houses).

Decorative window crowns are far less usual on masonry houses. Such Georgian houses often have changed brick patterns, or simple arches, above the windows. Adam masonry houses commonly have a flat lintel, keystone lintel, or keystone without a lintel set over the windows. These are usually of stone; stone sills are also sometimes used beneath the windows of Adam houses. Both Georgian and early Adam windows set in masonry are generally surrounded by a wooden frame (or architrave); these are usually omitted from Adam houses built after about 1800.

OCCURRENCE

Adam was the dominant style of the new United States from about 1780 to 1820, a period in which the population grew from 3 million to about 10 million and expanded to cover the area shown on the map. The style reached its zenith in the prosperous port cities of the eastern seaboard, particularly Boston, Salem, Newburyport, and Marblehead in Massachusetts; Newport, Providence, Warren, and Bristol in Rhode Island; Portland and Wiscasset in Maine; New Castle, Delaware; Portsmouth, New Hampshire; Philadelphia, Pennsylvania; New York, New York; Charleston, South Carolina; and Savannah, Georgia. Alexandria, Virginia, and Georgetown, District of Columbia, both near the newly developing national capital, also prospered during this period. High-style Adam houses are mostly concentrated in these areas, although scattered examples occur elsewhere.

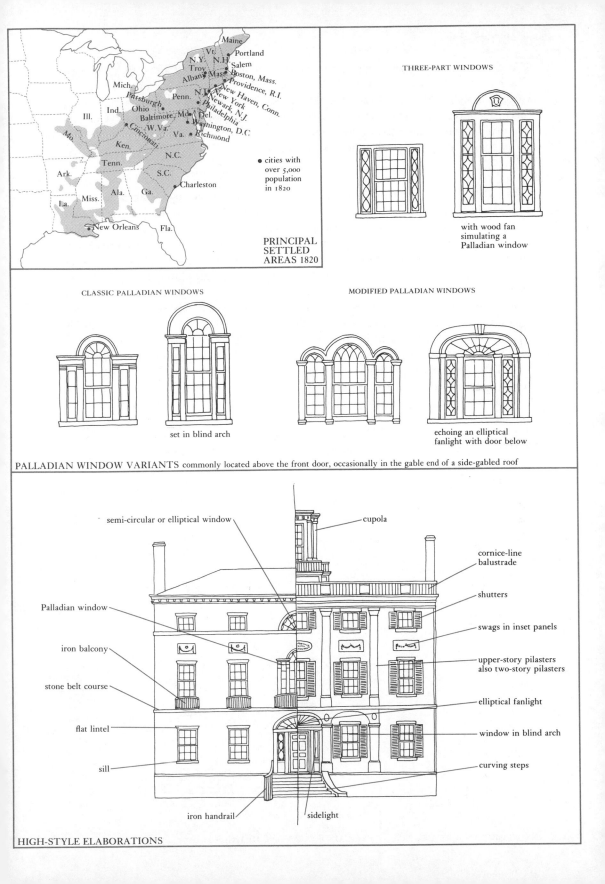

PRINCIPAL SETTLED AREAS 1820

- cities with over 5,000 population in 1820

THREE-PART WINDOWS

with wood fan simulating a Palladian window

CLASSIC PALLADIAN WINDOWS

set in blind arch

MODIFIED PALLADIAN WINDOWS

echoing an elliptical fanlight with door below

PALLADIAN WINDOW VARIANTS commonly located above the front door, occasionally in the gable end of a side-gabled roof

semi-circular or elliptical window

cupola

cornice-line balustrade

shutters

swags in inset panels

upper-story pilasters also two-story pilasters

elliptical fanlight

window in blind arch

curving steps

Palladian window

iron balcony

stone belt course

flat lintel

sill

iron handrail

sidelight

HIGH-STYLE ELABORATIONS

Thousands of vernacular examples survive throughout the settled areas; they are least common at the westward edges of expansion, where vernacular Georgian houses persisted throughout the period (occasional Georgian hangovers, some of landmark quality, occur in all regions). By the 1820s a more strictly classical style, the Greek Revival, was supplanting the Adam style. Still earlier, by about 1800, the related Early Classical Revival style was replacing Adam houses in the South.

COMMENTS

The Adam style was a development and refinement of the preceding Georgian style. Established first by wealthy merchants along the New England seaboard, it drew on contemporary European trends, particularly the work of the Adam brothers who, at that time, had the largest architectural practice in Britain. The eldest, Robert, had traveled to Italy and the Mediterranean to study classical buildings for himself. These studies, as well as those of others who reported on first-hand viewing, introduced a new interest in the early Greek and Roman monuments themselves, rather than as interpreted through the buildings of the Italian Renaissance.[1] Adam popularized a number of design elements (swags, garlands, urns, and various stylized geometric designs) that he had seen in his travels. He also incorporated into his interiors a diversity of spatial planning found in some classical ruins. Because of the breadth of his influence, what had formerly been called the Federal style is now becoming known simply as the American phase of the English Adam style.

It was during this era that the first true architects appeared on the American scene. Among the most notable of these, with their principal areas of work, were: Charles Bulfinch (Boston); William Jay (Savannah, Georgia); Benjamin H. Latrobe (his early work in Philadelphia and Virginia); Gabriel Manigault (Charleston, South Carolina); John McComb (New York); Samuel McIntire (Salem, Massachusetts); and Alexander Parris (Maine).

[1] The full flowering of this new concern for archeological classicism came in the contemporaneous Early Classical Revival and subsequent Greek Revival houses.

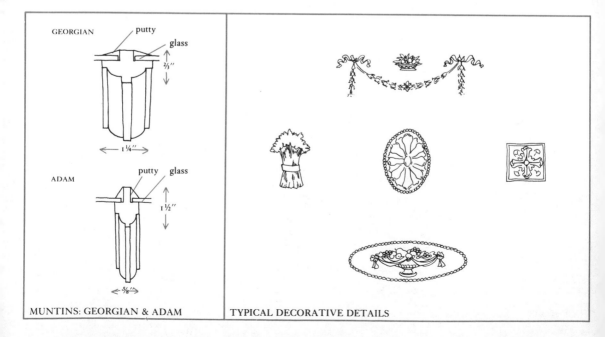

MUNTINS: GEORGIAN & ADAM

TYPICAL DECORATIVE DETAILS

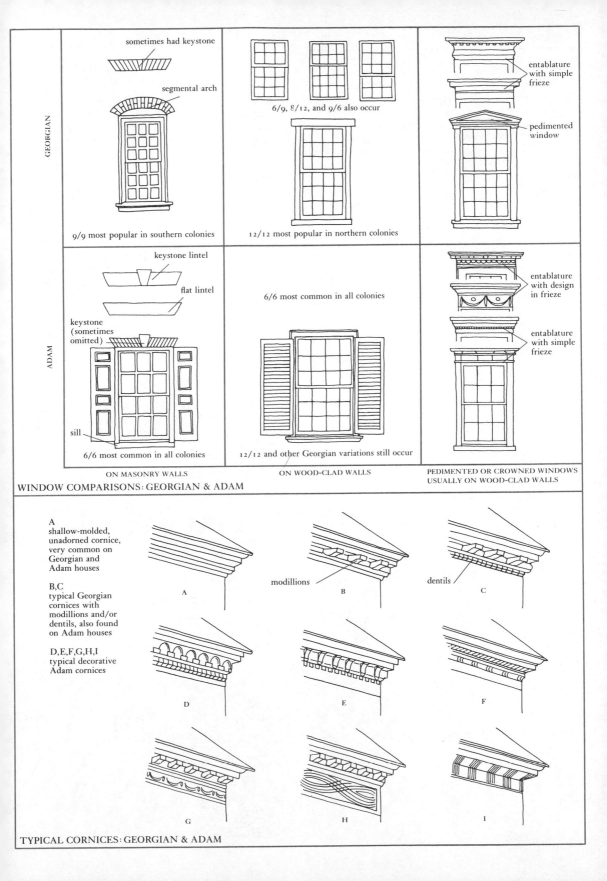

GEORGIAN

sometimes had keystone

segmental arch

9/9 most popular in southern colonies

6/9, 8/12, and 9/6 also occur

12/12 most popular in northern colonies

entablature with simple frieze

pedimented window

ADAM

keystone lintel

flat lintel

keystone (sometimes omitted)

sill

6/6 most common in all colonies

6/6 most common in all colonies

12/12 and other Georgian variations still occur

entablature with design in frieze

entablature with simple frieze

ON MASONRY WALLS

ON WOOD-CLAD WALLS

PEDIMENTED OR CROWNED WINDOWS USUALLY ON WOOD-CLAD WALLS

WINDOW COMPARISONS: GEORGIAN & ADAM

A shallow-molded, unadorned cornice, very common on Georgian and Adam houses

B,C typical Georgian cornices with modillions and/or dentils, also found on Adam houses

D,E,F,G,H,I typical decorative Adam cornices

A

modillions

B

dentils

C

D

E

F

G

H

I

TYPICAL CORNICES: GEORGIAN & ADAM

SIDE-GABLED ROOF

1. Providence, Rhode Island; ca. 1830. Seamans House.

2. Savannah, Georgia; 1808. Williams House. Note the exterior chimney, a common feature in the South.

3. Powhatan County, Virginia; early 19th century. Keswick. The simple three-ranked facade masks an elaborate H-shaped plan behind.

4. Somerset, Massachusetts; ca. 1800. Pettis House. This five-ranked wooden example has been elaborated with corner quoins. The slight overhang of the gable end is a holdover from Postmedieval building practice.

5. Longmeadow, Massachusetts; 1796. Colton House; attributed to Asher Benjamin, architect. Note the elaborate roof-line balustrade and Palladian window.

6. Alexandria, Virginia; ca. 1798. Lloyd House. An elaborate brick example with paired end chimneys, keystone lintels, and arched dormer windows.

7. New Castle, Delaware; 1801. Read House. A high-style example with roof balustrade, cornice-line modillions and dentils, keystone lintels, and elaborate Palladian window and door surround.

HIPPED ROOF, TWO-STORY

1. Auburn, Massachusetts; late 18th century. Chapin House. A simple wood-frame example. The 2/2 windows are later additions.

2. Columbia Falls, Maine; ca. 1818. Ruggles House; Aaron Sherman, architect. Note the flush, horizontal boards on the front facade and the swagged window heads.

3. Mappsville, Virginia, vicinity; ca. 1800. Wharton Place. The interior chimneys are separated by a flat roof deck with balustrade.

4. Providence, Rhode Island; ca. 1815. Burroughs House. Note the quoins. There are two balustrades on the roof.

5. Providence, Rhode Island; ca. 1801. Halsey House. The curved bays were added ca. 1825.

6. Damariscotta Mills, Maine; 1803. Kavanaugh House; Nicholas Codd, architect. This example has flush wood sheathing, a semi-circular entry porch, and a large octagonal cupola.

7. Greenfield, Massachusetts; 1796. Coleman House; Asher Benjamin, architect. Note the elaborate pilasters, Palladian window, and inset panels with swags.

8. Washington, District of Columbia; 1815. Tudor Place; William Thornton, architect. The garden front (shown) has an unusual circular portico and full-length three-part windows in blind arches. Note the five-part compound plan.

← 4

5

8

HIPPED ROOF, THREE-STORY

1. Portsmouth, New Hampshire; early 19th century. Barnes House. A wood-frame example with a minimum of exterior elaboration.

2. Washington, District of Columbia; 1819. Decatur House; Benjamin Latrobe, architect. A three-ranked brick example with flat lintels over the windows. The window height varies in the three stories.

3. Boston, Massachusetts; 1797. Otis House; attributed to Charles Bulfinch, architect. A high-style brick example with belt courses and keystone lintels. The Palladian and semi-circular windows align above the elaborate doorway.

4. Salem, Massachusetts; early 19th century. Phillips House. Note the quoins, Palladian window, and elaborated window crowns.

5. Providence, Rhode Island; 1806. Ives House; Caleb Ormsbee, architect. This example has roof-line and entry porch balustrades; there are matching fanlights on the first and second stories.

1

2

3

4

5

TOWN HOUSE

1. Easton, Maryland; late 18th century. Attached urban houses.

2. Savannah, Georgia; ca. 1820. Clark Houses. The paired doors on the left entrance are a later addition (note the glass panels).

3. Frederick, Maryland; 1799. Taney House. Note the side walls without windows to increase privacy in an urban setting. The 6/6 windows with lintels above and the curved patterning in the rectangular light over the door mark this example as an Adam house.

4. Libertytown, Maryland; ca. 1800. Jones House. Note the parapeted gables with double interior end chimneys.

5. Charleston, South Carolina; ca. 1809. Russell House. An unusual high-style example of compact town house form. Note the polygonal projection visible to the left of the house, the roof-line balustrade of alternating panels and balusters, and the full-width iron balcony and blind arches at second-floor level.

CENTERED GABLE

1. Baltimore, Maryland; ca. 1782. D'Annemours House. A three-ranked masonry example of a simple I-house plan (one room deep) with a rear wing.

2. Canterbury, Connecticut; ca. 1805. Payne House. This wood-frame example has notable pilasters set on pedestals at the corners and beside the slightly projecting center gable.

3. Frankfort, Kentucky; 1800. Liberty Hall. The centered gable covers three ranks of windows; gables of this width are frequent in high-style Adam houses but unusual in the preceding Georgian style.

4. Savannah, Georgia; 1819. Richardson House; William Jay, architect. Note the undulating entry porch roof and curved entry steps. The front door is also recessed into a curved niche.

5. Charleston, South Carolina; ca. 1822. Bennett House. Built in the typical Charleston-house form with the narrow end turned to the street. The principal facade, with a full-length porch, faces a side garden. Entry from the street is through a doorway leading to the porch.

6. Cazenovia, New York; 1807. Lorenzo House. The facade is elaborated by pilasters supporting decorative arches.

7. Clarkson, New York; ca. 1825. Palmer House. Full front-gabled Adam houses like this are uncommon; they are transitional to the Greek Revival style, which popularized the front-gabled form. Most Adam examples occur in western New York and in Ohio.

8. Mount Vernon, Virginia, vicinity; 1805. Woodlawn; William Thornton, architect. In this five-part compound plan, a large central house block is connected to two side dependencies by hyphens. This house has no projection or elaboration below the centered gable.

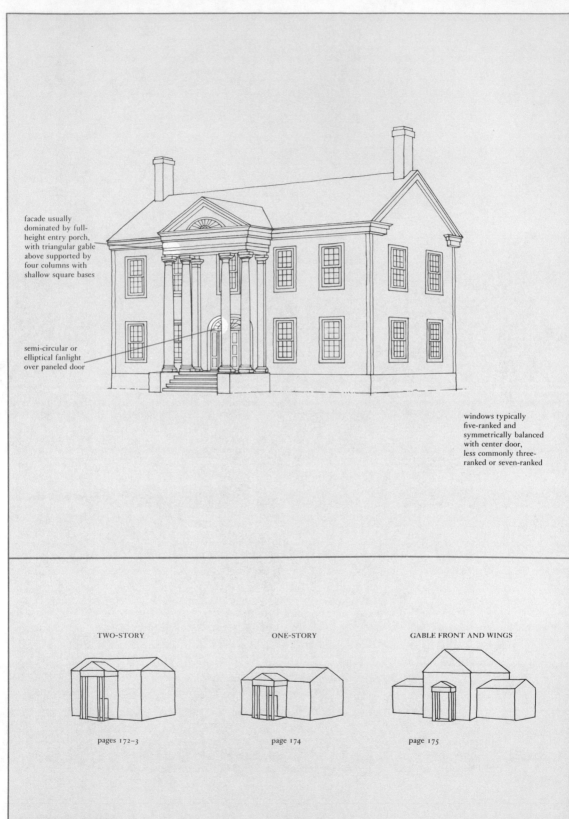

facade usually
dominated by full-
height entry porch,
with triangular gable
above supported by
four columns with
shallow square bases

semi-circular or
elliptical fanlight
over paneled door

windows typically
five-ranked and
symmetrically balanced
with center door,
less commonly three-
ranked or seven-ranked

TWO-STORY

ONE-STORY

GABLE FRONT AND WINGS

pages 172–3

page 174

page 175

PRINCIPAL SUBTYPES

Early Classical Revival

IDENTIFYING FEATURES

Entry porch (portico) dominating the front facade and normally equaling it in height; porch roof usually supported by four simple columns (Roman Doric or Tuscan types) each with a shallow square base (plinth); the columns support a prominent centered gable; a semi-circular or elliptical fanlight normally occurs above the paneled front door; windows aligned horizontally and vertically in symmetrical rows, usually five-ranked on front facade, less commonly three-ranked or seven-ranked.

PRINCIPAL SUBTYPES

Early Classical Revival houses are of three principal types:

TWO-STORY—Similar to one-story type, but with more imposing, two-story facades and entry porches.

ONE-STORY—These are simple, rectilinear houses with side-gabled or low-pitched hipped roofs having the characteristic full-height entry porch. They are commonly built several feet off the ground on tall foundations, which exaggerates the height of the front facade.

GABLE FRONT AND WINGS—Most Early Classical Revival houses are of the first two types with side-gabled or hipped roofs. In this less common variant, a two-story, front-gabled central block dominates the facade; this two-story unit is flanked by one-story wings on either side, making a three-part composition. This plan was introduced by Palladio in his 16th-century Italian pattern book and is called the Palladian three-part plan. In this subtype the dominant central block may have either a full-height, two-story entry porch or a smaller one-story entry porch.

VARIANTS AND DETAILS

Early Classical Revival houses closely resemble those of the succeeding Greek Revival period; the doorway, cornice line, and type of column are the three principal distinguishing features. In Early Classical Revival houses, the columns were generally of the Roman type (see page 181), although later transitional examples may have columns with Greek details. The Early Classical Revival house also usually lacks the wide band of trim at the cornice line seen on most Greek Revival houses; frequently a narrow line of dentils or modillions adorns the cornice. Like their Adam-style contemporaries, most Early Classical Revival examples have a prominent fanlight over the front door, a feature that became very rare during the subsequent Greek Revival. In addition, Early Classical Revival houses are likely to have Adam interior detailing.

The characteristic Early Classical entry porch shows considerable variation in detail. The porches may differ in: (1) The number of columns: four is most common, two is frequent, and five, six, eight, and ten occur less often. (2) The spacing of columns: even spacing is most common, but a frequent variation has a wider space between the two central columns framing the front entrance. (3) The treatment of columns and second-story porches on two-story examples: four variations occur in about equal overall abundance. The porches are most commonly placed only on the front facade as entry porches but may also appear both on the front and back, or on any combination of front, back, and side. Occasionally the entry porch is recessed inward (called a portico *in antis*). In all variants the centered gable (pediment) may be embellished with a semi-circular window (lunette); occasionally a round or oval window replaces the lunette or is found elsewhere on the facade. The entablature, or horizontal band above the columns and below the centered gable, is most often plain. If elaborated, it is with triglyphs, three closely spaced vertical lines repeated at intervals.

Wall materials may be either wood, brick, stucco, or stone, in order of decreasing frequency. Wall projections, which are only occasionally present, are never curved as in some contemporaneous Adam houses. Roof balustrades are rare, as are original dormers; when present, these are usually later additions. In most other details, Early Classical Revival houses resemble those of the contemporaneous Adam style (see Adam doors and windows, page 158). Many Georgian and early Adam houses, as well as simple folk houses, were updated during the early 19th century by the addition of a full-height Early Classical Revival entry porch. These modified examples may be difficult to distinguish from homes originally built in this configuration.

OCCURRENCE

This is a relatively uncommon style found in isolated examples throughout the areas settled by 1820 (see map, page 157). It is rare north of Pennsylvania; most examples occur in the southern states, particularly Virginia, where it had its most vocal champion in Thomas Jefferson. A handful of houses in the style were built in Virginia just before the Revolution, but most examples were constructed between 1790 and 1830. By 1830 the subsequent and more universally popular phase of classical revivalism, the Greek Revival, had replaced Early Classical models even in Virginia.

COMMENTS

Following the Revolution there was an immediate need for public buildings to house the newly organized government at both the state and national levels. It was natural to have taken Rome as a model, with its Republican ideas and monumental architecture, a choice that symbolized the mood and politics of the new country. Roman Revival architecture thus became fashionable. This was further emphasized by a concurrent neoclassical movement in France, the new country's principal ally in its fight for independence. The United States was not a mere follower in this movement, but led the way by erecting the first large public building in the new style, the Bank of Pennsylvania, completed in 1800 at Philadelphia. Among the prominent architects working in the style were William Jay (Savannah, Georgia); Benjamin H. Latrobe (Philadelphia, Baltimore, and Washington); Robert Mills (Charleston, South Carolina, and elsewhere); and William Thornton (Washington). Most influential of all, however, was Thomas Jefferson, who not only de-

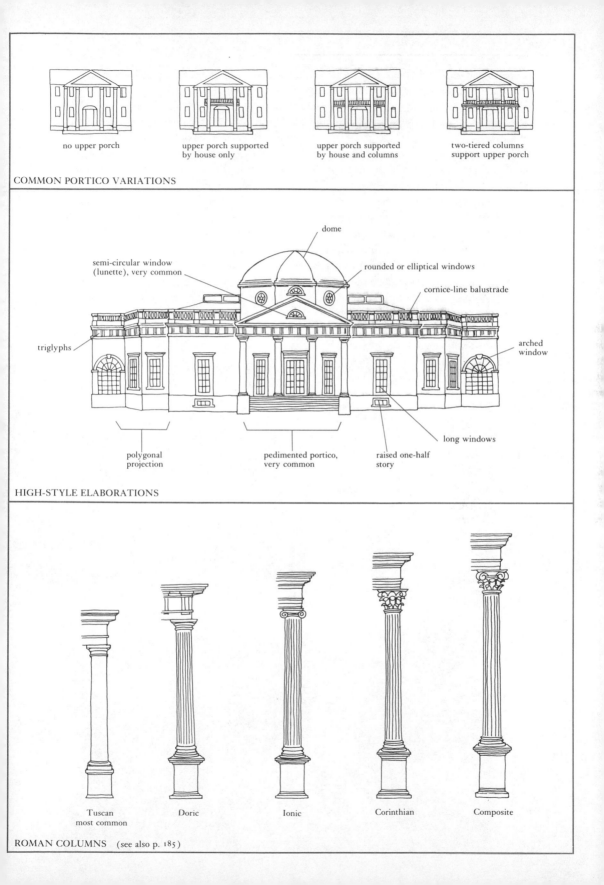

COMMON PORTICO VARIATIONS

no upper porch

upper porch supported
by house only

upper porch supported
by house and columns

two-tiered columns
support upper porch

HIGH-STYLE ELABORATIONS

dome

semi-circular window
(lunette), very common

rounded or elliptical windows

cornice-line balustrade

triglyphs

arched
window

long windows

polygonal
projection

pedimented portico,
very common

raised one-half
story

ROMAN COLUMNS   (see also p. 185)

Tuscan
most common

Doric

Ionic

Corinthian

Composite

signed Roman Revival buildings himself, but used the influence of his political office, and his considerable powers of personal persuasion, to push the United States toward his classical ideal. Jefferson thus shaped early Washington, D.C., the Virginia capitol at Richmond, and, almost single-handedly, the University of Virginia at Charlottesville. Because of his influence, the style is sometimes referred to as Jeffersonian Classicism.

Apart from Jefferson's influence on public architecture, his home, Monticello, his summer home, Poplar Forest, and other houses he designed for friends set the stage for Early Classical domestic architecture. These high-style examples probably sprang from Jefferson's familiarity with the writings of the Italian Renaissance architect Palladio (1508–80). Inspired by such high-style landmarks, typical Palladian entry porches were soon being built throughout the South, some at the time of original construction, but many also as additions to earlier houses.

A national sympathy for the Greek War of Independence (1821–30) and an increasing archeological understanding of the Greek roots of Roman architecture and culture made the years 1820–30 a transition to the succeeding Greek Revival style. Although relatively uncommon and primarily southern, the Early Classical Revival movement provided the background for this more pervasive classicism which dominated the new country for the next thirty years.

2

3

5

1

TWO-STORY

1. Beaufort, South Carolina; 1786. Tabby Manse. Built of tabby, a concrete-like mixture of oyster shell and lime mortar, covered with stucco. Note the delicate two-tiered entry porch with more slender columns above.

2. Berryville, Virginia, 1790. Annefield. Built of stone, this house has a two-tiered entry porch with a fanlight in the pediment. Note the upper balustrade formed in a Chinese Chippendale pattern.

3. Milledgeville, Georgia, vicinity; 1830. Boykin Hall; Daniel Pratt, architect. The relatively simple exterior contrasts with elaborate Adam detailing in the interior. The spindlework balustrade is probably a later addition.

4. Conetoe, North Carolina, vicinity; ca. 1820. Wilkinson House. A simple three-ranked wood-frame example with the exterior chimneys typical of the south. Note the lunette in the pediment; the porch balustrades are probably later additions.

5. Natchez, Mississippi, vicinity; 1812. Duncan House; Levi Weeks, architect. Weeks described this as "the first house in the territory on which was ever attempted any of the orders of [classical] architecture." The twin side wings were added after 1827.

6. Charleston, South Carolina; ca. 1816. Nicholson House; attributed to William Jay, architect. A unique example on a high, rusticated foundation. Note the unusual Gothic (pointed-arch) windows in the pediment, which contrast with the round-arch windows of the second story.

7. Warsaw, Virginia; ca. 1730 (entry porch ca. 1830). Sabine Hall. A well-documented case of a full-height entry porch with colossal columns added to an earlier (1730) house in an extensive exterior remodeling, which included lowering the roof.

4

6

7

ONE-STORY

1. Strasburg, Virginia; 1794. Belle Grove. Built of coursed ashlar limestone on a high basement.

2. Baltimore, Maryland; 1803. Homewood. Note the five-part compound plan with a large central block connected to distant wings by lower "hyphens." Decorative detailing in the gable is atypical.

3. Staunton, Virginia, vicinity; ca. 1818. Folly. Note the matching entry porch on the side facade.

4. Charlottesville, Virginia, 1770–1809. Monticello; Thomas Jefferson, architect. Note the octagonal dome and roof-line balustrade. The view shows the garden facade.

5. Bremo Bluff, Virginia, vicinity; ca. 1819. Bremo. A unique house with entry porches on each facade and dependencies connected by raised terraces.

1

2

3

5

GABLE FRONT AND WINGS

1. Halifax County, North Carolina; early 19th century. A small example, with careful detailing, built in the typical three-part plan.

2. Williamsburg, Virginia; ca. 1775. Semple House; attributed to Thomas Jefferson, architect. One of the earliest examples of the three-part plan, this house survives essentially as originally built.

3. Fayette, Missouri; 1833. Morrison House. Note the Palladian window and keystone lintels.

4. Lexington, Virginia; 1818. Stono. Note the front-gabled roof extended into a temple-form porch.

5. Louisville, Kentucky; ca. 1795. Spring Station. The porch on the right and porte cochere on the left are later additions. The columns on the proch have also been changed; the originals would have been thinner and more delicate.

Romantic Houses

1820–1880

During the preceding Colonial era, a single architectural style tended to dominate in each colony for long periods of time; Georgian houses, for example, were the fashion in the English colonies through most of the 18th century. Likewise the first popular Romantic style, the Greek Revival, dominated the newly independent United States through much of the first half of the 19th century. Architectural models evocative of Greek democracy were thought to be especially appropriate in the new republic, as it rejected traditional ties to England in the decades following the War of 1812.

By the 1840s, a new trend toward competition among *several* acceptable architectural fashions was taking shape. The harbinger of this movement was the publication in 1842 of the first popular pattern book of house styles—Andrew Jackson Downing's *Cottage Residences*. Downing showed full-facade drawings of several new fashions that he considered to be suitable alternatives to the prevailing Greek classicism. Medieval precedents were recommended in models that were to lead to the Gothic Revival style. Likewise, Italian Renaissance traditions were freely adapted in Downing's "Italianate" cottages. Now, for the first time, builders and home buyers had a choice. Soon neighborhoods of alternately Greek, Gothic, and Italianate houses became commonplace. Still more exotic fashions, based on Egyptian and Oriental precedents and on Swiss Chalets or octagonal shapes, also came to be advocated by Downing and others, but these never achieved wide acceptance. The simultaneous popularity of several architectural styles with differing antecedents was to persist as a dominant theme throughout the later history of American housing.

All of the Romantic styles originated and grew to popularity in the decades before 1860. The Greek Revival was dominant from about 1830 to 1850 (to 1860 in the South) and the Italianate from about 1850 until 1875. Gothic Revival houses were more complex to construct and were always less common than their Greek and Italian contemporaries. The Civil War marked the end of Greek classicism, but both Gothic and Italianate houses remained popular into the 1880s, sometimes in more elaborate versions than had appeared before the war. These later examples have been separated as High Victorian Gothic or High Victorian Italianate styles, but this distinction is difficult to recognize in field identification. Highly detailed early examples are not uncommon, nor are late survivors of the earlier, less elaborate interpretations.

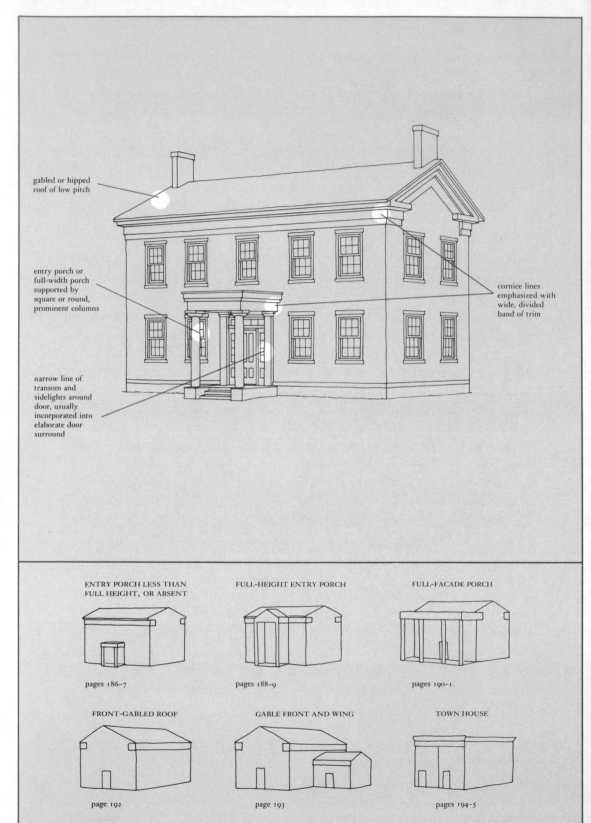

gabled or hipped
roof of low pitch

cornice lines
emphasized with
wide, divided
band of trim

entry porch or
full-width porch
supported by
square or round,
prominent columns

narrow line of
transom and
sidelights around
door, usually
incorporated into
elaborate door
surround

ENTRY PORCH LESS THAN
FULL HEIGHT, OR ABSENT

pages 186–7

FULL-HEIGHT ENTRY PORCH

pages 188–9

FULL-FACADE PORCH

pages 190–1

FRONT-GABLED ROOF

page 192

GABLE FRONT AND WING

page 193

TOWN HOUSE

pages 194–5

PRINCIPAL SUBTYPES

Greek Revival

IDENTIFYING FEATURES

Gabled or hipped roof of low pitch; cornice line of main roof and porch roofs emphasized with wide band of trim (this represents the classical entablature and is usually divided into two parts: the frieze above and architrave below); most have porches (either entry or full-width) supported by prominent square or rounded columns, typically of Doric style; front door surrounded by narrow sidelights and a rectangular line of transom lights above, door and lights usually incorporated into more elaborate door surround.

PRINCIPAL SUBTYPES

Six principal subtypes can be distinguished on the basis of porch and roof configurations:

ENTRY PORCH LESS THAN FULL HEIGHT, OR ABSENT—About 20 percent of Greek Revival houses have small entry porches which do not extend the full height of the facade. In some examples the entry porch is recessed *into* the facade. About 5 percent lack porches altogether.

FULL-HEIGHT ENTRY PORCH—This subtype has a dominant central porch extending the full *height*, but less than the full *width*, of the facade; it thus resembles the Early Classical Revival style from which the Greek Revival sprang. The Greek Revival version can usually be distinguished from its predecessor by the typical band of cornice trim and the rectangular lights, rather than a curving fanlight, over the entrance. As in the earlier style, many Greek Revival examples have a traditional classical pediment above the entry porch. In contrast to the earlier style, however, many Greek examples have flat-roofed entry porches. As in the entry porch less than full height, this type of entry porch also occurs recessed *into* the facade. About one-fourth of Greek Revival houses are of this subtype; like Early Classical Revival houses, these are most common in the southern states.

FULL-FACADE PORCH—In this configuration, the colonnaded porch occupies the full width and height of the facade. No pediment occurs above the porch, which is covered either by the main roof or, less commonly, by a flat or shed-style extension from it. In a few examples, the full-facade porch also extends around one or both sides of the house. This subtype makes up about one-fourth of Greek Revival houses. Like the preceding type, it is most common in the southern states.

FRONT-GABLED ROOF—All of the preceding subtypes have side-gabled or hipped roofs. In this subtype the gable end is turned 90 degrees to make the principal facade. In some high-style examples a full-width, colonnaded porch is present beneath the front gable, giving the house the appearance of a miniature Greek temple with its traditional classical pediment. Smaller entry porches are common on vernacular examples. This subtype is more common in the northeastern and midwestern states.

GABLE FRONT AND WING—In this subtype a front-gabled roof, as in the type just described, has a side wing (less commonly two wings) added; these are typically lower than the dominant front-gabled portion. This subtype rarely occurs outside of the northeastern states and is particularly common in western New York and Ohio.

TOWN HOUSE—A sixth subtype consists of narrow urban houses with Greek Revival detailing. These occur both with and without porches. They are most common in those port cities of the Atlantic and Gulf coasts that were expanding in the decades from 1830 to 1860. These include Boston; New York; Philadelphia; Washington; Richmond, Virginia; Savannah, Georgia; Mobile, Alabama; New Orleans, Louisiana; and Galveston, Texas.

VARIANTS AND DETAILS

The principal areas of elaboration in Greek Revival houses are cornice lines, doorways, porch-support columns, and windows:

CORNICE LINES—The wide band of trim beneath the cornice of both the main roof and the porch roofs is an almost universal feature of Greek Revival houses. Commonly the band is made up of undecorated boards, but complex incised decorations also occur. In gabled houses the trim band may be variously treated along the gabled walls. Post–1850 examples, particularly in the South, often have Italianate brackets added at the cornice line.

DOORWAYS—As in the preceding Georgian, Adam, and Early Classical Revival styles, elaborated door surrounds are a dominant feature of Greek Revival houses. The door itself is either single or paired and is most frequently divided into one, two, or four panels. The door is usually surrounded on sides and top by a narrow band of rectangular panes of glass held in a delicate, decorative frame. Door and glazed surround, in turn, are usually encased in a larger decorative enframement of wood or masonry. Not uncommonly door and glass are recessed behind the front wall, thus creating complex three-dimensional effects; free-standing columns are sometimes added to the inset portion.

COLUMNS—Classical columns for the support of porch roofs are a prominent feature of most Greek Revival houses. In some examples they dominate the entire facade; others retain only smaller entry porch columns. Although many Greek Revival houses have "correct" Greek columns, many also have Roman details; still more have vernacular adaptations with *no* clear classical precedent. The following guide to Classical Column Identification must therefore be used in combination with other typical features when identifying Greek Revival houses:

Classical columns are distinguished principally by their capitals (tops) and bases. Both Greek and Roman columns share three principal types of capitals which define the three familiar orders of classical architecture: Doric (plain capitals), Ionic (capitals with scroll-like spirals called volutes), and Corinthian (capitals shaped like inverted bells decorated with leaves). All three types are found in Greek Revival houses, as well as in most

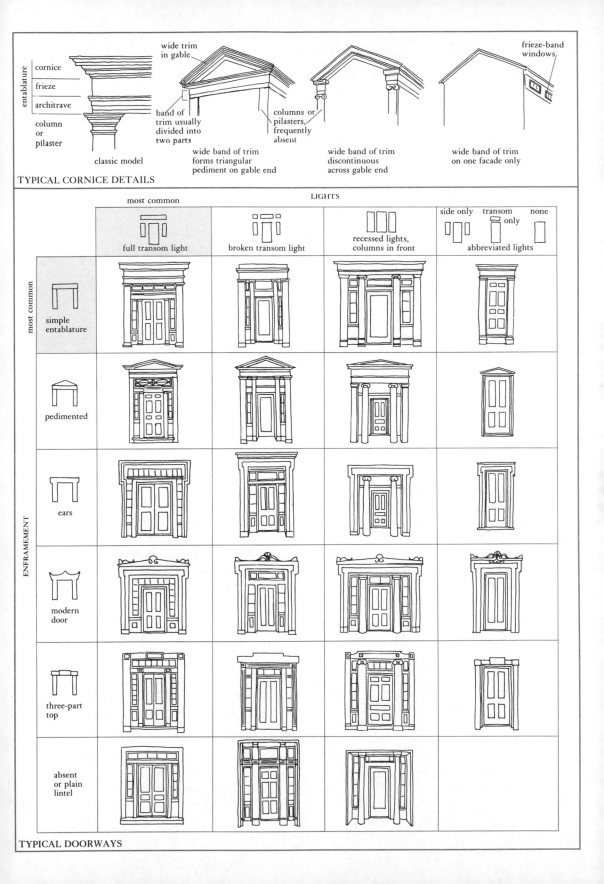

TYPICAL CORNICE DETAILS

entablature
- cornice
- frieze
- architrave

column
or
pilaster

classic model

wide trim
in gable

band of
trim usually
divided into
two parts

wide band of trim
forms triangular
pediment on gable end

columns or
pilasters,
frequently
absent

wide band of trim
discontinuous
across gable end

frieze-band
windows

wide band of trim
on one facade only

TYPICAL DOORWAYS

ENFRAMEMENT

LIGHTS

most common

	most common			side only transom none
	full transom light	broken transom light	recessed lights, columns in front	only abbreviated lights
most common — simple entablature				
pedimented				
ears				
modern door				
three-part top				
absent or plain lintel				

other classically influenced American styles. Greek and Roman examples of these three orders are distinguished by subtle differences in either the capitals or bases.

All columns of classical antiquity were round, as are many Greek Revival columns. Vernacular Greek Revival houses, on the other hand, commonly have *square* (and occasionally octagonal) columns, which were simple and inexpensive to construct from boards and moldings. Such columns generally lack classical capitals. About 40 percent of columns found on Greek Revival houses are square; the remaining 60 percent include about 40 percent Doric, 15 percent Ionic, and 5 percent Corinthian. Note that the Greek Doric column has no base, while the Roman version does. This distinction frequently will distinguish Greek Revival Doric columns from the Roman Doric columns of the Early Classical Revival. Note, however, that many Greek Revival houses retained Roman columns, particularly in the southern states, so that column type alone is seldom sufficient to identify the style.

Pilasters are also frequent Greek Revival features. They are most commonly used on the corners of frame houses but are occasionally found across the entire facade in lieu of free-standing columns.

WINDOWS—As in the preceding Adam style, Greek Revival window sashes most commonly had six-pane glazing. The rounded, three-part Palladian windows of Adam houses disappeared, to be replaced only occasionally by rectangular, tripartite examples. Small frieze-band windows, set into the wide trim beneath the cornice, are frequent. These are often covered with an iron or wooden grate fashioned into a decorative Greek pattern. Window surrounds were generally far less elaborate than doorways.

OCCURRENCE

Greek Revival was the dominant style of American domestic architecture during the interval from about 1830 to 1850 (to 1860 in the Gulf Coast states) during which its popularity led it to be called the National Style. It occurs in all areas settled by 1860, as noted on the map, and especially flourished in those regions that were being rapidly settled in the decades of the 1830s, '40s, and '50s. The style moved with the settlers from the older states as they crossed into Kentucky, Tennessee, and the Old Northwest Territory (today's Midwest). It followed the southern planters as they moved westward from the Old South into Alabama, Mississippi, and Louisiana. It even arrived on the west coast, sometimes disassembled into packages and shipped by way of Cape Horn! Each of the principal subtypes of the style shows geographic differences in frequency of occurrence, as noted above and in the maps.

Not surprisingly, the largest surviving concentrations of Greek Revival houses are found today in those states with the largest population growth during the period from 1820 to 1860. These are, in descending order of growth: New York, Pennsylvania, Ohio, Illinois, Virginia, Massachusetts, Indiana, Missouri, Tennessee, Alabama, Wisconsin, Georgia, Mississippi, Michigan, Texas, Kentucky, and Louisiana. New York gained about 2½ million persons during the interval while Louisiana gained about ½ million.

COMMENTS

The final years of the 18th century brought an increasing interest in classical buildings to both the United States and western Europe. This was first based on Roman models (see the Early Classical Revival chapter), but archeological investigation in the early 19th

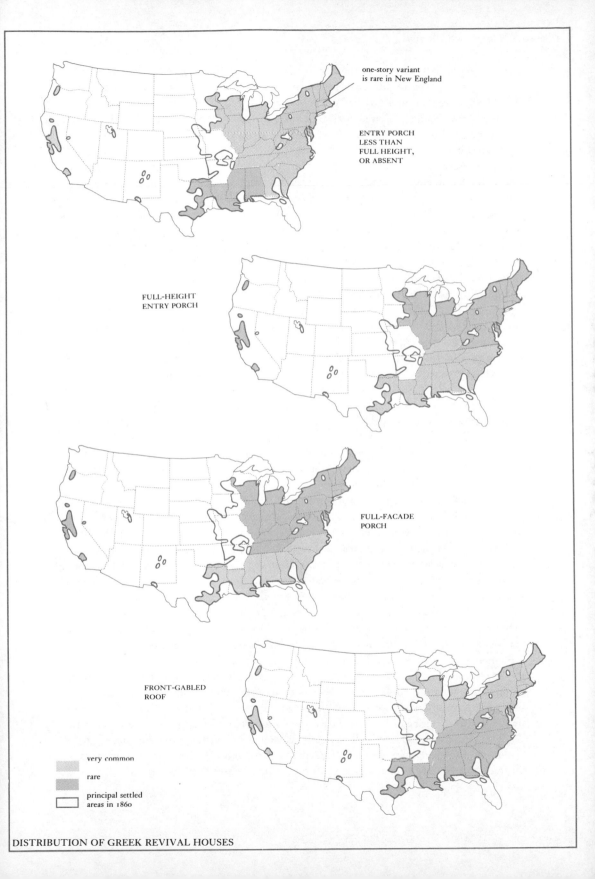

one-story variant
is rare in New England

ENTRY PORCH
LESS THAN
FULL HEIGHT,
OR ABSENT

FULL-HEIGHT
ENTRY PORCH

FULL-FACADE
PORCH

FRONT-GABLED
ROOF

very common

rare

principal settled
areas in 1860

DISTRIBUTION OF GREEK REVIVAL HOUSES

century emphasized Greece as the Mother of Rome which, in turn, shifted interest to Grecian models. Two additional factors enhanced Greek influence in this country. Greece's involvement in a war for independence (1821–30) aroused much sympathy in the newly independent United States; at the same time, the War of 1812 diminished American affection for British influence, including the still dominant Adam style in domestic architecture.

The Greek Revival began and ended in this country with public buildings built in Philadelphia. Among the first examples was the Bank of the United States (1818, William Strickland), and one of the last monuments was the Ridgeway Branch of the Philadelphia Library (1870, Addison and Hutton). Most domestic examples date from the period from 1830 to 1860. Among the earliest was a Greek remodeling of the Custis-Lee house in Arlington, Virginia, completed in 1820. The style was spread by carpenter's guides and pattern books, the most influential of which were written by Asher Benjamin (*The Practical House Carpenter; The Builder's Guide*) and Minard Lafever (*The Modern Builder's Guide; The Beauties of Modern Architecture*).

In addition to these guides for local carpenter-builders, there were a growing number of trained architects in America, some educated abroad, who designed high-style buildings in the fashionable Grecian mode. Among the most prominent were Benjamin H. Latrobe and his pupils Robert Mills and William Strickland; Strickland's own pupils Thomas U. Walter and Gideon Shryock; Ithiel Town, Alexander Jackson Davis (early work), John Haviland, Alexander Parris, and Isaiah Rogers.

One of the most familiar stereotypes in American architecture is the full-colonnaded Greek Revival mansion of the southern states. In this century these are sometimes called Southern Colonial houses, a historical inaccuracy since most were built long after American independence. This particular Greek Revival subtype does, however, have a little recognized colonial background, for it sprang, at least in part, from French colonial building practices. Early in their colonial expansions both the French and English appended broad living porches, a rarity in Europe, to houses built in tropical regions. The origins of these large *galeries* or verandahs are obscure, yet they appear wherever British or French colonists encountered warm climates, including the West Indies, Africa, India, and Australia. In the United States, most were built by the French in subtropical Louisiana. With the waning of French influence after the Louisiana Purchase in 1803, these forms slowly evolved in the Gulf Coast states into the full colonnaded Greek Revival form now sometimes known as Southern Colonial.

The decline of Greek Revival influence was gradual. In the more fashion-conscious urban centers of the Atlantic seaboard it began to be replaced by the Gothic Revival and Italianate movements in the 1840s. In the interior states, and in rural areas everywhere, it remained a dominant style for domestic buildings until the early 1860s.

An important and enduring legacy of the Greek Revival to American domestic architecture is the front-gabled house. Popularized during the ascendance of the Greek Revival style in the early 19th century, this became the predominant form for detached urban houses in cities of the Northeast and Midwest until well into the 20th century. There it occurs in unadorned folk versions, as well as in styled Gothic, Italianate, Queen Anne, and Shingle houses. In rural areas, the form of Greek Revival known as gable front and wing likewise remained a popular form for folk houses until the 1930s.

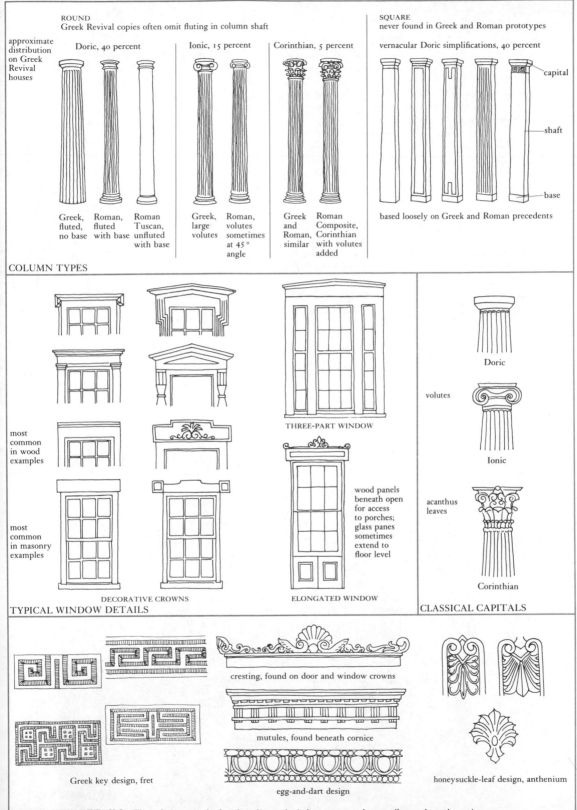

ROUND
Greek Revival copies often omit fluting in column shaft

approximate distribution on Greek Revival houses

Doric, 40 percent

Greek, fluted, no base

Roman, fluted with base

Roman Tuscan, unfluted with base

Ionic, 15 percent

Greek, large volutes

Roman, volutes sometimes at 45° angle

Corinthian, 5 percent

Greek and Roman, similar

Roman Composite, Corinthian with volutes added

SQUARE
never found in Greek and Roman prototypes

vernacular Doric simplifications, 40 percent

based loosely on Greek and Roman precedents

capital

shaft

base

COLUMN TYPES

most common in wood examples

most common in masonry examples

THREE-PART WINDOW

wood panels beneath open for access to porches; glass panes sometimes extend to floor level

DECORATIVE CROWNS

ELONGATED WINDOW

TYPICAL WINDOW DETAILS

Doric

volutes

Ionic

acanthus leaves

Corinthian

CLASSICAL CAPITALS

cresting, found on door and window crowns

mutules, found beneath cornice

Greek key design, fret

egg-and-dart design

honeysuckle-leaf design, anthenium

DECORATIVE DETAILS   These designs may be found on door and window crowns, columns, pilasters, beneath cornice, etc.

ENTRY PORCH LESS THAN FULL HEIGHT, OR ABSENT

1. Stafford, New York; 1835. Harmon House. A small wood-clad example with nicely detailed tripartite and frieze-band windows.

2. Beaufort, North Carolina; 1866. Croft House.

3. Marshall, Michigan; 1850. Montgomery House. This transitional example combines Italianate brackets under a wide eave overhang with Greek Revival door and window detailing.

4. New London, Connecticut; 1837. Barns House. Note how the wide band of trim forms a pediment on the gable end.

5. Ashville, New York; 1835. Smith-Bly House. This lavishly detailed house has four Ionic two-story pilasters across the front facade, carved window lintels, and an architrave at the entrance. The door is recessed with two small columns in front.

6. New London, Connecticut; mid-19th century. Note the small windows in the frieze band and the unusual Corinthian capitals on the pilasters and columns.

7. Rochester, New York; 1838–41. Woodside; Alfred M. Badger, architect-builder. This large five-ranked masonry example has a square cupola, topped by a round turret, which lights an interior stairway. Note the matching balusters at four different levels and the tripartite window lintels.

8. New Castle, Indiana; 1847. Murphy House. A simplified but nicely proportioned masonry example. Note the square columns on the entry porch and the absence of capitals on both columns and pilasters.

FULL-HEIGHT ENTRY PORCH

1. San Felipe, Texas; ca. 1838. Lambart House. A very simple one-story example. Note the very slender columns and pilasters. Such simplified details were usual in houses built far from centers of population.

2. Bastrop, Texas; ca. 1860. Reding House. A simple wood-clad two-story example.

3. Meriwether County, Georgia; 1852. Mark Hall. This house, similar to Figure 1, has heavier moldings and more substantial columns and pilasters.

4. Pittsford, New York; 1840. Kirby House. The entry porch without a pediment or hipped roof above is unusual. Note the Doric columns without bases.

5. Scott County, Kentucky; 1842. Glencrest. Note the exaggerated depth of the frieze and architrave over the entry porch.

6. Milledgeville, Georgia; 1838. Executive Mansion; Charles B. Clusky, architect-designer.

7. Natchez, Mississippi, vicinity. Homewood.

8. Belfast, Maine; 1840. White House; Calvin A. Ryder, architect. This full-height entry porch is a complex and subtle variation of the usual type. Note the elaborate cupola.

1

3

6

2

4

5

7

8

1

3

4

6   7

FULL-FACADE PORCH

1. Madison, Georgia; ca. 1859. Massey House. A simple one-story, wood-clad example.

2. Mobile, Alabama; 1851. Lowary House. This one-story cottage is more elaborated than Figure 1. Note the pedimented dormers and full-length windows with transoms.

3. Columbus, Mississippi; ca. 1836. Homewood.

4. Sparta vicinity, Georgia; ca. 1853. Smith House (Glen Mary). The main part is raised above a high masonry basement story, a pattern borrowed from earlier French Colonial houses of the rural south.

5. Geismar, Louisiana; 1841. Ashland; James Gallier, Sr., architect. The columns of this plantation house are four feet square and thirty feet high. The massive entablature hides a low-hipped roof.

6. New Iberia, Louisiana; 1834. Shadows-on-the-Teche. This handsome plantation house has a stairway exterior to the house and no interior halls, reflecting earlier French Colonial influences.

7. Selma, Alabama; 1853. Sturdivant Hall; Thomas Helm Lee, architect.

8. Nashville, Tennessee; 1853. Belle Meade. Note the parapet with cresting crowning the full-facade porch.

FRONT-GABLED ROOF

1. Breckinridge, Colorado; mid-19th century. A very simple house with just a hint of Greek Revival influence in its front-gabled form and pedimented door and windows.

2. Marietta, Georgia; ca. 1851. Brumby House.

3. Providence, Rhode Island; mid-19th century. Front-gabled examples commonly lack colonnaded porches but usually have pilasters and elaborate door and cornice details as in this example.

4. Middletown, Connecticut; 1828. Russell House; Ithiel Town, architect. This house is built of masonry covered with stucco scored to look like stone. Note the elaborate Corinthian capitals.

5. Andalusia, Pennsylvania; 1836 (porch and pediment). Andalusia. An earlier house to which a three-sided porch was added.

1

2

3

4

5

GABLE FRONT AND WING

1. Monroeville, Ohio; mid-19th century. This example, although quite small, has a colonnaded gable front and elaborate frieze-band windows.

2. Wellington vicinity, Ohio; mid-19th century. Here the frieze band is discontinuous across the gable front.

3. Buffalo, New York; mid-19th century. This imposing example has pilasters across the gable front and a two-story wing.

4. Jessamine County, Kentucky; mid-19th century. Bryant House. This brick example has a colonnaded gable front and two wings. Note that the wings have pilasters rather than the more common porch with columns as seen in the other examples.

TOWN HOUSE

1. New Orleans, Louisiana; mid-19th century. Note the exceptionally wide frieze band with windows.

2. Savannah, Georgia; 1845. Constantine House. A wood-clad example with simplified details.

3. Madison, Indiana; 1851. Costigan House. A small, two-ranked example with strong porch and window detailing.

4. St. Louis, Missouri; 1850. Sherrick House. Town houses with full-facade porches like this example were common along the Gulf Coast, particularly in New Orleans (this one slipped upriver). They may also have two tiers of one-story columns rather than the colossal ones illustrated.

5. Richmond, Virginia; 1847 and 1853. Lindon Row. A series of attached town houses.

6. Brooklyn, New York; ca. 1830. Tillary House. Note the tripartite windows and door lintels, curved top dormer windows, and elaborated frieze band.

7. Charleston, South Carolina; 1838. Roper House; attributed to E. B. White, architect. An outstanding example of the Charleston house, with narrow end turned to the street and wide porch along the side. An upper-story porch (omitted in this example) is commonly present.

8. New York, New York: 1833. Colonnade Row; attributed to Robert Higham, architect. A highly unusual row of town houses unified by free-standing columns; this example shows Renaissance influence in the placement of the columns above a rusticated lower story.

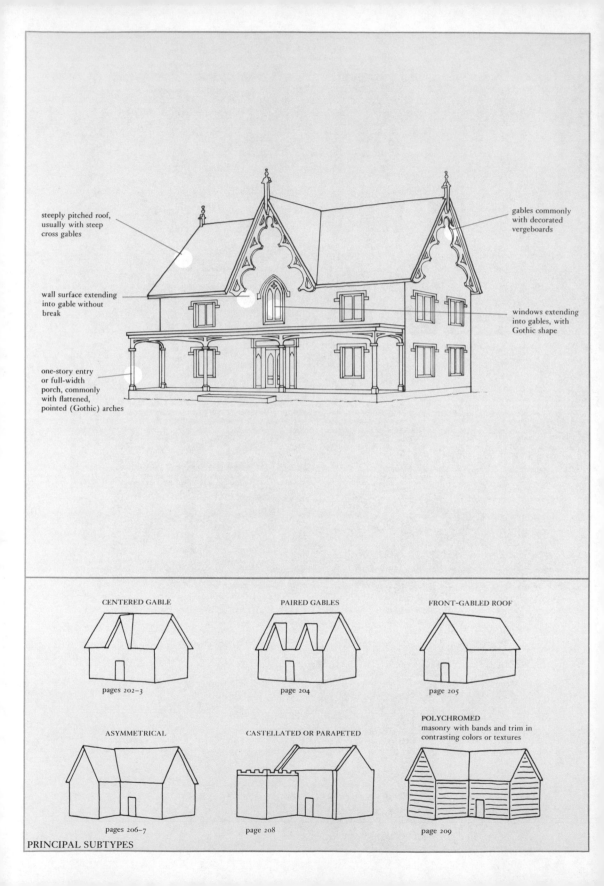

steeply pitched roof, usually with steep cross gables

gables commonly with decorated vergeboards

wall surface extending into gable without break

windows extending into gables, with Gothic shape

one-story entry or full-width porch, commonly with flattened, pointed (Gothic) arches

CENTERED GABLE

pages 202–3

PAIRED GABLES

page 204

FRONT-GABLED ROOF

page 205

ASYMMETRICAL

pages 206–7

CASTELLATED OR PARAPETED

page 208

POLYCHROMED
masonry with bands and trim in contrasting colors or textures

page 209

PRINCIPAL SUBTYPES

Gothic Revival

IDENTIFYING FEATURES

Steeply pitched roof, usually with steep cross gables (roof normally side-gabled, less commonly front-gabled or hipped; rarely flat with castellated parapet); gables commonly have decorated vergeboards; wall surface extending into gable without break (eave or trim normally lacking beneath gable); windows commonly extend into gables, frequently having pointed-arch (Gothic) shape; one-story porch (either entry or full-width) usually present, commonly supported by flattened Gothic arches.

PRINCIPAL SUBTYPES

Six principal subtypes can be distinguished on the basis of roof form, ground plan, or detailing:

CENTERED GABLE—These are symmetrical houses with side-gabled or hipped roofs having a prominent central cross gable. The plane of the cross gable may be either the same as the front wall or projected forward to make a small central wing. Smaller cross gables, or gable dormers, sometimes occur on either side of the dominant central gable. In some examples these are enlarged to give three identical cross gables. This subtype makes up over one-third of Gothic Revival houses.

PAIRED GABLES—Similar to the preceding subtype but with two, rather than one or three, cross gables. The two gables are sometimes extended forward into projecting wings. About 5 percent of Gothic Revival houses are of this type.

FRONT-GABLED ROOF—About 10 percent of Gothic Revival houses are simple gabled rectangles rotated so that the narrower gable end makes up the front facade. Some have additional cross gables added to the roof slope over the *side* walls, but many lack such cross gables.

ASYMMETRICAL—About one-third of Gothic Revival houses are of compound asymmetrical plan. L-shaped plans with cross-gabled roofs are the most common form, but there are many less regular variations. Small secondary cross gables, or gable dormers, were commonly added to one or more wings. After 1860, square towers were occasionally used.

CASTELLATED OR PARAPETED—The four preceding subtypes all have normal roof-wall junctions in which the eaves project outward beyond the wall. A fifth subtype, more closely based on English Medieval models, has either flat roofs with scalloped (castellated) parapets, or gabled roofs ending in high parapeted walls rather than overhanging eaves. Frequently both of these roof types occur on different parts of a single house. About 5 percent of Gothic Revival houses are of this type. These features are far more common on Gothic Revival churches and public buildings; most surviving houses are high-style landmarks.

POLYCHROMED—A final 5 percent of surviving Gothic Revival houses show distinctive linear patterns in masonry wall surfaces. These decorative polychrome patterns are produced by bands of contrasting color or texture in the brick or stonework, and occur principally around windows and as horizontal bands on wall surfaces. This feature is particularly characteristic of the last phase of the Gothic Revival, from about 1865 to 1880. It is sometimes treated as a separate style called High Victorian Gothic. Like the castellated or parapeted form, it is most common on churches and public buildings. The complex masonry construction was suitable only for high-style, landmark houses. These were once far more common in the prosperous industrial cities of the northeastern and midwestern states, but most have been destroyed.

VARIANTS AND DETAILS

Fanciful decorative ornamentation, cut from wood by the newly perfected scroll saw, is a dominant feature in most Gothic Revival houses. Windows, roof-wall junctions, porches, and doors were the principal sites for such decorations.

WINDOWS—Most Gothic Revival houses have at least one window with Gothic detailing. When only a single window is elaborated in this manner, it usually occurs in the most prominent gable. Such windows might have a pointed-arch shape or might consist of two or three such arches clustered together, or might even be designed as small projecting bay windows (oriels). Full-scale bay windows are also common on the first-floor level. In less elaborate houses, cut-out patterns were frequently used on or above rectangular windows to give a pointed-arch effect. A characteristic window crown called a drip-mold is found above many Gothic windows, both arched and square. Originally designed to protect windows from water running down the face of the building, this molding covers the top of the window and continues downward along the side before turning outward so that water will be deflected away from the window frame.

ROOF-WALL JUNCTIONS—Decorative vergeboards, making an inverted V beneath the eaves of the steep gables, are a distinctive feature of most wooden Gothic houses and came in almost as many designs as there were Gothic carpenter-builders. After about 1865 this feature became less popular and was generally replaced by decorative trusses at the apex of the gables. Gothic cornice detailing showed fundamental changes from the preceding classical styles (Georgian, Adam, Greek-Revival, etc.). The latter usually have boxed cornices with the rafters enclosed, while most Gothic Revival houses have open cornices with the rafters either exposed or sheathed parallel to the overlying roof.

PORCHES—One-story porches are found on about 80 percent of Gothic Revival houses.

DOORS—Doors commonly show pointed arches or other Gothic motifs as well as decorative crowns similar to those found on windows. Elaborate paneled doors are common but simple batten doors, mimicking modest Medieval prototypes, also occur.

WALL CLADDING AND DECORATIVE DETAILING—Gothic Revival houses are of both wooden

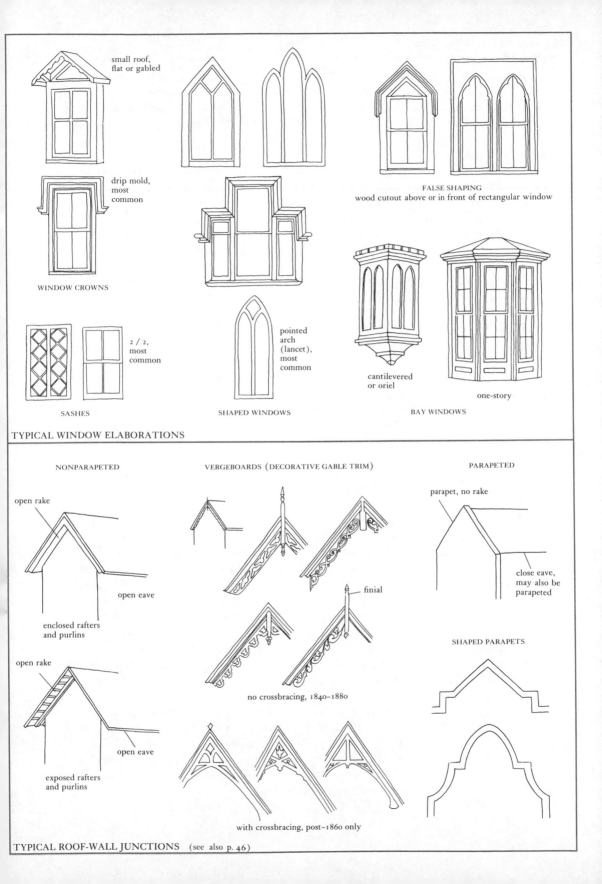

small roof, flat or gabled

drip mold, most common

WINDOW CROWNS

FALSE SHAPING
wood cutout above or in front of rectangular window

2 / 2, most common

SASHES

pointed arch (lancet), most common

SHAPED WINDOWS

cantilevered or oriel

one-story

BAY WINDOWS

TYPICAL WINDOW ELABORATIONS

NONPARAPETED

VERGEBOARDS (DECORATIVE GABLE TRIM)

PARAPETED

open rake

open eave

enclosed rafters and purlins

open rake

open eave

exposed rafters and purlins

finial

no crossbracing, 1840–1880

with crossbracing, post–1860 only

parapet, no rake

close eave, may also be parapeted

SHAPED PARAPETS

TYPICAL ROOF-WALL JUNCTIONS   (see also p. 46)

and masonry construction but wood-frame Carpenter Gothic examples predominate. These were usually covered with horizontal cladding, but vertical board-and-batten siding was also common. The latter material was widely advocated by contemporary pattern books for its verticality, which was considered suitably Gothic.

OCCURRENCE

Most Gothic Revival houses were constructed between 1840 and 1870; examples from the 1870s are less frequent. The style was never as popular as were houses in the competing Greek Revival or Italianate styles, yet scattered examples can still be found in most areas of the country settled before 1880. Surviving Gothic Revival houses are most abundant in the northeastern states, where fashionable architects originally popularized the style. They are less common in the South, particularly in the New South states along the Gulf Coast. In this region Greek Revival houses dominated the expansions of the 1840s and '50s, while the Civil War and Reconstruction all but halted building until the waning days of Gothic influence.

COMMENTS

The Gothic Revival began in England in 1749 when Sir Horace Walpole, a wealthy dilettante, began remodeling his country house in the Medieval style, complete with battlements and multiple pointed-arch windows. Over the next century, others followed his lead and such Picturesque country houses became common in England. Although a handful of earlier houses with Gothic detailing were built, the first documented, fully developed domestic example in America (Glen Ellen in Baltimore, Maryland) was designed by Alexander Jackson Davis in 1832. Davis was the first American architect to champion Gothic domestic buildings; his 1837 book, *Rural Residences*, was dominated by Gothic examples. This was also the first house plan book published in this country. Previous publications had shown details, parts, pieces, and occasional elevations of houses, but Davis's was the first to show three-dimensional views complete with floor plans. Davis's book had only a small circulation but his ideas were picked up by his friend, Andrew Jackson Downing, who expanded them in pattern books published in 1842 (*Cottage Residences*) and 1850 (*The Architecture of Country Houses*). Downing's writings were far more successful, because the author promoted them with tireless public speaking and personal energy. Downing thus became the popularizer of the style.

This style was seldom applied to urban houses for two reasons. First, the writings of Davis and Downing stressed its suitability as a *rural* style, compatible with the natural landscape; it was not promoted as appropriate for urban dwellings. Secondly, its emphasis on high, multiple gables and wide porches did not physically lend itself to narrow, urban lots. A few urban examples with Gothic door, window, or cornice detailing survive (figures 4, 5, page 209), but most urban houses of the era are in the contemporaneous Greek Revival or Italianate styles.

Gothic Revival was in declining favor for American domestic buildings after 1865, although a small rebirth of interest during the 1870s was stimulated by the writings of the English critic John Ruskin, who emphasized continental rather than English examples as models. This High Victorian Gothic phase was principally applied to public and religious buildings, although a few surviving landmark houses reflect its influence (see the paragraph on the polychromed subtype, above).

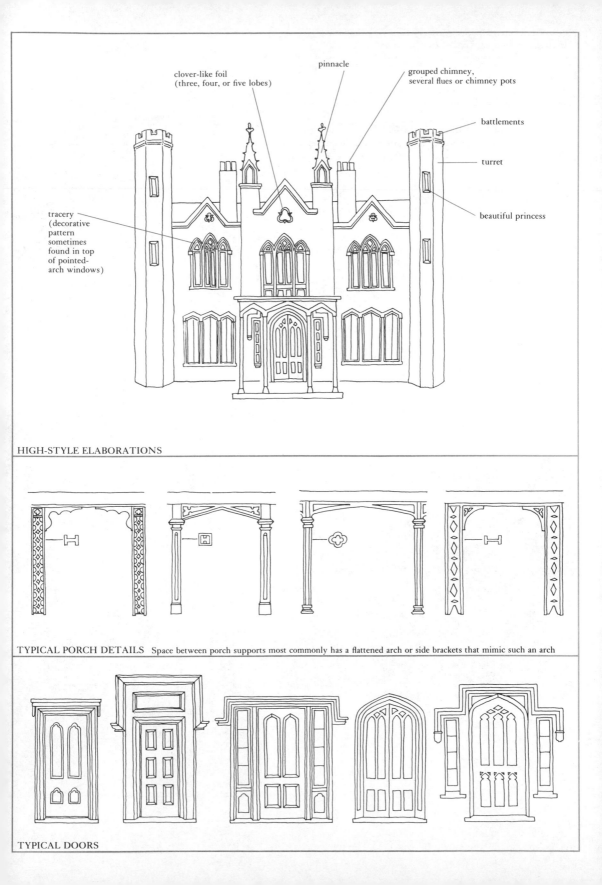

clover-like foil
(three, four, or five lobes)

pinnacle

grouped chimney,
several flues or chimney pots

battlements

turret

beautiful princess

tracery
(decorative
pattern
sometimes
found in top
of pointed-
arch windows)

HIGH-STYLE ELABORATIONS

TYPICAL PORCH DETAILS Space between porch supports most commonly has a flattened arch or side brackets that mimic such an arch

TYPICAL DOORS

CENTERED GABLE

1. Santa Clara, California; 1875. Landrum House. A small wood-clad example; the triangular pediments over the first-story windows are out of character.

2. Denison, Texas; ca. 1883. Eisenhower Birthplace. A small and simplified example. The centered gable has a matching gable on each side.

3. Jackson, Mississippi; 1857. Manship House. Note how the centered gable is extended forward from the main plane of the front facade to form a covered entrance.

4. Brownwood, Texas; ca. 1875. Adams House. This sandstone example has windows with flattened Tudor arches and drip-molds. The porch may have been modified.

5. Woodstock, Connecticut; 1846. Roseland. A landmark example with board-and-batten wood cladding, elaborate porch supports, oriel windows, and two facades elaborated with gables or gable dormers.

6. Salem, Massachusetts; 1851. Brooks House. An elaborately detailed house with foil windows, diamond-shape window panes, drip-molds, and castellations above the porch.

7. Wernersville, Pennsylvania; mid-19th century. A combination of the Gothic Revival form with Italianate cornice brackets and arched windows.

8. Rushford, Minnesota; ca. 1875. Note the decorative trusses at the apex of the gable and gable dormers (see also Figure 1); these are common on post-1865 examples.

1

3

6

7

2

4

5

8

PAIRED GABLES

1. Demopolis, Alabama; 1858. Ashe House. Both this house and Figure 3 have very delicate lacelike porches and vergeboard details.

2. Ashe County, North Carolina; ca. 1880. McGuire House. This very simple example has wood cladding that dramatically follows the lines of the paired gables. The porch shows later modifications.

3. Columbus, Mississippi; 1880. Episcopal Rectory.

4. Brunswick, Maine; 1849. Boody House; Gervase Wheeler, architect. This house has some applied stickwork (not visible in the photo) and is transitional from the Gothic Revival to the Stick style.

1   2

3   4

FRONT-GABLED ROOF

1. Georgtown, Colorado; mid-19th century. A very modest example complete with pointed arch window and drip-molds on all front windows and door.

2. Cleveland, Ohio; mid-19th century.

3. New Orleans, Louisiana; ca. 1869. Rountree House. An unusual example with a two-tiered porch and the full-length windows often found in Gulf Coast houses. The Tudor arches between the lower-story porch supports are carefully detailed.

4. Cuba, New York; mid-19th century. Note the wraparound porch and matching side gable.

1

ASYMMETRICAL

1. Hartford, Connecticut; mid-19th century. Although the Gothic decorated gable clearly dominates, a hodgepodge of secondary influences is evident—Italianate brackets, Second Empire tower, Queen Anne porch supports, and pedimented windows.

2. Southport, Connecticut; mid-19th century. Bulkley House. Although similar to Figure 1, the details here are mostly of Gothic inspiration.

3. Selma, Alabama; mid-19th century. A carefully detailed board-and-batten example.

4. Brown's Valley, Minnesota, vicinity; ca. 1885. Similar in form to Figure 3, the ornate trussed gables identify it as a later example.

5. Iowa City, Iowa; 1877. Jackson House.

6. Rochester, New York; mid-19th century. This house shows clearly the transition from the Gothic to the Stick style. Note the Gothic windows and door shapes with stickwork in the main gable and as supports under the upstairs bay windows.

7. Newport, Rhode Island; 1841. Kingscote; Richard Upjohn, architect (rear addition by Stanford White). A handsomely detailed house with entrance canopy, castellations over the bay window, drip-molds, and diamond-pane windows.

8. New Castle, Delaware; mid-19th century.

4

7

2

3

5

6

8

CASTELLATED OR PARAPETED

1. Aberdeen, Mississippi; ca. 1884. The Castle. A relatively modest wood-clad example, unusual for this subtype.

2. Fayette County, Kentucky; 1852. Ingelside; John McMurtry, architect.

3. Brookneal, Virginia, vicinity; 1848. Staunton Hill; John E. Johnson, designer. Note the symmetrical facade with its almost classical feeling.

4. Tarrytown, New York; 1838, major addition 1865. Lyndhurst; Alexander Jackson Davis, architect for both. This marble example is the finest Gothic Revival house surviving in this country—the result of a major 1865 addition to an earlier 1838 structure. Note the multiple parapets, castellations, pinnacles, foil windows, grouped chimneys, window tracery, and castellated tower. The interiors are equally elaborate.

1

2

3

4

POLYCHROMED

1. Philadelphia, Pennsylvania; 1894. Moore House; Wilson Eyre, architect. A late example with strong early Eclectic influences.

2. Detroit, Michigan; 1876. Gillis House; Brush and Mason, architects. Note the banded surround above the pointed arch window to the right. This was a favorite polychrome motif (see also Figure 5).

3. Cleveland, Ohio; ca. 1878. Winslow House. This example combines the towered Second Empire form with elaborate polychromed Gothic detailing.

4. Brooklyn, New York; 1848. The Gothic influence is seen in the door surround and drip-mold over the windows of these town houses. This example is not polychromed and is included to show a rare early Gothic town house. A roof addition and cornice modifications are evident in the house to the right.

5. New York, New York; 1874. Governor Tilden House; Calvert Vaux, architect. This town house example has elaborate polychromed detailing.

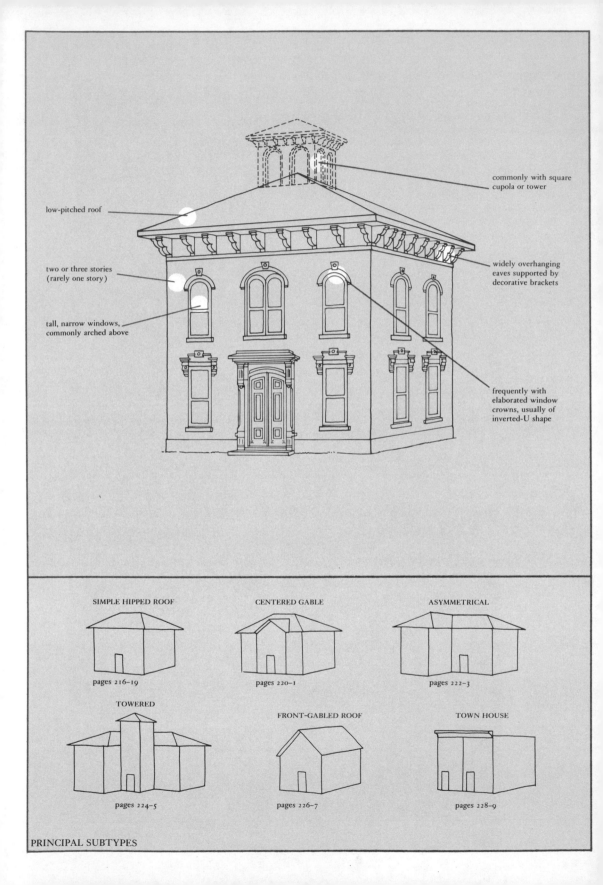

commonly with square cupola or tower

low-pitched roof

two or three stories (rarely one story)

tall, narrow windows, commonly arched above

widely overhanging eaves supported by decorative brackets

frequently with elaborated window crowns, usually of inverted-U shape

SIMPLE HIPPED ROOF

pages 216–19

CENTERED GABLE

pages 220–1

ASYMMETRICAL

pages 222–3

TOWERED

pages 224–5

FRONT-GABLED ROOF

pages 226–7

TOWN HOUSE

pages 228–9

PRINCIPAL SUBTYPES

Italianate

IDENTIFYING FEATURES

Two or three stories (rarely one story); low-pitched roof with widely overhanging eaves having decorative brackets beneath; tall, narrow windows, commonly arched or curved above; windows frequently with elaborated crowns, usually of inverted U shape; many examples with square cupola or tower.

PRINCIPAL SUBTYPES

Six principal subtypes can be distinguished:

SIMPLE HIPPED ROOF—These are square or rectangular box-shaped houses with hipped roofs that are uninterrupted except, in about half of the surviving examples, by a central cupola (these have been called cube and cupola houses). Facade openings are typically three-ranked, less commonly five-ranked, rarely two- or four-ranked. This is the most common subtype, making up about one-third of Italianate houses.

CENTERED GABLE—These are houses of both simple and compound plan having a front-facing centered gable. The usually rather small gable projects from a low-pitched hipped or side-gabled roof. Frequently the front wall beneath the gable extends forward as a prominent central extension. About 15 percent are of this type.

ASYMMETRICAL—These are compound-plan houses, usually L-shaped, without towers. Roofs are cross-hipped or cross-gabled. In a few examples the addition of a second forward-facing wing makes a U-shaped plan. About 20 percent of Italianate houses are of this type.

TOWERED—Only about 15 percent of Italianate houses have the square tower that is often considered to be characteristic of the Italian Villa. The tower is sometimes centered on the front facade or placed alongside it; more commonly, it occupies the position where the wing joins the principal section of an L-plan house. Typically, such towers have narrow paired windows with arched tops. Tower roofs are most commonly low-pitched and hipped; occasionally, steep mansard roofs are used instead.

FRONT-GABLED ROOF—In this subtype, Italianate detailing is added to the simple front-gabled rectangular box popularized by the Greek Revival style. This subtype, about 10 percent of surviving examples, is common on narrow lots in large cities.

TOWN HOUSE—Italianate styling, along with the related Second Empire style, dominated urban housing in the decades between 1860 and 1880. Italianate town houses are characterized by wide, projecting cornices with typical brackets; the cornice conceals a flat or low-pitched roof behind. Typical Italianate windows further distinguish these examples.

VARIANTS AND DETAILS

The principal areas of elaboration in Italianate houses are windows, cornices, porches (including porch-support columns), and doorways. Most American examples show a free intermixing of details derived from both informal rural models as well as formal Renaissance town houses.

WINDOWS—Italianate window sashes most commonly have one- or two-pane glazing. For the first time, arched and curved (segmentally arched) window tops became common, along with the traditional rectangular top. Window enframements show exuberant variation: U-shaped crowns, often with brackets, are most common; simple or pedimented crowns and complete decorated surrounds also occur. Paired and triple windows are frequent.

CORNICES—Large eave brackets dominate the cornice line of Italianate houses. These show an almost infinite variety of shapes and spacings. They are usually arranged either singly or in pairs, and are commonly placed on a deep trim band that is, itself, frequently elaborated with panels or moldings.

PORCHES AND PORCH-SUPPORT COLUMNS—Porches, although almost universally present, are relatively restrained in elaboration and are of single-story height. Small entry porches are most common; full-width porches are also frequent, although many of those seen today are later expansions or additions. The most common type of porch support is a square post with the corners beveled.

DOORWAYS—Paired as well as single doors are common. Large-pane glazing in the door itself, rather than small panes in a frame surrounding the door, first became common in Italianate houses. Doors occur in the same shapes as windows (rectangular, arched, segmentally arched); elaborate enframements above doors are similar to those over windows.

OCCURRENCE

The Italianate style dominated American houses constructed between 1850 and 1880. It was particularly common in the expanding towns and cities of the Midwest as well as in many older but still growing cities of the northeastern seaboard. In these decades San Francisco grew from a village to a principal American port; most of its earliest town houses were constructed of wood in this style. Many of these escaped the 1906 earthquake and fire to survive today. Italianate houses are least common in the southern states, where the Civil War, Reconstruction, and the 1870s depression led to little new building until after the style had passed from fashion.

COMMENTS

The Italianate style, along with the Gothic Revival, began in England as part of the Picturesque movement, a reaction to the formal classical ideals in art and architecture that had been fashionable for about two hundred years. The movement emphasized rambling, informal Italian farmhouses, with their characteristic square towers, as models for Italian-style villa architecture. Note that other, more formal, Italian models from the Renaissance or ancient Rome had led to the previous era of classicism. Italy, rather paradoxically, thus remained a principal source of artistic nurture during the reaction against the earlier ideals it had inspired.

Italianate houses built in the United States generally followed the informal rural models of the Picturesque movement. In America these Old World prototypes were variously modified, adapted, and embellished into a truly indigenous style with only

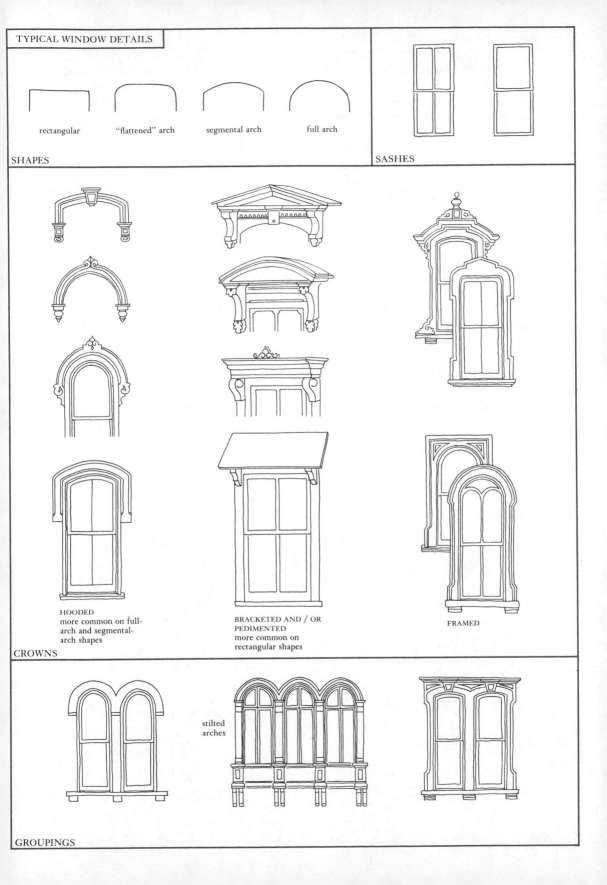

SHAPES

rectangular   "flattened" arch   segmental arch   full arch

SASHES

HOODED
more common on full-
arch and segmental-
arch shapes

BRACKETED AND / OR
PEDIMENTED
more common on
rectangular shapes

FRAMED

CROWNS

stilted
arches

GROUPINGS

hints of its Latin origin. Far less commonly, the formal Italian Renaissance town house, rather than the rural folk house, served as model; these were sometimes imported relatively intact. In purest form such Renaissance Revival houses are austere square or rectangular boxes with little decorative detailing save for formal window crowns (most typically a triangular pediment) and restrained cornice moldings. They are always of masonry (typically stone ashlar or stucco) and typically have horizontal belt courses and corner quoins. As in the originals, most American examples were town houses. Relatively few were built and only a handful survive. More commonly, one or more characteristics of the Renaissance town house were mixed with the general Italianate vernacular.

The first Italianate houses in the United States were built in the late 1830s; the style was popularized by the influential pattern books of Andrew Jackson Downing published in the 1840s and '50s (see the preceding chapter on Gothic Revival). By the 1860s the style had completely overshadowed its earlier companion, the Gothic Revival. Most surviving examples date from the period 1855–80; earlier examples are rare. The decline of the Italianate style, along with that of the closely related Second Empire style, began with the financial panic of 1873 and the subsequent depression. When prosperity returned late in the decade, new housing fashions—particularly the Queen Anne style—rose quickly to dominance.

Some writers have distinguished two chronological phases of Italianate styling: an earlier phase from the 1840s and '50s with relatively simple detailing and a later, more highly decorated phase from the 1860s and '70s (High Victorian Italianate). For domestic buildings, at least, this seems a rather artificial division. While the few surviving examples from the 1840s do have rather simple detailing, a survey of pattern book models and surviving examples shows a wide variation in decorative exuberance, with highly elaborated examples found from at least the early 1850s and simpler examples persisting through the 1870s.

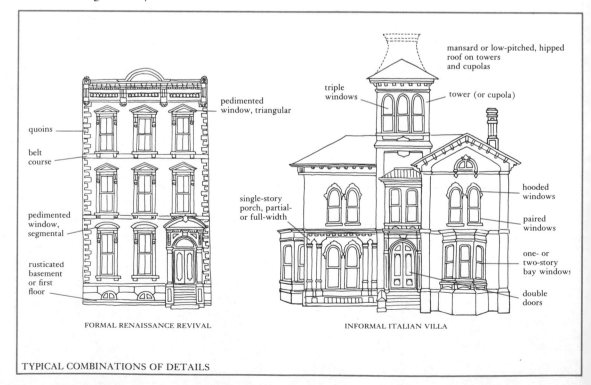

quoins

belt course

pedimented window, segmental

rusticated basement or first floor

pedimented window, triangular

FORMAL RENAISSANCE REVIVAL

mansard or low-pitched, hipped roof on towers and cupolas

triple windows

tower (or cupola)

single-story porch, partial- or full-width

hooded windows

paired windows

one- or two-story bay windows

double doors

INFORMAL ITALIAN VILLA

TYPICAL COMBINATIONS OF DETAILS

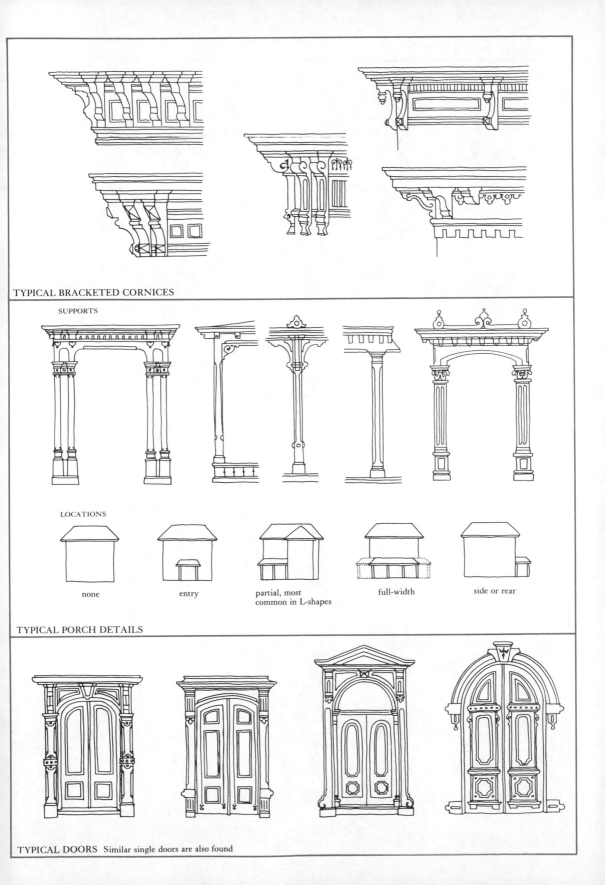

TYPICAL BRACKETED CORNICES

SUPPORTS

LOCATIONS

none   entry   partial, most   full-width   side or rear
                             common in L-shapes

TYPICAL PORCH DETAILS

TYPICAL DOORS Similar single doors are also found

1

2

4

6

7

SIMPLE HIPPED ROOF

1. Salisbury, North Carolina; mid-19th century. A simple masonry two-ranked example.

2. Hartford, Connecticut; mid-19th century.

3. Richmond, Virginia; 1857. Grant House. Note the heavy arched window hoods, also seen in Figure 5.

4. Austin, Texas; 1877. Tips House.

5. Cleveland, Ohio; 1862. Sanford House. Rear bay windows, seen here, and rear wings, one window wide (as in Figure 4), were common methods of bringing extra light and ventilation to narrow examples built on small city lots.

6. Savannah, Georgia; 1860. Mercer House; John S. Norris, architect. A lavishly detailed example with iron balconies, paired windows with elaborately bracketed hoods, and cornice brackets with double drops.

7. Providence, Rhode Island; 1853. Bowen House; Thomas Tefft, architect. This and Figure 8 reflect the more formal Renaissance town house tradition; note their cubic form, pedimented windows, quoins, and restrained entry porches.

8. St. Louis, Missouri; mid-19th century. Frost House. Note the rusticated first story (see additional comments under Figure 7).

3

5

8

SIMPLE HIPPED ROOF (con't)

9. Benicia, California; mid-19th century. A very simple, one-story, wood-clad example.

10. Austin, Texas; mid-19th century. A more elaborate one-story masonry example with quoins accenting the door, windows, and corners.

11. Louisville, Kentucky; mid-19th century. Note the use of segmentally arched windows on the first story with fully arched windows above.

12. Bloomington, Wisconsin; 1877. Ballantine House. The matching pair of bay windows on the front facade is unusual.

13. Salisbury, North Carolina; 1868. Murdoch-Wiley House. Occasionally the side-gabled roof form was substituted for the more typical Italianate hipped roof as in this example. Note the unusual use of paired brackets placed on top of pilasters.

14. Fort Smith, Arkansas; ca. 1880. Bonneville House. Note the handsome paired brackets and windows in the elaborated frieze band.

15. Macon, Georgia; 1860. Johnston House; James B. Ayres, architect. A large and elaborate three-story example raised on a full basement. An octagonal cupola and small round windows light the third story. Note the unusually heavy bracketed pediments above second-story windows on the front facade.

9

11

13

14

10

12

15

CENTERED GABLE

1. Selma, Alabama; mid-19th century. White House. A simple wood-clad example.

2. Oxford, Mississippi; 1878. Howry House. The two-story porches are unusual, as is their recessed position under the main roof of the house.

3. Raleigh, North Carolina; 1873. Andrews House; G. S. H. Appleget, architect. The small room on the left is a later addition.

4. Columbus, Indiana; 1864. Storey House; James Perkenson, architect. This three-ranked masonry example has simplified, but refined, detailing.

5. Richmond, Virginia; 1858. Haxall House. Contrast the ornate detailing here with the restrained detailing of Figure 4. Note the curved centered "gable," the cupola, and the pattern of paired and single windows.

6. Louisville, Kentucky; ca. 1870, porch ca. 1885. Field House. Bracketed and pedimented windows as well as quoins are used on both the main facade and the gabled central projection.

7. Richmond, Kentucky; 1864. Whitehall; Lewinski and McMurtry, architects. Note the unusual three-part design—a front-gabled central section is flanked by two wings, each with a centered gable; note also the full-height pilasters used across the entire facade.

8. Tarboro, North Carolina, vicinity; 1859. Coolmore Plantation. Rather than the more common centered gable, this unusual example has paired side gables. Note the cupola with centered gable.

7

2

3

5

6

8

ASYMMETRICAL

1. Selma, Alabama; mid-19th century. The simple gable-front-and-wing is a common Italianate form. Figures 2 and 3 are also examples of this type.

2. Clintonville, Kentucky; 1881. Crim House.

3. Salisbury, North Carolina; late 19th century.

4. Fort Smith, Arkansas; late 19th century. An unusual example showing Italianate detailing superimposed on a steeply pitched roof with a dominant front gable and dormer borrowed from the Gothic Revival.

5. Salem, Oregon; 1880. Port House. This narrow, deep house form was designed for a narrow urban lot.

6. Raleigh, North Carolina; ca. 1872. Merrimon House. This example has a second, more shallow wing and porch (left) added to the basic gable-front-and-wing form.

7. Oakland, California; mid-19th century. Camran House. Many asymmetrical Italianate examples are formed by the addition of a single large bay window to the basic cubic shape as in this example and Figure 8.

8. Penfield, New York; 1878. Hill and Hollow. A smaller version of Figure 7, this time executed in masonry with a cupola.

Romantic Houses: Italianate

TOWERED

1. South Stockton, New York; mid-19th century. Figures 1, 4, and 7 illustrate progressively more elaborate versions of a tower embraced by the wings of a gable-front-and-wing plan, a favorite Italianate arrangement.

2. Cherry Creek, New York; mid-19th century. Frost House. An unusual composition which builds from a one-story wing (in shadow at left) to the two-story central block to a three-story tower.

3. Hartford, Connecticut; mid-19th century.

4. Lexington, Kentucky; mid-19th century.

5. Marshalltown, Iowa; 1875. Although classical columns are frequently used as porch supports on Italianate houses (see figures 7 and 8), this large porch is probably a later addition (paired columns and columns raised on pedestals were uncommon before the 1890s).

6. Raleigh, North Carolina; ca. 1880. Centered towers are common in Second Empire houses, but Italianate examples, such as this, are unusual. Note how this placement produces a balanced, classical appearance even with the asymmetrical porch.

7. Portland, Maine; 1863. Morse House; Henry Austin, architect. An exceptional landmark example with numerous formal details. Note the segmental and the pedimented window crowns with brackets, as well as the quoins, classical columns, and balustrade.

8. San Antonio, Texas; ca. 1876, 1882, 1890. Norton House. In its final form this is a most unusual Italianate house based on formal Renaissance models.

4

7

FRONT-GABLED ROOF

1. Chicago, Illinois; mid-19th century.

2. Buffalo, New York; 1870–78. Tifft Houses. These examples show how the front-gabled form is well adapted to narrow urban lots.

3. New Orleans, Louisiana; mid-19th century. The bracketed wooden canopy over the second-story porch is a common New Orleans innovation on both one- and two-story houses. The full-length windows hark back to the earlier French Colonial building traditions of the region.

4. Washington, District of Columbia; mid-19th century. Although full-width porches are found throughout the country, they are most common in areas with hot summers.

5. Union Springs, Alabama; mid-19th century.

6. New London, Connecticut; mid-19th century.

7. Meriden, Connecticut; ca. 1868. Smith House. Cross gables extending outward the width of a single window or door are often added for light and ventilation toward the rear of front-gabled examples (see also Figure 8).

8. Iowa City, Iowa; 1882. Koza House. Note the unusually robust detailing of the bracketed cornice, flattened-arch window crowns, and door hood.

1

3

4

7

2

5

6

8

TOWN HOUSE

1. Benicia, California; mid-19th century. The cornice and parapet form a false front on this small, wood-clad example (see also Figure 5).

2. Savannah, Georgia; 1877.

3. Philadelphia, Pennsylvania; ca. 1865; Weightman House. An example inspired by formal Renaissance models.

4. Richmond, Virginia; mid-19th century.

5. San Francisco, California; ca. 1880. Stadtmuller House; P. R. Schmidt, architect. Most early Italianate California town houses have flat fronts, as in Figure 1. Later examples more often have elaborate ornamentation and large bay windows, as in this example.

6. Richmond, Virginia; 1861 and 1859. Putney Houses. Note how these detached townhouses are closely spaced with full windowless walls.

7. Pittsburgh, Pennsylvania; mid-19th century. Note the incised Eastlake detailing in the door surround and window crowns.

8. New York, New York; mid-19th century. Residential New York City was once dominated by blocks of attached Italianate brownstone townhouses such as these; some neighborhoods still have many surviving examples.

1

3　　4

5

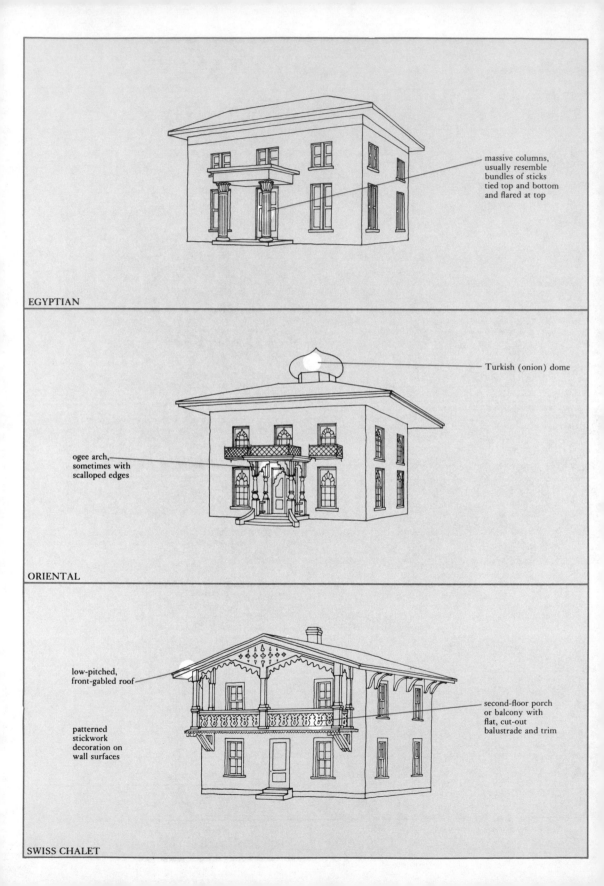

massive columns,
usually resemble
bundles of sticks
tied top and bottom
and flared at top

EGYPTIAN

Turkish (onion) dome

ogee arch,
sometimes with
scalloped edges

ORIENTAL

low-pitched,
front-gabled roof

patterned
stickwork
decoration on
wall surfaces

second-floor porch
or balcony with
flat, cut-out
balustrade and trim

SWISS CHALET

Exotic Revivals

Three principal types of exotic decorative ornament were occasionally used on romantic era houses: Egyptian, Oriental, and Swiss Chalet. These define three very rare styles, which, for convenience, will be treated here as subunits of a single Exotic Revival movement. The Egyptian and Oriental revivals were patterned after similar movements taking place in 19th-century Europe. The Swiss Chalet style, in contrast, was a romantic borrowing from contemporary Swiss domestic practice.

EGYPTIAN

The handful (probably fewer than a dozen) surviving domestic examples superimpose Egyptian columns on otherwise Greek Revival or Italianate forms. These columns resemble massive bundles of sticks tied together at the top and bottom and flared at the top.

The European Egyptian Revival sprang from Napoleon's Egyptian campaign (1798–99), coupled with a subsequent scholarly interest in Egypt as a source for the more familiar architecture of classical Greece and Rome. In Europe, as in this country, Egyptian motifs were most often applied to public buildings.

ORIENTAL

The several dozen surviving examples are mostly hipped-roof Italianate cubes with ogee arches (sometimes with scalloped edges added) and oriental trim. Another favored feature was the Turkish (onion) dome; few of these survive on domestic buildings.

The Oriental Revival was inspired by increasing exploration and trade in the Far East during the late 18th and early 19th centuries. Numerous detailed accounts of travels in India and China led to a new appreciation of the complexities of oriental architecture. The resulting use of Far Eastern motifs in Europe and America was the longest-lived of the exotic movements; occasional examples were built throughout the 19th century.

SWISS CHALET

Most of the few dozen surviving examples have low-pitched front-gabled roofs with wide eave overhangs. A second-story porch or balcony with flat, cut-out patterned balustrade and trim is characteristic, as is patterned stickwork decoration on exterior walls. Some examples superimpose Swiss porches and trim on Greek or Gothic Revival forms.

The style was introduced into the United States by the romantic popularizer Andrew Jackson Downing, whose pattern book, *The Architecture of Country Houses* (1850), showed several Swiss models suitable for "bold and mountainous" sites.

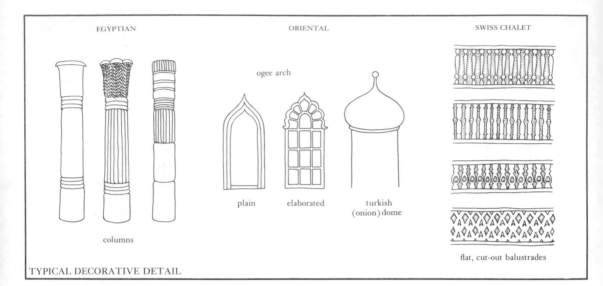

EGYPTIAN

ORIENTAL

SWISS CHALET

ogee arch

columns

plain

elaborated

turkish
(onion) dome

flat, cut-out balustrades

TYPICAL DECORATIVE DETAIL

3

4

5

1

EGYPTIAN

1. New Haven, Connecticut; 1837. Apthorp House; Alexander J. Davis, architect. Later additions surround the original cube house. The porch with its Egyptian columns is diminished by the additions above it.

2. Richmond, Virginia; 1847. Cabell House. The original house lacked both the bay windows and the porch balcony, making the two-story Egyptian columns still more prominent.

ORIENTAL

3. Rochester, New York; 1849. Brewster House. Oriental porch motif and window details on a cube-house form typical of the Italianate (see Figure 1 for an Egyptian counterpart).

4. Louisville, Kentucky; 1901. Discoe House. A very late example.

5. Church Hill, New York; 1874. Olana; Frederic E. Church, designer, Calvert Vaux, architect. An individualistic interpretation of the Exotic Revival by landscape painter Church.

SWISS CHALET

6. Chautauqua; New York, 1875; Miller House. Reported to have been precut in Akron, Ohio, and assembled on site.

7. Barrytown, New York, vicinity; 1867. Montgomery Place; Alexander Jackson Davis, architect.

8. Hartford, Connecticut; late 19th century.

2

6

7

8

Exotic Revivals 233

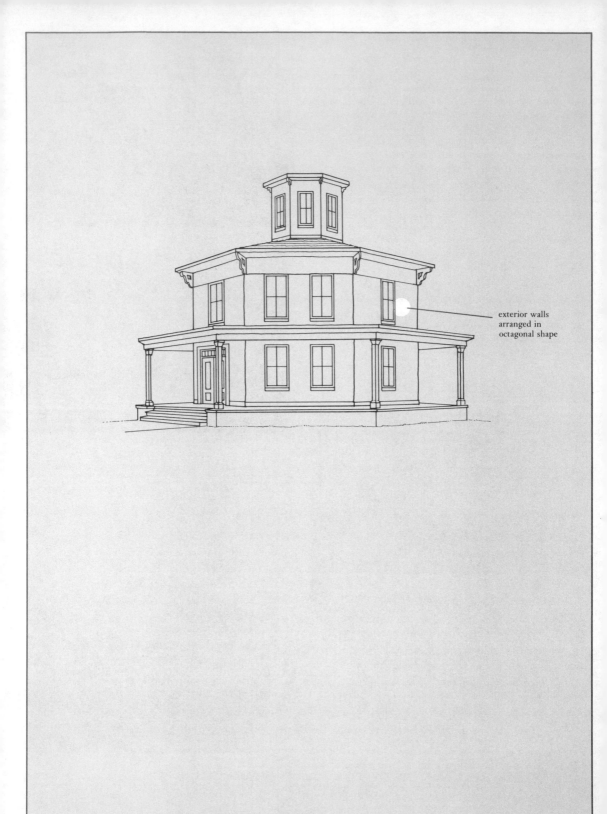

exterior walls
arranged in
octagonal shape

Octagon

The Octagon house is easily recognized by the eight-sided shape of the exterior walls. Most are two-story with low-pitched hipped roofs and wide eave overhangs; eave brackets are common. Occasional examples show six-, ten-, twelve-, or sixteen-sided forms; a few are round. About half have an octagonal cupola and most have porches. Many show Greek Revival, Gothic Revival, or Italianate decorative details; others lack detailing.

This is a very rare style; probably only a few thousand were originally built, mostly in New York, Massachusetts, and the Midwest. Several hundred of these survive; most were built in the decades of the 1850s and '60s.

The style owed its popularity to Orson S. Fowler, a lecturer and writer from Fishkill, New York, who in 1849 published an elaborate defense of its virtues entitled *The Octagon House, A Home for All.* Following Fowler, at least seven other pattern books of the 1850s also illustrated Octagon houses. Fowler stressed that an octagon encloses more floor space per linear foot of exterior wall than does the usual square or rectangle, thereby "reducing both building costs and heat loss through the walls." He also maintained that Octagons were superior to square houses in "increasing sunlight and ventilation" and in "eliminating dark and useless corners." As can be seen in the two typical plans shown in the accompanying drawings, he conveniently ignored interior room shapes, which were *not* octagonal and therefore still had "useless" corners, including triangular spaces not found in conventional shapes. Furthermore, much of this "increased sunlight and ventilation" went into pantries and closets; most rooms, in fact, have only a single exposure rather than the two commonly found in conventional houses. Such practical problems are undoubtedly responsible for the only modest success of the Octagon movement.

Fowler also advocated other improvements such as indoor plumbing, central heating, "board walls" made of lumber scraps and "gravel walls" of poured concrete. He was not generally concerned with decorative treatment beyond "the beauty of the octagon form itself," although many Octagons were built with decorative detailing. Fowler claimed his domestic use of the Octagon to be original but there were scattered earlier examples including Thomas Jefferson's summer house, Poplar Forest, completed in 1819. Octagonal wings and projections were also common in Adam houses (1780–1820).

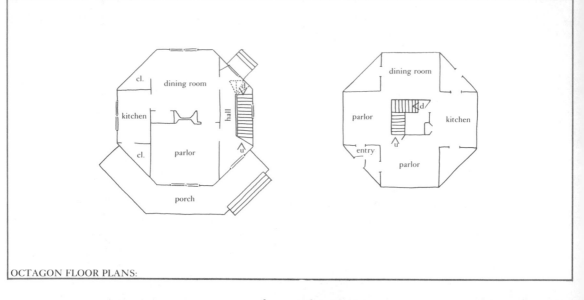

OCTAGON FLOOR PLANS:

2   3

6

OCTAGON

1. Eyota, Minnesota; ca. 1865. Mattison House. A small one-story example.

2. Williamson, New York; 1850. Sperry House. This house has twenty-inch-thick cobblestone walls that are covered with plaster. The porch is a later addition.

3. Geneva, New York; 1853. Moore House. Entrance steps, porch supports, and first- and second-story railings are all ornamental cast iron. Note the raised basement.

4. Hoosick Falls, New York; 1855. Estabrook House. The balustrade design is repeated in different scales on the roofs of the porch, the cupola, and the main house.

5. Wiscasset, Maine; 1855. Scott House. A two-and-one-half-story brick example with simple entry porch.

6. Monroe, Wisconsin; 1861. West House. This unusual house is a combination of several smaller octagonal sections rather than the usual large single octagon. Note the octagonal cupola, Italianate cornice detailing, and wraparound porch with cut-out balusters above.

7. Natchez, Mississippi, vicinity; 1862. Longwood; Samuel Sloan, architect. This landmark example shows Exotic Revival influence in the large onion dome and Italianate influence in the porch and the cornice detailing.

Victorian Houses

1860–1900

The long reign of Britain's Queen Victoria lasted from 1837 to 1901 and, in the most precise sense, this span of years makes up the Victorian era. In American architecture, however, it is those styles that were popular during the last decades of her reign—from about 1860 to 1900—that are generally referred to as "Victorian." During this period rapid industrialization and the growth of the railroads led to dramatic changes in American house design and construction. The balloon frame, made up of light, two-inch boards held together by wire nails, was rapidly replacing heavy-timber framing as the standard building technique. This, in turn, freed houses from their traditional box-like shapes by greatly simplifying the construction of corners, wall extensions, overhangs, and irregular ground plans. In addition, growing industrialization permitted many complex house components—doors, windows, roofing, siding, and decorative detailing—to be mass-produced in large factories and shipped throughout the country at relatively low cost on the expanding railway network. Victorian styles clearly reflect these changes through their extravagant use of complex shapes and elaborate detailing, features hitherto restricted to expensive, landmark houses.

Most Victorian styles are loosely based on Medieval prototypes. Multi-textured or multi-colored walls, strongly asymmetrical facades, and steeply pitched roofs are common features. Little attempt is made, however, at historically precise detailing. Instead, stylistic details are freely adapted from both Medieval and classical precedents. These exuberant mixtures of detailing, superimposed on generally Medieval forms, mean that most Victorian styles tend to overlap each other without the clear-cut stylistic distinctions that separate the Greek, Gothic, and Italianate modes of the preceding Romantic era. This architectural experimentation continued beyond Victorian times to reach a climax in the early decades of the 20th century when the first truly modern styles—Craftsman and Prairie—rose to popularity.

A second trend that was to end the Victorian era turned toward more precise copies of earlier styles, especially those of Colonial America. This movement began with the Centennial celebrations of 1876 and picked up momentum through the 1880s and '90s to become dominant in the 20th century. Its influence is evident in the borrowed Georgian and Adam details seen in many late Victorian houses built in the Shingle and Queen Anne styles.

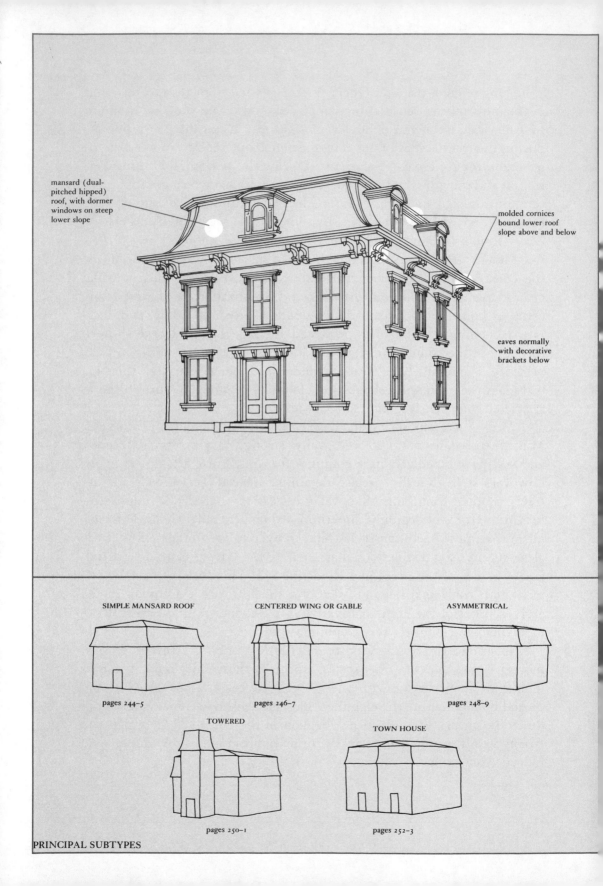

mansard (dual-
pitched hipped)
roof, with dormer
windows on steep
lower slope

molded cornices
bound lower roof
slope above and below

eaves normally
with decorative
brackets below

SIMPLE MANSARD ROOF

pages 244–5

CENTERED WING OR GABLE

pages 246–7

ASYMMETRICAL

pages 248–9

TOWERED

pages 250–1

TOWN HOUSE

pages 252–3

PRINCIPAL SUBTYPES

Second Empire

1855–1885

IDENTIFYING FEATURES

Mansard (dual-pitched hipped) roof with dormer windows on steep lower slope; molded cornices normally bound the lower roof slope both above and below; decorative brackets usually present beneath eaves.

PRINCIPAL SUBTYPES

Five principal subtypes can be distinguished:

SIMPLE MANSARD ROOF—These are symmetrical, either square or rectangular houses with the mansard roof uninterrupted except by dormers. Facade openings are typically three-ranked, less commonly five-ranked, and rarely two- or four-ranked. A few examples have central cupolas. This subtype makes up about 20 percent of Second Empire houses.

CENTERED WING OR GABLE—These are similar to the type just described but have either a centered gable, which usually echoes the mansard silhouette, or a mansard-roofed extension or wing centered on the front wall. About 20 percent of Second Empire houses in America are of this type.

ASYMMETRICAL—These are compound-plan houses, usually L-shaped, which lack towers. The forward-facing portion of the L may be either a full wing or merely a single strongly projecting bay window. About 20 percent of Second Empire houses are of this type.

TOWERED—About 30 percent of Second Empire houses have a rectangular or square tower. Sometimes it occupies the position where the wing joins the principal section of an L-plan house, but it is more commonly centered on the front facade. Occasionally it is placed off-center on the front or side facades. Typically the tower has a mansard roof with small dormer windows in each side.

TOWN HOUSE—Second Empire styling, along with the related Italianate style, dominated urban housing in the decades between 1860 and 1880. The mansard roof was particularly adapted to town houses, for it provided an upper floor behind the steep roof line, and thus made the structure appear less massive than most other styles with comparable interior space.

VARIANTS AND DETAILS

The style is characterized principally by its distinctive roof; five principal mansard silhouettes occur. Decorative patterns of color or texture are common in the roofing materials, as is iron cresting above the upper cornice. If a tower is present, it may have a roof silhouette different from that of the main house; the convex and ogee (S-curve) shapes, in particular, are more common on towers than on houses. Dormers and dormer windows appear in a great variety of styles. Beneath the distinctive roof line, Second Empire houses have details that are similar to those of the closely related Italianate style. Many show Italianate brackets at the cornice line; note, however, that Second Empire houses normally have less eave overhang than do Italianate examples. Window, door, and porch details are similar to those used in the Italianate style (see the drawings of those details in the Italianate chapter). Unelaborated windows, usually arched above, are also common on Second Empire houses but are rare in Italianate examples.

OCCURRENCE

Second Empire was a dominant style for American houses constructed between 1860 and 1880, although the first examples were built in the 1850s and late examples were not uncommon in the 1880s. The style was most popular in the northeastern and midwestern states. It is less common on the Pacific Coast and relatively rare in the southern states, although scattered examples survive in all regions settled before 1880.

COMMENTS

The contemporaneous Italianate and Gothic Revival styles were part of a Picturesque movement which looked to the romantic past for inspiration. In contrast, the Second Empire style was considered very modern, for it imitated the latest French building fashions. The distinctive roof was named for the 17th-century French architect François Mansart. Its use was extensively revived in France during the reign of Napoleon III (1852–70), France's Second Empire, from which the style takes its name. Exhibitions in Paris in 1855 and 1867 helped to popularize the style in England, from whence it spread to the United States. The boxy roof line was considered particularly functional because it permitted a full upper story of usable attic space. For this reason the style became popular for the remodeling of earlier buildings as well as for new construction. The Second Empire style was used for many public buildings in America during the Grant administration (1869–77) and has been facetiously called the General Grant style. It rapidly passed from fashion following the panic of 1873 and the subsequent economic depression.

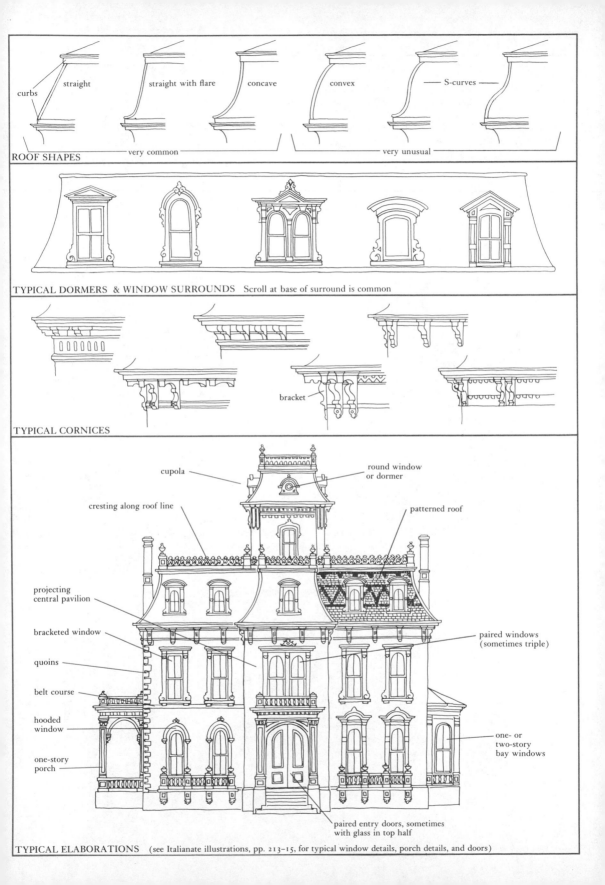

ROOF SHAPES

curbs — straight — straight with flare — concave — convex — S-curves

very common — very unusual

TYPICAL DORMERS & WINDOW SURROUNDS Scroll at base of surround is common

TYPICAL CORNICES

bracket

TYPICAL ELABORATIONS (see Italianate illustrations, pp. 213–15, for typical window details, porch details, and doors)

cupola

round window or dormer

cresting along roof line

patterned roof

projecting central pavilion

bracketed window

quoins

belt course

hooded window

one-story porch

paired windows (sometimes triple)

one- or two-story bay windows

paired entry doors, sometimes with glass in top half

SIMPLE MANSARD ROOF

1. Union Springs, Alabama; mid-19th century. The brackets above the central dormer and under the molded cornice at the roof top are an unusual feature.

2. Peru, Indiana; 1865–1870. Kilgore House. This small example has unusually elaborate detailing. Note the rusticated stone basement facade.

3. Cambridge, Massachusetts; 1860.

4. Cambridge, Massachusetts; 1864. Charles Wellington, builder. This example has paired first-story windows, plus matching entry and side porches.

5. St. Louis, Missouri; mid-19th century. Kayser House. An unusual stone facade.

6. Baltimore, Maryland; 1847. Pratt House. Note the roof cresting and entry porch with classical columns.

CENTERED WING OR GABLE

1. Hallettsville, Texas; ca. 1880. Lay House. Note the patterned roof shingles and the metal cresting at the roof line.

2. Fredonia, New York: ca. 1857. Pringle House. A small, earlier porch was replaced in 1929 by the one shown.

3. Cambridge, Massachusetts; 1863. Note how the shape of the centered gable echoes the mansard roof line.

4. Tarrytown, New York; ca. 1870. Arcularius House. The round-arched porte-cochere in the center front may be a later addition.

5. Savannah, Georgia; 1873. Hamilton House; J. D. Hall, architect. Note the quoins and the slender, paired windows.

6. Southport, Connecticut; mid-19th century. Pomeroy House. The paired windows in the dormers are an unusual feature.

7. St. Paul, Minnesota; 1873. Ramsey House. The hooded windows here and in Figure 2 show the strong Italianate detailing often seen in this style.

ASYMMETRICAL

1. Meriden, Connecticut; 1879. Renton House. In this example and in Figure 3, forward-facing wings create the asymmetrical facade.

2. Corning, New York; mid-19th century. In this example and in Figure 4, two-story bay windows create an asymmetrical facade.

3. Denver, Colorado; 1885. Knight House.

4. St. Louis, Missouri; ca. 1879. Blair-Huse House; George I. Barnett, architect.

5. Fort Smith, Arkansas; mid-19th century. Here and in Figure 7 a forward-facing wing is combined with a two-story bay window to create the asymmetry.

6. Cleveland, Ohio; mid-19th century. Roche House. Note the strongly hooded windows borrowed from the contemporary Italianate style.

7. Portland, Oregon; ca. 1870. Falling House. An elaborately detailed example with two principal facades, one with a porte-cochere and the other with a partial porch and two-story bay window.

1

3

6

TOWERED

1. Salem, Virginia; 1882. Evans House. Figures 1, 4, and 5 show symmetrical examples with a central tower. Note the contrasting shapes of the tower roof and main roof in this example.

2. Raleigh, North Carolina; ca. 1875. Heck House. Figures 2, 3, 6, and 8 show examples with a tower embraced between two wings of the house. Note the concave tower roof and the convex main roof in this example.

3. Rhinebeck, New York; mid-19th century. Wager House. Note window surrounds similar to one of the typical dormers illustrated. First-story windows are triple-hung.

4. Omaha, Nebraska; 1886. Cornish House. Note the projecting bays on each side of the centered tower.

5. Auburn, Maine; ca. 1880. Jordan House; Charles A. Jordan, architect-builder. Note the arcaded front porch, also seen in Figure 8.

6. Indianapolis, Indiana; 1862. Morris House; Diedrich A. Bohlen, architect. Note the differing window designs in the four-and-one-half-story tower, as well as the absence of the elaborate window surrounds commonly seen in the style.

7. Des Moines, Iowa; 1869. Hubbell House; William W. Boyington, architect. An extremely large and elaborately detailed example with two towers.

8. Woodbury, New Jersey; mid-19th century. Green House. The mansard roof of this house shows the rare S-curve shape. Note the extensive metal cresting on the roof line. Similar cresting, once present in many examples, has usually deteriorated and been removed. Note also the unusual cupola atop the tower.

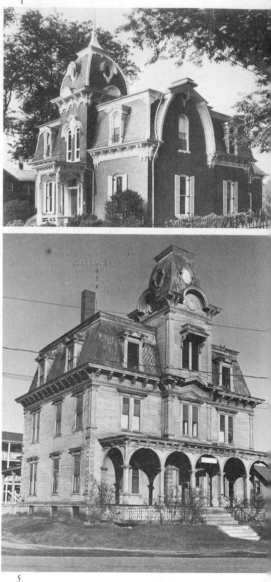

1

5

4

250

2

3

6, 7

8

TOWN HOUSE

1. Richmond, Virginia; mid-19th century. A detached urban example with a full-width porch.

2. St. Louis, Missouri; mid-19th century.

3. St. Louis, Missouri; mid-19th century. A row showing three different interpretations of the Second Empire detached town house. The roof on the center example may have been modified.

4. Washington, District of Columbia; mid-19th century. A row of three attached town houses.

5. Richmond, Virginia; mid-19th century. Note the slightly projecting entrance wing and side-facing bay window, an unusual feature in town houses.

6. New Haven, Connecticut; ca. 1871. A row of four attached town houses. Originally all matching, they have been somewhat modified by later alterations. The doorways, window hoods, and dormers are all heavily carved.

4

6

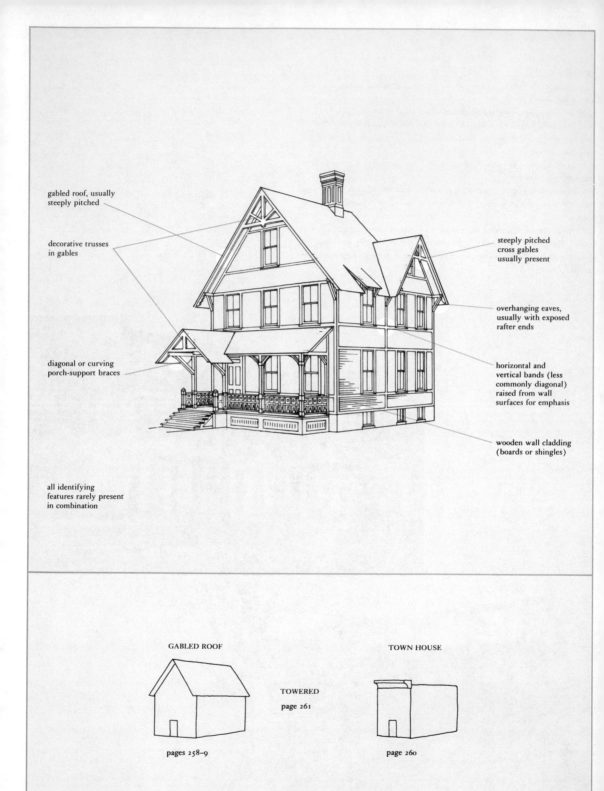

gabled roof, usually
steeply pitched

decorative trusses
in gables

diagonal or curving
porch-support braces

all identifying
features rarely present
in combination

steeply pitched
cross gables
usually present

overhanging eaves,
usually with exposed
rafter ends

horizontal and
vertical bands (less
commonly diagonal)
raised from wall
surfaces for emphasis

wooden wall cladding
(boards or shingles)

GABLED ROOF

pages 258–9

TOWERED
page 261

TOWN HOUSE

page 260

PRINCIPAL SUBTYPES

IDENTIFYING FEATURES

Gabled roof, usually steeply pitched with cross gables; gables commonly show decorative trusses at apex; overhanging eaves, usually with exposed rafter ends (normally replaced by brackets in town houses); wooden wall cladding (shingles or boards) interrupted by patterns of horizontal, vertical, or diagonal boards (stickwork) raised from wall surface for emphasis; porches commonly show diagonal or curved braces. (Few houses show all of these features in combination.)

PRINCIPAL SUBTYPES

Three principal subtypes occur:

GABLED ROOF—This subtype includes all examples of the style other than houses with towers and town houses with flat roofs. Both vertical and horizontal stickwork are normally present. Roofs may be either side- or front-gabled; secondary cross gables are common. A few examples have either mansard or steeply pitched hipped roofs. Late transitional examples may have hipped roofs with lower cross gables, a form that is more characteristic of the succeeding Queen Anne style.

TOWERED—These are similar to the type just described but with the addition of a square or rectangular tower.

TOWN HOUSE—These are flat-roofed urban houses with stick detailing. Normally they show only *vertical* stickwork terminating in brackets beneath an overhanging cornice. Most also have squared bay windows.

VARIANTS AND DETAILS

The style is defined primarily by decorative detailing—the characteristic multi-textured wall surfaces and roof trusses whose stickwork faintly mimics the exposed structural members of Medieval half-timbered houses. Varied patterns of wood siding and shingles are applied in the square and triangular spaces created by the stickwork. This detailing was applied to a variety of mid-19th-century house shapes; most show one-story porches, either entry or full-width. Other typical details are shown in the accompanying drawings.

OCCURRENCE

Although pattern books of the day show many examples of the style, relatively few were constructed in comparison with the contemporaneous Italianate or Second Empire styles. Gabled examples survive principally in the northeastern states and date from the 1860s and '70s (replacement of the characteristic wall patterns, and loss of other detailing, has undoubtedly obscured many examples). Surviving town houses are concentrated in San Francisco, where rapid growth and an abundance of lumber favored wooden urban houses. There the Stick tradition developed its own distinctive idiom, which appears to have peaked in the 1880s, after the style was passing from fashion in the Northeast.

COMMENTS

The Stick style is a transitional style which links the preceding Gothic Revival with the subsequent Queen Anne; all three styles are free adaptations of Medieval English building traditions. Unlike early Gothic Revival houses, the Stick style stressed the wall surface itself as a decorative element rather than merely as a plane with the principal decorative detailing applied at the doors, windows, or cornices. The later polychromed subtype of the Gothic Revival, like the Stick style, emphasized patterned wall surfaces, but was executed in masonry rather than wood. Because of this emphasis, the Stick style is considered by some authorities to be simply the wooden version of the polychromed or High Victorian Gothic. The emphasis on patterned wood walls seen in the Stick style was still further developed in the succeeding Queen Anne style.

The Stick style grew from the Picturesque Gothic ideals of Andrew Jackson Downing (page 200) and flourished in house pattern books of the 1860s and '70s. Although its proponents lauded the structural honesty of the style, the visible stickwork, unlike true half-timbering, was merely applied decoration with no structural relation to the underlying balloon-frame construction. During the 1880s the style was rapidly replaced by the closely related Queen Anne movement, which was to become far more influential and widespread.

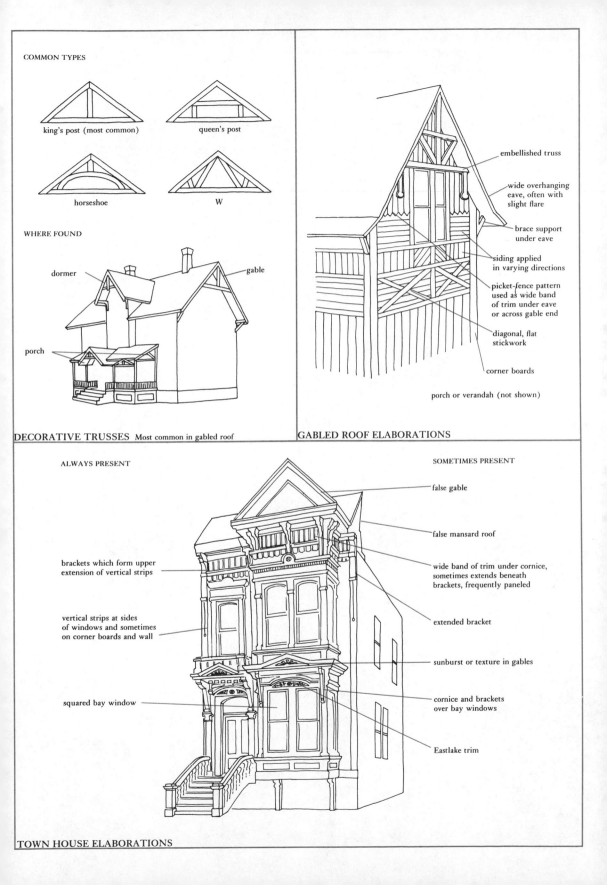

COMMON TYPES

king's post (most common)

queen's post

horseshoe

W

WHERE FOUND

dormer

gable

porch

DECORATIVE TRUSSES Most common in gabled roof

GABLED ROOF ELABORATIONS

embellished truss

wide overhanging eave, often with slight flare

brace support under eave

siding applied in varying directions

picket-fence pattern used as wide band of trim under eave or across gable end

diagonal, flat stickwork

corner boards

porch or verandah (not shown)

TOWN HOUSE ELABORATIONS

ALWAYS PRESENT

SOMETIMES PRESENT

brackets which form upper extension of vertical strips

vertical strips at sides of windows and sometimes on corner boards and wall

squared bay window

false gable

false mansard roof

wide band of trim under cornice, sometimes extends beneath brackets, frequently paneled

extended bracket

sunburst or texture in gables

cornice and brackets over bay windows

Eastlake trim

1

3

4

6

7

GABLED ROOF

1. Hartford, Connecticut; late 19th century. A very simple example with stick detailing only in the trussed gables and porch.

2. Wichita, Kansas; ca. 1878. Miller House. An example that is transitional from the Stick to the Queen Anne. The hipped roof has cross gables and the diagonal porch supports are turned spindles.

3. Portland, Oregon; late 19th century. Welty House. An example with vertical wood cladding in the gable, horizontal cladding on the main wall surfaces, and diagonal cladding below the first-story windows.

4. Honeoye Falls, New York; ca. 1875. Note the trusses supporting small roofs over the first-floor windows and the trussed balcony in the gable.

5. Benicia, California; late 19th century. This California house has low roof pitch and dominantly vertical stickwork.

6. New Bedford, Massachusetts; 1870. Smith House. The gable end has vertical, horizontal, and diagonal stickwork.

7. Newport, Rhode Island; 1863. Griswold House; Richard Morris Hunt, architect. A well-preserved landmark example; all the style's identifying features are present.

8. Cambridge, Massachusetts; 1878. The cut-away bay windows are precursors of a popular Queen Anne feature. The stickwork is confined to bands below the windows. Additional stickwork may well have originally been present on this and all other examples; such applied ornamentation is quite susceptible to deterioration and was commonly removed entirely rather than repaired or replaced.

5

8

TOWERED

1. Rochester, New York; late 19th century. The picket-fence pattern is used as trim under the eave line and across the gable end.

2. San Diego, California, 1887. Sherman House.

3. Fergus Falls, Minnesota; 1870. Clement House. Here the picket-fence pattern is used as frieze below the porch roof and below the tower eave.

4. Stony Creek, Connecticut; 1878. Villa Vista; Henry Austin, architect. Note the unusual two-tiered porch and the elaborate curving porch supports and decorative trussing.

5. Richfield Springs, New York; late 19th century. Hinds House. Note the very high pitch of the tower roof. Square towers are typical of Stick houses, whereas round towers are most common in the related Queen Anne style.

TOWN HOUSE

1. San Francisco, California; late 19th century. A double house (two identical attached houses).

2. San Francisco, California; late 19th century.

3. San Francisco, California; late 19th century. An unusual example of a narrow town house with a massive tower.

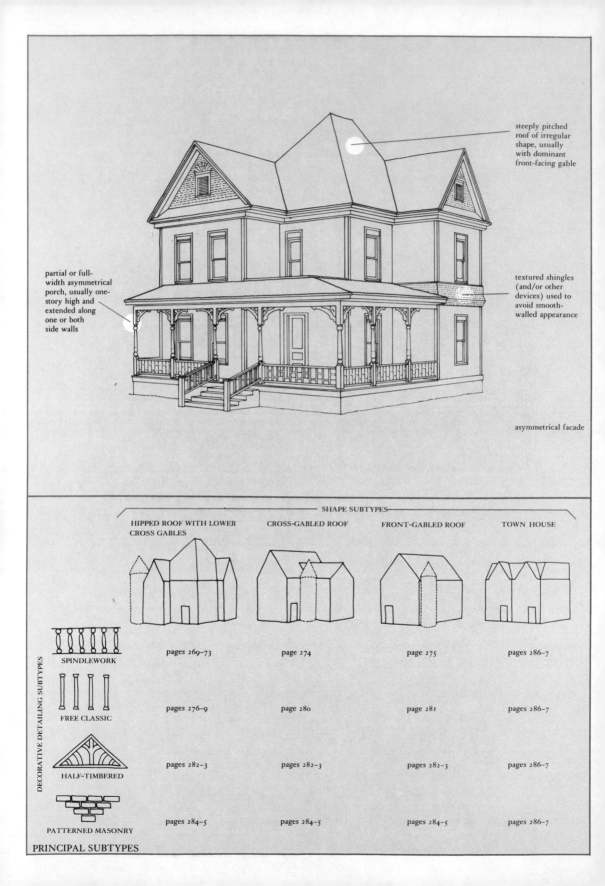

steeply pitched roof of irregular shape, usually with dominant front-facing gable

textured shingles (and/or other devices) used to avoid smooth-walled appearance

partial or full-width asymmetrical porch, usually one-story high and extended along one or both side walls

asymmetrical facade

PRINCIPAL SUBTYPES

SHAPE SUBTYPES

	HIPPED ROOF WITH LOWER CROSS GABLES	CROSS-GABLED ROOF	FRONT-GABLED ROOF	TOWN HOUSE
SPINDLEWORK	pages 269–73	page 274	page 275	pages 286–7
FREE CLASSIC	pages 276–9	page 280	page 281	pages 286–7
HALF-TIMBERED	pages 282–3	pages 282–3	pages 282–3	pages 286–7
PATTERNED MASONRY	pages 284–5	pages 284–5	pages 284–5	pages 286–7

DECORATIVE DETAILING SUBTYPES

IDENTIFYING FEATURES

Steeply pitched roof of irregular shape, usually with a dominant front-facing gable; patterned shingles, cutaway bay windows, and other devices used to avoid a smooth-walled appearance; asymmetrical facade with partial or full-width porch which is usually one story high and extended along one or both side walls.

PRINCIPAL SUBTYPES

Queen Anne houses are most conveniently subdivided into two sets of overlapping subtypes. The first is based on characteristic variations in *shape;* the second on distinctive patterns of *decorative detailing.*

SHAPE SUBTYPES

Four principal shape subtypes can be distinguished:

HIPPED ROOF WITH LOWER CROSS GABLES—Over half of all Queen Anne houses have a steeply hipped roof with one or more lower cross gables. Most commonly there are two cross gables, one front-facing and one side-facing, both asymmetrically placed on their respective facades. Unlike most hipped roofs, in which the ridge runs parallel to the front facade, Queen Anne hipped ridges sometimes run front-to-back, parallel to the side of the house. Others have pyramidal roofs with no ridge or merely a small flat deck crowning the hip. The hipped portion of the roof may have a gable-on-hip added; dormers and additional gables are common. A tower, when present, is most commonly placed at one corner of the front facade. The roof form of this subtype is among the most distinctive Queen Anne characteristics and occurs in examples ranging from modest cottages to high-style landmarks.

CROSS-GABLED ROOF—About 20 percent of Queen Anne houses have simple cross-gabled roofs without a central, hipped unit. These are normally of L-shaped plan; a tower, when present, is usually embraced within the L.

FRONT-GABLED ROOF—About 20 percent of Queen Anne houses have a full-width front gable which dominates the front facade. This form occurs most frequently in detached urban houses. A tower, when present, is usually placed at one corner of the front facade.

TOWN HOUSE—Detached Queen Anne urban houses usually have front-gabled roofs (as in the type just described). Attached row houses are uncommon but occur in both gabled and flat-roofed forms. Each attached unit may be individually distinguishable on the facade or may be part of a larger facade design.

DECORATIVE DETAILING SUBTYPES

Four principal subtypes can be distinguished on the basis of decorative detailing:

SPINDLEWORK—About 50 percent of Queen Anne houses have delicate turned porch supports and spindlework ornamentation, which most commonly occurs in porch balustrades or as a frieze suspended from the porch ceiling. Spindlework detailing is also used in gables and under the wall overhangs left by cutaway bay windows. Lacy, decorative spandrels and knob-like beads are also common ornamental elements in this subtype. Spindlework detailing is sometimes referred to as gingerbread ornamentation, or as Eastlake detailing (after Charles Eastlake, an English furniture designer who advocated somewhat similar design elements).

FREE CLASSIC—About 35 percent of Queen Anne houses use classical columns, rather than delicate turned posts with spindlework detailing, as porch supports. These columns may be either the full height of the porch or raised on a pedestal to the level of the porch railing; the railings normally lack the delicate, turned balusters of the spindlework type of Queen Anne house. Porch-support columns are commonly grouped together in units of two or three. Palladian windows, cornice-line dentils, and other classical details are frequent. This subtype became common after 1890 and has much in common with some early (asymmetrical) Colonial Revival houses (see pages 326–7).

HALF-TIMBERED—About 5 percent of Queen Anne houses have decorative half-timbering in gables or upper-story walls. Porch supports in this subtype are usually heavy turned posts with solid spandrels. Groupings of three or more windows are a common characteristic. This subtype occurs principally in the northeastern states and shares certain features with the early Tudor house (see page 355).

PATTERNED MASONRY—About 5 percent of Queen Anne houses have masonry walls with patterned brickwork or stonework and relatively little wooden detailing. Terra-cotta and stone decorative panels are frequently inset into the walls. Gable dormers, sometimes parapeted and shaped, are frequent. Examples of this subtype are usually high-style architect-designed houses which exhibit a wide variation in shape and detail. Most were built in large cities, particularly New York, Chicago, and Washington, D.C.; few have escaped subsequent demolition.

VARIANTS AND DETAILS

The Queen Anne, like the Stick style, uses wall surfaces as primary decorative elements. This is accomplished in two ways: (1) by avoiding plain flat walls through such devices as bays, towers, overhangs, and wall projections, and (2) by using several wall materials of differing textures wherever expanses of planar wall do occur.

DEVICES FOR AVOIDING FLAT WALL SURFACES—Irregularities in ground plan were facilitated by the widespread adoption of balloon framing techniques in the late 19th century (see page 36). Queen Anne houses make full use of this freedom by incorporating frequent bay windows and towers, as well as through the use of wall insets or projections which

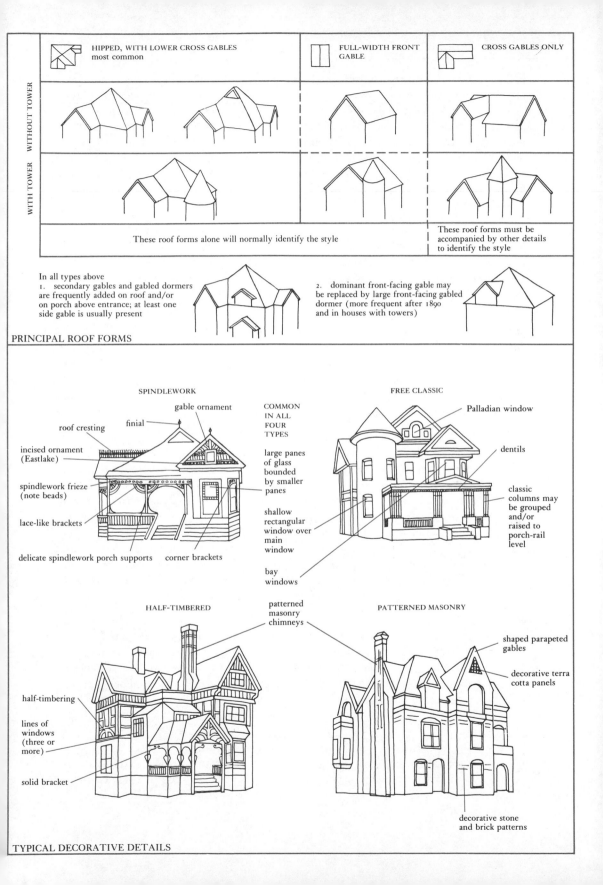

	HIPPED, WITH LOWER CROSS GABLES most common	FULL-WIDTH FRONT GABLE	CROSS GABLES ONLY
WITHOUT TOWER			
WITH TOWER			
	These roof forms alone will normally identify the style		These roof forms must be accompanied by other details to identify the style

In all types above
1. secondary gables and gabled dormers are frequently added on roof and/or on porch above entrance; at least one side gable is usually present

2. dominant front-facing gable may be replaced by large front-facing gabled dormer (more frequent after 1890 and in houses with towers)

PRINCIPAL ROOF FORMS

SPINDLEWORK

gable ornament

finial

roof cresting

incised ornament (Eastlake)

spindlework frieze (note beads)

lace-like brackets

delicate spindlework porch supports

corner brackets

COMMON IN ALL FOUR TYPES

large panes of glass bounded by smaller panes

shallow rectangular window over main window

bay windows

FREE CLASSIC

Palladian window

dentils

classic columns may be grouped and/or raised to porch-rail level

HALF-TIMBERED

patterned masonry chimneys

half-timbering

lines of windows (three or more)

solid bracket

PATTERNED MASONRY

shaped parapeted gables

decorative terra cotta panels

decorative stone and brick patterns

TYPICAL DECORATIVE DETAILS

provide random changes in the horizontal continuity of the wall plane. Other devices are used to avoid planar walls in *elevation*—that is, to provide a similar discontinuity of the wall plane *vertically;* these devices usually mimic the Medieval use of overhanging gables and upper stories. Particularly characteristic features are roof gables that overhang bay windows shaped into the wall below (cutaway bay windows). These occur in over half of all Queen Anne houses. In high-style examples entire gables or second stories are sometimes cantilevered out beyond the plane of the walls below. Many modest examples have less elaborate false overhangs; these are formed from moldings or pent roofs applied directly to the flat wall surfaces.

WALL TEXTURE VARIATIONS—Differing wall textures are a hallmark of Queen Anne houses. These are most commonly achieved with patterned wood shingles shaped into varying designs (note that this original shinglework patterning has been replaced by other materials on many surviving examples). In masonry houses, texture is obtained by using differing patterns of brick courses or brick of different colors; terra-cotta panels and other materials are also inserted for textural effect. A variety of materials are also commonly used on the different stories of Queen Anne houses (shingle over clapboard or over brick is most common).

PORCHES—Extensive one-story porches are common and accentuate the asymmetry of the facade. These always include the front entrance area and cover part or all of the front facade; they also commonly extend along one or both sides of the house. Second-story porches may be present; recessed porches sometimes occur in gables, second stories, or towers.

TOWERS—Towers are a common Queen Anne feature and may be round, square, or polygonal (the square form is the least common). These are of varying height and may rise from ground level, be cantilevered out at the second floor, or show other variations in position. In later examples the tower may appear to be less a separate design element than a mere bulge growing from the main mass of the house (see also the Shingle style, page 29). Round or polygonal wooden towers are particularly characteristic of the Queen Anne (round masonry towers may be Richardsonian Romanesque; square towers are more common on Stick, Italianate, or Second Empire houses). Towers placed at a front facade corner are most often Queen Anne, whereas those embraced within an L or centered on the front facade are equally common in several other styles.

OTHER DETAILS—Door and window surrounds tend to be simple in Queen Anne houses. Window sashes usually have only a single pane of glass; a frequent elaboration has a single large pane surrounded by additional small or rectangular panes on one or more sides. Some later examples have curved glass in tower windows. Doors commonly have delicate incised decorative detailing and a single large pane of glass set into the upper portion. Gables are commonly decorated with patterned shingles or more elaborate motifs.

OCCURRENCE

This was the dominant style of domestic building during the period from about 1880 until 1900; it persisted with decreasing popularity through the first decade of this century. In the heavily populated northeastern states the style is somewhat less common than elsewhere. There, except for resort areas, it is usually more restrained in decorative

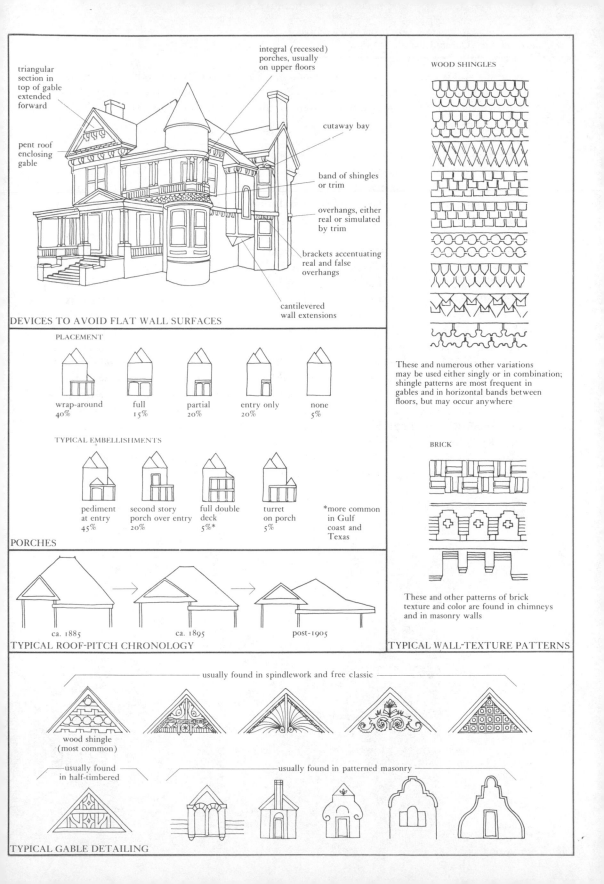

triangular section in top of gable extended forward

integral (recessed) porches, usually on upper floors

pent roof enclosing gable

cutaway bay

band of shingles or trim

overhangs, either real or simulated by trim

brackets accentuating real and false overhangs

cantilevered wall extensions

DEVICES TO AVOID FLAT WALL SURFACES

PLACEMENT

wrap-around 40%

full 15%

partial 20%

entry only 20%

none 5%

TYPICAL EMBELLISHMENTS

pediment at entry 45%

second story porch over entry 20%

full double deck 5%*

turret on porch 5%

*more common in Gulf coast and Texas

PORCHES

ca. 1885

ca. 1895

post-1905

TYPICAL ROOF-PITCH CHRONOLOGY

WOOD SHINGLES

These and numerous other variations may be used either singly or in combination; shingle patterns are most frequent in gables and in horizontal bands between floors, but may occur anywhere

BRICK

These and other patterns of brick texture and color are found in chimneys and in masonry walls

TYPICAL WALL-TEXTURE PATTERNS

— usually found in spindlework and free classic —

wood shingle (most common)

— usually found in half-timbered —

— usually found in patterned masonry —

TYPICAL GABLE DETAILING

detailing and is more often executed in masonry. Moving southward and westward the style increases steadily in dominance and ebullience; California and the resurgent, cotton-rich states of the New South have some of the most fanciful examples.

COMMENTS

The style was named and popularized by a group of 19th-century English architects led by Richard Norman Shaw. The name is rather inappropriate, for the historical precedents used by Shaw and his followers had little to do with Queen Anne or the formal Renaissance architecture that was dominant during her reign (1702–14). Instead, they borrowed most heavily from late Medieval models of the preceding Elizabethan and Jacobean eras. The half-timbered and patterned masonry American subtypes are most closely related to this work of Shaw and his colleagues in England. The spindlework and free classic subtypes are indigenous interpretations.

The half-timbered Watts-Sherman house built at Newport, Rhode Island, in 1874 is generally considered to be the first American example of the style. A few high-style examples followed in the 1870s and by 1880 the style was being spread throughout the country by pattern books and the first architectural magazine, *The American Architect and Building News.* The expanding railroad network also helped popularize the style by making pre-cut architectural details conveniently available through much of the nation.

The earliest American examples followed Shaw's early, half-timbered designs, but during the 1880s the inventive American spindlework interpretation became dominant. Throughout the 1880s and '90s a relatively few high-style urban examples continued to imitate Shaw's later English models, which were executed in masonry. In the decade of the 1890s the free classic adaptation became widespread. It was but a short step from these to the early, asymmetrical Colonial Revival houses which, along with other competing styles, fully supplanted the Queen Anne style after about 1910.

4

SPINDLEWORK:
HIPPED ROOF WITH LOWER CROSS GABLES

1. Biloxi, Mississippi; ca. 1900. A very simple example. Additional corner-bracket detailing was probably once present above the cutaway bay window, but is now missing (see the corner brackets still present on figures 2 and 5). The low roof pitch indicates a late construction date.

2. Santa Clara, California; late 19th century. Note the gable-on-hip roof (also present in figures 1 and 5); these were most common on one- and one-and-one-half-story examples.

3. Union Springs, Alabama; late 19th century. Note the unusual dormer.

4. Clement, North Carolina, vicinity; ca. 1912. Autry House. The symmetrical placement of the two gables is unusual, as is the steep roof pitch in such a late example.

5. Cripple Creek, Colorado; 1896. Miller House. This one-and-one-half-story example has unusually fine detailing.

6

7

9

10

12

SPINDLEWORK: HIPPED ROOF
WITH LOWER CROSS GABLES (cont.)

6. Atlanta, Georgia; ca. 1893. Martin Luther King Birthplace.

7. Greensburg, Indiana; 1885–90. Woodfill House.

8. Meriden, Connecticut; c. 1890. Cahill House. Note the second-story porch over the entrance; the central hipped roof is mostly obscured behind the front gable.

9. San Antonio, Texas; 1886. This masonry example has a two-tiered porch and unusually low pitched gables, which hide a low-pitched hipped roof behind.

10. Union Springs, Alabama; late 19th century.

11. Muncie, Indiana; 1885–90. Kitselman House. Note the use of large curved wood arches rather than the more common lacy spandrels or spindlework frieze.

12. Fleischmanns, New York; 1895. Note the integral upstairs porch beneath the principal roofline and the turreted lower porch roof.

13. Elkader, Iowa; 1889. Stemmer House. Note the elaborate gable detailing; the hipped portion of the roof is hidden behind the gables.

8

11

13

14

16

19

15

SPINDLEWORK:
HIPPED ROOF WITH LOWER CROSS GABLES (cont.)

14. Lovelady, Texas, ca. 1895. Nelms House. Note the curved roof on the tower; such roofs are far less common than straight-sided examples.

15. Cambridge, Massachusetts; 1889. Note the absence of the typical front-facing gable; a hipped dormer is used here instead.

16. Santa Cruz, California; 1891. Gray House. Note how the tower is interrupted at the first-story level by a band of shingles and at the second-story level by a band of roofing. This clearly illustrates the typical Queen Anne aversion to smooth wall surfaces. Figures 17 and 18 also show interrupted towers.

17. San Francisco, California; 1886. Haas House. The central hipped roof is hidden by gables and tower. Note the unusually elaborate details of the wall surfaces.

18. Union Springs, Alabama; late 19th century. Note the S-shaped curve of the tower roof.

19. Laurens, South Carolina; ca. 1896. Davis House. Note the porch-roof turret and the delicate beaded spindlework frieze extending around the entire porch.

17   18

Victorian Houses: *Queen Anne*

SPINDLEWORK: CROSS-GABLED ROOF

1. Biloxi, Mississippi; ca. 1900. Even this small example has an ornamented and textured gable and cutaway bay window to avoid smooth wall surfaces. Compare this with page 312, Figure 1, a Folk Victorian example of similar shape.

2. Hartford, Connecticut; late 19th century.

3. New Haven, Connecticut; late 19th century.

4. Hillsboro, Texas; late 19th century. Note the wide gable overhang. The gable detailing and square tower are transitional to the closely related Stick style.

5. Orange, New Jersey; ca. 1880. Dodd House. Note the roof cresting, patterned chimney, and heavy turned porch supports. This early east coast example resembles many houses of the half-timbered Queen Anne subtype, but lacks half-timbered detailing.

SPINDLEWORK: FRONT-GABLED ROOF

1. Chicago, Illinois; late 19th century.

2. Rochester, New York; late 19th century. Front-gabled forms may have shallow cross gables extending outward the width of a single door or window, as seen in this example.

3. New Haven, Connecticut; late 19th century.

4. St. Paul, Minnesota; ca. 1896. Stevens House. This early photograph shows the elaborate wall-texture detailing that was originally present on many modest houses, but that rarely survives today.

5. Cambridge, Massachusetts; 1886. Parry House. Note the brick first story with wood shingling above. The porch has been modified.

FREE CLASSIC:
HIPPED ROOF WITH LOWER CROSS GABLES

1. Salisbury, North Carolina; late 19th century. Brown House.

2. Eutaw, Alabama; late 19th century. Note the Palladian window and recessed arch under the gable.

3. Salisbury, North Carolina; late 19th century. Gaskill House.

4. Dallas, Texas; ca. 1900. Arnold House. The shingled porch-support arches are unusual.

5. Cleveland, Ohio; late 19th century. Note the upper-story window sashes with a single central pane of glass surrounded by smaller panes.

6. Jacksonville, Oregon; 1893. Nunan House. The hipped central roof is hidden by the front gable in this photograph. Note the dominant, elaborately detailed front chimney.

7. Concord, North Carolina; late 19th century.

8. Warsaw, Indiana; ca. 1894. Wood House. Note the transoms above the windows, a frequent Queen Anne feature that often had decorative beveled or colored glass glazing.

1

4

5

7

9

11

12

14   15

FREE CLASSIC:
HIPPED ROOF WITH LOWER CROSS GABLES (cont.)

9. Union Springs, Alabama; late 19th century.

10. Dallas, Texas; ca. 1899. Wilson House.

11. Santa Clara, California; late 19th century.

12. New Haven, Connecticut; late 19th century.

13. Kirksville, Missouri; late 19th century. Still House. Note the shingled gable wall curving into the gable window, a motif that is more common in the Shingle style. Although of masonry, this house lacks patterning in the brick-wall surfaces. This and the classical columns differentiate it from the patterned masonry subtype.

14. New London, Connecticut; late 19th century. Note the unusual flared eaves and the decorative frieze beneath the gable.

15. Montgomery, Alabama; late 19th century. Note the dramatically exaggerated S-curved roof of the tower.

16. Concord, North Carolina; late 19th century. Although asymmetrical, this house has a centered entry and a suggestion of classical balance; it is transitional to some early examples of the Colonial Revival style.

13

16

FREE CLASSIC: CROSS-GABLED ROOF

1. Cambridge, Massachusetts; 1890. The siding and shutters are later additions.

2. Marshall, Michigan; 1884. Page House. Note the matching front and side porches with grouped columns set on pedestals. The short, broad tower is less common than more slender versions.

FREE CLASSIC: FRONT-GABLED ROOF

1. New Haven, Connecticut; late 19th century.

2. Hartford, Connecticut; late 19th century. Note the use of board siding on the first story, with shingles above, a common pattern. The two front doors indicate that this is a "two-decker" duplex with separate dwelling units on the first and second floors.

3. Denver, Colorado; late 19th century. Note the elaborate Palladian window with decorative swags that recur above the second-story porch.

4. San Francisco, California; late 19th century. Many San Francisco Queen Anne houses combine classical columns with elaborate spindlework detailing used elsewhere on the facade.

1

HALF-TIMBERED

1. Buffalo, New York; late 19th century. Note the row of multiple windows in the gable; such window rows are common only in this subtype (see also figures 2, 4, 6, 7, and 8).

2. Chicago, Illinois; 1888. Miller House; G. A. Garnsey, architect. Shows the close relationship of this subtype to the Tudor style that grew from it. The multiple wall materials (stone, stucco, wood, and wood shingles) and many changes in wall plane mark this house as Queen Anne.

3. Brookline, Massachusetts; late 19th century; E. A. P. Newcomb, architect.

4. Hartford, Connecticut; 1884. Day House; Francis Kimball, architect. Note the light-colored limestone walls banded with brownstone.

5. Brookline, Massachusetts; ca. 1880. Toby House. Note the paneled brick chimney (see also figures 1, 4, 6, 7, and 8); these are most common on half-timbered and patterned brick examples, although simply decorated chimney *tops* are seen in all subtypes.

6. Newport, Rhode Island; 1878. Baldwin House; Potter and Robinson, architects.

7. Rochester, New York; ca. 1880. Cutler House.

8. Newport, Rhode Island; 1876. Watts-Sherman House; H. H. Richardson, architect. This is regarded as the first American Queen Anne house.

4

6

2

3

5

7

8

PATTERNED MASONRY

1. New Haven, Connecticut; 1886. Treat House. It is hard to photograph the textured patterns in the dark red brick, typical of this subtype, in a manner that shows up well in reproduction.

2. Herkimer, New York; late 19th century. Suiter House.

3. New Haven, Connecticut; ca. 1895. Note the cornice patterns formed by the brickwork.

4. Hartford, Connecticut; late 19th century. George Keller, architect. The extensive full-width or wrap-around porches common on the spindle-work and free classic subtypes are rare on patterned masonry houses; usually only an entry porch is present, as seen here.

5. Hartford, Connecticut; late 19th century. The one-story wooden projection on the right is a later addition.

6. Cincinnati, Ohio; 1882. Bell House; S. Hannaford, architect. An example with stone, rather than brick, walls. Note the shaped, parapeted gables, a rare but characteristic feature of this subtype.

7. Chicago, Illinois; ca. 1884. Wells House; Wheelock and Clay, architects. Note extensive roof cresting here and in Figure 4.

8. Rochester, New York; ca. 1883. Harvey Ellis, architect. An American copy of a design by the English proponent of the Queen Anne style, Richard Norman Shaw.

1

4

7

TOWN HOUSE

1. Boston, Massachusetts; 1880. Note the false gable with a mansard roof behind. Sculptured terra-cotta tiles add richness to this facade.

2., 3. Savannah, Georgia; 1892. McMillan Houses. A row of attached town houses behind one unified facade. Figure 3 is a close-up detail of the patterned brickwork executed in two colors of brick.

4. Rochester, New York; 1870s. These are half-timbered examples.

5. Hartford, Connecticut; 1888.

6. Washington, District of Columbia; late 19th century. Many miles of these simplified, patterned brick row houses were built in eastern cities. Note the false gable roof; these have deteriorated and been removed from many remaining examples.

7. Cleveland, Ohio; ca. 1890.

8. Camden, New Jersey; 1886. Taylor House; Wilson Eyre, architect. A unique town house of limestone and brick with a large, shaped, parapeted gable.

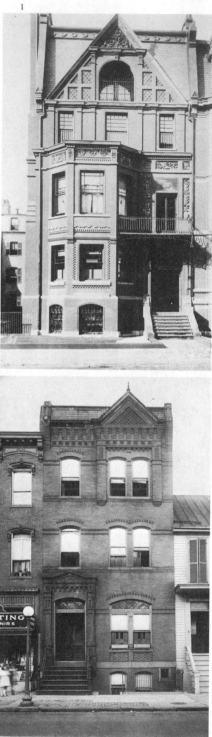

1

4

6

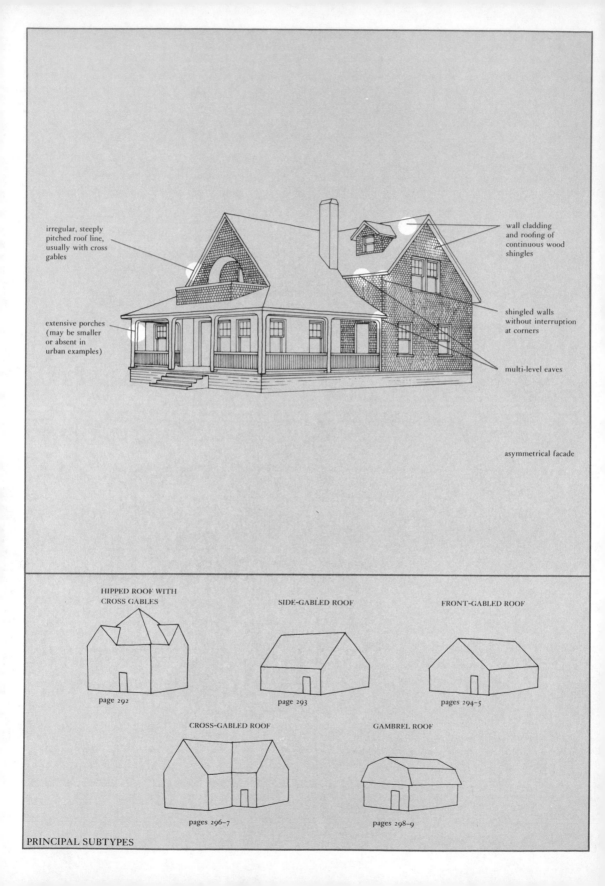

irregular, steeply pitched roof line, usually with cross gables

wall cladding and roofing of continuous wood shingles

extensive porches (may be smaller or absent in urban examples)

shingled walls without interruption at corners

multi-level eaves

asymmetrical facade

HIPPED ROOF WITH CROSS GABLES

page 292

SIDE-GABLED ROOF

page 293

FRONT-GABLED ROOF

pages 294–5

CROSS-GABLED ROOF

pages 296–7

GAMBREL ROOF

pages 298–9

PRINCIPAL SUBTYPES

IDENTIFYING FEATURES

Wall cladding and roofing of continuous wood shingles (shingled walls may occur on second story only; original wooden roofing now replaced by composition shingles on most examples); shingled walls without interruption at corners (no corner boards); asymmetrical facade with irregular, steeply pitched roof line; roofs usually have intersecting cross gables and multi-level eaves; commonly with extensive porches (may be small or absent in urban examples).

PRINCIPAL SUBTYPES

Five principal subtypes can be distinguished:

HIPPED ROOF WITH CROSS GABLES—About 15 percent of Shingle houses have hipped roofs with lower cross gables. Asymmetrical gable arrangements, similar to the typical Queen Anne shape, are most common, but Shingle houses may also show paired, symmetrical cross gables.

SIDE-GABLED ROOF—About 20 percent of Shingle houses have side-gabled roofs; many of these have asymmetrically placed towers on the front facade.

FRONT-GABLED ROOF—About 20 percent of Shingle houses have a front gable which dominates the main facade; subordinate cross gables and towers may be added.

CROSS-GABLED ROOF—About 20 percent of Shingle houses have cross-gabled roofs; most are of L or T plan and have secondary cross gables and dormers intersecting the principal roof line. Subordinate hipped sections may also be added.

GAMBREL ROOF—About 25 percent of Shingle houses have gambrel roofs. Normally a full second story is incorporated into the steeper, lower slope of the gambrel, giving a one-story appearance. Gambreled cross gables are usually present.

VARIANTS AND DETAILS

Unlike most of the 19th-century styles that preceded it, the Shingle does not emphasize decorative detailing at doors, windows, cornices, porches, or on wall surfaces. Instead it aims for the effect of a complex shape enclosed within a smooth surface (the shingled exterior) which unifies the irregular outline of the house. Most variants and details are designed to enhance either the irregularity of the shape or the uniformity of its surface. Decorative detailing, when present, is used sparingly.

Towers, found in about one-third of Shingle houses, are more likely to appear as partial bulges or as half-towers rather than as fully developed elements. Tower roofs are frequently blended into the main volume of the house by a continuous roof line. Porch supports are most commonly either slender, unadorned wooden posts or massive piers of stone or shingle cladding. Window surrounds are simple; bay windows, multiple windows, and walls curving into windows are common. Massive Romanesque or Syrian arches (see page 303) may be used on porches or entrances. Palladian windows and simple classical columns, both borrowed from the contemporaneous early phases of the Colonial Revival, are the most common decorative details.

OCCURRENCE

Most Shingle houses were built between 1880 and 1900, with a relatively few examples dating from the late 1870s and from the first decade of this century. The style began and reached its highest expression in seaside resorts of the northeastern states. Fashionable summer destinations such as Newport, Cape Cod, eastern Long Island, and coastal Maine had numerous architect-designed cottages in the style, many of which survive today. From this fashionable base, well publicized in contemporary architectural magazines, the style spread throughout the country, and scattered examples can be found today in all regions. It never gained the wide popularity of its contemporary, the Queen Anne style, and thus Shingle houses are relatively uncommon except in coastal New England.

COMMENTS

The Shingle style, like the Stick and spindlework Queen Anne, was a uniquely American adaptation of other traditions. Its roots are threefold: (1) From the Queen Anne it borrowed wide porches, shingled surfaces, and asymmetrical forms. (2) From the Colonial Revival it adapted gambrel roofs, rambling lean-to additions, classical columns, and Palladian windows. (3) From the contemporaneous Richardsonian Romanesque it borrowed an emphasis on irregular, sculpted shapes, Romanesque arches, and, in some examples, stone lower stories (some scholars consider the Shingle to be merely the wooden phase of the masonry Richardsonian Romanesque, but the styles also have many dissimilarities).

The Shingle style was an unusually free-form and variable style; without the ubiquitous shingle cladding it would be difficult to relate many of its different expressions. One reason for this great range of variation is that it remained primarily a high-fashion, architect's style, rather than becoming widely adapted to mass vernacular housing, as did the contemporaneous Queen Anne. Among the innovative designers working in the style were Henry Hobson Richardson and William Ralph Emerson of Boston; John Calvin Stevens of Portland, Maine; McKim, Mead & White, Bruce Price, and Lamb and Rich of New York; Wilson Eyre of Philadelphia; and Willis Polk of San Francisco.

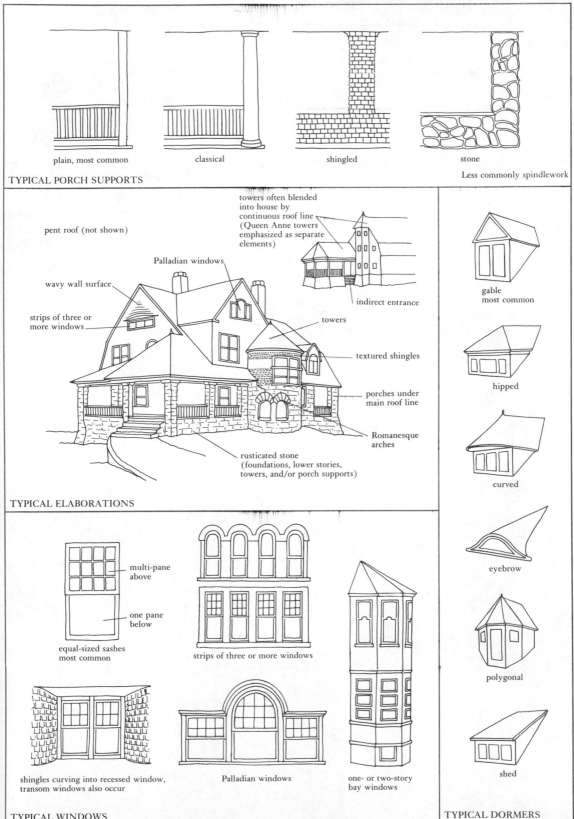

TYPICAL PORCH SUPPORTS

plain, most common

classical

shingled

stone

Less commonly spindlework

TYPICAL ELABORATIONS

pent roof (not shown)

wavy wall surface

strips of three or more windows

Palladian windows

towers often blended into house by continuous roof line (Queen Anne towers emphasized as separate elements)

indirect entrance

towers

textured shingles

porches under main roof line

Romanesque arches

rusticated stone (foundations, lower stories, towers, and/or porch supports)

TYPICAL DORMERS

gable most common

hipped

curved

eyebrow

polygonal

shed

TYPICAL WINDOWS

multi-pane above

one pane below

equal-sized sashes most common

strips of three or more windows

shingles curving into recessed window, transom windows also occur

Palladian windows

one- or two-story bay windows

HIPPED ROOF WITH CROSS GABLES

1. Dallas, Texas; late 19th century. Bookhout House. A transitional house with Queen Anne form, but Shingle porches and porte cochere.

2. New London, Connecticut; late 19th century. Note the varied dormer shapes—hipped, eyebrow, and gabled; the Palladian motif created above the line of gable windows; and the extensive porch with Romanesque arches.

3. Brookline, Massachusetts; late 19th century. E. A. P. Newcomb, architect. Note the rounded bay and oriel windows.

4. Blue Ridge Summit, Pennsylvania; late 19th century. Menz House. A large, symmetrical example.

5. Hartford, Connecticut; late 19th century. A unique Shingle house with a Tudor-influenced castellated tower and shaped, parapeted gables.

1

2

3

4

5

SIDE-GABLED ROOF

1. Emporia, Kansas; late 19th century. The wide shingles on this house are probably later additions.

2. Lexington, Kentucky; late 19th century. Note the three different dormer shapes crowded into the front roof.

3. Buffalo, New York; ca. 1885. Note the elaborate detailing of the side gable and the way the enormous tower seems to grow from the roof.

4. Brookline, Massachusetts; late 19th century. This early photograph shows the elaborate original wall detailing that has been lost over the years in most examples, as in Figure 5.

5. New Haven, Connecticut; 1900. Richard Williams, architect. This house has lost its original wood-shingled roof and diamond window panes (a few can still be seen in the side windows). Note the strong horizontal emphasis—it was once even more pronounced, with a porte cochere extending to the side.

FRONT-GABLED ROOF

1. Louisville, Kentucky; late 19th century. A modest urban example.

2. Montauk, New York; late 19th century. Benson House. A seaside example with extensive porches.

3. Newport, Rhode Island; late 19th century. Richardson House.

4. New Haven, Connecticut; 1889. A massive front gable that clearly dominates the small, shallow side gable marks this example as the front-gabled, rather than cross-gabled, subtype of the style.

5. Corning, New York; late 19th century. The tower and front facade are united by the extended front wall and the upper band of windows.

6. Corning, New York; late 19th century. Note the paneled chimney and patterned shingles.

7. Dallas, Texas; 1909. Miller House.

8. Bristol, Rhode Island; 1887. Low House; McKim, Mead and White, architects. A now-demolished landmark example of the style.

CROSS-GABLED ROOF

1. Baltimore, Maryland; late 19th century. The Gothic (pointed arch) windows are unusual in Shingle houses.

2. Meriden, Connecticut; ca. 1890. Hale House. Note the Romanesque arched entry porch.

3. Kansas City, Missouri; late 19th century.

4. Brookline, Massachusetts; late 19th century. The half-timbered detailing seen here and in Figure 7 is unusual in Shingle houses.

5. Cleveland, Ohio; late 19th century. McNairy House. This house, with its colonnaded porch, Palladian window, and overall symmetry shows a strong classical influence.

6. Newport, Rhode Island; 1883. Bell House; McKim, Mead and White, architects.

7. Tuxedo Park, New York; late 19th century. This large house lacks the unified facade seen in most examples of the style.

GAMBREL ROOF

1. Nebraska City, Nebraska; late 19th century. Morton House. The off-center doorway and the asymmetrical upper story emphasize the unusual roof form: the left half is gambreled, the right gabled.

2. Cincinnati, Ohio; late 19th century. The walls of these two houses have unusually large shingles.

3. Kansas City, Missouri; 1890. Alderson House. An uncommon three-story example.

4. Emporia, Kansas; late 19th century.

5. Wichita, Kansas; 1887.

6. New Haven, Connecticut; late 19th century. Note the dramatic use of windows of varying shape in the dominant front gambrel (also see Figure 5).

7. Salisbury, North Carolina; late 19th century. The cantilevered balcony over the entry is unusual.

8. Gainesville, Texas; late 19th century. Although this house has a side-gabled roof, the dominant front-facing gambrel places it in the gambrel subtype.

3

6

8

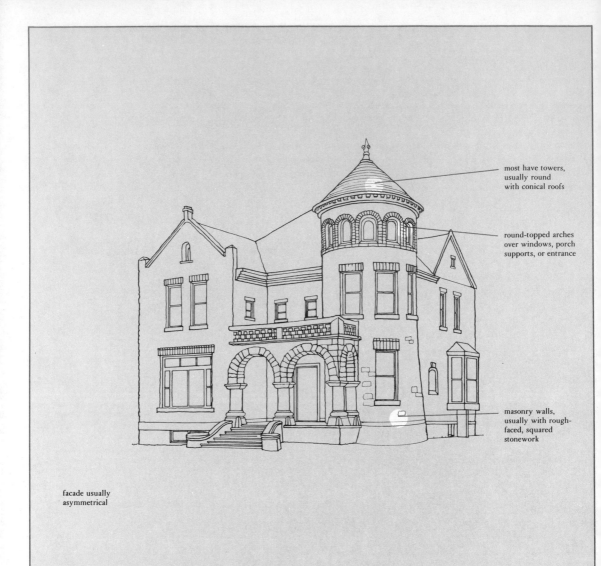

most have towers,
usually round
with conical roofs

round-topped arches
over windows, porch
supports, or entrance

masonry walls,
usually with rough-
faced, squared
stonework

facade usually
asymmetrical

**HIPPED ROOF WITH
CROSS GABLES**

pages 304–5

OTHER ROOF FORMS
page 306

TOWN HOUSE
page 307

PRINCIPAL SUBTYPES

Richardsonian Romanesque

IDENTIFYING FEATURES

Round-topped arches occurring over windows, porch supports, or entrance; masonry walls, usually with rough-faced, squared stonework; most have towers which are normally round with conical roofs; facade usually asymmetrical.

PRINCIPAL SUBTYPES

Three principal subtypes can be distinguished:

HIPPED ROOF WITH CROSS GABLES—About two-thirds of Richardsonian Romanesque houses have hipped roofs with one or more lower cross gables. Most commonly there are two cross gables, one front-facing and the other side-facing, each asymmetrically placed on its respective facade. This shape is similar to the typical Queen Anne roof form.

OTHER ROOF TYPES—A variety of other roof forms also occur on Richardsonian Romanesque houses. Among the most frequent are side-gabled, cross-gabled, mansard, and simple hipped roofs.

TOWN HOUSE—Richardsonian Romanesque was frequently used for detached urban houses, which typically have front-gabled or mansard roofs; attached row houses in this style are less common.

VARIANTS AND DETAILS

Richardsonian Romanesque houses are always of masonry and usually show at least some rough-faced, squared (ashlar) stonework. Frequently two or more colors or textures of stone or brick are combined to create decorative wall patterns. Wide, rounded (Romanesque) arches are a key identifying feature of the style. These may occur above windows or porch supports or over entryways. Most commonly the arches rest on squat columns, but some are supported on massive piers or are incorporated directly into wall surfaces. Column capitals and wall surfaces may be ornamented with floral or other decorative details. Windows are usually deeply recessed into the masonry wall and have only a single pane of glass per sash. The characteristic arched windows sometimes have small decorative columns (colonnettes) on each side. Groupings of three or more arched or rectangular windows occur in over half of the examples.

Towers occur in about 75 percent of Richardsonian Romanesque houses; these are most commonly round, although polygonal and squared versions are found. A second tower occurs in about 15 percent. Tower roofs are usually conical, but may be convex. Dormers are present in about half of Richardsonian Romanesque houses. Most commonly these are parapeted and gabled wall dormers, but hipped dormers, eyebrow dormers, and other variations occur.

OCCURRENCE

The innovative Boston architect Henry Hobson Richardson (1838–86) designed houses during the 1860s and '70s in the then fashionable Second Empire, Queen Anne, or Stick styles; in 1879–80 he executed the first of his few Romanesque houses, the rectory for his monumental Trinity Church in Boston. Richardson's Romanesque adaptations became very popular for large public buildings during the 1880s but he completed only a few more houses in the style before his premature death in 1886. Other architects, following Richardson's lead, also designed houses in the '80s, but these were uncommon. In 1888, a sympathetic monograph on Richardson's life and work was published which greatly increased interest in the style. Most domestic examples are an outgrowth of this revival and were built in the 1890s. Because they were always of solid masonry construction (masonry veneering techniques were not yet perfected), Richardsonian Romanesque houses were much more expensive to build than were those Late Victorian styles which could be executed in wood. For this reason, they are mostly architect-designed landmarks and were never common. Scattered examples occur throughout the country but are most frequent in the larger cities of the northeastern states.

COMMENTS

In the middle decades of the 19th century, European Romanesque models were sometimes used for American public and commercial buildings (the Romanesque Revival style), but these precedents reached American *houses* only in a later 19th-century form shaped by the powerful personality and talent of Henry Hobson Richardson. Born in Louisiana, Richardson attended Harvard and then studied architecture at the prestigious École des Beaux-Arts in Paris (he was only the second American to do so). He returned to the United States after the Civil War and opened an office in New York, which he subsequently moved to Boston. During the 1870s he evolved his strongly personal style, which incorporated Romanesque forms and which, like its mid-century predecessor, was applied principally to large public buildings. Unlike the earlier and more correct Romanesque revival, Richardson borrowed from many sources. He incorporated the polychromed walls seen in the contemporary late Gothic Revival (see page 209). His arches are frequently not truly Romanesque but Syrian, an early Christian form which springs from ground level rather than from a supporting pedestal. Most importantly, he stressed unusual, sculpted shapes which give his buildings great individuality. His followers were usually less inventive; most houses in this style merely add Romanesque detailing to the typical hipped-with-cross-gables shape of the then dominant Queen Anne style.

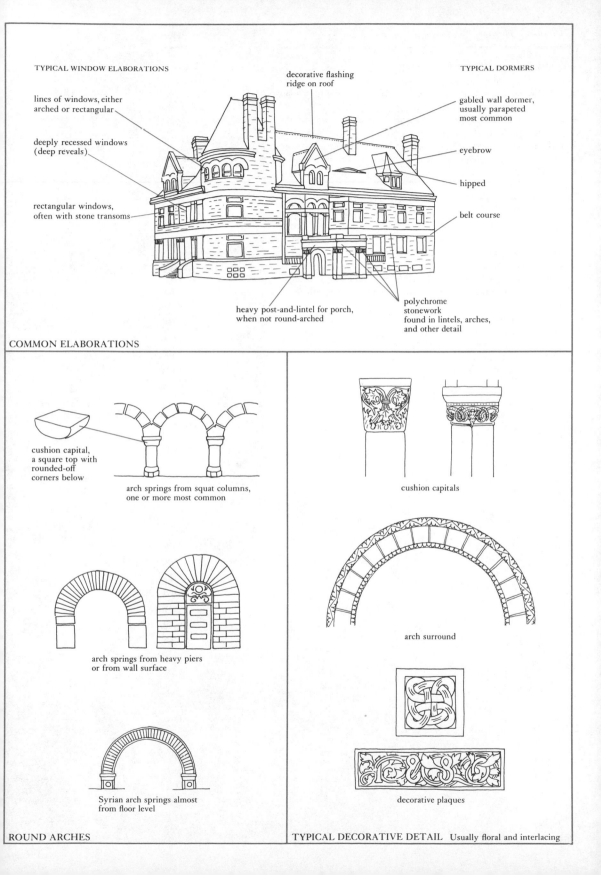

TYPICAL WINDOW ELABORATIONS

TYPICAL DORMERS

decorative flashing
ridge on roof

lines of windows, either
arched or rectangular

gabled wall dormer,
usually parapeted
most common

deeply recessed windows
(deep reveals)

eyebrow

hipped

rectangular windows,
often with stone transoms

belt course

heavy post-and-lintel for porch,
when not round-arched

polychrome
stonework
found in lintels, arches,
and other detail

COMMON ELABORATIONS

cushion capital,
a square top with
rounded-off
corners below

arch springs from squat columns,
one or more most common

cushion capitals

arch springs from heavy piers
or from wall surface

arch surround

Syrian arch springs almost
from floor level

decorative plaques

ROUND ARCHES

TYPICAL DECORATIVE DETAIL Usually floral and interlacing

HIPPED ROOF WITH CROSS GABLES

1. St. Charles, Missouri; 1885. Atkinson House. This example is unusual in lacking rough-faced stonework in the facade above the foundation level.

2. Richmond, Virginia; late 19th century.

3. Lexington, Kentucky; late 19th century. Dark red brick and white stone detailing provide startling contrast in this exuberant example. Note the tiny Romanesque-arched basement window at the left, the inventive open arch of the porch, and the exaggerated width of the stone window arches.

4. Provo, Utah; 1892. Reed House. Note the eyebrow dormer.

5. Cleveland, Ohio; 1883. Everett House; Charles F. Schweinfurth, architect. The Romanesque arch appears here stair-stepped diagonally across the facade from porte cochere to gable. Note the windows with transom above at the second-story level and the band of alternating windows and columns at the third-story level.

6. Savannah, Georgia; 1891. Tiedeman House; A. Eichberg, architect. Note the contrasting trim of light colored stone. As in Figure 7, there are wall dormers around the tower roof.

7. Richmond, Virginia; late 19th century. The polychromed walls show contrasting light brick and dark stonework.

8. Louisville, Kentucky; 1894. Conrad House; Clark and Loomis, architects. Two towers with differing roof shapes are used here. Note the floral detailing in the gable, and elsewhere on the facade.

1

4

6

OTHER ROOF TYPES

1. St. Louis, Missouri; 1886. Lionberger House; Henry Hobson Richardson, architect. One of Richardson's fortress-like designs.

2. St. Louis, Missouri; late 19th century. The wide roof overhang is unusual in the style.

3. Chicago, Illinois; 1886. Glessner House; Henry Hobson Richardson, architect. Another of Richardson's few domestic designs, this presents a fortress-like face to the street.

4. Kerrville, Texas; ca. 1895. Shreiner House; Alfred Giles, architect. In this example a full Romanesque facade with a two-tiered porch and end towers has been added to two earlier houses to make a single larger dwelling.

5. Washington, District of Columbia; 1880. Heurich House, J. G. Myers, architect. The facade rises a full three stories in this landmark example.

TOWN HOUSE

1. Louisville, Kentucky; late 19th century. A simple, front-gabled example. It would be hard to miss the Romanesque arches.

2. Louisville, Kentucky; late 19th century. Groups of columns support the Romanesque arches in this front-gabled example.

3. Richmond, Virginia; late 19th century. Here the mansard roof provides a background for the wall dormer and tower.

4. St. Paul, Minnesota; 1887. Riley Row, Wilcox and Johnston, architects. Attached Romanesque town houses are unusual; groups with many uniform units, such as this, are very rare.

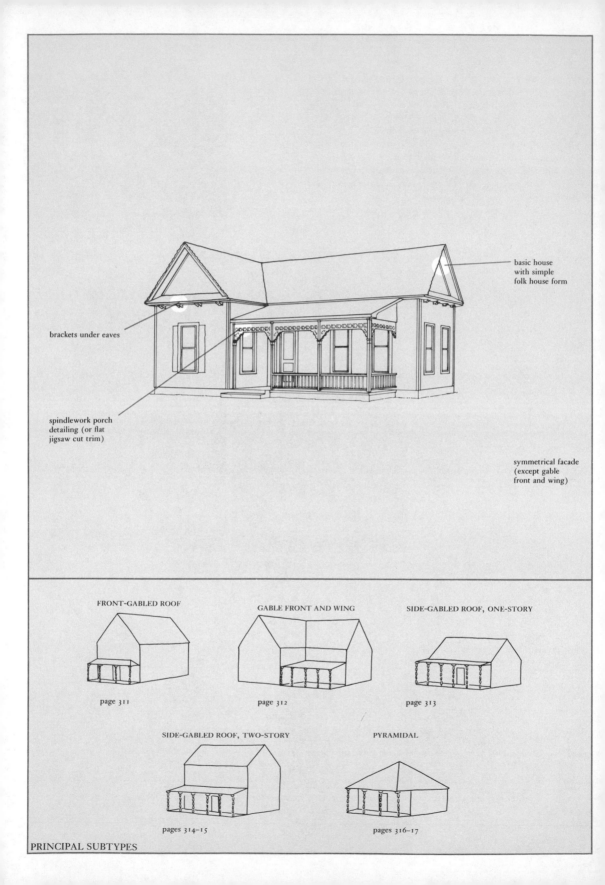

basic house
with simple
folk house form

brackets under eaves

spindlework porch
detailing (or flat
jigsaw cut trim)

symmetrical facade
(except gable
front and wing)

PRINCIPAL SUBTYPES

FRONT-GABLED ROOF

page 311

GABLE FRONT AND WING

page 312

SIDE-GABLED ROOF, ONE-STORY

page 313

SIDE-GABLED ROOF, TWO-STORY

pages 314–15

PYRAMIDAL

pages 316–17

Folk Victorian

IDENTIFYING FEATURES

Porches with spindlework detailing (turned spindles and lace-like spandrels) or flat, jig-saw cut trim appended to National Folk (post-railroad) house forms (see page 89); symmetrical facade (except gable-front-and-wing subtype); cornice-line brackets are common.

PRINCIPAL SUBTYPES

Five principal subtypes occur. These are closely related to the subtypes of National Folk (post-railroad) houses.

FRONT-GABLED ROOF—Like their pure folk counterparts, two-story, front-gabled forms with Victorian detailing are most common in the northeastern states, while one-story, narrow shotgun forms are generally found in the urban South.

GABLE FRONT AND WING—Both one- and two-story Victorian versions of this popular folk form are found throughout the country but are particularly common in the southern states.

SIDE-GABLED ROOF, ONE-STORY—This common subtype includes Victorian versions of both the hall-and-parlor (one room deep) and massed, side-gabled (two or more rooms deep) folk forms. It is widely distributed through the country.

SIDE-GABLED-ROOF, TWO-STORY—Most examples of this subtype are I-houses (one room deep) to which Victorian detailing in varying degrees of exuberance was added. They are common in all parts of the country.

PYRAMIDAL—Both one- and two-story versions of this folk form were often given Victorian detailing in the southern states but are relatively rare elsewhere.

VARIANTS AND DETAILS

The style is defined by the presence of Victorian decorative detailing on simple folk house forms, which are generally much less elaborated than the Victorian styles that they attempt to mimic. The details are usually of either Italianate or Queen Anne inspiration; occasionally the Gothic Revival provides a source. The primary areas for the application of this detailing are the porch and cornice line. Porch supports are commonly either Queen Anne–type turned spindles, or square posts with the corners beveled (chamfered) as in many Italianate porches. In addition, lace-like spandrels are frequent and turned balusters may be used both in porch railings and in friezes suspended from the porch ceiling (see pages 265 and 267). The roof-wall junction may be either boxed or open. When boxed, brackets are commonly found along the cornice. Centered gables are often added to side-gabled and pyramidal examples. Window surrounds are generally simple or may have a simple pediment above. Most Folk Victorian houses have some Queen Anne spindlework detailing but are easily differentiated from true Queen Anne examples by the presence of symmetrical facades and by their lack of the textured and varied wall surfaces characteristic of the Queen Anne.

OCCURRENCE

The style is common throughout the country; the five subtypes show differing patterns of distribution as noted in the descriptions of each above.

COMMENTS

Like that of the National Folk forms on which they are based, the spread of Folk Victorian houses was made possible by the railroads. The growth of the railroad system made heavy woodworking machinery widely accessible at local trade centers, where they produced inexpensive Victorian detailing. The railroads also provided local lumber yards with abundant supplies of pre-cut detailing from distant mills. Many builders simply grafted pieces of this newly available trim onto the traditional folk house forms familiar to local carpenters. Fashion-conscious homeowners also updated their older folk houses with new Victorian porches. These dwellings make strong stylistic statements and are therefore treated here as distinctive styled houses, rather than pure folk forms. After about 1910 these Symmetrical Victorian houses, as they are sometimes called, were replaced by the Craftsman, Colonial Revival, and other fashionable eclectic styles.

FRONT-GABLED ROOF

1. New Orleans, Louisiana; late 19th century. A shotgun form, one room wide, with Italianate windows and Queen Anne spindlework porch and gable detailing.

2. New Orleans, Louisiana; late 19th century. A narrow, two-ranked shotgun, with Italianate windows and brackets. Note the hipped front roof that replaces the more usual front gable.

3. Fernandez, Florida; late 19th century. A large two-story front-gabled form with a two-tiered porch. This example has flat jigsaw-cut upper balustrade and gable trim.

4. New London, Connecticut; late 19th century. An inventive craftsman's interpretation of spindlework porch detailing.

1

2

3   4

GABLE FRONT AND WING

1. Bartlett, Texas; late 19th century. This example has modest spindlework porch detailing, with a typical Queen Anne pent roof beneath the gables. The porches in this subtype are usually confined within the L formed by the gable and wing as seen here and in figures 2 and 3.

2. Sinclairville, New York, vicinity; late 19th century.

3. Hillsboro, Texas; late 19th century. An inventive craftsman's version of a spindlework porch. Note the shingled gable and bracketed window hood to the right. Slight differences in roof pitch and height between the gable front portion and the wing, as well as differing gable and window detailing in the two portions, probably indicate that they were built at different times. Gable-front-and-wing forms were often the result of such melding.

4. Little River, South Carolina; ca. 1910. Ellis House. Note the contrast between the body of the house, a simple two-story folk form with little detailing, and the elaborate spindlework porch with paired gables.

5. Laurens, South Carolina; late 19th century. Huff House. This example has unusually elaborate spindlework detailing and eave brackets. The high-pitched gable is less common than the lower-pitched ones seen in the other examples. Note how the porch roof has been extended upward to simulate a full-scale Victorian tower.

1

3

2

5

4

SIDE-GABLED ROOF, ONE-STORY

1. Bastrop, Texas; 1890. Elzner House.

2. Rosin, North Carolina; ca. 1890. McPhail House. Centered front gables are common in this subtype (see also figures 3 and 4).

3. San Antonio, Texas; ca. 1880. Kuhn House.

4. St. Francois County, Missouri; late 19th century. Graves House. The projecting central wing of this carefully detailed example is unusual.

5. Galveston, Texas; 1893. Eimar House. Note the typical Queen Anne cutaway corners to the right. First stories raised high above the ground are common along the Gulf Coast.

1

3

2

5

4

SIDE-GABLED ROOF, TWO-STORY

1. Annapolis, Maryland; late 19th century. A simple side-gabled town house with modest spindlework porch detailing.

2. Canton, Mississippi; late 19th century. Two-tiered, full-facade porches such as this are common in the South (see also Figure 6).

3. Lansing, North Carolina, vicinity; ca. 1890. Howell House. Here a two-tiered, full-height entry porch is added to an I-house form. Full-height entry porches on Folk Victorian houses are always two-tiered; two-story columns would indicate a classically influenced, styled house.

4. Laurens, South Carolina; late 19th century. Easterby House. Like Figure 3, this I-house also has Italianate brackets and bay windows.

5. Clinton, Missouri, vicinity; ca. 1879. Noble House. An I-house with modified Victorian porch detailing.

6. Waveland, Mississippi, late 19th century. The elaborate jig-saw cut porch detailing of this example shows Gothic influence in the paired gables.

7. Hampton, South Carolina; ca. 1880. Here a full-width, one-story porch is combined with a two-story entry porch.

8. Henderson County, North Carolina; 1877. Elliott House. An unusually elaborate I-house. If this transitional example had arched windows or other Italianate detailing in addition to the eave brackets, it would clearly belong to the Italianate, rather than the Folk Victorian, style.

4

3

7

PYRAMIDAL ROOF

1. Midway, North Carolina, vicinity; ca. 1880. McLamb House. A five-ranked, hipped-roof I-house with eave brackets and modest spindlework porch detailing.

2. Biloxi, Mississippi, ca. 1900.

3. San Antonio, Texas; 1903. Pancoast House. Note the flat, jig-saw cut porch frieze elaborated with stars, a frequent motif in the Lone Star state.

4. McPhersonville, South Carolina; late 19th century. Gregorie House. Two-tiered, full facade porches, such as this, are common throughout the South.

5. Brunson, South Carolina; ca. 1875. Brunson House. This example has small eave brackets and flat, jig-saw cut porch decoration.

6. Woodville, Texas; ca. 1880. Cruse House. This example adds centered gables to the low-pitched hipped roof. It is quite large for a Folk Victorian; most houses of this size and detailing more closely followed one of the stylish modes of the day.

1

4

6

Eclectic Houses

1880–1940

The Eclectic movement draws on the full spectrum of architectural tradition—Ancient Classical, Medieval, Renaissance Classical, or Modern—for stylistic inspiration. Unlike the free stylistic mixtures that dominated the preceding Victorian era, the Eclectic movement stresses relatively pure copies of these traditions as originally built in different European countries and their New World colonies. In Eclecticism many different styles vie with one another in a sort of friendly competition within which the sharpest lines are drawn between historical or "period" styles and "modern" styles that eschew earlier precedents.

The Eclectic movement began quietly in the last decades of the 19th century as fashionable, European-trained architects began to design landmark period houses for wealthy clients. These were mostly in the Italian Renaissance, Chateauesque, Beaux Arts, Tudor, or Colonial Revival styles. The trend gained momentum with Chicago's Columbian Exposition of 1893, which stressed correct historical interpretations of European styles. This early emphasis on period styles was interrupted and almost overwhelmed by the first wave of architectural modernism which, in the form of the Craftsman and Prairie styles, dominated American houses built during the first two decades of this century.

World War I brought an abrupt end to this first phase of the Modern movement. After the war, fashions in domestic architecture shifted quickly toward the period styles which had hitherto been favored principally in architect-designed landmarks. Here, as in Victorian times, a change in technology facilitated a change in fashion. The European models for period styles were almost exclusively built of solid masonry, often with elaborate patterns of decorative stonework or brickwork exposed on the facades. Most American houses, in contrast, were of wooden-framed construction; solid masonry was generally confined to the most expensive dwellings. In the early 1920s, inexpensive techniques were perfected for adding a thin veneer of brick or stone to the exterior of the traditional balloon-framed house. Soon even modest cottages began to mimic, in brick veneer, the masonry facades of Old World landmarks. The resulting burst of period fashions drew on the complete historical spectrum of European and Colonial American housing styles and dominated domestic building during the 1920s and '30s. In the mid-1930s the beginning of a new wave of modernism appeared. Although the resulting Modernistic and International styles remained rather rare and avant garde, their Modern descendants were destined to dominate American housing in the decades immmediately following World War II.

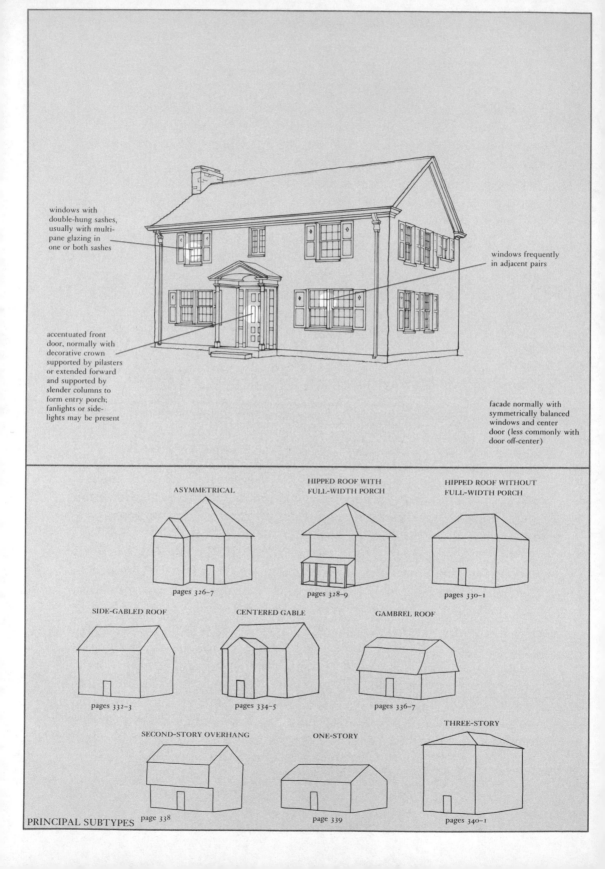

windows with double-hung sashes, usually with multi-pane glazing in one or both sashes

windows frequently in adjacent pairs

accentuated front door, normally with decorative crown supported by pilasters or extended forward and supported by slender columns to form entry porch; fanlights or side-lights may be present

facade normally with symmetrically balanced windows and center door (less commonly with door off-center)

ASYMMETRICAL

pages 326–7

HIPPED ROOF WITH FULL-WIDTH PORCH

pages 328–9

HIPPED ROOF WITHOUT FULL-WIDTH PORCH

pages 330–1

SIDE-GABLED ROOF

pages 332–3

CENTERED GABLE

pages 334–5

GAMBREL ROOF

pages 336–7

SECOND-STORY OVERHANG

page 338

ONE-STORY

page 339

THREE-STORY

pages 340–1

PRINCIPAL SUBTYPES

IDENTIFYING FEATURES

Accentuated front door, normally with decorative crown (pediment) supported by pilasters, or extended forward and supported by slender columns to form entry porch; doors commonly have overhead fanlights or sidelights; facade normally shows symmetrically balanced windows and center door (less commonly with door off-center); windows with double-hung sashes, usually with multi-pane glazing in one or both sashes; windows frequently in adjacent pairs.

PRINCIPAL SUBTYPES

Nine principal subtypes can be distinguished. Some examples may be almost identical to their colonial (particularly Georgian and Adam) prototypes. Clues for distinguishing Revival copies from early originals are given below under Variants and Details.

ASYMMETRICAL—About 10 percent of Colonial Revival houses have asymmetrical facades, a feature rarely seen on their colonial prototypes. These asymmetrical examples range from rambling, free-form houses resembling the free classic Queen Anne style (see pages 276–9) to simple boxes with asymmetrical window or porch arrangements. Prior to 1900 this subtype accounted for about one-third of all Colonial Revival houses. After 1910 few examples were constructed until the 1930s, when irregular facades reappeared with less elaborate detailing. These were, in part, inspired by the desire for attached garages, which were difficult to incorporate within a balanced facade.

HIPPED ROOF WITH FULL-WIDTH PORCH—About one-third of Colonial Revival houses built before about 1915 are of this subtype, which is sometimes called the Classic Box. These have a one-story, full-width porch with classical columns, which is added to a symmetrical, two-story house of square or rectangular plan. Two-story pilasters are common at the corners; dormers, hipped or gabled, are usually present. Doors may be centered or placed to the side. These houses have both Neoclassical and Colonial Revival influences, but lack the full-height porches of typical Neoclassical houses.

HIPPED ROOF WITHOUT FULL-WIDTH PORCH—About 25 percent of Colonial Revival houses are simple two-story rectangular blocks with hipped roofs; porches are usually absent or, if present, are merely small entry porches covering less than the full facade width. This subtype, built throughout the Colonial Revival era, predominates before about 1910. On early examples, the colonial detailing tended to be highly exaggerated and of awkward proportions; fanciful, pedimented dormers were particularly favored. After about 1910 detailing became more "correct" by closely following Georgian or Adam precedents.

SIDE-GABLED ROOF—About 25 percent of Colonial Revival houses are simple, two-story rectangular blocks with side-gabled roofs. As in the type just described, the details tend to be exaggerated prior to 1910 and more "correct" afterward. This subtype was built throughout the Colonial Revival era but predominates after about 1910.

CENTERED GABLE—Less than 5 percent of Colonial Revival houses have a centered front gable added to either a hipped or side-gabled roof. These uncommon Revival houses mimic high-style Georgian or Adam prototypes. Scattered examples were built throughout the Colonial Revival era.

GAMBREL ROOF—About 10 percent of Colonial Revival houses have gambrel roofs. Most are one story with steeply pitched gambrels containing almost a full second story of floor space; these have either separate dormer windows or a continuous shed dormer with several windows. A full-width porch may be included under the main roof line or added with a separate roof. This subtype is known as Dutch Colonial, but very few examples closely follow early Dutch precedent. From about 1895 to 1915 the most common form has a front-facing gambrel roof, occasionally with a cross gambrel at the rear. These are influenced by the typical gambrels of the earlier Shingle style (see pages 298–9). Side gambrels, usually with long shed dormers, became the predominant form in the 1920s and '30s.

SECOND-STORY OVERHANG—This subtype is loosely based on Postmedieval English prototypes (see page 107), commonly built with the second story extended slightly outward to overhang the wall below. The subtype was relatively rare until the 1930s, when stylized, side-gabled examples (called Garrison Colonial houses) became very popular. These persisted into the 1950s. Unlike their early prototypes, these typically have masonry-veneered first stories with wooden wall claddings above. Georgian- or Adam-inspired doorways are commonly mixed with decorative pendants or other Postmedieval details.

ONE-STORY—The preceding subtypes are all based on familiar two-story prototypes, but one-story Colonial Revival houses are also common. These are generally Cape Cod cottages, loosely patterned after early wooden folk houses of eastern Massachusetts, usually with the addition of Georgian- or Adam-inspired doorways. These were built throughout the Colonial Revival era but were most common in the 1920s and '40s

THREE-STORY—A small percentage of Colonial Revival houses are three stories high. These include both narrow urban houses and more typical forms modeled after three-story Adam prototypes, common in parts of New England (see page 164). These typically have low-pitched, hipped roofs which appear almost flat; Adam fanlights are usual over entrances. In the early decades of this century, narrow urban houses were becoming less common in all but the largest cities. In those populous cities where urban houses persisted, Colonial Revival detailing remained popular through the 1920s.

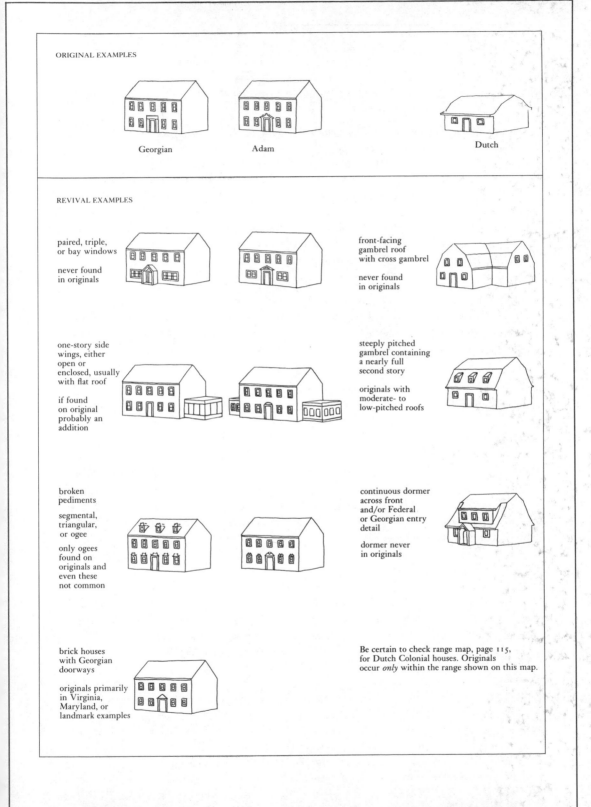

ORIGINAL EXAMPLES

Georgian

Adam

Dutch

REVIVAL EXAMPLES

paired, triple,
or bay windows

never found
in originals

front-facing
gambrel roof
with cross gambrel

never found
in originals

one-story side
wings, either
open or
enclosed, usually
with flat roof

if found
on original
probably an
addition

steeply pitched
gambrel containing
a nearly full
second story

originals with
moderate- to
low-pitched roofs

broken
pediments

segmental,
triangular,
or ogee

only ogees
found on
originals and
even these
not common

continuous dormer
across front
and/or Federal
or Georgian entry
detail

dormer never
in originals

brick houses
with Georgian
doorways

originals primarily
in Virginia,
Maryland, or
landmark examples

Be certain to check range map, page 115,
for Dutch Colonial houses. Originals
occur *only* within the range shown on this map.

DISTINGUISHING THE COLONIAL REVIVAL HOUSE FROM GEORGIAN, ADAM, & DUTCH ORIGINALS

VARIANTS AND DETAILS

As in their Georgian and Adam prototypes, the principal areas of elaboration in Colonial Revival houses are entrances, cornices, and windows.

ENTRANCES—The illustrations of Georgian and Adam entrances on pages 155 and 158 include most variants found on colonial prototypes; some common additional variations favored on Colonial Revival houses are illustrated here. Broken pediments, rare on colonial originals, were particularly favored by the Revivalists. Entrance details on careful Colonial Revival copies can be distinguished from originals only by their regular, machine-made finish, which contrasts with the slightly irregular hand finishes of early examples. On less precise Colonial Revival copies, door surrounds are typically flatter than the originals; that is, less wood and fewer and shallower moldings are used to gain a similar frontal effect but less depth and relief are apparent when viewed from the side.

CORNICES—In original Georgian and Adam houses the cornice is an important identifying feature. It is almost always part of a boxed roof-wall junction with little overhang, and is frequently decorated with dentils or modillions (see page 155). These are also typical of many Colonial Revival examples. Some, however, have open eaves and rake, or even exposed rafters, features never found on original colonial houses.

WINDOWS—As in the originals, most Colonial Revival windows are rectangular in shape with double-hung sashes. In the more accurate copies, each sash has six, eight, nine, or twelve panes. Equally common are multi-pane upper sashes hung above lower sashes that have only a single large pane, a pattern never seen on colonial originals. Where bay windows, paired windows, or triple windows (except the Adam Palladian type) are present, they clearly signify a Colonial Revival house rather than an original.

OTHER DETAILS—All common wall materials were used, but masonry predominates in high-style examples. Vernacular examples were generally of wood before about 1920, with masonry progressively more common as veneering techniques became widespread in the 1920s. High-style elaborations of Georgian and Adam originals may also occur on landmark Colonial Revival copies.

OCCURRENCE

This was a dominant style for domestic building throughout the country during the first half of this century. The different subtypes were not, however, equally common throughout this long period, but shifted with changing fashion (see each subtype above). After briefly passing from favor in mid-century, the style has recently reappeared in somewhat different form as a dominant Neoeclectic style (see page 489).

COMMENTS

The term "Colonial Revival," as used here, refers to the entire rebirth of interest in the early English and Dutch houses of the Atlantic seaboard. The Georgian and Adam styles form the backbone of the Revival, with secondary influences from Postmedieval English or Dutch Colonial prototypes. Details from two or more of these precedents are freely combined in many examples so that pure copies of colonial houses are far less common than are eclectic mixtures.

COLONIAL REVIVAL SUB-TYPES	YEARS WHEN MOST FREQUENTLY BUILT						
	1880	1890	1900	1910	1920	1930	1940
ASYMMETRICAL	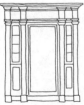 →						
HIPPED ROOF WITH FULL-WIDTH PORCH		→					
SIDE-GABLED & HIPPED WITHOUT FULL-WIDTH PORCH — with exaggerated details	 →						
with more accurate and/or simpler details			 →				→
vernacular brick examples Hipped predominate pre-1910, gabled predominate post-1910				ca. 1915- introduction of brick veneer	 →		→
ONE-STORY					□□□ →		→
GAMBREL OR DUTCH COLONIAL — front or cross gambrel		□□□ →					
side gambrel					▱ →		→
SECOND-STORY OVERHANG					⌂ →		→

 sidelights without fanlight above, uncommon on originals

portico with *curved* underside (roof may be gable or curved), on few originals

broken triangular and segmental pediments: rare on originals; broken ogee pediments occasionally on originals

broken pediments, not usually over fanlights on originals

 heavily elaborated entrances, not common on American originals (copied from English Georgian)

pediments without supporting pilasters, not on originals

REVIVAL ENTRANCES: SOME COMMON WAYS THEY VARY FROM ORIGINALS

In the years between 1880 and 1900 the Colonial Revival movement also influenced two other architectural styles: Queen Anne and Shingle. In the Queen Anne this produced the free classic subtype, which grades into the closely related asymmetrical Colonial Revival house. In the Shingle style, the shingled walls and rambling forms were thought to evoke early shingled houses with shed and lean-to additions. Moreover, colonial details such as Palladian windows were used in many examples.

The Philadelphia Centennial of 1876 is credited with first awakening an interest in our colonial architectural heritage. In 1877 the fashionable architects McKim, Mead, White, and Bigelow took a widely publicized tour through New England to study original Georgian and Adam buildings at first hand. By 1886 they had executed two landmark houses in the style—the Appleton House (1883–84) in Lennox, Massachusetts, and the Taylor House (1885–86) in Newport, Rhode Island. These important examples typify the two subtypes that were most common before 1910: the asymmetrical form with superimposed colonial details and the more authentic symmetrical hipped roof shape; details in both tended to have exaggerated proportions.

These early examples of Colonial Revival were rarely historically correct copies but were instead free interpretations with details inspired by colonial precedents. During the first decade of this century, Colonial Revival fashion shifted toward carefully researched copies with more correct proportions and details. This was encouraged by new methods of printing that permitted wide dissemination of photographs in books and periodicals. In 1898 *The American Architect and Building News* began an extensive series called "The Georgian Period: Being photographs and measured drawings of Colonial Work with text." This was joined in 1915 by the *White Pine Series of Architectural Monographs*, which was dominated by photographs of colonial buildings. These and similar ventures led to a wide understanding of the prototypes on which the Revival was based. Colonial Revival houses built in the years between 1915 and 1935 reflect these influences by more closely resembling early prototypes than did those built earlier or later. The economic depression of the 1930s, World War II, and changing postwar fashions led to a simplification of the style in the 1940s and '50s. These later examples are most often of the side-gabled type, with simple stylized door surrounds, cornices, or other details that merely suggest their colonial precedents rather than closely mirroring them.

4   5

ASYMMETRICAL

1. Cambridge, Massachusetts; 1897. Note the exaggerated broken pediments on the dormers.

2. Brookline, Massachusetts; ca. 1900. Note the two-story wing set at an angle to the left and the almost centered gable with Palladian window below to the right.

3. Salisbury, North Carolina; 1898. The line between some late free classic Queen Anne houses and some early Colonial Revival examples is not a sharp one: compare this photo with the similar transitional example shown in Figure 16, page 279. The Palladian window and Adamesque swags link this house more closely with the Colonial Revivial movement.

4. Hartford, Connecticut; ca. 1900. This early example shows Craftsman influence in its open eaves with exposed rafters.

5. Dallas, Texas; 1937. Hershfelt House.

6. Dallas, Texas; 1939. Bowers House. Later asymmetrical examples mostly date from the 1930s and commonly have either gabled roofs with side wings, as in this house, or forward-facing gable-fronted wings as in Figure 5.

1

2

3

6

HIPPED ROOF WITH FULL-WIDTH PORCH

1. Galveston, Texas; ca. 1911. Lawrence House. On narrow urban lots a front-gabled roof occasionally replaces the more common hipped roof.

2. Dallas, Texas; ca. 1910. This early, two-ranked house with an off-center entrance is adapted from the simple four-square folk plan with a pyramidal roof.

3. Ashe County, North Carolina; ca. 1920. Livesy House. This example, like figures 5, 6, and 7, has a centered entrance and a three-ranked facade, indicating the likelihood of a central-hall plan rather than the simple four-square plan seen in figures 2 and 4.

4. Buffalo, New York; ca. 1900. Foster House. A simple, early two-ranked example; note the corner pilasters.

5. Union Springs, Alabama; ca. 1910. Note the elaborate pedimented entranceway moved to the front of the porch, rather than around the doorway as in Colonial examples. Less grand pediments are seen in figures 2 and 3.

6. Winston-Salem, North Carolina; ca. 1910. Note the grouped columns on pedestals. This pattern of porch supports was uncommon before about 1900.

7. Brooklyn, New York; 1900. John J. Petit, architect. Paired windows and a front door with sidelights, but no fanlight, are common Revival details seen clearly in this example.

8. Buffalo, New York; ca. 1900. White House. An unusually elaborate example with roof and upper porch balustrades, upper-story bay windows, and a heavily detailed cornice with a solid railing above.

1

4

7

2

3

6

5

8

HIPPED ROOF WITHOUT FULL-WIDTH PORCH

1. San Francisco, California; ca. 1900. A fine early example with exaggerated pediments on the dormers, an overwide entablature above the entry-porch columns, an overwide belt course, and triple windows with decorative transoms on the first story. Such details never appear on more correct, later examples like figures 3 and 5.

2. Cincinnati, Ohio; 1920s. Such austere examples emphasize the shift to more correct copies of Colonial dwellings.

3. Buffalo, New York; 1920s. A later example, more traditionally scaled than figures 1, 4, and 7.

4. St. Louis, Missouri; ca. 1914. O'Neil House. Note the paired dormer pediments, oval windows, and large, curved window bays.

5. Montgomery, Alabama; 1920s. Like Figure 3, this house is more traditionally scaled. Elaborated windows above the entrance were unusual on original Georgian and Adam houses, but are common in Revival examples.

6. Dallas, Texas; 1938. Varner House. This Regency variation of the Colonial Revival, loosely based on English rather than American precedents, was popular in the 1930s. The octagonal window, simplified door surround, and unusually plain roof-wall junction are typical of this variant.

7. Brookline, Massachusetts; ca. 1900. E. A. P. Newcombe, architect. Another early example with exaggerated detailing. Note the dormers with Palladian windows and broken pediments, the two colonnaded upstairs balconies, and the very deep entry porch.

8. Atlanta, Georgia; 1922. McDuffie House. A very large and elaborate example. Note the pilasters, roof-line balustrade, and arched windows.

1

4

7

1

4

SIDE-GABLED ROOF

1. Baltimore, Maryland; ca. 1910. A very simple, two-ranked example.

2. Louisville, Kentucky; 1920s. Side porches are common on Colonial Revival houses (see figures 3, 4, and 7).

3. Louisville, Kentucky; 1930s. Another Regency house (see also page 331, Figure 6). This type of metal entry porch, with a canopy roof is a characteristic Regency feature.

4. Kansas City, Missouri; 1910s. Although at first glance this looks like an accurate copy, the roof overhang is too wide and the windows too broad for an original colonial house.

5. Cleveland, Ohio; 1920s. The entry porch with a curved underside is a favored Revival detail.

6. Dallas, Texas; 1941. Young House. Small round windows (above the entry here and in the gable end of Figure 3) were widely used in the late 1930s, '40s, and early '50s on Colonial Revival houses and on other styles.

7. Dallas, Texas; 1919. Thomson House. This example was inspired by the Middle Colonies Georgian house. Note the pent roof and the hood over the entry. The side porch to the left has a summer sleeping porch above with windows on three sides. These were especially favored in the South where they appear in many early 20th-century styles.

8. Cambridge, Massachusetts; 1903. John W. Ames, architect. This house demonstrates that reasonably accurate Colonial copies were being designed in the early years of the Revival; those with exaggerated detailing were, however, far more common.

9. Louisville, Kentucky; 1920s. The garden facade of a very large example. Note the door surround with the pediment extending over the sidelights but lacking a fanlight. Although this combination was never used in colonial houses, the example here faithfully captures the spirit of a Georgian or Adam doorway.

7   8

CENTERED GABLE

1. Buffalo, New York; ca. 1900. Harrover House. Centered gables that cover three ranks of window or door openings (here and in Figure 8) are less common than those that are only one or two ranks wide.

2. Dallas, Texas; 1938. Lincoln House. The simplicity of detailing on this house is typical of examples from the 1930s and '40s.

3. Buffalo, New York; 1920s.

4. Madison, Wisconsin; 1896. Ely House.

5. Cleveland, Ohio; 1910s. The open overhanging eaves and the entry porch with trellised roof are borrowed from the Craftsman movement.

6. Buffalo, New York; 1910s. Note the fine detailing: the entrance with a rounded door, the sidelights without fanlight, the wide classical pediment, the Palladian and bay windows; and the carefully executed dormers.

7. Des Moines, Iowa; 1905. W. W. Witmer House; Liebbe, Nourse and Rasmussen, architects. Note the first-story windows crowned with broken pediments (see also Figure 4). Although common above the main entrance, such pediments became rare on windows and dormers after about 1910.

8. Raleigh, North Carolina; 1935. Tatton Hall; William Lawrence Bottomley, architect. A five-ranked central block is flanked by one-story wings (obscured by trees and shadows in the photograph) in this landmark example.

1

4

7

2

3

5

6

8

GAMBREL ROOF

1. Louisville, Kentucky; 1920s. Figures 1, 4, and 7 are typical examples of the popular Dutch Colonial house of the 1920s and '30s. The side-gambrel shape, most often with a full-width shed dormer (see also figures 2 and 7), is the most common form.

2. Durham, North Carolina; 1920s. This is a less common cross-gambrel form of the Dutch Colonial. Note the flared eaves, here and in figures 1, 4, 7, and 8. These mimic the Flemish eaves of many Dutch Colonial originals.

3. Lexington, Kentucky; ca. 1910. This cross-gambrel form, with wood cladding, was a popular pattern-book design during the period from about 1905 to 1915.

4. Cincinnati, Ohio; 1920s.

5. Union, South Carolina; ca. 1910. Figures 5, 8, and 9 are all early gambrel-roof designs showing varying degrees of adventuresomeness. They are clearly descendants of the free-form gambrel designs of the preceding Shingle style.

6. Washington, District of Columbia; ca. 1900. An early example with a full-front gambrel. Note the Adamesque swags on the porch frieze.

7. St. Louis, Missouri; 1920s.

8. Cleveland, Ohio; ca. 1910.

9. New Haven, Connecticut; 1910. Brown and Von Beren, architects.

1

4

7

8

2

3

5

6

9

SECOND-STORY OVERHANG

1. Cambridge, Massachusetts; 1940. This Garrison Colonial subtype was especially popular in the latest phases of the Colonial Revival, from about 1935 to 1955. The overhang required a wood-sided second floor since cantilevered brick veneering was very difficult to construct. Here brick is used only on the front facade of the first story.

2. Dallas, Texas; 1953. Wilson House. Unlike their Colonial precedents, most Revival examples have a brick-sided first story.

3. Mission Hills, Kansas; 1930s. This example shows more detailing (door surround, wall dormers, centered gable) than is typical for the subtype.

4. Dallas, Texas; 1951. Voss House. Note the two tall bay windows; these were very popular during the 1950s.

ONE-STORY

1. Greeleyville, South Carolina; ca. 1910. Wilder House. See the comments on Figure 2.

2. Louisville, Kentucky; 1920s. This is a typical example of the Cape Cod cottage. Figure 1 is an earlier Cape Cod, which lacks the proportions of the Colonial originals (note the lower roof pitch, oversized dormers, and extra width and height of the front facade). The Cape Cod is the most common form of one-story Colonial Revival house. As a form, it originated in the early 18th century and continued with few changes through the 1950s.

3. Dallas, Texas; 1929. Randall House. This house has a formal, Adam-inspired entry porch and doorway.

4. Decatur, Indiana; ca. 1935. A modest asymmetrical interpretation of the Cape Code.

5. Macon, Georgia; 1912. Stetson House. Note the lower one-story wings; this finely detailed example, like Figure 3, was inspired by more pretentious Colonial antecedents than the typical Cape Cod examples shown in figures 1, 2, and 4.

1

2

3

4

5

THREE-STORY

1. Cambridge, Massachusetts; 1900. John A. Hasty, architect. Not a single-family house, but a triple-decker (one dwelling unit on each of three floors), this has the exuberant detailing associated with early examples. Note the broken pediments on the roof and over the central second-story window.

2. Cambridge, Massachusetts; 1916. J. W. Ames, architect. Figures 2 and 4 are both modeled after the three-story Adam subtype that was popular in New England (see pages 163–4).

3. Richmond, Virginia; 1910s. A three-story detached urban house with full-width porch.

4. Cambridge, Massachusetts; 1911. President's House, Harvard University; G. Lowell, architect.

5. Washington, District of Columbia; 1915. Woodrow Wilson House.

6. Buffalo, New York; ca. 1890–1910. The Midway. A group of town houses with distinctive detailing. Note the broken-pediment dormers on the house on the left; the simple and more accurate Adam detailing on the center house; and the entry porch, blind arches with swags, and roof-line parapet on the house on the right.

7. New York, New York; 1909–1926. Pyne, Filley, Sloane, and Davison Houses; McKim, Mead and White, Delano and Aldrich, and Walker and Gillette, architects for various houses. A remarkable surviving row of large attached town houses with detailing drawn from Georgian and Adam precedents.

3

6

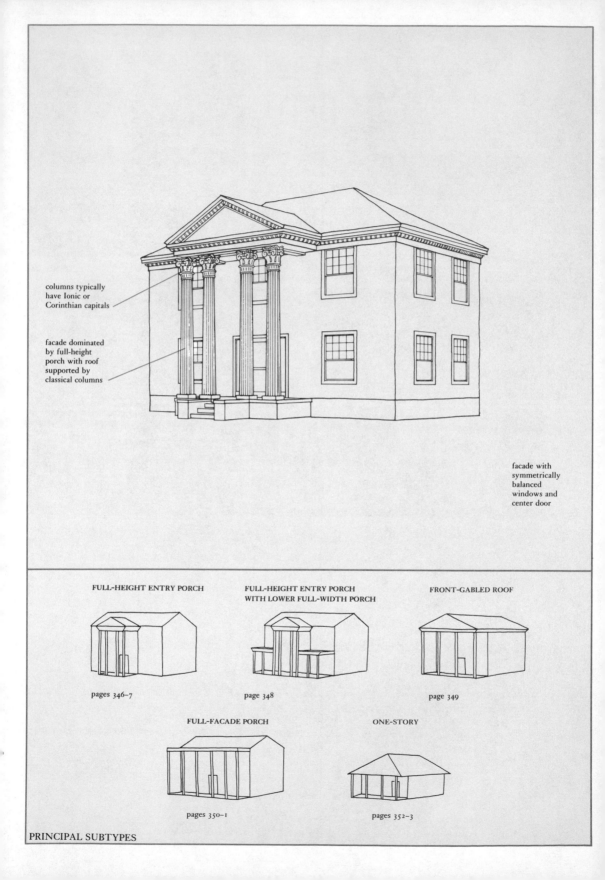

columns typically
have Ionic or
Corinthian capitals

facade dominated
by full-height
porch with roof
supported by
classical columns

facade with
symmetrically
balanced
windows and
center door

FULL-HEIGHT ENTRY PORCH

pages 346–7

**FULL-HEIGHT ENTRY PORCH
WITH LOWER FULL-WIDTH PORCH**

page 348

FRONT-GABLED ROOF

page 349

FULL-FACADE PORCH

pages 350–1

ONE-STORY

pages 352–3

PRINCIPAL SUBTYPES

Neoclassical

IDENTIFYING FEATURES

Facade dominated by full-height porch with roof supported by classical columns; columns typically have Ionic or Corinthian capitals; facade shows symmetrically balanced windows and center door.

PRINCIPAL SUBTYPES

Five principal subtypes can be distinguished:

FULL-HEIGHT ENTRY PORCH—This common subtype has a dominant central entry porch extending the full height, but less than the full width, of the facade. It closely resembles certain Early Classical Revival and Greek Revival subtypes. As in both of these earlier styles, the entry porch may have a classical pediment and gabled roof above or, as in the Greek Revival only, the porch roof may be flat. Some Neoclassical examples have curved, semi-circular entry porches with flat roofs, a variation unusual on earlier prototypes.

FULL-HEIGHT ENTRY PORCH WITH LOWER FULL-WIDTH PORCH—In this relatively uncommon subtype, a full-width, one-story porch is added to the full-height entry porch just described. This dual-level entry porch is without precedent in the earlier classical styles. Most examples were built from 1895 to 1915; few, after World War I.

FRONT-GABLED ROOF—In this uncommon subtype, the full-facade, colonnaded porch beneath the front-facing gable gives the house the appearance of a miniature Greek temple. This form was very common in Greek Revival houses, but makes up only a small percentage of Neoclassical examples.

FULL-FACADE PORCH—In this subtype, as in the one just described, a colonnaded porch occupies the full width and height of the facade. Here, however, the porch is not covered by a traditional pedimented gable but instead either by the principal (side-gabled or hipped) roof, or by a flat or shed extension from such a roof. This subtype became particularly popular in the period from about 1925 to 1950. These later examples normally have slender columns without elaborate capitals or fluted surfaces.

ONE-STORY—One-story Neoclassical cottages, a common subtype, usually have hipped roofs with prominent central dormers. The colonnaded porch may be either full- or partial-width and may be included under the main roof or have a separate flat or shed roof.

VARIANTS AND DETAILS

The principal areas of elaboration in Neoclassical houses are porch-support columns, cornices, doorways, and windows.

PORCH-SUPPORT COLUMNS—In Neoclassical houses built before about 1920, the columns are generally more ornate than those of Early Classical Revival or Greek Revival prototypes. Corinthian or Ionic capitals, or mixtures of the two, are found in about 75 percent of Neoclassical houses but in only 20 percent of Greek Revival examples. This change was made possible by the introduction of mass-produced capitals prefabricated of molded plaster or composition materials. Fluted column shafts are common in early houses. After about 1925, very slender, unfluted (often square) columns began to be used, primarily on houses with full-facade porches. Those usually lack capitals and their proportions readily distinguish them from earlier Neoclassical and Greek Revival examples.

DOORWAYS—Doors commonly have elaborate, decorative surrounds based on Greek Revival, Adam, or even Georgian precedents (see pages 155 and 201). Those with Georgian or Adam doorways are easily distinguished, because original examples very rarely had full-height, two-story columns (although some have had such porches added later). Greek Revival–type doorways may be more easily confused with original examples.

CORNICES—Neoclassical houses usually have a boxed eave with a moderate overhang, frequently with dentils or modillions beneath; a wide frieze band is occasionally found beneath the cornice. These are loosely based on Adam or Greek Revival precedents.

WINDOWS—Windows are rectangular with double-hung sashes. Examples following early precedent have six or nine panes to each sash; others have a multi-pane or single-pane upper sash and a single-pane lower sash. The presence of bay windows, paired windows, triple windows (except the Palladian type), transomed windows, or arched windows differentiate Neoclassical from Greek Revival or Early Classical Revival examples.

OTHER DETAILS—Many elaborations found on Early Classical Revival and Greek Revival houses also occur in Neoclassical examples. Roof-line balustrades, in particular, are much more common in Neoclassical houses than in the earlier styles.

OCCURRENCE

Neoclassical was a dominant style for domestic building throughout the country during the first half of the 20th century. Never quite as abundant as its closely related Colonial Revival contemporary, it had two principal waves of popularity. The first, from about 1900 to 1920, emphasized hipped roofs and elaborate, correct columns. The later phase, from about 1925 to the 1950s, emphasized side-gabled roofs and simple, slender columns. During the 1920s, the style was overshadowed by other Eclectic fashions.

COMMENTS

This revival of interest in classical models dates from the World's Columbian Exposition, held in Chicago in 1893. The exposition's planners mandated a classical theme, and many of the best-known architects of the day designed dramatic colonnaded buildings arranged

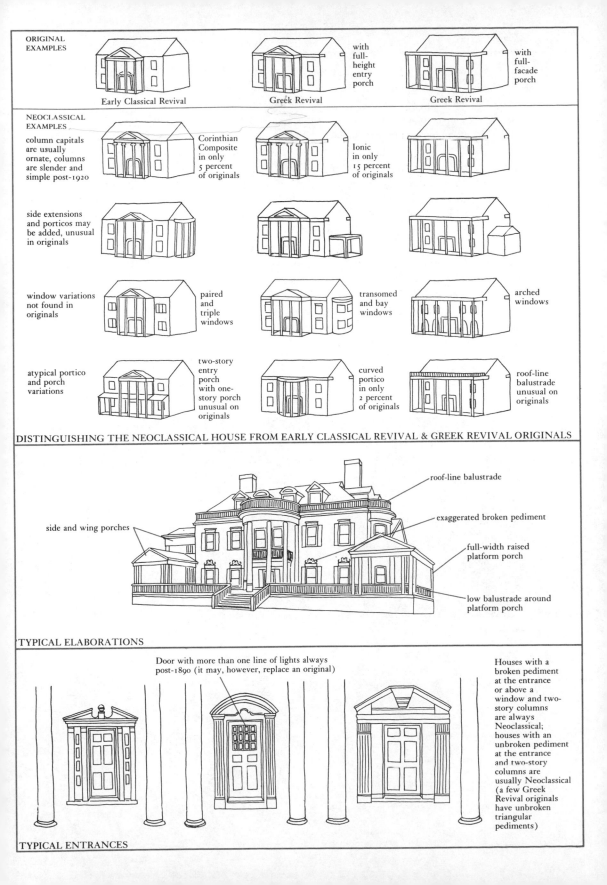

ORIGINAL EXAMPLES

Early Classical Revival

Greek Revival — with full-height entry porch

Greek Revival — with full-facade porch

NEOCLASSICAL EXAMPLES

column capitals are usually ornate, columns are slender and simple post-1920

Corinthian Composite in only 5 percent of originals

Ionic in only 15 percent of originals

side extensions and porticos may be added, unusual in originals

window variations not found in originals

paired and triple windows

transomed and bay windows

arched windows

atypical portico and porch variations

two-story entry porch with one-story porch unusual on originals

curved portico in only 2 percent of originals

roof-line balustrade unusual on originals

DISTINGUISHING THE NEOCLASSICAL HOUSE FROM EARLY CLASSICAL REVIVAL & GREEK REVIVAL ORIGINALS

roof-line balustrade

exaggerated broken pediment

full-width raised platform porch

side and wing porches

low balustrade around platform porch

TYPICAL ELABORATIONS

Door with more than one line of lights always post-1890 (it may, however, replace an original)

Houses with a broken pediment at the entrance or above a window and two-story columns are always Neoclassical; houses with an unbroken pediment at the entrance and two-story columns are usually Neoclassical (a few Greek Revival originals have unbroken triangular pediments)

TYPICAL ENTRANCES

around a central court. The exposition was widely photographed, reported, and attended; soon these Neoclassical models became the latest fashion throughout the country.

The central buildings of the exposition were of monumental scale and inspired countless public and commercial buildings in the following decades. The designs of smaller pavilions representing each state of the Union were more nearly domestic in scale and in them can be seen the precedents for most Neoclassical houses. Those of Ohio, Utah, and South Dakota, for example, all had semi-circular, full-height entry porches. Nebraska and Kentucky were represented by more traditional full-height porches with triangular pediments. The Connecticut pavilion had a full-height entry porch with a lower full-width porch. All of these drew heavily on the country's previous interest in the Early Classical Revival and Greek Revival styles. The Virginia pavilion was a copy of Mount Vernon, whose full-facade porch, among the first in the country, had been added in 1784 to an earlier Georgian house. The presence of this replica at the fair, and the original's wide familiarity as the nation's premier museum house, contributed to the incorrect impression that such porches were somehow colonial. Thus did Georgian, Adam, Early Classical Revival, and Greek Revival traditions, which originally spanned a century and a half of the nation's history, become fused into the eclectic Neoclassical style.

3   4

7

FULL-HEIGHT ENTRY PORCH

1. Dallas, Texas; 1936. Bell House. A typical later example with side-gabled roof, roof-line balustrade, and simple square columns.

2. Dallas, Texas; 1940. Musgrove House. A late example with a side-gabled roof and slender columns. The somewhat awkward-looking projection of the entry porch results from the omission of an entablature under the pediment.

3. Raleigh, North Carolina; 1903. Goodwin House; William P. Rose, architect. This early example has fluted columns with Roman Ionic capitals. Note the variety of pediments—segmental over the lower-story windows, broken-ogee over the entrance fanlight, and triangular over the arched upper-story window.

4. Montgomery, Alabama; 1907. Governor's Mansion. An elaborately detailed early example. Note the composite capitals on the pilasters and columns. These and the arched and double windows are never seen on earlier classical styles.

5. Dallas, Texas; 1933. Lee House. Here the entry porch (or portico) has been recessed into the body of the house; this is known as a portico in antis (see also Figure 6).

6. Kansas City, Missouri; 1930s. Slender columns, side-gabled roof, and roof-line balustrade mark this as a late example.

7. New London, Connecticut, ca. 1910. An unusual gambrel-roof example. The triple windows, broken pediment occurring with full-height columns, and the curved entry porch with balustrade all mark this as a Neoclassical example.

8. Louisville, Kentucky; 1910s. This entry porch is both recessed into the body of the house and extended outward. Note the keystone lintels over the upper-story windows and three-part lintels over the lower-story triple windows.

1

2

5

6

8

347

FULL-HEIGHT ENTRY PORCH WITH LOWER FULL-WIDTH PORCH

1. Dallas, Texas; ca. 1900. Harris House. In many examples the full-width lower porch is built independently, passing behind the tall entry porch as here and in Figure 4. In this example the lower porch even has a pediment at the entry.

2. Dallas, Texas; 1905. Baird House. In this example, the lower porch attaches to the tall entry porch; where they meet, both are supported by the same columns.

3. Eufaula, Alabama; ca.1910. This example is somewhat unusual in that no colossal columns are used for the full-height entry; instead a second tier of one-story columns occurs above the lower porch.

4. Taylor, Texas; ca. 1910. This brick example has a tiled roof; the triple columns supporting the full-height porch are unusual.

FRONT-GABLED ROOF

1. Jamestown, New York; 1906. The fanlight over the front door distinguishes this example and that in Figure 2 from a Greek Revival original.

2. Brooklyn, New York; 1905. George Hitchings, architect. This house has a cross-gabled roof behind the dominant front gable. Note the unusual use of corner quoins next to the pilasters.

3. Little Rock, Arkansas; 1906. Haliburton Houses. Although not front-gabled, the hipped roof with front-to-back ridge gives these houses a similar look. As with most examples of this subtype, they were designed for narrow urban lots.

FULL-FACADE PORCH

1. Buffalo, New York; ca. 1910. Geir House.

2. Buffalo, New York; ca. 1930. The porch is recessed under the main roof of the house. The small entry porch with balustrade is an unusual addition. The simple square columns mark this as a late example.

3. Buffalo, New York; 1895. Williams House; Stanford White, architect. A green copper roof accents this landmark house.

4. Jackson, Mississippi, ca. 1910. A richly detailed house with tiled roof, paired balconies, and multiple swags.

5. Dallas, Texas; 1922. Warren House. Note the full-length casement windows opening onto the porch and recessed side wings.

6. Salisbury, North Carolina; ca. 1910. The forward extension in the central part of a full-facade porch (seen here and in figures 3 and 4) is a Neoclassical feature not used during the earlier classical revivals.

7. Mission Hills, Kansas; ca. 1930. The side-gabled form and slender, simplified columns indicate a late date for this example.

8. Union Springs, Alabama; 1920s. Note the one-story side wing to the left with a roof-line balustrade matching that of the main house.

2

5

7

8

ONE-STORY

1. Louisville, Kentucky; ca. 1910. An unusual early example.

2. Louisville, Kentucky; ca. 1910. Kettig House.

3. Dallas, Texas; 1929. Ohrum House. A late example with slender, square porch supports.

4. Smithfield, North Carolina; ca. 1910. Figures 4, 5, and 7 are all variations of the most common early form of the subtype. Note that all have hipped roofs, centered dormers, and full-facade porches. This example has a porch under a separate roof.

5. Selma, Alabama; ca. 1910.

6. Dallas, Texas; 1947. Marsh House. The entry porch is recessed into the house (portico in antis). A cupola has been added to suggest a miniature Mount Vernon.

7. Dallas, Texas; 1914. Gordon House. Note how the porch is under the main roof and the columns are set on pedestals.

8. Dallas, Texas; 1939. Harrison House. A one-story version of the most common late Neoclassical house with side-gabled roof, full-facade porch, and roof-line balustrade.

3

6

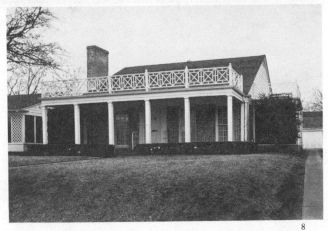

8

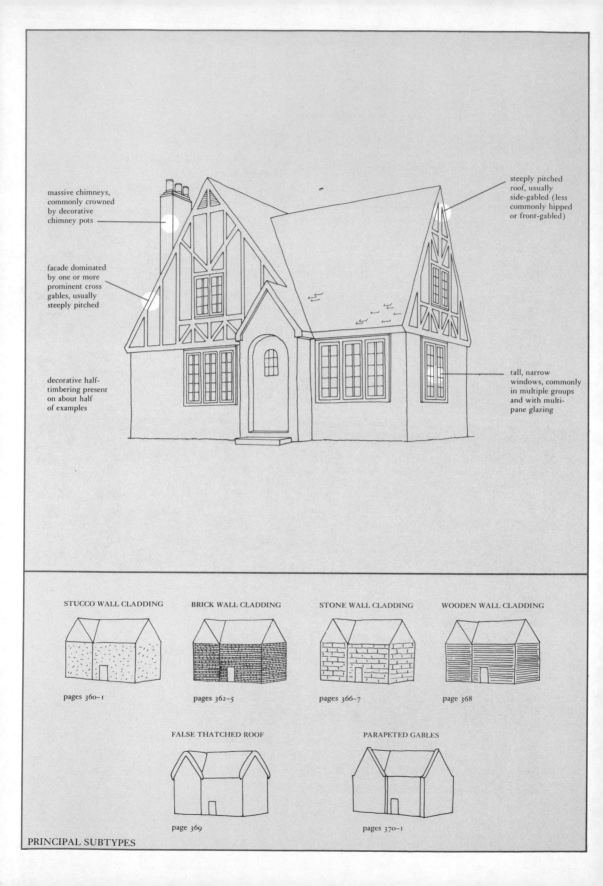

massive chimneys, commonly crowned by decorative chimney pots

steeply pitched roof, usually side-gabled (less commonly hipped or front-gabled)

facade dominated by one or more prominent cross gables, usually steeply pitched

decorative half-timbering present on about half of examples

tall, narrow windows, commonly in multiple groups and with multi-pane glazing

STUCCO WALL CLADDING

pages 360–1

BRICK WALL CLADDING

pages 362–5

STONE WALL CLADDING

pages 366–7

WOODEN WALL CLADDING

page 368

FALSE THATCHED ROOF

page 369

PARAPETED GABLES

pages 370–1

PRINCIPAL SUBTYPES

IDENTIFYING FEATURES

Steeply pitched roof, usually side-gabled (less commonly hipped or front-gabled); facade dominated by one or more prominent cross gables, usually steeply pitched; decorative (i.e., not structural) half-timbering present on about half of examples; tall, narrow windows, usually in multiple groups and with multi-pane glazing; massive chimneys, commonly crowned by decorative chimney pots.

PRINCIPAL SUBTYPES

Six principal subtypes can be distinguished:

STUCCO WALL CLADDING—A relatively small percentage of Tudor houses have stucco walls. These are most common on modest examples built before the widespread adoption of brick and stone veneering techniques in the 1920s. In the early decades of the century wood-frame houses could be most easily disguised as masonry by applying stucco cladding over the wooden studs; many early Tudor houses used this technique, both with and without false half-timbering.

BRICK WALL CLADDING—This is the most common Tudor subtype. Walls of solid brick masonry were sometimes used on landmark examples early in this century, but brick became the preferred wall finish for even the most modest Tudor cottages after masonry veneering became widespread in the 1920s. Brick first-story walls are commonly contrasted with stone, stucco, or wooden claddings on principal gables or upper stories. False half-timbering occurs on about half the houses in this style, with infilling of stucco or brick between the timbers and, quite often, elaborate decorative patterns in the arrangement of timbers or brick.

STONE WALL CLADDING—Stone trim is common on Tudor houses of all subtypes but only a relatively small proportion have stone as the principal wall material. Like the ones just described, these were principally large landmark houses before 1920. During the 1920s and '30s, modest, stone-veneered cottages appeared. In this subtype, brick, stucco, or wooden trim is frequent on gables or second stories, as is false half-timbering.

WOODEN WALL CLADDING—Earlier American styles based on English Medieval precedents (Gothic Revival, Stick, Queen Anne) were executed predominantly in wood, whereas principal walls with wooden cladding are uncommon on Tudor houses. Modest examples are occasionally seen with weatherboard or shingled walls; stuccoed gables with half-timbering may be added above.

FALSE THATCHED ROOF—This rare but very distinctive subtype attempts to mimic with modern materials the picturesque thatched roofs of rural England. Typically, composition roofing materials are rolled around eaves and rakes to suggest a thick layering of thatch. The original composition materials frequently had irregular surface textures, also suggesting thatch, but these have usually been replaced by later coverings with regular shingled patterns. Such roofs were occasionally used on Tudor houses of all types, from modest cottages to grand landmarks.

PARAPETED GABLES—This distinctive subtype is based on the more formal English building traditions of Late Medieval times. In these, the walls of the characteristic front-facing gables rise in a parapet above the roof behind. In side-gabled examples the principal gables are usually similarly parapeted. Shaped Flemish gables are common as are flat-roofed towers and bays having castellated parapets. Elaborate facade detailing of Gothic or Renaissance inspiration is quite common; false half-timbering is unusual. This Jaco-bethan style, as it has been called, was common in architect-designed landmarks built from about 1895 to 1915, particularly in the northeastern states. After World War I, less formal, more picturesque early English models dominated architectural fashion, although scattered parapeted landmarks continued to be built through the 1930s.

VARIANTS AND DETAILS

The Tudor style is loosely based on a variety of early English building traditions ranging from simple folk houses to Late Medieval palaces. Most houses in this style emphasize high-pitched, gabled roofs and elaborated chimneys of Medieval origin, but decorative detailing may draw from Renaissance or even the modern Craftsman traditions.

GABLES—Parapeted gables are characteristic of one distinctive subtype, as noted above. When gables are not parapeted, there is usually a slight overhang of the gable roof; plain or decorated vergeboards may be present. Overlapping gables with eave lines of varying height are common.

HALF-TIMBERING—Decorative (i.e., false) half-timbering, mimicking Medieval infilled timber framing (see page 40), is a common detail. Many different designs and patterns are found; most have stucco infilling between the timbers, but brick, often arranged in decorative patterns, is also used.

CHIMNEYS—Large, elaborated chimneys are favorite Tudor details; these are commonly placed in prominent locations on the front or side of the house. The lower part of the chimney may be decorated with complex masonry or stone patterns and the top commonly has a separate chimney pot for each flue. Multiple shafts of the chimney itself, representing the number of flues contained within, are also used.

DOORWAYS—These are favorite places for adding Renaissance detailing. Small tabs of cut stone may project into surrounding brickwork, giving a quoin-like effect. Simple round-arched doorways with heavy board-and-batten doors are also common. Tudor (flattened pointed) arches are often used in door surrounds or entry porches.

WINDOWS—Windows are typically casements of wood or metal, although more traditional double-hung sash windows are also common. Windows are frequently grouped into strings of three or more, which are most commonly located on or below the main gable or

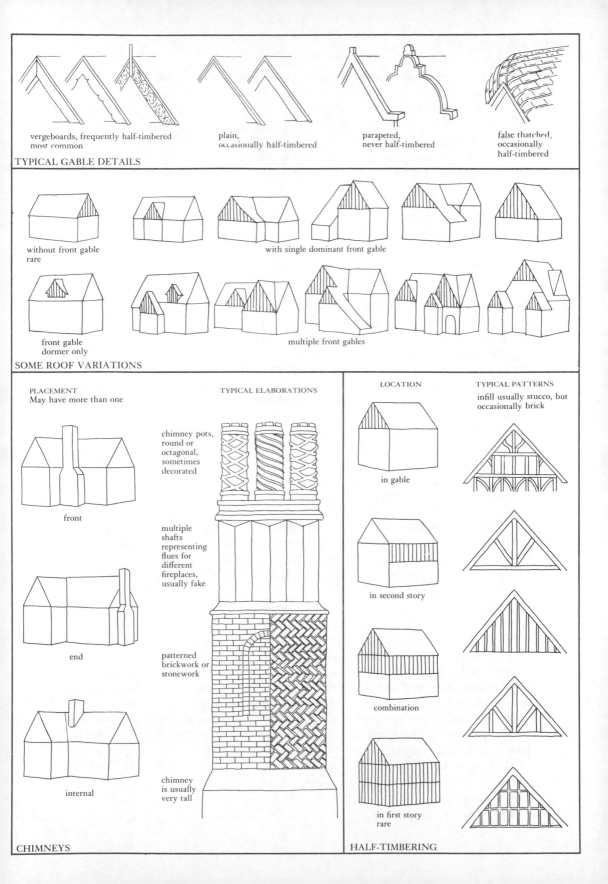

vergeboards, frequently half-timbered
most common

plain,
occasionally half-timbered

parapeted,
never half-timbered

false thatched,
occasionally
half-timbered

TYPICAL GABLE DETAILS

without front gable
rare

with single dominant front gable

front gable
dormer only

multiple front gables

SOME ROOF VARIATIONS

PLACEMENT
May have more than one

front

end

internal

TYPICAL ELABORATIONS

chimney pots,
round or
octagonal,
sometimes
decorated

multiple
shafts
representing
flues for
different
fireplaces,
usually fake

patterned
brickwork or
stonework

chimney
is usually
very tall

CHIMNEYS

LOCATION

in gable

in second story

combination

in first story
rare

TYPICAL PATTERNS
infill usually stucco, but
occasionally brick

HALF-TIMBERING

on one- or two-story bays; small transoms are sometimes present above the main windows. Stone mullions may divide casements and transoms in high-style examples.

OTHER DETAILS—Use of a variety of wall materials is common, both for different vertical units and for different stories; patterned brickwork and stonework is common. Upper stories and gables may overhang lower stories. Castellated parapets are sometimes present. Front-facade porches are generally either small entry porches or are absent entirely. Side porches are frequent.

OCCURRENCE

This dominant style of domestic building was used for a large proportion of early 20th-century suburban houses throughout the country. It was particularly fashionable during the 1920s and early '30s when only the Colonial Revival rivaled it in popularity as a vernacular style.

COMMENTS

The popular name for the style is historically imprecise, since relatively few examples closely mimic the architectural characteristics of Tudor (early 16th-century) England. Instead, the style is loosely based on a variety of late Medieval English prototypes, ranging from thatch-roofed folk cottages to grand manor houses. These traditions are freely mixed in their American Eclectic expressions but are united by an emphasis on steeply pitched, front-facing gables which, although absent on many English prototypes, are almost universally present as a dominant facade element in Tudor houses. About half have ornamental false half-timbering, a characteristic they share with some examples of the earlier Stick and Queen Anne styles, which also drew heavily on Medieval English precedent. Unlike these styles, which were usually executed with wooden (board or shingle) wall cladding, most Tudor houses have stucco, masonry, or masonry-veneered walls.

The earliest American houses in the style date from the late 19th century. These tended to be architect-designed landmarks which, like the first American Queen Anne houses built twenty years earlier, rather closely copied English models. Many were patterned after late Medieval buildings with Renaissance detailing that were popular during the reigns of Elizabeth I (1558–1603) and James I (1603–25), the Elizabethan and Jacobean eras of English history. Architectural historians have proposed the contracted term "Jacobethan" style for these early Tudor landmarks. Most fall into the parapeted gable subtype described above.

The uncommon Tudor landmarks of the Jacobethan type were joined in the decades from 1900 to 1920 by less pretentious Tudor houses which superimposed steep gables, half-timbering, or other typical detailing upon otherwise symmetrical facades (most commonly with full front gables). These modest early examples, unlike most Tudor houses, tend to have walls clad with weatherboard, shingles, or stucco (applied over wooden lath), thus avoiding the expense of solid masonry construction. Still relatively uncommon before World War I, the style expanded explosively in popularity during the 1920s and '30s as masonry veneering techniques allowed even the most modest examples to mimic closely the brick and stone exteriors seen on English prototypes. They show endless variations in overall shape and roof form and are most conveniently subdivided on the basis of their dominant facade materials (brick, stone, stucco, or wood). The style quickly faded from fashion in the late 1930s but has become popular in somewhat modified form during the Neoeclectic movement of the 1970s and '80s.

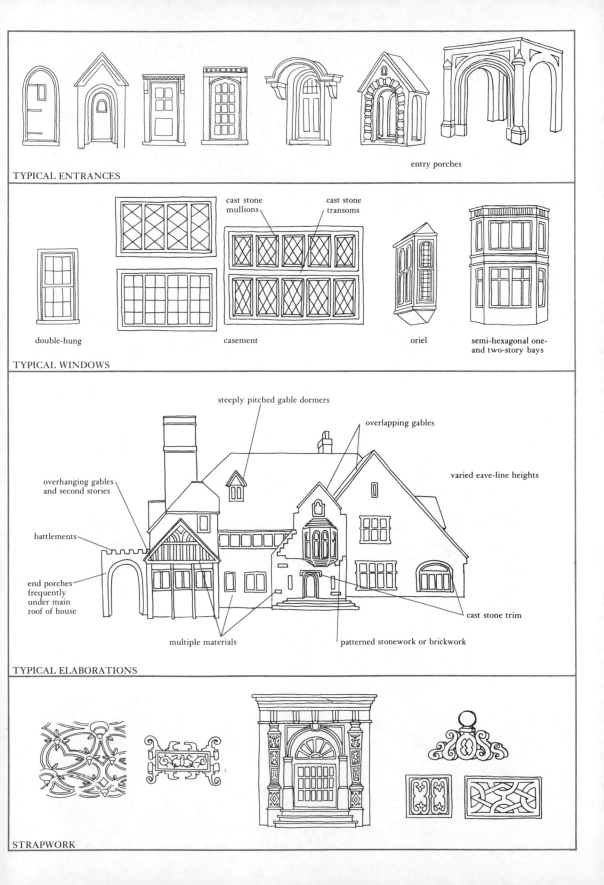

TYPICAL ENTRANCES

entry porches

TYPICAL WINDOWS

double-hung

cast stone mullions

cast stone transoms

casement

oriel

semi-hexagonal one- and two-story bays

TYPICAL ELABORATIONS

steeply pitched gable dormers

overlapping gables

varied eave-line heights

overhanging gables and second stories

battlements

end porches frequently under main roof of house

multiple materials

patterned stonework or brickwork

cast stone trim

STRAPWORK

STUCCO WALL CLADDING

1. Lexington, Kentucky; 1920s.

2. Ashtabula, Ohio; 1910s. Note the wall dormers, an unusual Tudor feature, the brick tabbed door surround, the quoins and the chimney detailing.

3. Louisville, Kentucky; 1910s. Such examples, with the dominant front gable capped by a hip, suggest Continental, rather than British, precedents. They were sometimes referred to as Germanic Cottages by eclectic builders.

4. Cleveland, Ohio; 1920s. This example retains the original roof of rough-cut slate. Note the unusually low eave line and the massive front chimneys.

5. Montgomery, Alabama; 1910s. Many early Tudor houses were symmetrical or nearly so, as in this example.

6. Americus, Georgia; 1920s.

7. Louisville, Kentucky; 1910s. Wymond House. This landmark example has wood-shingle walls above the rough-finished stucco of the first story. Note the multiple groups of casement windows and the shed dormer to the left, contrasting with the hipped dormers on the right.

8. Pittsford, New York; 1920s. Note the decorated vergeboards in the gables and the second-story overhang above the entry.

BRICK WALL CLADDING

1. Chevy Chase, Maryland; 1930s. The stone of the gabled wing contrasts with the brick walls of the rest of house (see Figure 5 below).

2. Durham, North Carolina; 1930s. A late example with relatively little decorative detailing.

3. Hartford, Connecticut, 1910s. A brick lower story with wood-shingled walls above. The symmetrical form seen here is common in pre-1920 examples, but rare after.

4. St. Louis, Missouri; 1920s.

5. Raleigh, North Carolina; 1920s. In placing houses into Tudor subtypes we have used the dominant first-story wall material as the principal criterion. Other materials are commonly used on upper stories (or portions thereof) and for dominant design elements, such as the entry, front gable, or chimney. This unusual example has about equal proportions of brick, stone, and wood on the front facade. Brick slightly dominates the first story as well as the side and back walls not seen in the photograph.

6. Kansas City, Missouri; 1920s. Here a brick chimney, entry area, and foundation walls are used with rough-stuccoed gables and upper story.

7. Toledo, Ohio; 1920s. A landmark example with multiple gables and chimneys and a Renaissance-inspired door surround.

8. Cleveland, Ohio; 1920s. Note the finely detailed entry gable with very tall leaded glass windows, vergeboard, and decorative paneling. The curved roof line over the bay window is a distinctive but relatively rare Tudor feature.

1

4

7

BRICK WALL CLADDING (cont.)

9. Hartford, Connecticut; 1910s.

10. Mendon, Utah; ca. 1935.

11. Dallas, Texas; 1920s. Note the open entry porch beneath an upper-story room. This reflects a common Medieval building practice and is also seen in some Postmedieval English and Gothic Revival examples.

12. St. Louis, Missouri; 1920s. Note that brick, rather than the more usual stucco, is used here as fill in the decorative half-timbering (see also Figure 15).

13. Salisbury, North Carolina; 1910s. An early, symmetrical example with exposed rafters (see Figure 14).

14. Louisville, Kentucky; 1910s. Open eaves with exposed rafters, seen here and in Figure 13, indicate a house with Craftsman influence. These were generally built before about 1915. The early date of this example is confirmed by the symmetrical form. Such elaborate half-timbered effects are also rare on later examples.

15. Cleveland, Ohio; 1920s. A landmark example with multiple rows of casement windows.

16. Hartford, Connecticut; 1910s.

10

13

14

16

STONE WALL CLADDING

1. Lexington, Kentucky; 1930s. Note how the distinctive form (side-gabled roof with the facade dominated by a prominent, steep cross gable and a massive chimney) marks this as a Tudor house even with little additional detailing.

2. Lexington, Kentucky; 1920s.

3. Louisville, Kentucky; 1920s. Note the pair of unusually tall and steeply pitched gables.

4. Durham, North Carolina; 1930s.

5. Durham, North Carolina; 1920s. The Tudor arch of the doorway is also seen in Figure 3.

6. Dallas, Texas; 1920s. Note the oriel window above the entry. Brick is used for window surrounds and in a decorative diamond pattern in the main gable.

7. Cleveland, Ohio; remodeled 1924. S. Weringen House; Philip L. Small, architect. This landmark example has a three-story bay window with castellations above and an irregular slate roof.

1

4

6

WOODEN WALL CLADDING

1. Taylor, Texas; 1930s. The arched extension of the front-gabled wall extending beyond the main house to the right is called an "arcaded wing wall." This is a feature found on both Tudor and Spanish Eclectic houses (see also Figure 3).

2. Kansas City, Missouri; 1930s. An unusually tall and steeply pitched front-gabled roof forms the principal facade. Note the pedimented entry; varying interpretations of classical doorways were added to Tudor house forms in the 1930s.

3. Ste. Genevieve, Missouri; 1920s. It is easy to identify the simple side-gabled form in this example and to see how the addition of the gabled entry, massive front chimney, and dominant front gable converts it to Tudor styling.

4. St. Louis, Missouri; 1920s.

5. Buffalo, New York; 1910s. An early symmetrical example with a full front-gabled roof. Note the open eaves with exposed rafters, borrowed from contemporaneous Craftsman houses. Decorative half-timbering, seen here and in Figure 4, is uncommon on Tudor houses with only wooden wall cladding.

1

3

2

5

4

FALSE THATCHED ROOF

1. Portland, Oregon; 1920s. This steeply pitched roof with curved dormer and curved gable roof gives a convincing imitation of thatch. The roofing material is probably a replacement of the original.

2. St. Louis, Missouri; 1920s. The tightly wrapped roof edge seen here is less common and less convincing than the more gently rolled edge of the other examples shown. Note the undulating texture of the original composition roofing material, visible on the left gable.

3. Cleveland, Ohio; 1920s. False-thatched-roof examples are more likely to have symmetrical facades than other Tudor subtypes (see also figures 4 and 5). The original roofing material has probably been replaced here and in Figure 4.

4. Cleveland, Ohio; 1920s.

5. Cedarhurst, New York; 1910s. This atypical example lacks the front-facing gable usually found on Tudor houses. The trellised front entry shows some Craftsman influence. The original composition roofing is shown; note the textured pattern which closely simulates thatch.

PARAPETED GABLES

1. Richmond, Virginia; 1910s. This finely detailed example was designed for a relatively narrow urban lot.

2. Chicago, Illinois; 1902. Goodyear House; W. C. Zimmerman, architect.

3. Cleveland, Ohio; 1910s. An unusual interpretation with flat roof and castellations all around.

4. St. Louis, Missouri; 1910s. Note the shaped Flemish gables and tabbed window and door surrounds.

5. Concord, North Carolina; 1920s. Both figures 5 and 6 are symmetrical interpretations.

6. Buffalo, New York; 1910s. Albright House. The multiple chimneys with paired flues and the lines of casement windows with stone transoms are features seen in many examples of this subtype.

7. Tuxedo Park, New York; 1910s. Mitchell House. Note the flat-roofed tower with castellations, shaped Flemish gables and the Renaissance-influenced door surround with columns and pediment.

1

3

4

6

2

5

7

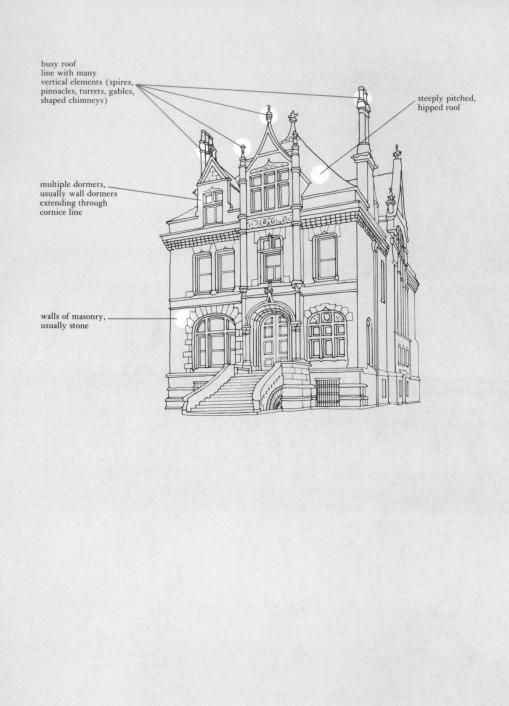

busy roof
line with many
vertical elements (spires,
pinnacles, turrets, gables,
shaped chimneys)

steeply pitched,
hipped roof

multiple dormers,
usually wall dormers
extending through
cornice line

walls of masonry,
usually stone

Chateauesque

IDENTIFYING FEATURES

Steeply pitched hipped roof; busy roof line with many vertical elements (spires, pinnacles, turrets, gables, and shaped chimneys); multiple dormers, usually wall dormers extending through cornice line; walls of masonry (usually stone).

VARIANTS AND DETAILS

The steeply pitched hipped roofs are sometimes truncated above by a flat roof deck; others rise to a high pyramidal apex or hipped ridge. Towers and turrets have steep candle-snuffer roofs. Dormer roofs are usually steep, parapeted gables. Ornamental metal cresting is sometimes used along roof ridges or above cornice lines; the latter generally have elaborate moldings. Gables, doorways, windows, and other facade elements are commonly ornamented with shallow relief carving or Gothic tracing. Windows are usually divided by stone mullions into narrow vertical units with smaller transoms above. Windows and doorways may be arched; the arches often have a characteristic Gothic basket-handle shape.

OCCURRENCE

Chateauesque is a rare style used primarily for architect-designed landmark houses. Scattered examples are found throughout the country but are most frequent in the larger cities of the northeastern states. Most of these date from the late 1880s and '90s. Elsewhere the fashion persisted through the first decade of this century.

COMMENTS

The Chateauesque is loosely based on monumental 16th-century chateaus of France, which combined earlier Gothic elements with that century's increasingly fashionable trend toward Renaissance detailing. As in the originals, Chateauesque houses show varying mixtures of Gothic and Renaissance detail. The style was popularized in this country by Richard Morris Hunt, the first American architect to study at France's prestigious École des Beaux-Arts. In France, a mid-19th-century revival of buildings in the chateau (or François I) style undoubtedly influenced Hunt, who returned to advocate similar buildings for his wealthy clients. Among these were the Vanderbilts, for whom he designed several Chateauesque houses, culminating in Biltmore, George W. Vanderbilt's North Carolina country house completed in 1895, which rivaled its early French prototypes in size and splendor. The Chateauesque style required massive masonry construction and elaborate, expensive detailing and was therefore unsuitable for vernacular imitation. It thus remained a relatively rare, architect-designed fashion throughout its brief period of popularity.

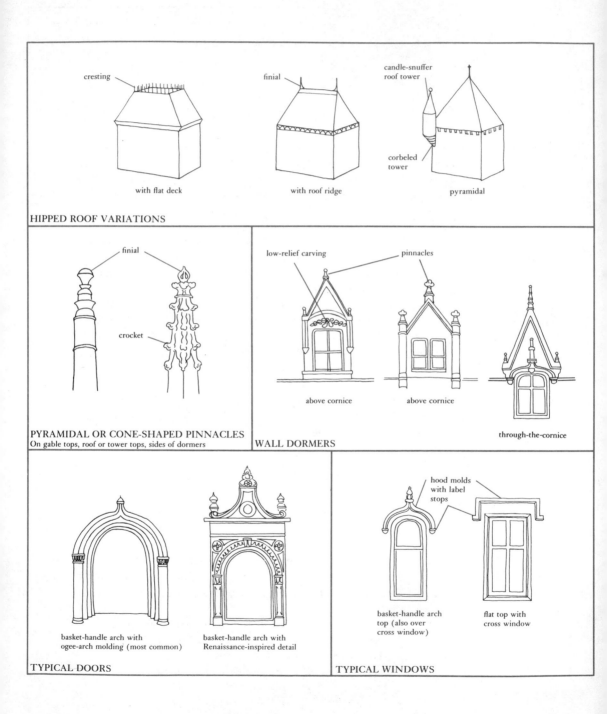

HIPPED ROOF VARIATIONS

cresting

with flat deck

finial

with roof ridge

candle-snuffer roof tower

corbeled tower

pyramidal

PYRAMIDAL OR CONE-SHAPED PINNACLES
On gable tops, roof or tower tops, sides of dormers

finial

crocket

WALL DORMERS

low-relief carving

pinnacles

above cornice

above cornice

through-the-cornice

TYPICAL DOORS

basket-handle arch with ogee-arch molding (most common)

basket-handle arch with Renaissance-inspired detail

TYPICAL WINDOWS

hood molds with label stops

basket-handle arch top (also over cross window)

flat top with cross window

374

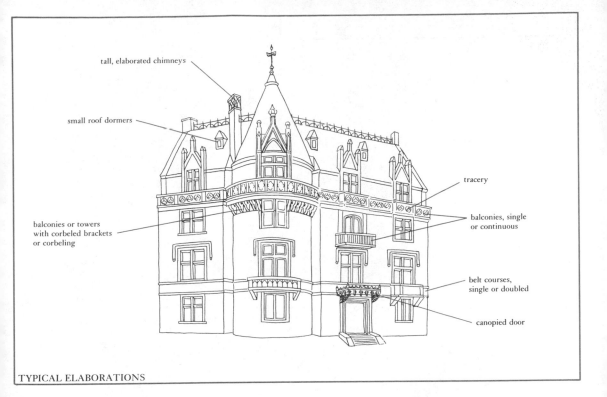

tall, elaborated chimneys

small roof dormers

balconies or towers
with corbeled brackets
or corbeling

tracery

balconies, single
or continuous

belt courses,
single or doubled

canopied door

TYPICAL ELABORATIONS

CHATEAUESQUE

1. Boston, Massachusetts; 1890s. An attached town house; note the through-the-cornice wall dormer.

2. Louisville, Kentucky; 1890s. The paired wall dormers begin above the cornice in this detached town house.

1   2

3

5

6

9

CHATEAUESQUE (cont.)

3. Montgomery, Alabama; 1906. Sabel House. The pyramidal hipped roof is also seen in figures 4 and 7.

4. Chicago, Illinois; ca. 1880. Byram House; Burnham and Root, architects. The entrance door is in a basket-handle arch surrounded by ogee-arch molding.

5. Milwaukee, Wisconsin; ca. 1900. Goldberg House. Note the delicate tracery above the dormers.

6. St. Louis, Missouri; ca. 1900. Note the elaborately sculpted dormer detailing.

7. Cincinnati, Ohio; 1890s. The rough-faced stone of this house is more common in Richardsonian Romanesque houses; Chateauesque examples are more often of brick or smooth-faced stone.

8. New Haven, Connecticut; 1896. Joseph W. Northrup, architect.

9. Asheville, North Carolina; 1895. Biltmore; Richard Morris Hunt, architect. This, the ultimate Chateauesque landmark, is located in a setting of gardens worthy of the French originals.

10. Salisbury, North Carolina; 1890s. Wallace House.

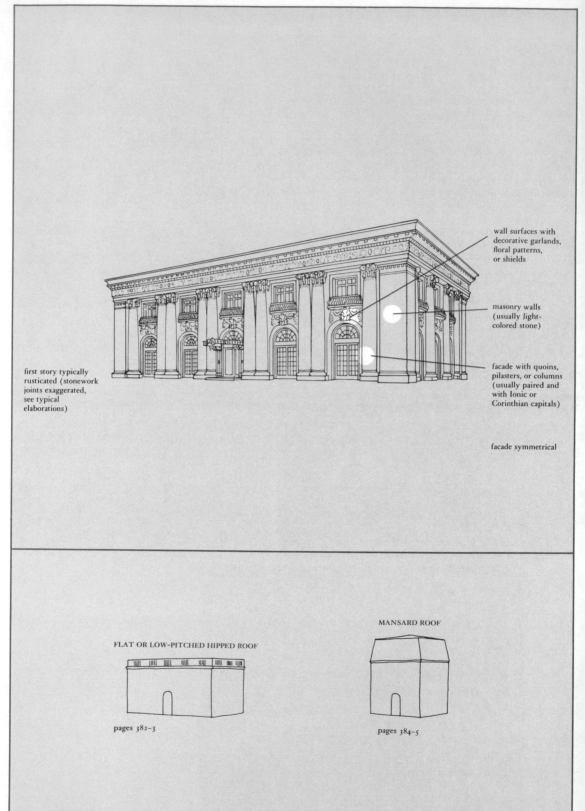

wall surfaces with
decorative garlands,
floral patterns,
or shields

masonry walls
(usually light-
colored stone)

facade with quoins,
pilasters, or columns
(usually paired and
with Ionic or
Corinthian capitals)

facade symmetrical

first story typically
rusticated (stonework
joints exaggerated,
see typical
elaborations)

FLAT OR LOW-PITCHED HIPPED ROOF

pages 382–3

MANSARD ROOF

pages 384–5

PRINCIPAL SUBTYPES

Beaux Arts

IDENTIFYING FEATURES

Wall surfaces with decorative garlands, floral patterns, or shields; facade with quoins, pilasters, or columns (usually paired and with Ionic or Corinthian capitals); walls of masonry (usually smooth, light-colored stone); first story typically rusticated (stonework joints exaggerated); facade symmetrical.

PRINCIPAL SUBTYPES

Two principal subtypes can be distinguished:

FLAT OR LOW-PITCHED HIPPED ROOF—This more common of the two subtypes is based on Italian or northern European Renaissance models. Examples lacking full-height, two-story columns are similar to some landmark Italian Renaissance houses, which, however, lack the elaborate decorative detailing typifying the Beaux Arts. This detailing also generally serves to distinguish colonnaded Beaux Arts houses from closely related Neoclassical examples, which, in addition, seldom have the paired columns typical of the Beaux Arts.

MANSARD ROOF—This subtype is loosely based on 17th- and 18th-century French Renaissance models that have distinctive mansard (dual-pitched hipped) roofs with dormer windows on the steep lower slope. These may resemble earlier Second Empire houses with similar roofs, which are, however, generally of smaller scale with walls of wood or brick, rather than stone, and without the distinctive facade decoration of Beaux Arts examples.

VARIANTS AND DETAILS

The Beaux Arts is a classical style and has many of the same details found in other styles of Renaissance classical inspiration, which, however, seldom have the exuberant surface ornamentation that characterizes the Beaux Arts. Entry porches with roofs supported by classical columns are common. Cornice lines are accented by elaborate moldings, dentils, and modillions. Roof-line balustrades and balustraded window balconies are common, as are elaborated window crowns and surrounds. Classical quoins, pilasters, and columns are almost universal.

OCCURRENCE

Houses in the Beaux Arts style are usually architect-designed landmarks and were built principally in the prosperous urban centers where turn-of-the-century wealth was concentrated. New York, Boston, Washington, D.C., St. Louis, and San Francisco had many examples, as did Newport, Rhode Island, a favorite summer playground for the affluent. Among the earliest domestic examples was The Breakers (page 383) designed by Richard Morris Hunt in 1892, for Cornelius Vanderbilt in Newport. Most domestic examples were built before 1915 but the style persisted until the economic depression of the 1930s. Isolated examples occur throughout the country.

COMMENTS

The term "Beaux Arts" (the approximate French equivalent of "Fine Arts") is used by architectural historians in two different senses. Some use it to describe the entire 1885–1920 period of elaborate eclectic styles because these tended to be advocated by Americans who studied at France's École des Beaux-Arts, the era's premier school of architecture. A more limited meaning, followed here, stresses only one eclectic tradition among the many that were then popular. This is based on classical precedents elaborated by lavish decorative detailing, and was perhaps the most typical of the many styles inspired by study at the École. More than any other style (except perhaps the Chateauesque), the Beaux Arts expressed the taste and values of America's industrial barons at the turn of the century. In those pre–income tax days, great fortunes were proudly displayed in increasingly ornate and expensive houses. Many were of such a size that they were impossible to maintain in later eras of economic recession and higher taxes. Most of the grandest have been destroyed but some are preserved as schools, club houses, or museums. The Preservation Society of Newport County, in particular, has saved several of the most elaborate examples as public museums.

Another concern of the École des Beaux-Arts was for formal planning of the spacial relationships between buildings. This influence provided the impetus for the City Beautiful movement which was prevalent at the turn of the century. The first major example was the planning, supervised by Richard Morris Hunt, for the World's Columbian Exposition in Chicago in 1893. Soon cities such as Cleveland, Philadelphia, and Washington, D.C. implemented monumental planning for their city centers. On a domestic scale this interest in formal design expressed itself in planned suburbs with extensive parks and boulevards lined with landmark houses.

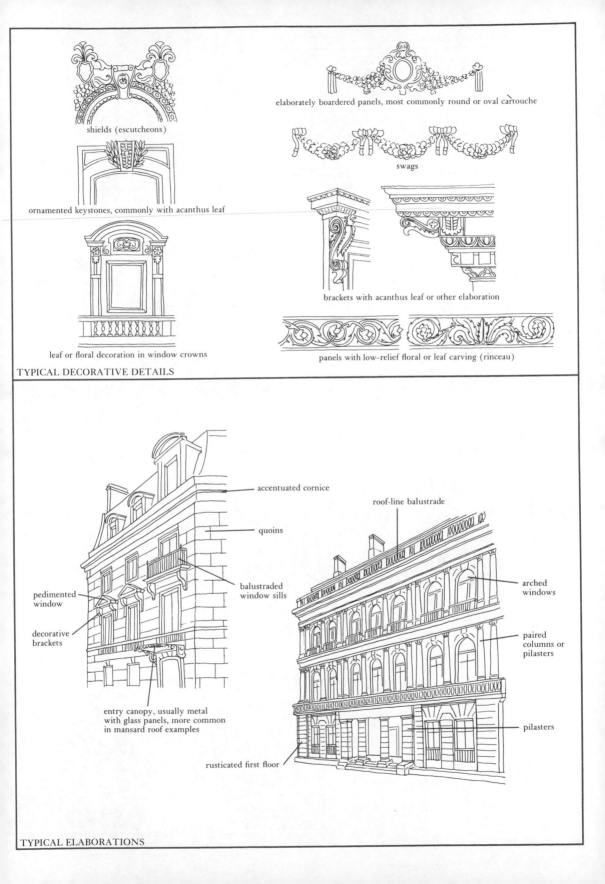

shields (escutcheons)

elaborately boardered panels, most commonly round or oval cartouche

swags

ornamented keystones, commonly with acanthus leaf

brackets with acanthus leaf or other elaboration

leaf or floral decoration in window crowns

panels with low-relief floral or leaf carving (rinceau)

TYPICAL DECORATIVE DETAILS

accentuated cornice

roof-line balustrade

quoins

pedimented window

balustraded window sills

arched windows

decorative brackets

paired columns or pilasters

entry canopy, usually metal with glass panels, more common in mansard roof examples

rusticated first floor

pilasters

TYPICAL ELABORATIONS

FLAT OR LOW-PITCHED HIPPED ROOF

1. Louisville, Kentucky; 1901. Ferguson House.

2. Cincinnati, Ohio; ca. 1910. Note the wide frieze with windows and floral swags.

3. Dallas, Texas; 1906. Alexander House. This example lacks the floral ornamentation typical of the style, but the paired columns with bands and flat roof with attic windows indicate a Beaux Arts, rather than Neoclassical, inspiration.

4. Cleveland, Ohio; 1914. Tremaine House; Frederic W. Striebinger, architect. This example, and figures 6 and 8, reflect a common Renaissance form in which a main block is flanked by symmetrical front-projecting wings. As in Figure 8, an arcaded porch is here set between the wings.

5. Frankfort, Kentucky; 1914. Governor's Mansion.

6. Newport, Rhode Island; 1902. Rosecliff; McKim, Mead and White, architects.

7. St. Louis, Missouri; 1899. Hills House. An example with a low-pitched hipped roof. Note the flat-roof portico on the left, pedimented portico on the front, and semi-circular portico to right.

8. Newport, Rhode Island; 1892. The Breakers; Richard Morris Hunt, architect (seaside facade). Low-pitched hipped roofs, usually covered with tiles as seen here, also occur in Beaux Arts houses. In other details these are similar to flat-roof examples. Unfortunately the photograph cannot show the numerous small floral details in this Beaux Arts landmark.

2

4

6

8

MANSARD ROOF

1. Washington, District of Columbia; 1907. Bliss House; A. Goenner, architect. Attached Beaux Arts town houses such as this are found principally in the larger cities of the Northeast. The mansard roof is particularly favored for urban houses because it reduces the apparent height of upper-floor living space.

2. Washington, District of Columbia; 1909. Fahnestock House; Nathan C. Wyeth, architect.

3. Washington, District of Columbia; 1901. Walsh House; Henry Andersen, architect.

4. Montgomery, Alabama; ca. 1910. Sabel House. A rare example built far from the urban centers of the Northeast.

5. Buffalo, New York; 1920s. The curved central wing is unusual in this late example.

6. New York, New York; 1905. DeLamar House; C. P. H. Gilbert, architect. This example has the paired side wings that are seen more frequently in the flat-roof subtype.

7. Washington, District of Columbia; 1909. Moran House; George Oakley Totten, Jr., architect. The entryways of this subtype rarely have the colonnaded entry porches seen in the flat-roof subtype. Here only a simple glass canopy is used over the entrance door.

2

3

6

7

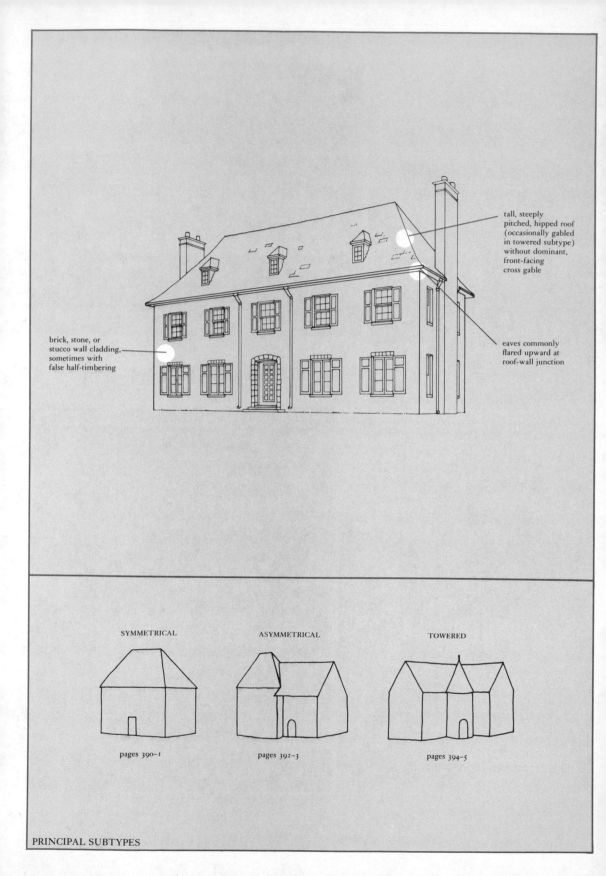

tall, steeply
pitched, hipped roof
(occasionally gabled
in towered subtype)
without dominant,
front-facing
cross gable

eaves commonly
flared upward at
roof-wall junction

brick, stone, or
stucco wall cladding,
sometimes with
false half-timbering

SYMMETRICAL

ASYMMETRICAL

TOWERED

pages 390–1

pages 392–3

pages 394–5

PRINCIPAL SUBTYPES

French Eclectic

IDENTIFYING FEATURES

Tall, steeply pitched hipped roof (occasionally gabled in towered subtype) without dominant front-facing cross gable; eaves commonly flared upward at roof-wall junction; brick, stone, or stucco wall cladding, sometimes with decorative half-timbering.

PRINCIPAL SUBTYPES

Three principal subtypes can be recognized; each shows a great variety of detailing and wall materials:

SYMMETRICAL—In this subtype, the massive hipped roof, normally with the ridge paralleling the front of the house, dominates a symmetrical facade with centered entry. Facade detailing is usually rather formal, inspired by smaller French manor houses rather than grand chateaus or modest farmhouses. Wings are frequently added to the sides of the main block.

ASYMMETRICAL—This is the most common subtype and includes both picturesque examples based on rambling French farmhouses as well as more formal houses similar to the symmetrical subtype, but with off-center doorways and asymmetrical facades.

TOWERED—This common subtype is immediately identifiable by the presence of a prominent round tower with a high, conical roof. The tower generally houses the principal doorway. Decorative half-timbering is particularly common in this subtype, which is loosely patterned after similar farmhouses from the province of Normandy in northwestern France; Eclectic builders often called these Norman Cottages.

VARIANTS AND DETAILS

Based upon precedents provided by many centuries of French domestic architecture, the style shows great variety in form and detailing but is united by the characteristic roof. (Only the Spanish Eclectic style, similarly based upon a long and complex architectural tradition, approaches it in variety.) Informal domestic building in northwestern France (particularly Normandy and Brittany) shares much with Medieval English tradition. The use of half-timbering with a variety of different wall materials, as well as roofs of flat tile, slate, stone, or thatch, are common to both. As a result, French Eclectic houses often resemble the contemporaneous Tudor style based on related English precedent. French examples, however, normally lack the dominant front-facing cross gables characteristic of the Tudor. In contrast to these generally informal, rural prototypes, many French Eclectic houses show formal Renaissance detailing resembling that of the English Georgian.

Doors in informal examples are usually set in simple arched openings; doors in symmetrical and formal houses may be surrounded by stone quoins or more elaborate Renaissance detailing (pilasters, pediments, etc.). Windows may be either double-hung or casement sashes, the latter sometimes with small leaded panes. Full-length casement windows with shutters (French doors) are sometimes used. Three distinctive types of dormers are common.

OCCURRENCE

This relatively uncommon style is found throughout the country in Eclectic suburbs of the 1920s and '30s. Out of fashion during the 1940s and '50s, a Neoeclectic emphasis on French models has been gathering momentum since the 1960s (see page 490).

COMMENTS

Many Americans served in France during World War I, and their first-hand familiarity with the prototypes probably helped popularize the style. In addition, a number of photographic studies of modest French houses were published in the 1920s, giving architects and builders many models to draw from. Pre-1920 examples are rare and are usually of the formal, symmetrical type. These were usually inspired by the earlier and more pretentious Chateauesque or Beaux Arts traditions.

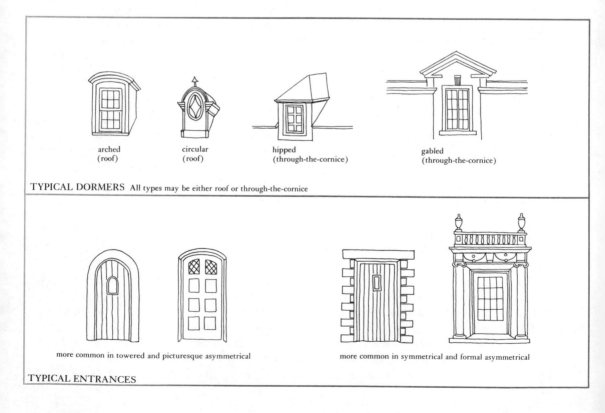

arched
(roof)

circular
(roof)

hipped
(through-the-cornice)

gabled
(through-the-cornice)

TYPICAL DORMERS All types may be either roof or through-the-cornice

more common in towered and picturesque asymmetrical

more common in symmetrical and formal asymmetrical

TYPICAL ENTRANCES

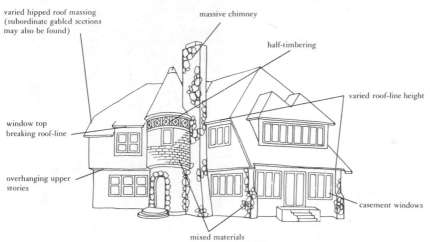

varied hipped roof massing
(subordinate gabled sections
may also be found)

massive chimney

half-timbering

varied roof-line height

window top
breaking roof-line

overhanging upper
stories

casement windows

mixed materials
(i.e., stone with brick)

MORE COMMON IN SYMMETRICAL SUBTYPE

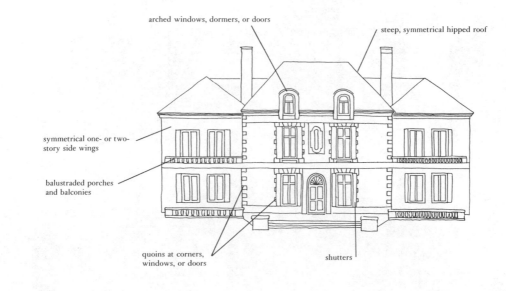

arched windows, dormers, or doors

steep, symmetrical hipped roof

symmetrical one- or two-
story side wings

balustraded porches
and balconies

quoins at corners,
windows, or doors

shutters

TYPICAL ELABORATIONS

SYMMETRICAL

1. Buffalo, New York; 1920s. This example has been turned 90° to adapt to a narrow urban lot. What would ordinarily be the side facade faces the street and has been elaborated with shutters and a dormer.

2. Dallas, Texas; 1941. Evans House.

3. Dallas, Texas; 1924. Hall House.

4. Cleveland, Ohio; 1920s. Although the main block of this house appears symmetrical, a close look will reveal the right side to be narrower than the left. The open eave with exposed rafters is uncommon in French Eclectic houses.

5. Buffalo, New York; 1920s. This house has two identical forward-facing wings; the left one is hidden behind a tree in the photograph. The through-the-cornice wall dormers have windows placed higher in the wing than those in the taller main block.

6. Dallas, Texas; ca. 1917. Lewis House; Hal Thomson, architect. This house has Renaissance detailing borrowed from the Beaux Arts movement. Note the columns beside the door and in the side wings, the pediment over the entry at roof level, the balustrades on porch, over door, and in the roof section. The pitch of the hipped roof is also lower than in most examples of the style.

7. St. Louis, Missouri; 1914. Mallinckrodt House; James P. Jamieson, architect. A strong Chateauesque influence is evident in the door surround, dormers, and roof ornaments of this early example.

ASYMMETRICAL

1. Louisville, Kentucky; 1920s. Note the irregular quoins around the door and windows.

2. Richmond, Virginia; 1920s. A formal example with a shallow-projecting wing that is difficult to distinguish in the photograph. The house is designed for a narrow urban lot.

3. Cincinnati, Ohio; 1920s. Note the varied eave-line heights, massive chimney, and two types of through-the-cornice wall dormers. Compare this informal, picturesque house with Figure 7, a formal, Renaissance-inspired example.

4. Cleveland, Ohio; 1920s. Examples based on informal French models sometimes affect Medieval half-timbering as here.

5. Dallas, Texas; 1930s.

6. St. Louis, Missouri; 1910s.

7. Washington, District of Columbia; 1904. Graff House; Jules Henri de Sibour, architect. This house has formal Renaissance detailing; note the regular quoins, keystone lintels, cornice-line dentils, and pedimented dormers.

8. Dallas, Texas; 1930s. Note the decorative brick pattern of the entryway.

2

5

6

8

TOWERED

1. Raleigh, North Carolina; 1930s. Note the three slightly different dormers.

2. Dallas, Texas; 1937. Gilliland House. This example is unusual in not having the entrance in the tower (see also Figure 8). Note the two chimneys of differing shapes and materials and also that none of the five windows are identical.

3. Mission Hills, Kansas; 1930s.

4. Kansas City, Missouri; 1930s.

5. Buffalo, New York; 1930s. The regular, formal placement of the windows is not typical of this subtype.

6. Kansas City, Missouri; 1930s. Note the multi-colored slate roof, tower overhang, massive chimney, and tiny band of half-timbering on the tower.

7. Cleveland, Ohio; 1930s. Here a stone tower is combined with walls of half-timbered stucco or brick. Note the curving secondary hipped roof, simulating thatch, above the bay windows.

8. Tuxedo Park, New York; 1930s. Kent House. This landmark example has several towers and an unusually tall roof—note the double row of dormers.

3   4

6   7

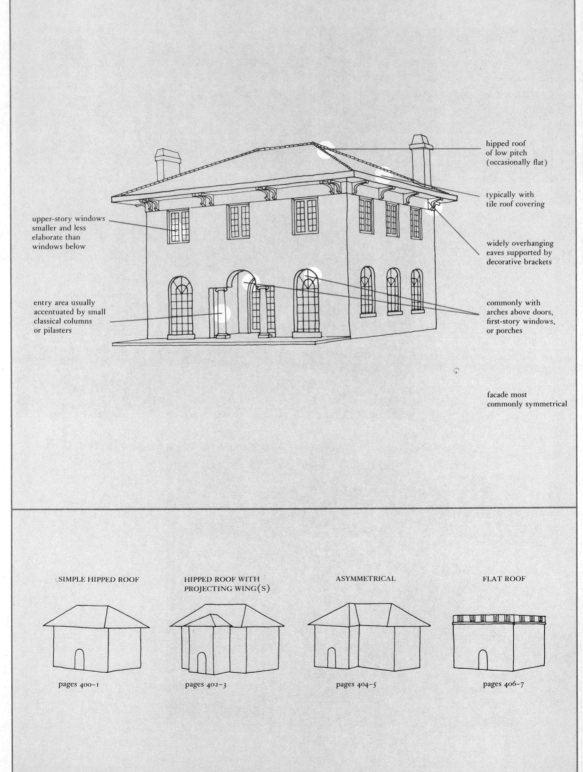

hipped roof
of low pitch
(occasionally flat)

typically with
tile roof covering

widely overhanging
eaves supported by
decorative brackets

upper-story windows
smaller and less
elaborate than
windows below

entry area usually
accentuated by small
classical columns
or pilasters

commonly with
arches above doors,
first-story windows,
or porches

facade most
commonly symmetrical

SIMPLE HIPPED ROOF

HIPPED ROOF WITH
PROJECTING WING(S)

ASYMMETRICAL

FLAT ROOF

pages 400–1

pages 402–3

pages 404–5

pages 406–7

PRINCIPAL SUBTYPES

Italian Renaissance

IDENTIFYING FEATURES

Low-pitched hipped roof (flat in some examples); roof typically covered by ceramic tiles; upper-story windows smaller and less elaborate than windows below; commonly with arches above doors, first-story windows, or porches; entrance area usually accented by small classical columns or pilasters; facade most commonly symmetrical.

PRINCIPAL SUBTYPES

Four principal subtypes can be distinguished:

SIMPLE HIPPED ROOF—Over half of Italian Renaissance houses have a simple hipped roof with a flat, symmetrical front facade. Full-width porches, often with massive square piers as porch supports, are frequent in examples built before 1920.

HIPPED ROOF WITH PROJECTING WING(S)—Many Italian Renaissance houses have either a small central wing projecting forward from the front facade, or two small wings at either end of the facade with a recessed central block in between.

ASYMMETRICAL—A relatively small proportion of Italian Renaissance houses have unbalanced, asymmetrical facades. Usually the asymmetry involves only door and window placement on an otherwise symmetrical building of simple square or rectangular plan. Less commonly L plans or more complex shapes are used.

FLAT ROOF—Many high-style Italian Renaissance houses have flat roofs, usually with a prominent, dentiled cornice and roof-line balustrade. Typically the first story is rusticated (finished as exaggerated stonework courses), while the floors above have smooth wall finishes. Facades are symmetrical. These are almost always architect-designed landmarks built of stone; they are closely related to flat-roofed, Beaux Arts style houses, which are similar but add more elaborate facade detailing.

VARIANTS AND DETAILS

Details are borrowed more or less directly from the Italian originals. Among the most characteristic are recessed entry porches and full-length first-story windows with arches above. The roof, except when flat, commonly has broadly overhanging, boxed eaves; normally the eaves have decorative brackets beneath. These features of the roof-wall junction are helpful in distinguishing Italian Renaissance houses from related Mediterranean styles with tiled roofs. Mission houses usually have wide eave overhangs, but these are commonly open rather than boxed-in. Spanish Eclectic houses normally have little or no eave overhang. Eave brackets are rare on both Mission and Spanish Eclectic houses. Common decorative details include quoins, roof-line balustrades, pedimented windows, classical door surrounds, molded cornices, and belt courses. Stucco, masonry, or masonry-veneered walls are universal; wooden wall claddings are never used. Note that similar details appear in several earlier styles with Renaissance roots, particularly the Georgian, Adam, and Italianate. Because of these similarities, Italian Renaissance houses sometimes resemble Georgian- or Adam-inspired examples of the contemporaneous Colonial Revival.

OCCURRENCE

The Italian Renaissance style is found in early 20th-century houses throughout the country but is considerably less common than the contemporary Craftsman, Tudor, or Colonial Revival styles. Primarily a style for architect-designed landmarks in major metropolitan areas prior to World War I, vernacular interpretations spread widely with the perfection of masonry veneering techniques; most of these date from the 1920s. The style steadily declined in popularity through the 1930s, and post-1940 examples are rare.

COMMENTS

The latest revival of interest in Italian Renaissance domestic models began with the landmark Villard Houses in New York (McKim, Mead & White, 1883). Other fashionable architects used the style in the late 1880s and '90s as a dramatic contrast to the Gothic-inspired Shingle or Queen Anne styles. These Second Renaissance Revival houses tended to mimic more closely their Italian predecessors than did the free interpretations of the preceding Italianate style. There are several reasons for this increased authenticity. By the late 19th century a great many American architects, and their clients, had visited Italy and thus had some first-hand familiarity with the original models. Furthermore, improved printing technology provided ready access to excellent photographic documentation of these models. The earlier Italianate style, in contrast, was usually based on pattern book drawings by professionals with no first-hand knowledge of Italian buildings. In addition, many houses of the earlier Italianate style had wooden wall cladding, whereas later examples invariably mimic the stuccoed or masonry walls of their original Italian prototypes. The perfection of masonry veneering techniques after World War I made this possible in even the most modest examples of the style.

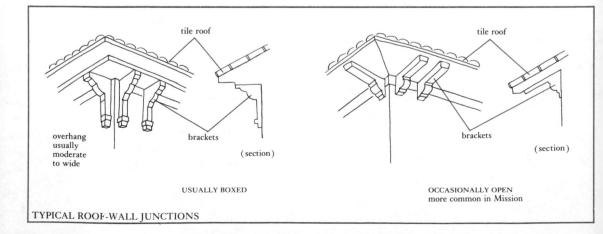

tile roof

tile roof

overhang usually moderate to wide

brackets

brackets

(section)

(section)

USUALLY BOXED

OCCASIONALLY OPEN
more common in Mission

TYPICAL ROOF-WALL JUNCTIONS

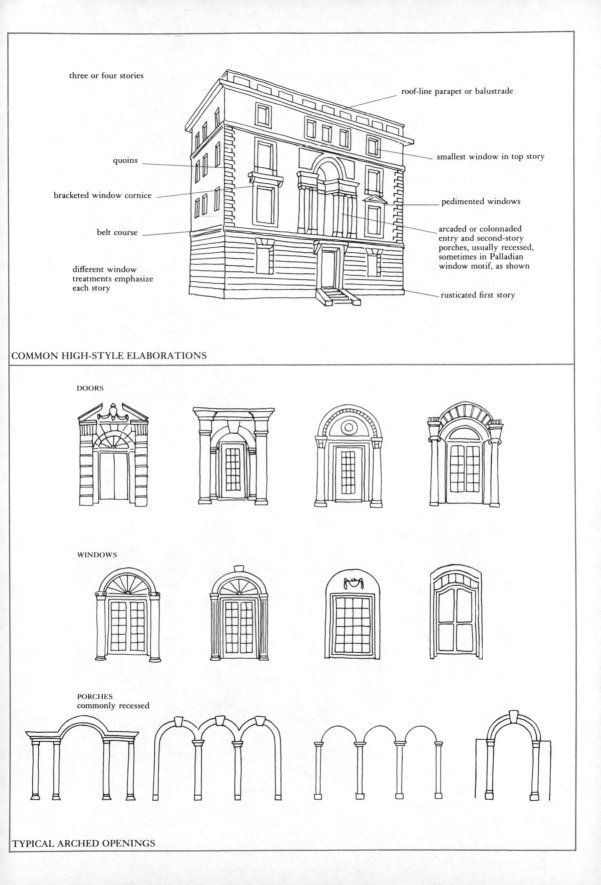

three or four stories

roof-line parapet or balustrade

quoins

smallest window in top story

bracketed window cornice

pedimented windows

belt course

arcaded or colonnaded entry and second-story porches, usually recessed, sometimes in Palladian window motif, as shown

different window treatments emphasize each story

rusticated first story

COMMON HIGH-STYLE ELABORATIONS

DOORS

WINDOWS

PORCHES
commonly recessed

TYPICAL ARCHED OPENINGS

SIMPLE HIPPED ROOF

1. Kansas City, Missouri; ca. 1910. A simple stucco interpretation with Spanish influence in the door surround.

2. Montgomery, Alabama; 1920s. An unusual one-story example with an elaborate entry porch bounded by paired pilasters.

3. Montgomery, Alabama; 1910s. This example has paired cornice-line brackets and a triple-arched entry porch with balusters above.

4. Shelbyville, Kentucky; ca. 1920. Note the cornice-line brackets and full-length arched windows on the first story.

5. Washington, District of Columbia; 1910. MacVeagh House; Nathan Wyeth, architect. This landmark town house now has a carriage porch added at the entry.

6. New Orleans, Louisiana; ca. 1905. Weis House; MacKenzie and Goldstein, architects. This example shows Prairie influence in its heavy square brick piers and Beaux Arts influence in the paired columns and the elaborated shields ornamenting the brick piers.

7. Cincinnati, Ohio; ca. 1910. Note the attic-story windows, the quoins, and the second-story windows with triangular pediments above and balustraded balconies below.

8. Louisville, Kentucky; 1908. Rostrevor; Loomis and Hartman, architects. A large five-ranked stone example with an unusual recessed entry porch. Note that the shape of the porch echoes that of a Palladian window (see also Figure 2).

1

3

6

7

HIPPED ROOF WITH PROJECTING WING(S)

PROJECTING CENTRAL WING

1. Montgomery, Alabama; ca. 1920. A simple three-ranked brick example. Note the recessed entry with Palladian motif, full-length French doors set in blind arches, and one-story side wings.

2. Buffalo, New York; ca. 1920. This example is unusual in lacking wide overhanging eaves.

3. New Orleans, Louisiana; ca. 1910. This elaborate stucco example has quoins and recessed upper and lower porches in the front wing.

PROJECTING SIDE WINGS

4. Wichita, Kansas; ca. 1920. The tall window to the left of the front door probably lights the stairway.

5. Kansas City, Missouri; 1913. Halpin House; John W. McKecknie, architect. Made of concrete clad with cut stone, this house is unusual in having elaborated, arched windows in the upper story rather than the lower.

6. Saratoga, California, vicinity; ca. 1920. Phelan House. This large house has little decorative detailing. The raised terrace with balustrade, a typical feature, is also seen in figures 2 and 4.

7. Richmond, Virginia; ca. 1920. This unusual example has a three-story central block with two-story wings projecting forward.

8. Dallas, Texas; 1920. Ragland House.

1

3

5

7

ASYMMETRICAL

1. St. Louis, Missouri; 1920s. This simple brick example has lower-story windows in blind arches and a side entrance.

2. Durham, North Carolina; 1920s. This stucco example is a simpler version of its neighbor shown in Figure 3.

3. Durham, North Carolina; 1920s. A seven-ranked brick example with asymmetrical recessed porch.

4. Louisville, Kentucky; 1920s. This example has Beaux Arts detailing over the door and arched windows.

5. Kansas City, Missouri, 1910s. An unusual feature for this style is the prominent front chimney.

6. Montgomery, Alabama; 1910s. The taller, projecting section recalls the towers of the Italianate style.

7. St. Louis, Missouri; 1910s. Note the prominent Palladian-motif entry and angled side wings.

8. Montgomery, Alabama, 1910s.

1

4   5

7

FLAT ROOF

1. Dallas, Texas; 1909. Hill House. A Prairie–Italian Renaissance hybrid. Remove the brackets and add a hipped roof with overhanging eaves and you would have a house similar to those on pages 444–5.

2. Richmond, Virginia; ca. 1910. A detached, three-ranked town house. There is actually a low-pitched roof behind the roof-line balustrade.

3. Washington, District of Columbia; ca. 1910.

4. St. Louis, Missouri; ca. 1910. Note the solid roof parapet, rather than the more usual balustrade, and the recessed Palladian entry.

5. St. Louis, Missouri; ca. 1910. Note the rusticated first story, the triangular and segmental pediments above the second-story windows, and the upper-story pilasters. An unusual note is the unaccented entry at the left side of this absolutely symmetrical house; a bay window is used where one would expect the entry.

6. Savannah, Georgia; 1917. Armstrong House; Henrik Wallis, architect. A colonnaded, curved side porch or gallery is visible to the right. Arcaded and colonnaded porches such as these are sometimes called "loggias" (see pages 402–5 for other examples). A similar one-story side wing porch is seen in Figure 7.

7. St. Louis, Missouri; ca. 1900. Faust House. The balustrade on the side porch roof is a typical Italian Renaissance elaboration. Such balustrades can be found at the roof line, on balconies, on entry- or side-porch roofs, and along the perimeter of platform porches. The individual balusters usually resemble small bowling pins bounded by moldings above and below. Solid and wrought-iron railings are also found. In this example some floral details are present over the first-story windows. Full-scale floral detailing would place this, or other houses on this page, in the contemporary Beaux Arts style.

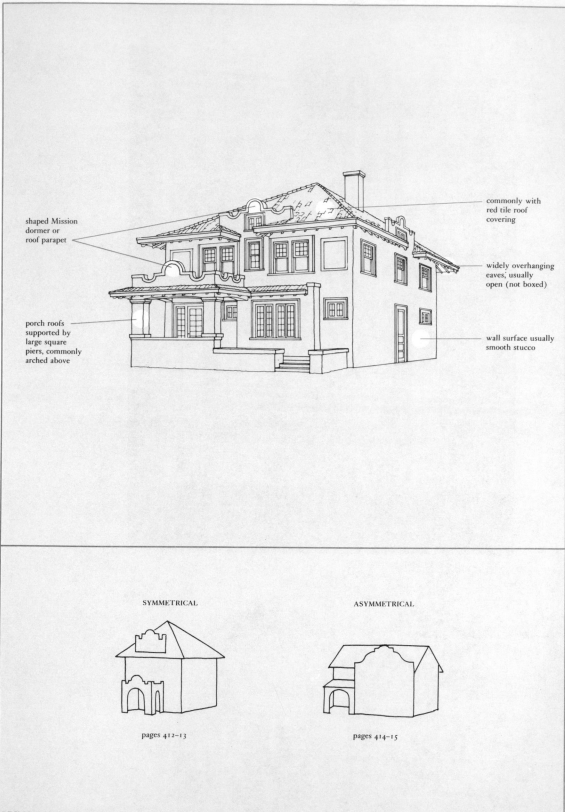

shaped Mission
dormer or
roof parapet

commonly with
red tile roof
covering

widely overhanging
eaves, usually
open (not boxed)

porch roofs
supported by
large square
piers, commonly
arched above

wall surface usually
smooth stucco

SYMMETRICAL

ASYMMETRICAL

pages 412–13

pages 414–15

PRINCIPAL SUBTYPES

Mission

IDENTIFYING FEATURES

Mission-shaped dormer or roof parapet (these may be on either main roof or porch roof); commonly with red tile roof covering; widely overhanging eaves, usually open; porch roofs supported by large, square piers, commonly arched above; wall surface usually smooth stucco.

PRINCIPAL SUBTYPES

Two principal subtypes can be distinguished:

SYMMETRICAL—About half of Mission houses have balanced, symmetrical facades. These are most commonly of simple square or rectangular plan with hipped roofs.

ASYMMETRICAL—The remaining half of Mission houses have asymmetrical facades of widely varying form. Most typically the facade asymmetry is superimposed on a simple square or rectangular plan. Elaborate, rambling compound plans are found on some landmark examples.

VARIANTS AND DETAILS

A great variety of shaped dormers and roof parapets mimic those found on some Spanish Colonial mission buildings. Few are precise copies of the original models. Most examples have prominent one-story porches either at the entry area or covering the full width of the facade; these sometimes have arched roof supports to simulate the arcades of Hispanic buildings. Mission-like bell towers occur on a few landmark examples. Quatrefoil windows are common; decorative detailing is generally absent, although patterned tiles, carved stonework, or other wall surface ornament is occasionally used. Some examples have unusual visor roofs. These are narrow, tiled roof segments cantilevered out from a smooth wall surface (similar to the pent roofs seen in some Georgian or Queen Anne houses). They most commonly occur beneath the parapets of flat roofs.

OCCURRENCE

California was the birthplace of the Mission style and many of its landmark examples are concentrated there. The earliest were built in the 1890s; by 1900 houses in this style were spreading eastward under the influence of fashionable architects and national builders' magazines. Although never common outside of the southwestern states, scattered examples were built in early 20th-century suburbs throughout the country. Most date from the years between 1905 and 1920.

COMMENTS

One scholar has noted that the style "is the Californian counterpart" of the Georgian-inspired Colonial Revival that was then gaining popularity in the northeastern states. Rather than copy the East's revival of its own colonial past, California turned to its Hispanic heritage for inspiration. Several California architects began to advocate the style in the late 1880s and early 1890s. It received further impetus when the Santa Fe and Southern Pacific railways adopted the style for stations and resort hotels throughout the West. Most commonly, typical Hispanic design elements (shaped parapets, arches, quatrefoil windows, etc.) were borrowed and freely adapted to adorn traditional shapes. In a few landmark examples, however, the forms of the early missions, including twin bell towers and elaborate arcades, were faithfully followed in domestic designs. In still other examples, innovative architects designed Mission buildings with many features borrowed from the contemporary Craftsman and Prairie movements; some even anticipate the simplicity of the subsequent International style. The style quickly faded from favor after World War I as architectural fashion shifted from free, simplified adaptations of earlier prototypes to more precise, correct copies. From this concern grew the Spanish Eclectic style which drew inspiration from a broader spectrum of both Old and New World Spanish buildings.

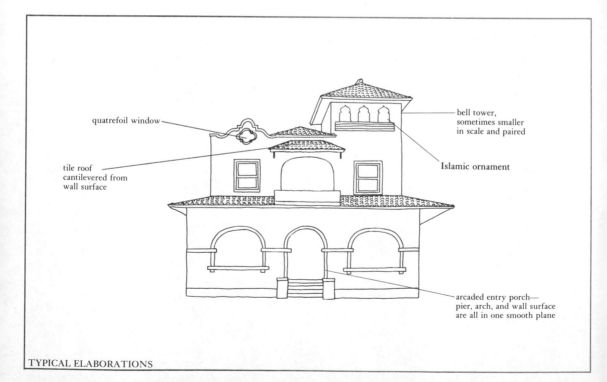

quatrefoil window

tile roof
cantilevered from
wall surface

bell tower,
sometimes smaller
in scale and paired

Islamic ornament

arcaded entry porch—
pier, arch, and wall surface
are all in one smooth plane

TYPICAL ELABORATIONS

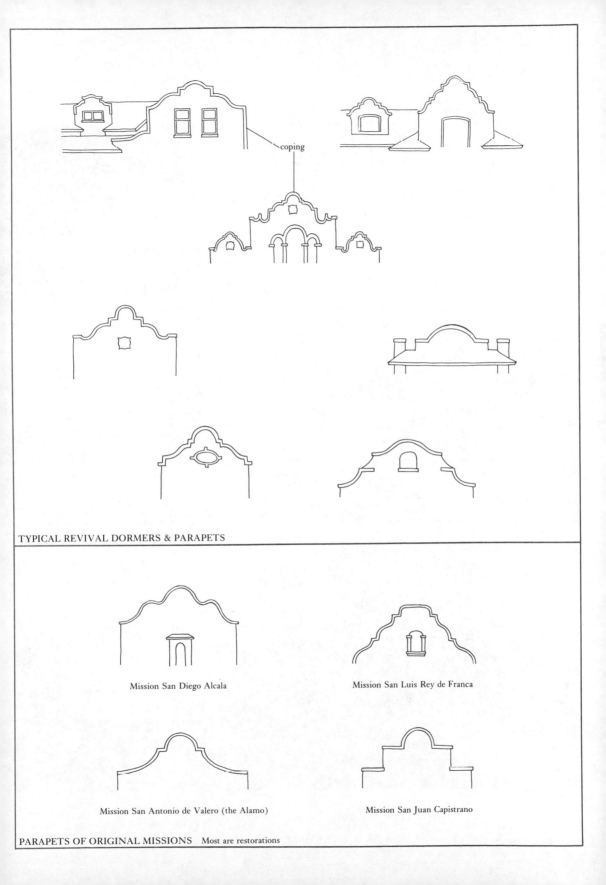

coping

TYPICAL REVIVAL DORMERS & PARAPETS

Mission San Diego Alcala

Mission San Luis Rey de Franca

Mission San Antonio de Valero (the Alamo)

Mission San Juan Capistrano

PARAPETS OF ORIGINAL MISSIONS   Most are restorations

SYMMETRICAL

1. Dallas, Texas; 1912. Bianchi House.

2. Hammond, Louisiana; ca. 1910. Preston House. The wood wall cladding is unusual. Although open eaves are most common in the style, boxed eaves also occur, usually with brackets below as seen here and in Figure 3.

3. Dallas, Texas; 1913. Harris House. This house originally had a second shaped parapet above the two central piers.

4. Kansas City, Missouri; ca. 1910. This house shows the four-square shape that was popular in various styles built from about 1900 to 1915.

5. Oklahoma City, Oklahoma; ca. 1910.

6. Washington, District of Columbia; 1902. Barney House; Waddy B. Wood, architect. A rare example of a Mission town house.

7. Louisville, Kentucky; ca. 1910. Caperton House.

8. Redlands, California; 1901. Burrage House; Charles Bingham, architect. This landmark house is a full-scale copy of a Spanish mission, complete with bell towers and arcaded side wings.

1

3

4

7

2

5

6

8

ASYMMETRICAL

1. Fort Smith, Arkansas; ca. 1910. In this example the entire side gable of the main roof is covered by a shaped parapet.

2. Oklahoma City, Oklahoma; ca. 1910. Here a flat roof is surrounded by a parapet with a projecting visor roof beneath; the porch roof repeats this pattern on a smaller scale.

3. Salisbury, North Carolina; ca. 1910. The recessed arcaded porch on the second story creates asymmetry on this otherwise balanced facade.

4. Kansas City, Missouri; ca. 1910. The bell tower is unusual on relatively modest examples such as this.

5. White Plains, New York; ca. 1910. Scholz House.

6. Redlands, California; 1903. Holt House. The decorative detailing is unusually exuberant for the Mission style, which normally stresses smooth, flat wall surfaces.

7. Kansas City, Missouri; ca. 1910. Few Mission houses are built of stone; brick and stucco are the most common materials.

8. Fullerton, California; ca. 1915. Note the Exotic influence in the recessed porch over the entry, and in the porch columns. This house looks symmetrical, but the right and left sides of the facade are quite different. Compare it to Figure 7, p. 412, where the house looks asymmetrical because of its wings, but has an absolutely symmetrical central block.

2

6

5

8

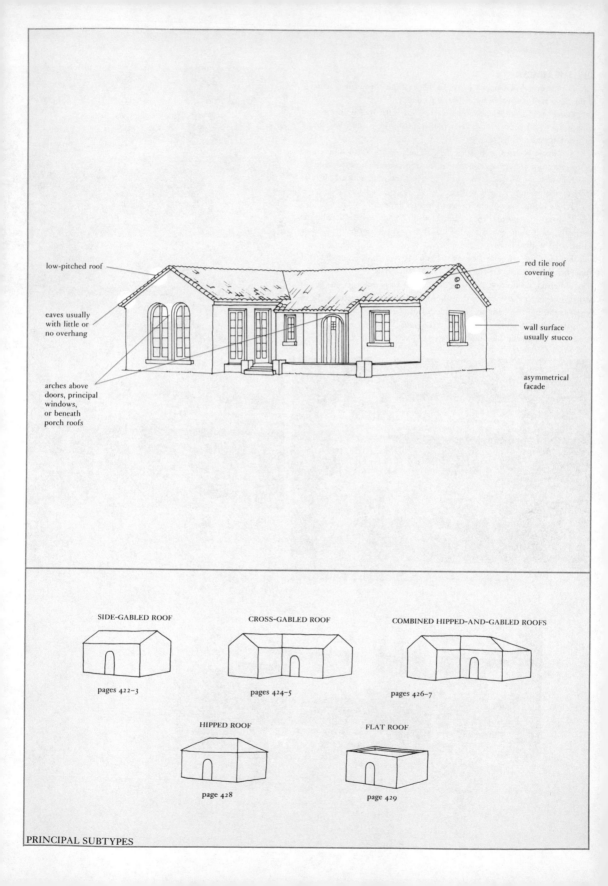

low-pitched roof

eaves usually
with little or
no overhang

arches above
doors, principal
windows,
or beneath
porch roofs

red tile roof
covering

wall surface
usually stucco

asymmetrical
facade

SIDE-GABLED ROOF

pages 422–3

CROSS-GABLED ROOF

pages 424–5

COMBINED HIPPED-AND-GABLED ROOFS

pages 426–7

HIPPED ROOF

page 428

FLAT ROOF

page 429

PRINCIPAL SUBTYPES

Spanish Eclectic

IDENTIFYING FEATURES

Low-pitched roof, usually with little or no eave overhang; red tile roof covering; typically with one or more prominent arches placed above door or principal window, or beneath porch roof; wall surface usually stucco; facade normally asymmetrical.

PRINCIPAL SUBTYPES

Five principal subtypes can be distinguished:

SIDE-GABLED ROOF—About 20 percent of Spanish Eclectic houses have side-gabled roofs. Many of these are multi-level with taller, side-gabled sections bounded by lower, side-gabled wings.

CROSS-GABLED ROOF—About 40 percent of Spanish Eclectic houses have cross-gabled roofs with one prominent, front-facing gable. These are usually L-plan houses; one-story and two-story forms are both common, as are examples with wings of differing heights.

COMBINED HIPPED-AND-GABLED ROOFS—Some landmark examples have rambling, compound plans in which different units have separate roof forms of varying heights arranged in an irregular, informal pattern. Typically both hipped and gabled roofs are used in combination, a pattern which mimics the varied roof forms of Spanish villages.

HIPPED ROOF—About 10 percent of Spanish Eclectic houses have low-pitched hipped roofs. These are generally two-story forms with simple rectangular plans.

FLAT ROOF—About 10 percent of Spanish Eclectic houses have flat roofs with parapeted walls. These typically show combinations of one- and two-story units. Narrow, tile-covered shed roofs are typically added above entryways or projecting windows. This subtype, loosely based on flat-roofed Spanish prototypes, resembles the Pueblo Revival house.

VARIANTS AND DETAILS

The style uses decorative details borrowed from the entire history of Spanish architecture. These may be of Moorish, Byzantine, Gothic, or Renaissance inspiration, an unusually rich and varied series of decorative precedents. The typical roof tiles are of two basic types: Mission tiles, which are shaped like half-cylinders, and Spanish tiles, which have an S-curve shape. Both types occur in many variations depending on the size of the tiles and the patterns in which they are applied. Dramatically carved doors are typical of Spanish architecture; these are more common on high-style Spanish Eclectic houses but also occur on modest examples. Doors are usually emphasized by adjacent spiral columns, pilasters, carved stonework, or patterned tiles. Less elaborate entrance doors of heavy wood panels, sometimes arched above, are also common. Doors leading to exterior gardens, patios, and balconies are usually paired and glazed with multiple panes of rectangular glass. Many examples have at least one large focal window. These are commonly of triple-arched or parabolic shape and may be filled with stained glass of varying design. Decorative window grilles of wood or iron are common, as are similar balustrades on cantilevered balconies, which occur in a variety of shapes and sizes. Other typical details include tile-roofed (and otherwise decorated) chimney tops; brick or tile vents; fountains; arcaded walkways (usually leading to a rear garden); and round or square towers.

OCCURRENCE

Spanish Eclectic is most common in the southwestern states, particularly California, Arizona, and Texas, and in Florida, all regions where original Spanish Colonial building occurred and continued into the 19th century. Landmark houses in this style are rare outside of Florida and the Southwest but, as in the related Mission style which preceded it, scattered vernacular examples are found in suburban developments throughout the country. During the 1920s, many new communities in Florida and southern California were planned in the Spanish Eclectic style, and older towns (such as Santa Barbara, California) sought to affect a Spanish Colonial image.

COMMENTS

Domestic buildings of Spanish precedent built before about 1920 are generally free adaptations in the Mission style. It was not until the Panama-California Exposition, held in San Diego in 1915, that precise imitation of more elaborate Spanish prototypes received wide attention. The exposition was designed by Bertram Grosvenor Goodhue, who had previously authored a detailed study of Spanish Colonial architecture. Goodhue wanted to go beyond the then prevalent Mission interpretations and emphasize the richness of Spanish precedents found throughout Latin America. Inspired by the wide publicity given the exposition, other fashionable architects soon began to look directly to Spain for source material. There they found a still longer and richer sequence of architectural traditions which became melded into a style that they continued to call the Spanish Colonial Revival. Because of its broad roots we prefer the more inclusive name Spanish Eclectic. The style reached its apex during the 1920s and early 1930s and passed rapidly from favor during the 1940s.

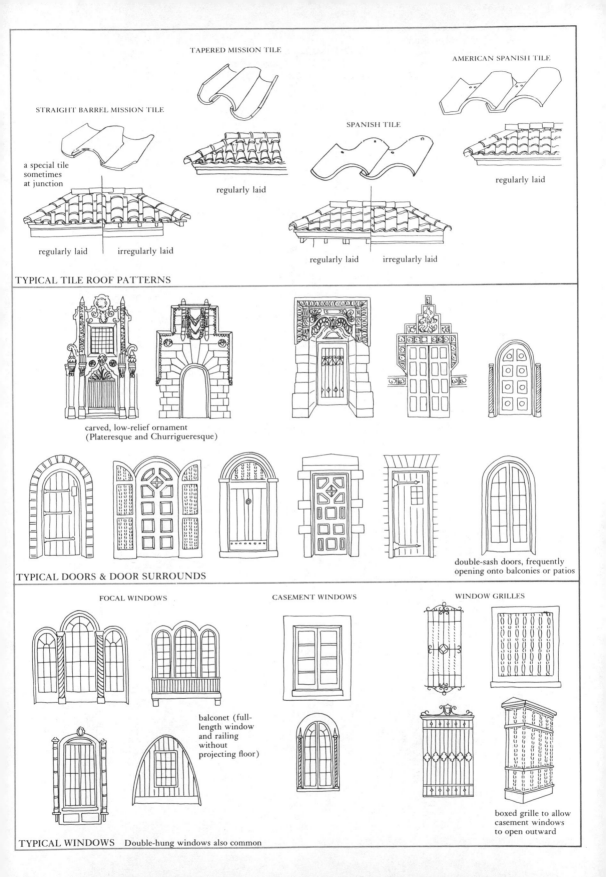

TAPERED MISSION TILE

AMERICAN SPANISH TILE

STRAIGHT BARREL MISSION TILE

SPANISH TILE

a special tile
sometimes
at junction

regularly laid

regularly laid

regularly laid

regularly laid   irregularly laid

regularly laid   irregularly laid

TYPICAL TILE ROOF PATTERNS

carved, low-relief ornament
(Plateresque and Churrigueresque)

double-sash doors, frequently
opening onto balconies or patios

TYPICAL DOORS & DOOR SURROUNDS

FOCAL WINDOWS

CASEMENT WINDOWS

WINDOW GRILLES

balconet (full-
length window
and railing
without
projecting floor)

boxed grille to allow
casement windows
to open outward

TYPICAL WINDOWS   Double-hung windows also common

elaborated chimney tops,
often with small tiled roof

towers, round or square

stucco or tile
decorative vents

arcaded wing wall

balconies, open or roofed,
with wood or iron railings

COMMON ELABORATIONS

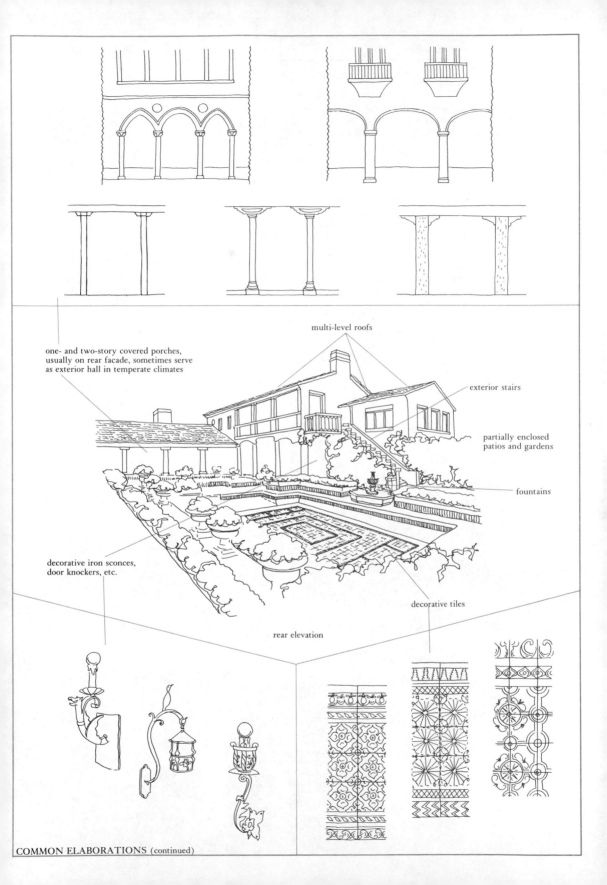

multi-level roofs

one- and two-story covered porches,
usually on rear facade, sometimes serve
as exterior hall in temperate climates

exterior stairs

partially enclosed
patios and gardens

fountains

decorative iron sconces,
door knockers, etc.

decorative tiles

rear elevation

COMMON ELABORATIONS (continued)

SIDE-GABLED ROOF

1. Wichita, Kansas; 1930s. The projecting door surround is atypical.

2. New Orleans, Louisiana; 1920s. The doorway is surrounded by low-relief carving of Plateresque inspiration. Note the elaborate window grills.

3. Wichita, Kansas; 1930s. The unadorned main block, with its short broad chimney and paucity of windows, resembles a smaller version of Figure 4.

4. Santa Barbara, California; 1916. El Hogar; George Washington Smith, architect. Inspired by the houses of southern Spain, this example presents an austere facade to the world (few windows and little ornamentation) but opens into an elaborate garden behind.

5. Dallas, Texas; 1930s. Note the spiraled columns beside the entry and the lower-story windows.

6. Dallas, Texas; 1932. Shurtz House.

7. Dallas, Texas; 1926. Green House; Thomson and Swane, architects. Although similar to Figure 4 in basic form, this example adds numerous double-hung windows to the front facade, giving it a less authentic look. Note the strongly textured stucco walls.

8. Mission Hills, Kansas; 1920s. This house shows symmetrical Renaissance influences in its centered doorway with quoined door surround.

1

3   4

7

2

5

6

8

Eclectic Houses: Spanish Eclectic

CROSS-GABLED ROOF

1. Delano, California; 1930s. Simple one-story examples similar to this dominate many 1930s neighborhoods in Florida and California.

2. Santa Barbara, California; 1923. Burke House; George Washington Smith, architect. Note the restrained facade with large expanses of windowless wall. The small house-shaped chimney capping at the right is a favorite Spanish Eclectic detail.

3. Louisville, Kentucky; 1930s. Note the strong textured pattern of the stucco walls.

4. Dallas, Texas; 1936. Baty House. This small example is complete with a bell tower, a focal window with stained glass, and a front entry court enclosed by a low stone wall.

5. St. Louis, Missouri; 1930s.

6. Oklahoma City, Oklahoma; 1930s.

7. Dallas, Texas; 1947. Cox House. This late example illustrated the trend toward the sprawling one-story Ranch style, which was inspired by Spanish Colonial prototypes.

8. Dallas, Texas; 1934. Cohn House. Note the recessed arcaded porch and the tiny roof extensions over the upper-story windows to the right.

4

3

7

2

5

6

8

COMBINED HIPPED-AND-GABLED ROOFS

1. Dallas, Texas; 1938. Turner House. Note the overhanging balcony and enclosed entry court.

2. Dallas, Texas; 1932. Kaufman House. This house combines hipped-, gabled-, shed-, and flat-roofed units.

3. Montecito, California; 1916. Bliss House; Carleton Winslow, Sr., architect. Note the bell tower and multiple-arched chimney crowns.

4. Santa Barbara, California; ca. 1930. Villa Eseanado. Note the ornate Renaissance-inspired entryway and the differing roof heights of the three wings, which enclose an interior courtyard.

5. Santa Barbara, California; 1925. Dreyfus House; W. Maybury Somervell, architect. This landmark example, with its varying roof forms, resembles an entire block of a Spanish village.

6. Palm Beach, Florida; 1927. Mar-A-Lago; Adison Mizner, architect. A major landmark of the style.

7., 8. Montecito, California; 1930. Dieterich House; Adison Mizner, architect. These photographs illustrate the elaborate courtyards found in most landmark examples. Figure 7 shows an automobile entry court and Figure 8 an interior courtyard. Note the fountain, arcaded gallery, and decorative paving.

2

4

5

7

8

HIPPED ROOF

1. Palo Alto, California; 1930s. Kennedy House.
2. Morgan Hill, California; 1930s. Fountain Oaks.
3. Corning, New York; 1930s.
4. Dallas, Texas; 1942. Luse House. Note the elaborate door surround, the two focal window areas, and the corner quoins.
5. Dallas, Texas; 1932. Bounds House. Note the roof-top cupola, centered visor roof echoed on the porte cochere, and massive door surrounds with spiraled columns.

FLAT ROOF

1. Santa Barbara, California; ca. 1930. Figures 1 and 2 are typical of smaller examples built by the thousands in California suburbs during the 1920s and '30s. The flat roof with decorative tiles along the parapet is typical, as is the arched entryway with either gabled or flat roof.

2. Santa Barbara, California; ca. 1920.

3. St. Louis, Missouri, 1930s. Figures 3, 4, and 5 combine both one- and two-story sections. Note the small shed roofs over the windows and the shed-roof entryways.

4. Durham, North Carolina; 1930s.

5. Independence, Missouri; 1930s.

low-pitched,
gabled roof

two stories

second-story
balcony, usually
cantilevered
and covered by
principal roof

IDENTIFYING FEATURES

Two stories, with low-pitched gabled roof (occasionally hipped); second-story balcony, usually cantilevered and covered by principal roof.

VARIANTS AND DETAILS

Roofs are usually covered with wooden shingles but are occasionally tiled. Wall cladding materials are either stucco, brick, or wood (weatherboard, shingle, or vertical board-and-batten). The first and second stories frequently have different cladding materials, with wood over brick being the most common pattern. Door and window surrounds sometimes mimic the Territorial examples of their Spanish Colonial prototypes; paired windows and false shutters are common. Doors may show Colonial Revival influences. One variant substitutes balcony columns and balustrades of cast iron for the more typical wooden detailing. These are sometimes called Creole French houses.

COMMENTS

The Monterey style is a free revival of the Anglo-influenced Spanish Colonial houses of northern California. These blended Spanish adobe construction with pitched-roof, massed-plan English shapes brought to California from New England. The revival version similarly fuses Spanish Eclectic and Colonial Revival details. Earlier examples, built from about 1925 to 1940, tend to favor Spanish detailing; those from the 1940s and '50s typically emphasize English Colonial details. Scattered examples occur throughout the country in suburbs built during the second quarter of this century.

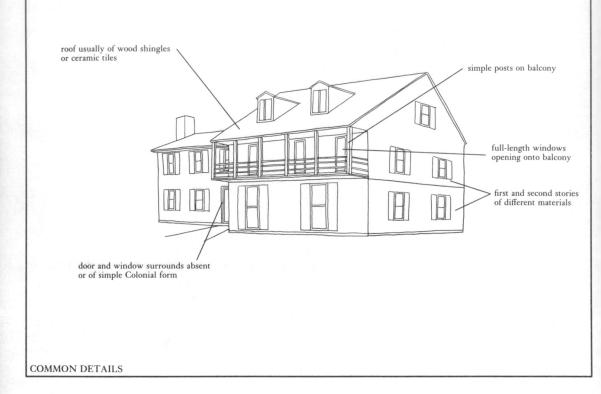

roof usually of wood shingles
or ceramic tiles

simple posts on balcony

full-length windows
opening onto balcony

first and second stories
of different materials

door and window surrounds absent
or of simple Colonial form

COMMON DETAILS

4

MONTEREY

1. Dallas, Texas; 1937. Braly House. This example, with its tiled roof and parabolic focal window, is transitional to the Spanish Eclectic style.

2. Montecito, California; 1929. Morphy House; Roland Coate, Sr., architect. Note the asymmetrical placement of doors and windows and the shaped ends of the heavy beams supporting the balcony.

3. Kansas City, Missouri; 1930s. Most examples of the style have three-ranked facades. When a broader facade was desired, a separate parallel wing was added, as here.

4. Dallas, Texas; 1930s.

5. Dallas, Texas; 1951. Bywaters House. In the late 1940s and '50s the simple wood balcony railings and roof supports of the style were commonly replaced by lacy cast iron, leading to a variant called the Creole French style by its builders. These were, of course, inspired by the iron balconies of New Orleans. Asymmetrical interpretations of these Creole French houses, usually with front-facing gable wings, were also popular.

1

3

2

5

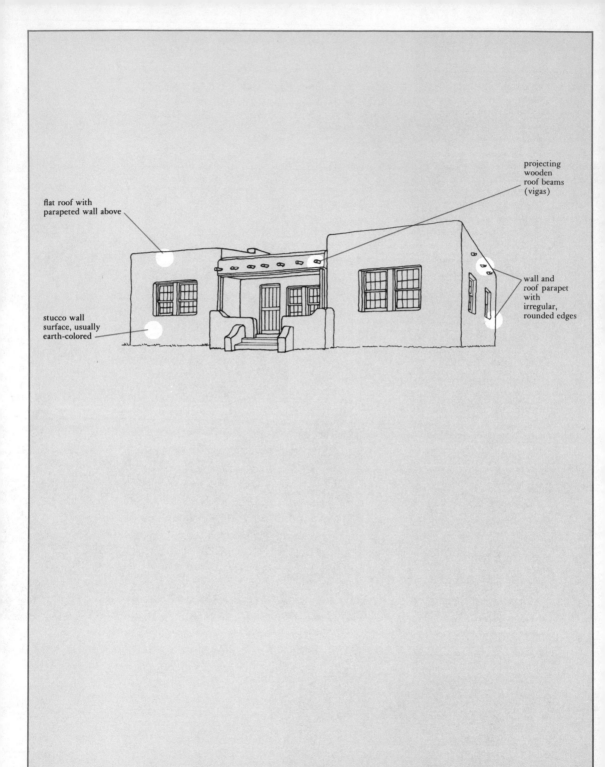

flat roof with
parapeted wall above

projecting
wooden
roof beams
(vigas)

wall and
roof parapet
with
irregular,
rounded edges

stucco wall
surface, usually
earth-colored

Pueblo Revival

1910–present

IDENTIFYING FEATURES

Flat roof with parapeted wall above; wall and roof parapet with irregular, rounded edges; projecting wooden roof beams (vigas) extending through walls; stucco wall surface, usually earth-colored.

VARIANTS AND DETAILS

Pueblo Revival houses imitate the hand-finishes of their Native American prototypes. Corners are blunted or rounded and wall surfaces are given irregular, stuccoed textures. In addition, rough-hewn vigas (roof beams), window lintels, and porch supports carry out the hand-built theme. The stepped-back roof line of the original pueblos is often used.

COMMENTS

Like the contemporary Mission movement, the Pueblo Revival draws on local historical precedents for inspiration. The buildings are a mixture of influences from both flat-roofed Spanish Colonial buildings and Native American pueblos (see pages 73 and 136–7). For this reason some architectural historians have proposed the name "Pueblo–Spanish Revival" for the style. The earliest examples were built in California around the turn of the century. The style became most popular, however, in Arizona and New Mexico, areas where the original prototypes survive. It is particularly common in Albuquerque and Santa Fe, where it persists today, in part because of the requirements of special design controls in historic districts. Scattered examples occur throughout the southwestern states, most of which date from the 1920s and '30s. A variation, introduced in New Mexico about 1920, could be more aptly termed the Territorial Revival. Although executed in abode it picked up the form and detail of the Anglo-Spanish Colonial Territorial house (page 130) with roof parapets topped by fired brick and wooden decorative details influenced by the Greek Revival movement.

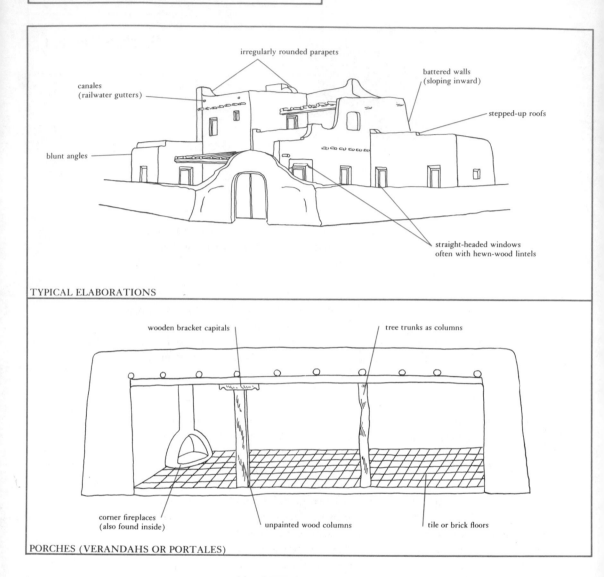

irregularly rounded parapets

battered walls
(sloping inward)

canales
(railwater gutters)

stepped-up roofs

blunt angles

straight-headed windows
often with hewn-wood lintels

TYPICAL ELABORATIONS

wooden bracket capitals

tree trunks as columns

corner fireplaces
(also found inside)

unpainted wood columns

tile or brick floors

PORCHES (VERANDAHS OR PORTALES)

4

PUEBLO REVIVAL

1., 2. Santa Fe, New Mexico; 1920s. John Gaw Meem, architect. The closeup shows the irregular rounded edges of the roof parapet and walls, the irregular stucco texture, and the inset window lintels. Note the difference between the two projecting roof beams (vigas) and the rainwater gutter (canale) immediately to the left. In the full view the stepped up effect (emphasized by the heavy shadows) begins with the garden wall at lower left and continues to the first- and second-story sections. Note the inward curving profile of the walls at right.

3. Sante Fe, New Mexico; 1930s.

4. Santa Fe, New Mexico; 1930s. This landmark example has stepped roofs and strongly rounded edges to walls and roofs. Note the ladder, the only stairway of the original Pueblos.

5. Sante Fe, New Mexico; 1930s.

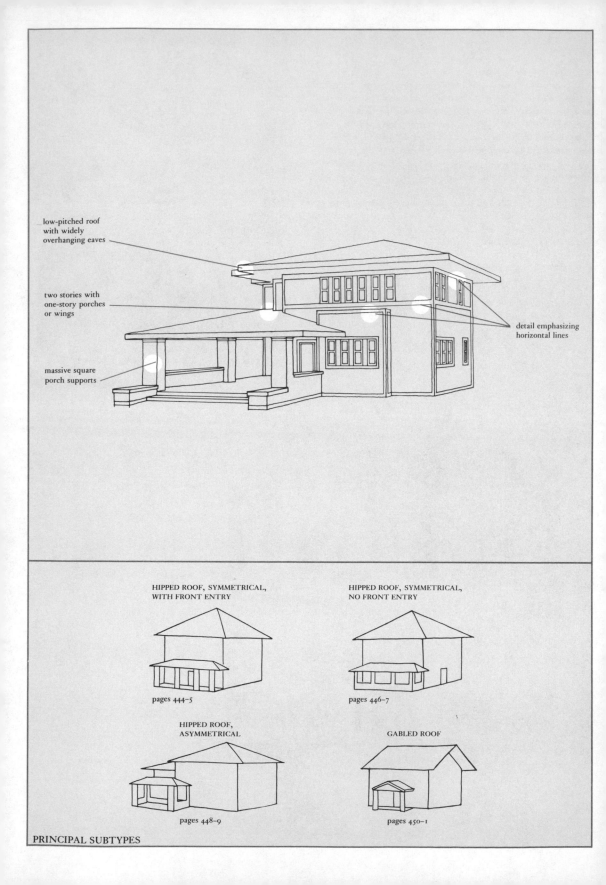

low-pitched roof
with widely
overhanging eaves

two stories with
one-story porches
or wings

massive square
porch supports

detail emphasizing
horizontal lines

HIPPED ROOF, SYMMETRICAL,
WITH FRONT ENTRY

pages 444–5

HIPPED ROOF, SYMMETRICAL,
NO FRONT ENTRY

pages 446–7

HIPPED ROOF,
ASYMMETRICAL

pages 448–9

GABLED ROOF

pages 450–1

PRINCIPAL SUBTYPES

Prairie

IDENTIFYING FEATURES

Low-pitched roof, usually hipped, with widely overhanging eaves; two stories, with one-story wings or porches; eaves, cornices, and facade detailing emphasizing horizontal lines; often with massive, square porch supports.

PRINCIPAL SUBTYPES

Four principal subtypes can be distinguished:

HIPPED ROOF, SYMMETRICAL, WITH FRONT ENTRY—This subtype, which is sometimes called the Prairie Box or American Foursquare, has a simple square or rectangular plan, low-pitched hipped roof, and symmetrical facade. One-story wings, porches, or carports are clearly subordinate to the principal two-story mass. The entrance, which may be centered or off-center, is a conspicuous focal point of the facade. This was the earliest Prairie form and developed into the most common vernacular version. In vernacular examples, hipped dormers are common, as are full-width, single-story front porches and double-hung sash windows. Many show Mission or Italian Renaissance secondary details, such as tiled roofs or cornice-line brackets.

HIPPED ROOF, SYMMETRICAL, NO FRONT ENTRY—Similar to the type just described but with inconspicuous entrances and facades dominated by horizontal rows of casement windows having sharply defined vertical detailing. This is a favorite form for smaller, architect-designed Prairie houses and also for those built on narrow urban lots.

HIPPED ROOF, ASYMMETRICAL—Most high-style examples are of this form. Typically a single two- or three-story, hipped-roof mass is contrasted with equally dominant, but lower, wings, porches, or carports with hipped roofs. The front entrance is usually inconspicuous, the facade being dominated by horizontal rows of casement windows having sharply defined vertical detailing. Many variations occur, but in all cases the facade is asymmetrical; most have masonry walls.

GABLED ROOF—In this subtype, gables replace the more typical hipped roofs. High-style examples typically have both front-facing and side gables, each with exaggerated eave overhangs. In some, the gables have swept-back profiles with the peaks projecting beyond the lower edges. The pitch of the roof edges may also be flattened to give a pagoda-like effect. Vernacular examples usually have simple front- or side-gabled roofs. Tudor secondary influences are common, particularly false half-timbering in gables.

VARIANTS AND DETAILS

Massive square or rectangular piers of masonry used to support porch roofs are an almost universal feature of high-style examples. They remain common in vernacular examples, which also show squared wooden imitations. The characteristic horizontal decorative emphasis is achieved by such devices as: (1) contrasting caps on porch and balcony railings, (2) contrasting wood trim between stories, (3) horizontal board-and-batten siding, (4) contrasting colors on eaves and cornice, and (5) selective recessing of only the horizontal masonry joints. Other common details in both landmark and vernacular examples include window boxes or flattened pedestal urns for flowers; geometric patterns of small-pane window glazing (usually in leaded casement windows in high-style examples and upper sashes of wooden-muntin, double-hung windows in vernacular houses); broad, flat chimneys; contrasting wall materials or trim emphasizing the upper part of the upper story; and decorative friezes or door surrounds consisting of bands of carved geometric or stylized floral (Sullivanesque) ornamentation.

OCCURRENCE

The Prairie style originated in Chicago and landmark examples are concentrated in that city's early 20th-century suburbs, particularly Oak Park and River Forest, and in other large midwestern cities. Vernacular examples were spread widely by pattern books and popular magazines; they are common in early 20th-century suburbs throughout the country. Most were built between 1905 and 1915; the style quickly faded from fashion after World War I.

COMMENTS

This is one of the few indigenous American styles. It was developed by an unusually creative group of Chicago architects that have come to be known as the Prairie School. Frank Lloyd Wright's early work is in this style and he is the acknowledged master of the Prairie house. Wright was unusual in that he early turned his creative genius toward the problems of domestic architecture rather than public buildings. His 1893 Winslow House was perhaps the first Prairie house; it is a symmetrical rectangle (see page 444). It was not until about 1900 that he began to use the asymmetrical hipped form, which he continued to develop until about 1913. As Wright explained, "Democracy needed something basically better than the box." Many of the other Prairie architects worked either with Wright himself or with his earlier employer and teacher, Louis Sullivan. Others absorbed Wright's and Sullivan's influence simply by being in Chicago. Among the most important were George W. Maher, Robert C. Spencer, Jr., Thomas E. Tallmadge, John S. Van Bergen, Vernon S. Watson, Charles E. White, Jr., Eben E. Roberts, Walter Burley Griffin, William Drummond, F. Barry Byrne, George G. Elmslie, and William G. Purcell.

Outside of the Chicago area, numerous local architects produced creditable and sometimes outstanding Prairie houses throughout the midwestern states and, less commonly, in other regions. The style in its vernacular form was spread throughout the country by pattern books published in the Midwest. It is among the more short-lived styles, having grown, flourished, and declined in the years between 1900 and 1920.

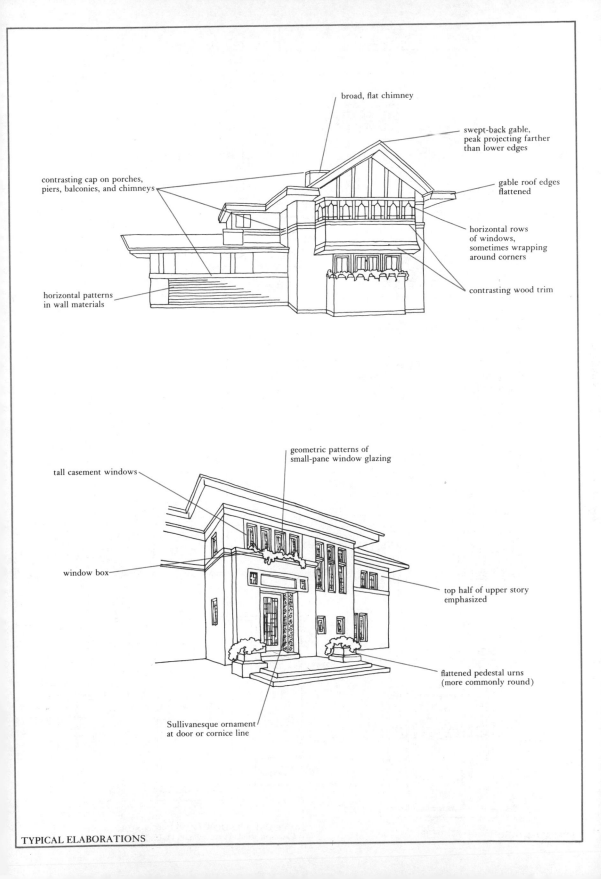

broad, flat chimney

swept-back gable,
peak projecting farther
than lower edges

gable roof edges
flattened

contrasting cap on porches,
piers, balconies, and chimneys

horizontal rows
of windows,
sometimes wrapping
around corners

horizontal patterns
in wall materials

contrasting wood trim

geometric patterns of
small-pane window glazing

tall casement windows

window box

top half of upper story
emphasized

flattened pedestal urns
(more commonly round)

Sullivanesque ornament
at door or cornice line

TYPICAL ELABORATIONS

SULLIVANESQUE
stylized floral and circular geometric

WRIGHTIAN
angular geometric

column capitals

terra cotta medallion

column elaboration and capitals

leaded glass windows

DECORATIVE DETAIL

FOUND IN BOTH CRAFTSMAN & PRAIRIE

TYPICAL DOORS

TYPICAL WINDOW GLAZING & SURROUNDS
Casement windows common on Prairie high-style examples

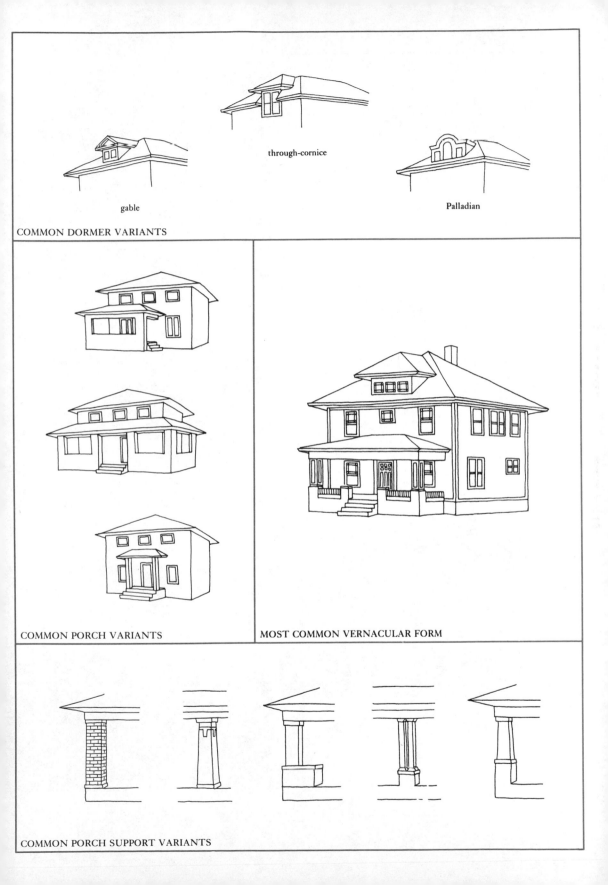

through-cornice

gable

Palladian

COMMON DORMER VARIANTS

COMMON PORCH VARIANTS

MOST COMMON VERNACULAR FORM

COMMON PORCH SUPPORT VARIANTS

HIPPED ROOF, SYMMETRICAL, WITH FRONT ENTRY

1. Dallas, Texas; ca. 1920. Jones House. Aluminum siding has been added to the walls and porch supports.

2. Dallas, Texas; 1910. Harrison House. This example has a door surround of stylized Sullivanesque floral ornament (not visible in the photograph). Note the Wrightian column capitals.

3. Gowanda, New York; ca. 1910. Houses of concrete blocks simulating stone, as seen here, were widely advocated by early 20th-century pattern books as a novel new building method. Note the through-the-cornice wall dormer.

4. Dallas, Texas; ca. 1910. The four-square plan, which was very popular during the period from about 1900 to 1920, is indicated by the two ranks of windows and the off-center entrance.

5. Louisville, Kentucky; ca. 1910. One-story Prairie examples like this are uncommon; one-story houses of the period were usually built in the Craftsman style.

6. Lexington, Kentucky; ca. 1910. Note the uncoursed stone used for the lower two-thirds of the house, with stucco walls above.

7. River Forest, Illinois; 1893. Winslow House; Frank Lloyd Wright, architect. This is Wright's first Prairie house and is much simpler than his later examples, most of which have asymmetrical hipped roofs. This house, and similar examples, provided the model for most later pattern book and builder interpretations of the style. Note how the horizontal effect is emphasized by the thin bricks and trim band above (subtle decorative patterning in the dark upper wall is not visible in the photograph).

8. Fort Dodge, Iowa; 1903. Butler House; Nourse and Rasmussen, architects.

1

4

6

7

1

2

4

6

HIPPED ROOF, SYMMETRICAL, NO FRONT ENTRY

1. Wichita, Kansas; ca. 1910.

2. Buffalo, New York; ca. 1910. Note the flat flower pots at the entrance to the right.

3. St. Louis, Missouri; ca. 1910. The entry is in the right wing; a porte cochere, in the left.

4. Buffalo, New York; ca. 1910. Figures 2 and 4 are both set on fairly narrow urban lots with entrance doors on the side. The porch windows may be early additions that maintain the spirit of the original windows.

5. Racine, Wisconsin; 1905. Hardy House; Frank Lloyd Wright, architect. Note the wide, low chimney with dark coping at the top. The vertical emphasis here is particularly pronounced.

6. Lake Minnetonka, Minnesota; 1913. Decker House (garden facade); Purcell, Feick and Elmslie, architects. Note the ribbon of leaded casement windows across the second story.

7. Milwaukee, Wisconsin; 1916. Bogk House; Frank Lloyd Wright, architect. This house, done after Wright's principal Prairie years, has the simple box-like shape of some of his earlier houses.

3

5

7

HIPPED ROOF, ASYMMETRICAL

1. Kansas City, Missouri; ca. 1910. One-story examples such as this are very uncommon.

2. Mission Hills, Kansas; ca. 1915. This house has a strong horizontal emphasis in the linear pattern of the lower-story masonry, the dark band above, and the differing wall material of the upper one-third.

3. St. Louis, Missouri; ca. 1910. Note the massive chimney with narrow side toward the street (see also Figure 7).

4. Lexington, Kentucky; ca. 1915. Note the similarity in form between this example and Figure 5. This one, however, is pure Prairie with boxed eaves and ribbons of casement windows.

5. Dallas, Texas; 1910. Parker House. This wood-clad example shows Craftsman influence in the open eaves with exposed rafters and in the stickwork between the porch supports. Note the decorative transom over the first-story windows.

6. Wichita, Kansas; 1917. Allen House; Frank Lloyd Wright, architect. In this late example, Wright includes an interior garden not found in earlier Prairie houses.

7. Minneapolis, Minnesota; 1913. Purcell, Feick and Elmslie, architects. This house has particularly dramatic ribbons of decorative casement windows.

8. Buffalo, New York; 1904. Martin House; Frank Lloyd Wright, architect. Note the variety of hipped roofs and heavy masonry piers on this major Prairie landmark. The copings along low walls provide horizontal emphasis. Greenery overflows from planting boxes and planters placed at several levels.

1

5

4

7

GABLED ROOF

1. Kansas City, Missouri; ca. 1910. Figures 1 and 2 are front-gabled examples. This one has a stone lower story, with wooden shingles above. Narrow lot size dictates few extensions.

2. Dallas, Texas; ca. 1920. Jeremiah House. This late example is dominated by a wide front gable, although there is a hipped roof unit hidden behind. The wide lot allows for a one-story porte cochere and porch wings not present in Figure 1.

3. Dallas, Texas; 1918. Peck House. This side-gabled example has a band of Sullivanesque trim below the porch eave.

4. Kansas City, Missouri; ca. 1910.

5. Montgomery, Alabama; ca. 1910. Note the four heavy piers ending two-thirds the way up the walls.

6. Oak Park, Illinois; 1912. Eastabrook House; Tallmadge and Watson, architects. Figures 6, 7, and 8 are cross-gabled examples; this is the simplest. Note the double-gabled roof on the left wing.

7. Pine Bluff, Arkansas; 1903. Macmillan House; Hugh Mackie Gorden Garden, architect. This photo shows clearly the open eave with enclosed rafters that is typical of this subtype (particularly those examples designed by architects). This contrasts with the open eave having exposed rafters that is found in contemporaneous Craftsman houses.

8. Grand Rapids, Michigan; 1910. Amberg House; Marion Mahony and Frank Lloyd Wright, architects.

2

4   5

8

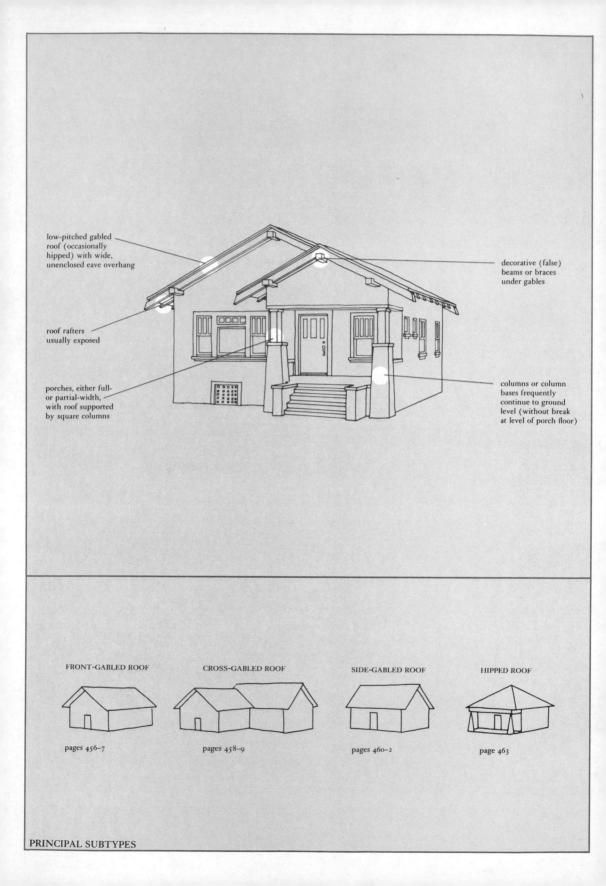

low-pitched gabled roof (occasionally hipped) with wide, unenclosed eave overhang

decorative (false) beams or braces under gables

roof rafters usually exposed

porches, either full- or partial-width, with roof supported by square columns

columns or column bases frequently continue to ground level (without break at level of porch floor)

FRONT-GABLED ROOF

CROSS-GABLED ROOF

SIDE-GABLED ROOF

HIPPED ROOF

pages 456–7

pages 458–9

pages 460–2

page 463

PRINCIPAL SUBTYPES

Craftsman

IDENTIFYING FEATURES

Low-pitched, gabled roof (occasionally hipped) with wide, unenclosed eave overhang; roof rafters usually exposed; decorative (false) beams or braces commonly added under gables; porches, either full- or partial-width, with roof supported by tapered square columns; columns or pedestals frequently extend to ground level (without a break at level of porch floor).

PRINCIPAL SUBTYPES

Four principal subtypes can be distinguished:

FRONT-GABLED ROOF—About one-third of Craftsman houses are of this subtype. Porches, which may either be full- or partial-width, are almost evenly divided between those sheltered beneath the main roof and those with separate, extended roofs. Most examples of this subtype are one-story, but one-and-a-half- and two-story examples are not uncommon; dormers are found in only about 10 percent of this subtype.

CROSS-GABLED ROOF—Cross-gabled examples make up about one-fourth of Craftsman houses. Of these, three-quarters are one-story examples; dormers occur on about 20 percent. Porches are varied, but by far the most common type is a partial-width, front-gabled porch, its roof forming the cross gable.

SIDE-GABLED ROOF—About one-third of Craftsman houses are of this subtype. Most are one-and-a-half stories high with centered shed or gable dormers. Porches are generally contained under the main roof, sometimes with a break in slope. Two-story examples commonly have added, full-width porches. This subtype is most common in the northeastern and midwestern states.

HIPPED ROOF—These make up less than 10 percent of Craftsman houses; they are almost equally divided between one- and two-story examples. This subtype is similar to some simple Prairie houses, which normally lack the exposed rafters and other typical Craftsman details.

VARIANTS AND DETAILS

PORCH ROOF SUPPORTS—Columns for supporting the porch roofs are a distinctive and variable detail. Typically short, square upper columns rest upon more massive piers, or upon a solid porch balustrade. These columns, piers, or balustrades frequently begin directly at ground level and extend without break to a level well above the porch floor. Commonly the piers or columns have sloping (battered) sides. Materials used for piers, columns, and solid balustrades are varied. Stone, clapboard, shingle, brick, concrete block, or stucco are all common; they frequently occur in combination.

ROOF-WALL JUNCTIONS—Among the most distinctive features of the style are the junctions where the roof joins the wall, which are almost never boxed or enclosed. The roof has a wide eave overhang; along *horizontal* edges the actual rafter ends are exposed, or false rafter ends are added. These are sometimes cut into decorative shapes. Along the sloping, or rake, edges, three or more beams (usually false) extend through the wall to the roof edge. These are either plain or embellished by a triangular knee brace.

OTHER DETAILS—Craftsman doors and windows are similar to those used in vernacular Prairie houses (see page 442). Dormers are commonly gabled, with exposed rafter ends and braces such as are found at the main roof-wall junction. The most common wall cladding is wood clapboard; wood shingles rank second. Stone, brick, concrete block, and stucco are also used, most frequently in the northern and midwestern states. Secondary influences such as Tudor false half-timbering, Swiss balustrades or Oriental roof forms are also sometimes seen.

OCCURRENCE

This was the dominant style for smaller houses built throughout the country during the period from about 1905 until the early 1920s. The Craftsman style originated in southern California and most landmark examples are concentrated there. Like vernacular examples of the contemporaneous Prairie style, it was quickly spread throughout the country by pattern books and popular magazines. The style rapidly faded from favor after the mid-1920s; few were built after 1930.

COMMENTS

Craftsman houses were inspired primarily by the work of two California brothers—Charles Sumner Greene and Henry Mather Greene—who practiced together in Pasadena from 1893 to 1914. About 1903 they began to design simple Craftsman-type bungalows; by 1909 they had designed and executed several exceptional landmark examples that have been called the "ultimate bungalows." Several influences—the English Arts and Crafts movement, an interest in oriental wooden architecture, and their early training in the manual arts—appear to have led the Greenes to design and build these intricately detailed buildings. These and similar residences were given extensive publicity in such magazines as the *Western Architect, The Architect, House Beautiful, Good Housekeeping, Architectural Record, Country Life in America,* and *Ladies' Home Journal,* thus familiarizing the rest of the nation with the style. As a result, a flood of pattern books appeared, offering plans for Craftsman bungalows; some even offered completely pre-cut packages of lumber and detailing to be assembled by local labor. Through these vehicles, the one-story Craftsman house quickly became the most popular and fashionable smaller house in the country. High-style interpretations are rare except in California, where they have been called the Western Stick style. One-story vernacular examples are often called simply bungalows or the Bungaloid style.

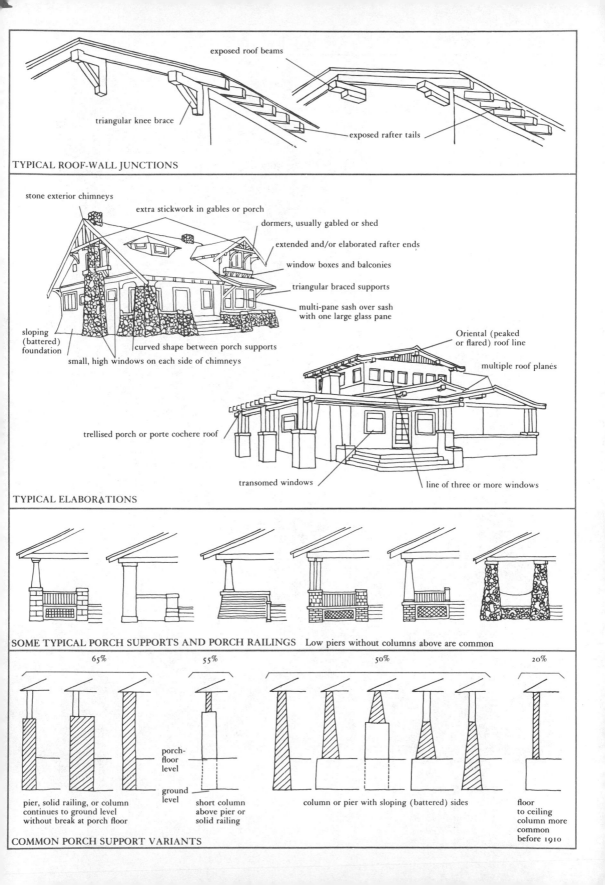

TYPICAL ROOF-WALL JUNCTIONS

exposed roof beams

triangular knee brace

exposed rafter tails

TYPICAL ELABORATIONS

stone exterior chimneys

extra stickwork in gables or porch

dormers, usually gabled or shed

extended and/or elaborated rafter ends

window boxes and balconies

triangular braced supports

multi-pane sash over sash
with one large glass pane

sloping
(battered)
foundation

curved shape between porch supports

small, high windows on each side of chimneys

Oriental (peaked
or flared) roof line

multiple roof planes

trellised porch or porte cochere roof

transomed windows

line of three or more windows

SOME TYPICAL PORCH SUPPORTS AND PORCH RAILINGS Low piers without columns above are common

65%   55%   50%   20%

porch-
floor
level

ground
level

pier, solid railing, or column
continues to ground level
without break at porch floor

short column
above pier or
solid railing

column or pier with sloping (battered) sides

floor
to ceiling
column more
common
before 1910

COMMON PORCH SUPPORT VARIANTS

FRONT-GABLED ROOF

1. Holmes County, Florida; 1910s. Here a Craftsman porch is attached to a simple folk form.

2. Canton, Mississippi; 1910s. The porch roof is a separate gabled element in this very common version of the subtype.

3. Lexington, Kentucky; 1910s. Note the doubled porch supports set on a closed porch railing. There is a section of hipped roof in the front with a gable above.

4. Kansas City, Missouri; 1910s. This stucco example has three front facing gables, all with half-timbered detailing.

5. Jackson, Mississippi; 1910s. This photograph emphasizes the triangular knee braces commonly used in the gable ends of Craftsman houses. The slightly tapered porch-roof supports, extending from ground level, are of irregular brick masonry. Note how the main roof extends over the porch.

6. Kansas City, Missouri; 1910s. A large two-story example of stone and stucco. The gable encompassing the entire second story is unusual.

7. Emporia, Kansas; 1910s. This is a more typical two-story form than Figure 6. Note the matching roof-support columns and gables over the entry and porte cochere.

8. Pasadena, California; 1906. Bentz House; Greene and Greene, architects. An early construction photograph of a relatively small-scale design by the masters of the style.

CROSS-GABLED ROOF

1. Abbeville, South Carolina; 1920s. Modest examples with Craftsman detailing, such as this, were common in outlying areas into the early 1930s.

2. San Jose, California; 1910s. The two picture windows in this house are obvious later alterations.

3. Kansas City, Missouri; 1910s. Note the triple front-facing gables.

4. Ardmore, Oklahoma; 1910s. Note the similarity between this and Figure 7. Examples with the single room on the second story were called airplane bungalows, presumably because they afforded a panoramic view.

5. Louisville, Kentucky; 1910s. Brick Craftsman houses were less common than wood; most occur in the larger cities of the Northeast and the Midwest. Fire codes in some cities, Denver and Chicago for example, prohibited wooden exteriors.

6. Wichita, Kansas; 1910s. Note the tapered porch supports that rise from ground level and are made of rough-faced stone.

7. Santa Barbara, California; ca. 1910.

8. Pasadena, California; 1908. Gamble House; Greene and Greene, architects. A garden view of one of the great landmarks of the style. Note the numerous low-pitched gables, open porches, and exposed wooden structural elements. (In this case they *are* structural, not just added decoration as in most Craftsman houses.)

1

4

6

7

2 3

5

8

SIDE-GABLED ROOF

1. Dallas, Texas; 1915. Lorrimer House. The typical exposed rafter ends show clearly here.

2. Salisbury, North Carolina; 1913. Rock House. Entry porches such as this are less common than full-width porches.

3. Durham, North Carolina; 1910s. The wide expanse of porch without porch supports allows an unrestricted view from the front windows (see also figures 4, 7, and 8).

4. Louisville, Kentucky; 1910s. Side-gabled Craftsman houses frequently have the attic area finished for bedrooms. Light comes from windows in the gable and from large centered dormers (see also Figures 2, 3, 7, and 8).

5. Dallas, Texas; 1920. Clem House. Note the half-timbering in the gables and the use of paired, tapering porch supports atop the wide pedestals.

6. Dallas, Texas; 1917. Wheaton House. Large round columns, such as this, are seen in Craftsman pattern books, but are uncommon in actual examples.

7. Lexington, Kentucky; 1910s.

8. Kansas City, Missouri; 1910s. The balcony gives this example a Swiss Chalet feel.

1

4

3

6

SIDE-GABLED (cont.)

9. Dallas, Texas; 1914. Cranfill House.

10. Dallas, Texas; 1911. Defreese House. Note the full-width two-tiered porch. The typical triangular knee braces are clearly visible along the side gable.

11. Wichita, Kansas; ca. 1920. Lewis House.

12. Buffalo, New York; 1910s. Note the contrasting stonework of the first and second stories and the shed dormers with matching shed-roof porch.

9

10

11

12

HIPPED ROOF

   1. Dallas, Texas; 1910s.

   2. Washington, District of Columbia; 1910s. Note the trellised entry porch. Similar porches were also used as side or wing porches in many examples of the style.

   3. Dallas, Texas; 1912. Gibbs House. Note the porte cochere with a sleeping porch above. This was a typical addition to the main-house block in early 20th-century houses.

   4. Dallas, Texas; 1917. Burgoyne House. This house shows the close relationship of the subtype with simple Prairie houses built in the four-square shape. The unenclosed eaves distinguish this example from similar Prairie forms; the porch supports are clearly Craftsman, but these are also used frequently on Prairie houses.

1

2

3

4

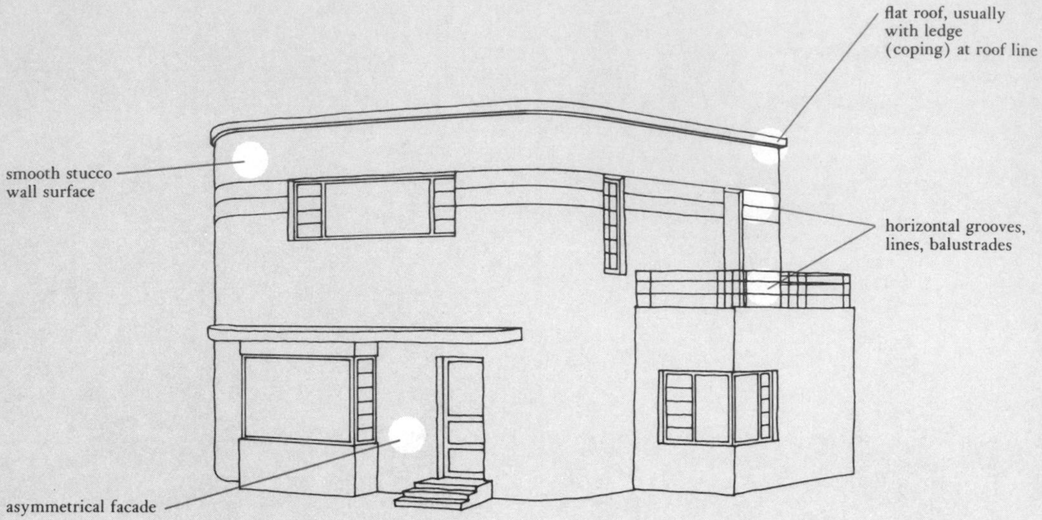

flat roof, usually
with ledge
(coping) at roof line

smooth stucco
wall surface

horizontal grooves,
lines, balustrades

asymmetrical facade

ART MODERNE (streamline modernistic)

towers and other
vertical projections

zigzags and other
geometric and
stylized motifs

smooth stucco
wall surface

ART DECO ("zigzag" modernistic)

Modernistic

IDENTIFYING FEATURES

ART MODERNE—Smooth wall surface, usually of stucco; flat roof, usually with small ledge (coping) at roof line; horizontal grooves or lines in walls and horizontal balustrade elements give a horizontal emphasis; facade usually asymmetrical.

ART DECO—Smooth wall surface, usually of stucco; zigzags, chevrons, and other stylized and geometric motifs occur as decorative elements on facade; towers and other vertical projections above the roof line give a vertical emphasis.

VARIANTS AND DETAILS

ART MODERNE—One or more corners of the building may be curved; windows frequently are continuous around corners; glass blocks are often used in windows, or as entire sections of wall; small round windows are common.

OCCURRENCE

The Modernistic styles were built from about 1920 to 1940. The earlier form was the Art Deco, which was common in public and commercial buildings in the 1920s and early 1930s. It was, however, extremely rare in domestic architecture; we know of only a few surviving houses, although it was frequently used for apartment buildings. After about 1930, Art Moderne became the prevalent Modernistic form. Although never common, many houses were built in the style; scattered examples can be found throughout the country.

COMMENTS

The Modernistic styles received their first major impetus in 1922 when the Chicago *Tribune* held a world-wide competition for a headquarters building in Chicago. Although the first prize went to a Gothic design, the second prize went to an Art Deco design by a young Finnish architect, Eliel Saarinen. His design was widely publicized and much of the architectural profession felt that he deserved the first prize; the style quickly became the latest architectural fashion. Shortly after 1930 another, more diffuse influence affected the Modernistic style—the beginning of streamlined industrial design for ships, airplanes, and automobiles. The smooth surfaces, curved corners, and horizontal emphasis of the Art Moderne style all give the feeling that airstreams could move smoothly over their them; thus they were streamlined. In most building types, both the horizontal, streamlined Art Moderne and the vertical, zigzagged Art Deco influences occur in combination. In houses, however, the streamline influences predominate. Many examples resemble the contemporaneous International style, in which decorative detailing was reduced to the barest minimum.

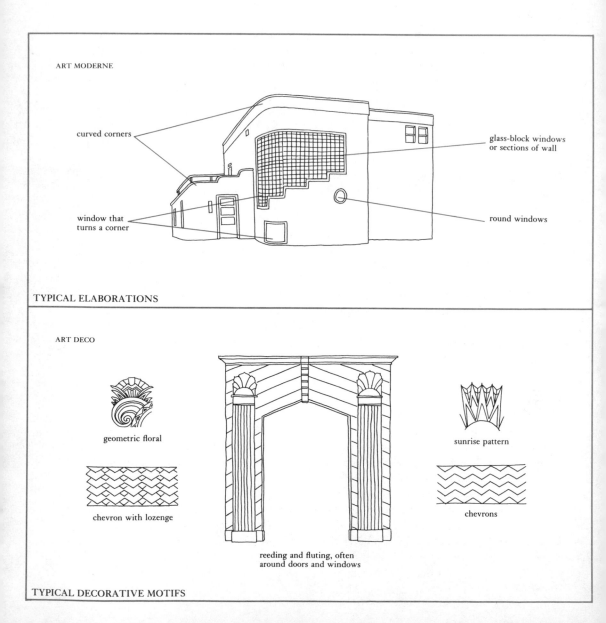

ART MODERNE

curved corners

glass-block windows
or sections of wall

window that
turns a corner

round windows

TYPICAL ELABORATIONS

ART DECO

geometric floral

sunrise pattern

chevron with lozenge

chevrons

reeding and fluting, often
around doors and windows

TYPICAL DECORATIVE MOTIFS

MODERNISTIC

1. San Francisco, California; ca. 1930. A very rare example of an Art Deco house; note the geometric decorative details and vertical roof projections.

2. Toledo, Ohio; 1930s. This popular Art Moderne design is almost symmetrical.

3. San Antonio, Texas; 1930s. Note the entry area with its round window, curved glass-brick window, and curved porch roof with coping above the entry.

4. Fergus Falls, Minnesota; 1937. Lee House; Foss and Co., architects. The brick wall cladding is atypical of the style. Note the extensive horizontal railings and curved one-story section.

5. Des Moines, Iowa; 1937. Butler House; Kraetsch and Kraetsch, architects. This landmark example has several curved sections and a dramatic frieze of horizontal grooves. Note also the varied angles and corner windows in the section to the left.

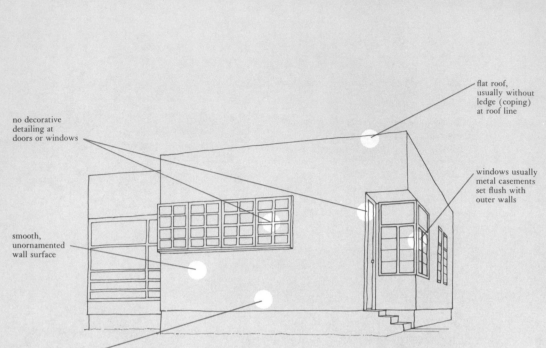

flat roof,
usually without
ledge (coping)
at roof line

no decorative
detailing at
doors or windows

windows usually
metal casements
set flush with
outer walls

smooth,
unornamented
wall surface

asymmetrical facade

International

IDENTIFYING FEATURES

Flat roof, usually without ledge (coping) at roof line; windows (usually metal casements) set flush with outer wall; smooth, unornamented wall surfaces with no decorative detailing at doors or windows; facade asymmetrical.

VARIANTS AND DETAILS

In many high-style International style houses, walls are not used for structural support; instead the exterior walls are curtains hung over a structural steel skeleton. Similarly, interior walls are mere partitions allowing great flexibility in room layout. Freeing exterior walls from structural demands allowed facade treatments that had not been feasible earlier; long ribbons of windows, sometimes wrapping around building corners, are common. Large, floor-to-ceiling plate glass windows are also used. Where interior functions do not require windows, they are replaced by large, blank expanses of exterior wall. Smooth wall surfaces are favored. These are usually of stucco, but smooth board walls (and, less commonly, brick) are also used. Cantilevered projections are much favored; sections of roof, balcony, or second stories may jut dramatically over the wall below, thus dramatizing the non-supporting nature of the walls.

OCCURRENCE

This avant-garde and primarily architect-designed style is relatively rare. Most landmark examples date from the 1930s and occur principally in fashionable suburbs in the northeastern states and in California. Following World War II, certain elements of the style became softened into a more widespread vernacular called the Contemporary style (see pages 482–3). During the 1970s a group known as the New York Five (Charles Gwathmey, Michael Graves, John Hejduk, Richard Meier, and Peter Eisenman) began a revival of interest in the International house that has continued to the present day.

COMMENTS

In the decades separating World Wars I and II, Americans tended to prefer period houses that reflected past traditions, while European architects emphasized radically new designs that came to be known as International style architecture. Le Corbusier in France, Oud and Rietveld in Holland, Walter Gropius and Mies van der Rohe in Germany were all working without historic precedent, trying to exploit the materials and technology of the day. During the 1930s these ideas were introduced into the United States by several distinguished practitioners who emigrated to escape the developing chaos in Europe. The structural and theoretical concepts they brought had a profound influence in America. At the base of this revolution was the use of a structural skeleton, generally of steel, that could be covered by a thin, non-structural skin. With this developed the theory of regularity. Asymmetrical facades were believed to gain coherence by having some visible expression of the regular structural skeleton behind. This has application to only the grandest houses, however, for most are too small to make steel-skeleton construction economically practical. Instead it was another theory of the Internationalists that influenced domestic buildings. Le Corbusier had stressed the idea of the house as a "machine for living." In a world of rapidly advancing technology this idea was appealing; all superfluous ornament could be stripped away, the latest machinery installed in kitchens and bathrooms, and true efficiency brought to the home. The phrase caught on and became the battle cry for International style house design. Functionalism, emphasizing how a building served its inhabitants, was of prime importance; traditional elements of the house that were merely decorative, rather than functional, were to be discarded. This idea was greatly to influence American domestic building in the following decades.

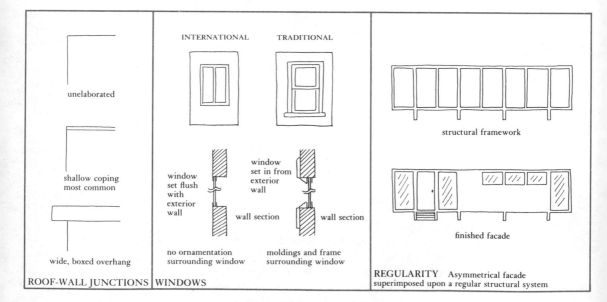

ROOF-WALL JUNCTIONS: unelaborated / shallow coping most common / wide, boxed overhang

WINDOWS: INTERNATIONAL / TRADITIONAL / window set flush with exterior wall / window set in from exterior wall / wall section / wall section / no ornamentation surrounding window / moldings and frame surrounding window

REGULARITY Asymmetrical facade superimposed upon a regular structural system: structural framework / finished facade

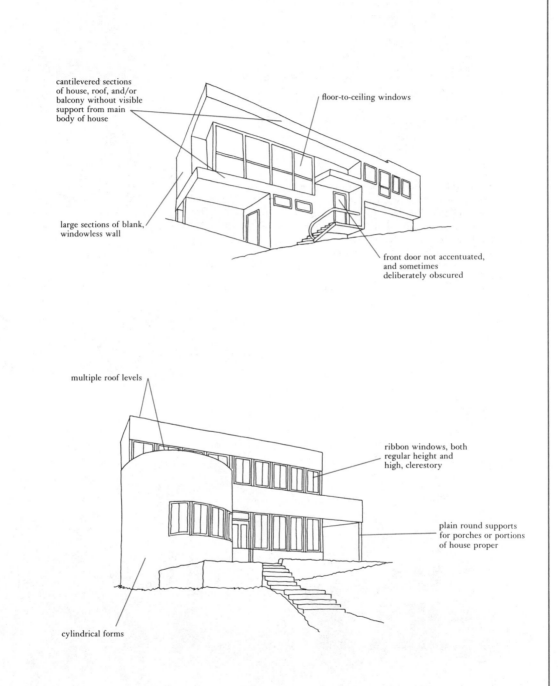

cantilevered sections of house, roof, and/or balcony without visible support from main body of house

floor-to-ceiling windows

large sections of blank, windowless wall

front door not accentuated, and sometimes deliberately obscured

multiple roof levels

ribbon windows, both regular height and high, clerestory

plain round supports for porches or portions of house proper

cylindrical forms

COMMON ELABORATIONS

INTERNATIONAL

1. Cambridge, Massachusetts; 1949. G. D. Solberg, architect. A small, simple example with atypical wood cladding in the upper story. Note the cantilevered overhang above the entry.

2. Los Angeles, California; 1938. Richard Lind, architect. Note the blank expanses of wall in three different planes, the garage incorporated into the facade design, and the cantilevered section of roof.

3. Los Angeles, California; 1936. Fitzpatrick House; R. M. Schindler, architect. Note the multiple, cantilevered roof sections and large expanses of glass window walls.

4. Cambridge, Massachusetts; 1935. Bowers House; Howard T. Fisher, architect.

5. Los Angeles, California; 1934. Buck House; R. M. Schindler, architect.

6. Cambridge, Massachusetts; 1937. Carl Koch and Edward T. Stone, architects. Note the ribbon window in an otherwise blank expanse of wall and the cut-away section at right with a recessed entry.

7. Dallas, Texas; 1981. Note the wall at right, extending forward as a decorative element, and also the use of the windowless curved element.

8. Kenwood, Minnesota; 1970. Horty, Elving and Associates, architects. Wood cladding is common in later International houses. Note the stepped effect of the massing in this example. The only similar massing occurs in the Pueblo Revival style.

9. Deephaven, Minnesota; 1973. Rappaport House; Milo H. Thompson, architect. Note the very long ribbon window.

1

4

7

8

American Houses
Since 1940

The Eclectic movement—with its alternating emphasis on period designs that mimic the past and Modern designs that shun historic precedent—has continued to dominate American domestic building in the decades since 1940. The first phases of this Eclecticism, treated in detail in the preceding section of the book, saw an early 20th-century modernism (the Craftsman and Prairie movements) abruptly supplanted after World War I by an emphasis on period designs. World War II reversed this pattern as postwar taste quickly shifted from the period houses of the 1920s and '30s to new Modern styles of the '50s. (Paradoxically, European reactions were exactly the opposite. After World War I Europeans widely embraced modernism while following World War II they embarked on a course of precise restoration and rebuilding of the past.)

The Modern houses of the 1950s and '60s, mostly in the Ranch, Split-level, or Contemporary styles, grew from the earlier phases of Eclectic modernism and sometimes echo details borrowed from the preceding Craftsman, Prairie, Modernistic, and International styles. They were, nevertheless, innovative new styles that largely shaped the burgeoning suburban landscapes of mid-20th-century America.

As in the earlier phases of Eclecticism, these Modern styles of the 1950s and '60s have come to be supplanted, during the '70s and '80s, by a new taste for period styles based on earlier architectural traditions. Unlike the period houses of the 1920s and '30s that inspired them, however, these Neoeclectic fashions make little attempt to closely copy European or Colonial prototypes. Instead, they borrow prominent historical details (for example Tudor half-timbering, Georgian doorways, and Queen Anne spindlework porches) and freely adapt them to contemporary forms and materials. The result is a new wave of historically based styles that is the dominant theme in American house design as we move into the last decades of the century.

The years since 1940 have also witnessed a dramatic change in the nature of American folk housing—those dwellings meant to provide basic shelter with little regard for changing stylistic fashions. Early 20th-century folk dwellings were generally small, unadorned houses built by the same techniques of balloon framing seen in their stylish neighbors. Beginning with the Quonset huts of World War II, these traditional houses have been largely replaced by prefabricated, factory-built dwellings, especially the ubiquitous mobile home, the dominant folk house of contemporary America.

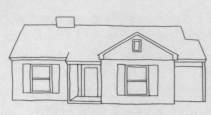

MINIMAL TRADITIONAL

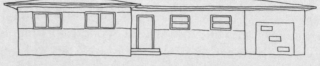

RANCH

SPLIT-LEVEL

CONTEMPORARY

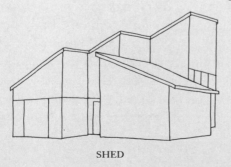

SHED

Modern

Most domestic building ceased between 1941 and 1945 as the United States prepared for and fought World War II. When construction resumed in 1946, houses based on historical precedent were largely abandoned in favor of new variations of the modern styles that had only begun to flourish in the pre-war years. The earliest of these, the Minimal Traditional style, was a simplified form loosely based on the previously dominant Tudor style of the 1920s and '30s. Like Tudor houses, these generally have a dominant front gable and massive chimneys, but the steep Tudor roof pitch is lowered and the facade is simplified by omitting most of the traditional detailing. These houses first became popular in the late 1930s and were the dominant style of the post-war '40s and early '50s. By the early 1950s they were being replaced by the Ranch style, which dominated American domestic building through the '60s and is still popular in many parts of the country. These are one-story houses with very low-pitched roofs and broad, rambling facades. Some lack decorative detailing, but most have decorative shutters, porch-roof supports, or other detailing; these are usually loosely based on colonial precedents. Also during the 1950s the closely related Split Level style, with half-story wings and sunken garages, began to emerge. These generally have some traditional decorative detailing but their unusual form clearly marks them as modern houses. A somewhat less common modern style, the Contemporary, completely eschews traditional form and detail, and was particularly favored in architect-designed houses of the 1950s, '60s, and early '70s. These generally have wide eave overhangs and either flat roofs or low-pitched roofs with broad, low, front-facing gables. Exposed supporting beams and other structural members are common. Contrasting wall materials and textures, and unusual window shapes and placements are also typical features. The most recent of the modern styles is the Shed style. Like the Contemporary, this style eschews traditional detail and is most common in architect-designed houses of the late 1960s and '70s. It is characterized by one or more shed-roofed elements, usually of moderate to high pitch, which dominate the facade and give the effect of several geometric forms shoved together.

The five styles described above are by far the most common modern styles built since 1940. Many additional modern designs have, however, appeared through this period. Some have been dominated by regional design considerations or legacies, while others have been inspired by energy-conservation considerations or by new and experimental advances in building technology.

MINIMAL TRADITIONAL (ca. 1935–50)

With the economic Depression of the 1930s came this compromise style which reflects the form of traditional Eclectic houses, but lacks their decorative detailing. Roof pitches are low or intermediate, rather than steep as in the preceding Tudor style. Eaves and rake are close, rather than overhanging as in the succeeding Ranch style. Usually, but not always, there is a large chimney and at least one front-facing gable, both echoing Tudor features. In fact, many examples suggest Tudor cottages with the roof line lowered and detailing removed. These houses were built in great numbers in the years immediately preceding and following World War II; they commonly dominate the large tract-housing developments of the period. As the photographs show, they were built of wood, brick, stone, or a mixture of these wall-cladding materials. Although most were relatively small one-story houses, occasional two-story examples are also seen. More commonly, two-story houses of the period have extra detailing and represent late examples of one of the traditional Eclectic styles, usually Colonial Revival or Monterey.

RANCH (ca. 1935–75)

This style was originated in the mid-1930s by several creative California architects. It gained in popularity during the 1940s to become the dominant style throughout the country during the decades of the '50s and '60s. The popularity of "rambling" Ranch houses was made possible by the country's increasing dependence on the automobile. Streetcar suburbs of the late-19th and early-20th centuries still used relatively compact house forms on small lots because people walked to nearby streetcar lines. As the automobile replaced streetcars and buses as the principal means of personal transportation in the decades following World War II, compact houses could be replaced by sprawling designs on much larger lots. Never before had it been possible to be so lavish with land, and the rambling form of the Ranch house emphasizes this by maximizing facade width (which is further increased by built-in garages that are an integral part of most Ranch houses).

The style is loosely based on early Spanish Colonial precedents of the American southwest, modified by influences borrowed from Craftsman and Prairie modernism of the early 20th century.

Asymmetrical one-story shapes with low-pitched roofs dominate. Three common roof forms are used: the hipped version is probably the most common, followed by the cross-gabled, and, finally, side-gabled examples. There is usually a moderate or wide eave overhang. This may be either boxed or open, with the rafters exposed as in Craftsman houses. Both wooden and brick wall cladding are used, sometimes in combination. Builders frequently add modest bits of traditional detailing, usually loosely based on Spanish or English Colonial precedents. Decorative iron or wooden porch supports and decorative shutters are the most common. Ribbon windows are frequent as are large picture windows in living areas. Partially enclosed courtyards or patios, borrowed from Spanish houses, are a common feature. These private outdoor living areas to the rear of the house are a direct contrast to the large front and side porches of most late 19th- and early 20th-century styles.

RANCH (continued)

SPLIT LEVEL (ca. 1955–75)

This style rose to popularity during the 1950s as a multi-story modification of the then dominant one-story Ranch house. It retained the horizontal lines, low-pitched roof, and overhanging eaves of the Ranch house, but added a two-story unit intercepted at mid-height by a one-story wing to make three floor levels of interior space. An elaborate theory of interior planning grew around this form. Families were felt to need three types of interior spaces: quiet living areas, noisy living and service areas, and sleeping areas. The Split Level form made it possible to locate these on separate levels. The lower level usually housed the garage and, commonly, the "noisy" family room with its television, which was becoming a universal possession. The mid-level wing contained the "quiet" living areas and the upper level the bedrooms.

The style shows a wide variety of wall cladding, often mixed in a single house. Decorative detailing of vaguely colonial inspiration is somewhat more usual than on Ranch houses, probably because of the taller facades. Although found throughout the country, Split Level houses are less common in the southern and western states than elsewhere.

CONTEMPORARY (ca. 1940–80)

This style was the favorite for architect-designed houses built during the period from about 1950 to 1970. It occurs in two distinctive subtypes based on roof shapes: flat or gabled. The flat-roofed subtype is a derivation of the earlier International Style and houses of this subtype are sometimes referred to as American International. They resemble the International in having flat roofs and no decorative detailing, but lack the stark white stucco wall surfaces, which are usually replaced by various combinations of wood, brick, or stone. Landscaping and integration into the landscape are also stressed, unlike the pristine white International house that was meant to be set upon the landscape as a piece of sculpture.

The gabled subtype is more strongly influenced by the earlier modernism of the Craftsman and Prairie styles. It features overhanging eaves, frequently with exposed roof beams. Heavy piers may support gables. As in the flat-roofed subtypes, various combinations of wood, brick, and stone wall cladding are used and traditional detailing is absent. Both subtypes are most commonly one-story forms although two-story versions are not infrequent.

SHED (ca. 1960–present)

This style originated in the early 1960s as an outgrowth of the designs, writings, and teaching of several creative architects, among them Charles Moore and Robert Venturi. Although their work shows varying influences and forms, the distinctive feature that has been picked up by architects and builders throughout the country is the multi-directional shed roof, often accompanied by additional gabled roof forms. In shape these houses represent a new development in American domestic architecture for they appear to be assembled from two or more gabled and shed-roofed forms joined together. The effect is of colliding geometric shapes. Venturi and Moore primarily use wood-shingle wall cladding, but most interpretations of the style use board siding (applied either horizontally, vertically, or diagonally) or brick veneer. Roof-wall junctions are usually smooth and simple, with little or no overhang; usually a single board is used for a cornice. The entrance is generally recessed and obscured. Windows tend to be relatively small and are asymmetrically placed on each facade. The overall effect is of bold diagonals, counterpointed shapes, and multiple massing.

OTHER

In the decades since 1940, architects have introduced many other types of modern houses, but none have been so widely accepted as those already discussed. Some of these have been based on a desire to utilize new materials or building technologies. There have been few basic changes in house construction since the development of balloon framing in the mid 19th century and the perfection of masonry veneering in the early 20th, as a look at any new housing development under construction will confirm. Many attempts have been made to change this by introducing new building techniques. For example, houses have been suspended from poles (Figure 1) or built of such non-traditional materials as metal (Figure 2), precast concrete, or concrete sprayed on steel skeletons. None have seriously challenged more traditional methods of house construction. Another design consideration—energy conservation—has dominated many architects' house designs since the early 1970s. Almost all rely on either the sun's energy or the stable temperature and insulating effects of the earth (or both) to reduce energy requirements. Some are passive solar houses (using no mechanical systems, only natural air flow; the vertical design of Figure 4 facilitates this), others are active solar houses with mechanical distribution of heat and cooling, while still others stress thick coverings of earth for insulation. The solar collectors, air-flow systems, heavy insulation, lack of windows, and earth covering used in these techniques create unique facade designs that may bear little resemblance to traditional houses.

While most other modern houses simply continue regional design legacies or revive older design traditions, there are architects and clients who simply want a house that is different—a fantasy or extraordinary design that is clearly one-of-a-kind (figures 3 and 5).

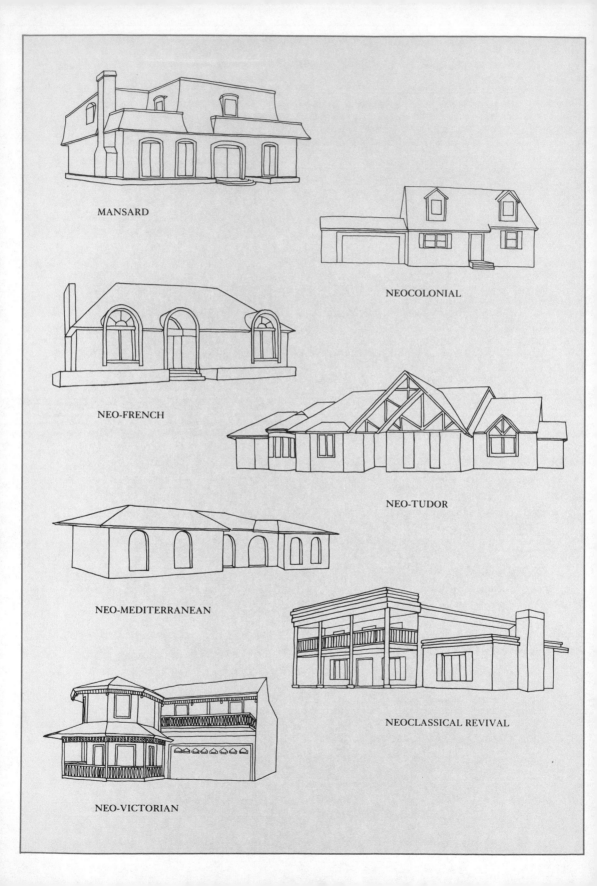

MANSARD

NEOCOLONIAL

NEO-FRENCH

NEO-TUDOR

NEO-MEDITERRANEAN

NEOCLASSICAL REVIVAL

NEO-VICTORIAN

Neoeclectic

ca. 1965 to present

Although some pre-1940 Eclectic styles continued to be built into the early 1950s, the decades between 1950 and 1970 were dominated by the Modern styles discussed in the previous section. By the late 1960s, however, the fashions of domestic architecture were shifting back toward styles based on traditional, rather than modern, architectural shapes and detailing. The first popular style to emerge in this Neoeclectic phase of architectural taste was the Mansard, named for its characteristic roof form. Widely used by home builders in the 1960s, the mansard roof was not limited to houses, but swept shopping centers, apartment houses, and smaller commercial buildings as well. A second dominant Neoeclectic style is the Neocolonial, very free adaptations of English Colonial precedents that grew from the preceding, and generally more historically precise, Colonial Revival style. Neocolonial houses occur throughout the post-1940 period but sharply increased in popularity with the expansion of Neoeclecticism through the 1970s. The Neo-French style appeared about 1970 and by the early '80s was among the most fashionable throughout the country, reaching a level of popularity never achieved by its pre-1940 French Eclectic forebears. The style is particularly characterized by high hipped roofs and through-the-cornice-dormers (usually with rounded tops). The Neo-Tudor style has been a favorite since about 1970. Like its more correctly detailed pre-1940 predecessors, it has dominant, steeply pitched front gables, usually with half-timbered detailing.

Three additional Neoeclectic styles have not yet gained the popularity of the four already discussed. The Neo-Mediterranean includes free interpretations of the earlier Italian Renaissance, Spanish Eclectic, Mission, or Monterey styles; most examples have stucco walls, rounded arches, and red tile roofs. The Neoclassical Revival style borrows full-height columns from the preceding Neoclassical style, but freely applies them to a variety of house forms with little concern for historically accurate detailing. Its most common expression is seen in Neoclassical entry porches added to the one-story Ranch house form. The Neo-Victorian style is the most recent traditional revival. Most examples show free interpretations of Queen Anne spindlework porch detailing.

The fashion for Neoeclectic houses spread rapidly during the 1970s after a quiet beginning in the late '60s. Most American architectural styles began with high-fashion architect-designed landmark houses or public buildings which, in turn, inspired new designs for more modest houses. The Neoeclectic movement, in contrast, appears to have been first introduced by builders of modest houses who sensed the public's resurgent interest in traditional designs. The architectural profession, on the other hand, has been slow to abandon its emphasis on experimental modern styles. As a result, individually designed Neoeclectic landmark houses remain relatively uncommon.

MANSARD (ca. 1960–present)

Interior designers have long known that the cheapest way to obtain a dramatic effect in a room is to change wall surfaces with a bright coat of paint or an unusual wallpaper. The mansard roof applies this principle to house facades. Builders in the early 1960s learned that a relatively inexpensive way to get a dramatic decorative effect was to construct slightly sloping upper wall surfaces to be covered with shingles or other decorative roofing materials. This technique was apparently first used in apartment projects in Florida and the southwest and then spread rapidly to houses. The style was particularly favored in the late 1960s and early '70s but has persisted into the '80s with modifications. Early versions, for example, seldom have through-the-cornice windows, a common feature on more recent examples.

1

2

3

4

5

NEOCOLONIAL (ca. 1950–present)

This style grades into the preceding Colonial Revival style but differs in showing less concern for precisely copying Colonial prototypes. For example, widely overhanging eaves and metal windows, both absent on more correct Colonial Revival houses, are commonly used. Likewise, little attempt is made to closely mimic original Georgian or Adam detailing. Instead, very free interpretations of colonial door surrounds, colonnaded entry porches, and dentiled cornices are used. House forms, too, are seldom precisely colonial. Roof pitches may be either lower or steeper than was typical in original examples. Facades, although usually symmetrical, also lack the regularly spaced patterns of window placement seen in Georgian and Adam houses. The style has been continuously popular but never dominant. It was overshadowed by the Ranch and other modern styles through the 1950s and '60s and by other Neoeclectic styles during the '70s and early '80s.

1

2

3

4

5

NEO-FRENCH (ca. 1970–present)

This style has steadily grown in popularity through the 1970s to become a dominant Neoeclectic fashion. The most characteristic feature is a steeply pitched, hipped roof. Facades may be either one or two stories high and either symmetrical or, more commonly, asymmetrical. Doors and windows are frequently round or segmentally arched above; they commonly extend upward through the cornice line. As in other Neoeclectic fashions, little attempt is made to closely follow French prototypes. These free Neo-French interpretations are thus easily distinguised from their more correct pre-1940 predecessors of the French Eclectic style.

NEO-TUDOR (ca. 1965–present)

The Neo-Tudor, like its pre-1940 Tudor predecessors, is characterized by dominant front-facing gables with steeply pitched roofs; these almost always have decorative half-timbered detailing in Neo-Tudor houses. Slender windows, frequently in groups of four or more and sometimes with diamond-shaped panes, are also common, as in pre-1940 Tudor houses. The earlier examples of the style are usually one-story Ranch house forms with Tudor detailing added. During the 1970s two-story adaptations became common. As in other Neoeclectic styles, the Neo-Tudor is a very free interpretation of traditional designs; unlike its Tudor antecedent, there is little attempt at precisely mimicking Medieval forms or detailing.

NEO-MEDITERRANEAN (ca. 1970–present)

Neoeclectic houses of Spanish or Italian inspiration are less common than are Neo-French, Neo-Tudor or Neocolonial versions. Neo-Mediterranean designs may be loosely based on either Spanish Eclectic and Mission precedents (figures 1–4) or the Italian Renaissance style (Figure 5). Tile roofs (now usually made of light composition materials rather than heavy clay) are usual as are stucco walls and round-arched windows and doorways. As in their pre-1940 predecessors, the style is most common in California and the southwest.

2

4

NEOCLASSICAL REVIVAL (ca. 1965–present)

Although this is not yet a major Neoeclectic style, it has been gaining in favor through the 1970s. In the late 1960s and early '70s the most frequent Neoclassical influence was a pedimented portico grafted onto a one-story, rambling Ranch house form (Figure 2). More recently, two-story adaptations have become common. As in other Neoeclectic styles, most examples are very free adaptations of earlier traditions. In this style, however, there is a recent trend toward more nearly correct interpretations as illustrated in figures 1 and 5).

1

2

4

3

5

NEO-VICTORIAN (ca. 1975–present)

This most recent Neoeclectic style is still relatively rare, but appears to be gaining in popularity. As fewer actual Victorian houses survive, builders have begun to recreate fanciful new versions, most of which stress spindlework porch detailing borrowed from the 19th-century Queen Anne style. Figure 4, publicized as a local Bicentennial House, is a 1976 rebuilding of a simple hipped-roof Prairie design. It combines a number of Victorian influences. Note how Figure 2 mimics the cross-gabled hipped-roof form seen in many Queen Anne houses.

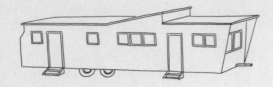

MOBILE HOMES

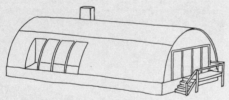

QUONSET HUTS

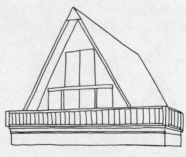

A-FRAMES

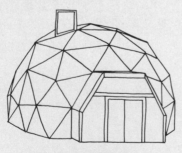

GEODESIC DOMES

Contemporary Folk

ca. 1940 to present

Contemporary Folk houses, like those of the past, reflect the continuing need for basic, economical shelter without concern for fashionable stylistic design or detailing. In the decades since 1940, the traditional folk house forms discussed in earlier chapters have been largely replaced by a new type of relatively inexpensive, prefabricated housing— the *mobile home*. Like many earlier folk forms, mobile homes are normally of linear plan—that is, made up of a single line of rooms. This shape allows them to be placed either long side to the road, as in the traditional hall-and-parlor plan or, where land is more expensive, on narrow lots with the short end to the road as in the traditional shotgun plan. Mobile homes grew from earlier house trailers, designed to be pulled behind ordinary automobiles (see illustration). As larger designs became popular (figures 1, 2, and 3) the form lost much of its mobility; most now must be moved by special trucks with warning vehicles ahead because of width. For this reason they are infrequently moved once sited; most remain permanently in place. Because they are factory-built, with all appliances and sometimes even the furnishings included, mobile homes have now become the cheapest and simplest means of acquiring basic housing, as their wide popularity attests.

At least three other types of modern folk houses have been in common use since 1940. The first is the quonset hut: a half-cylindrical framework covered by corrugated metal that was widely used for housing and other purposes in the 1940s, during and immediately following World War II. Surviving examples used as dwellings are now extremely rare. A second type of modern folk house—the A-frame—is used more for vacation and second homes than for permanent dwellings (Figure 4). In this structure, sidewalls and roof-wall junctions are omitted; instead, the gabled roof continues to ground level on two sides. This all-roof form is relatively simple to construct and can be adapted to a variety of materials, but its advantages are offset by the awkward interior spaces created by the design. A third modern folk type is the geodesic dome (figures 5 and 6). Popularized by the eloquent advocacy of Buckminster Fuller, domes received a great boost by being used for the United States pavilion at Montreal World's Fair of 1967. The form consists of a rigid geometric frame of metal or plastic covered by either a flexible skin or rigid panels. In spite of its structural simplicity, the form has achieved only limited popularity for dwellings.

For Further Reference

The selected works included here are those that we believe will be among the most helpful to readers seeking additional information about houses of a particular style or region. The first section lists important references on the general topic of American houses. This is followed by five lists of works treating more specific subjects ("House Form and Structure" through "Eclectic and Modern Houses"); these are arranged to parallel the generally chronological organization of the book. Four succeeding sections list selected "Regional and Local Guides" that cover a range of architectural styles as found in a particular part of the country. (Note that local works treating only a single style or period may be listed in the preceding chronological sections rather than with the regional and local guides of broader scope.) Only a few important examples of pattern books (works showing sample house plans and elevations) have been included from among the many thousands of such publications. These are labeled "[pattern book]" in the lists. A comprehensive survey of all such works published before 1895 can be found in Henry-Russell Hitchcock's *American Architectural Books*, rev. ed (New York: Da Capo Press, 1976). The far more numerous examples from this century still await bibliographic research. A final section, "House Preservation and Restoration," is included to guide those wishing to conserve the original architectural character of older houses as they adapt them to contemporary living.

GENERAL WORKS

Andrews, Wayne. *Architecture, Ambition, and Americans*, rev. ed. New York: Free Press, 1978.

Blumenson, John J.-G. *Identifying American Architecture*, rev. ed. Nashville, Tennessee: American Association for State and Local History, 1981.

Davidson, Marshall B. *Notable American Houses*. New York: American Heritage Publishing Co., 1971.

Fitch, James Marston. *American Building 1: The Historical Forces That Shaped It*, 2nd ed. Boston: Houghton Mifflin Co., 1966.

Foley, Mary Mix. *The American House*. New York: Harper & Row, 1980.

Gowans, Alan. *Images of American Living*. Philadelphia: J. B. Lippincott, 1964.

Handlin, David P. *The American Home*. Boston: Little, Brown and Co., 1979.

Harrison, Henry S. *Houses*. Chicago: National Association of Realtors, 1973.

Hilowitz, Beverley, and Susan Eikov Green. *Historic Houses of America*, rev. ed. New York: Simon and Schuster, 1980.

Hunt, William Dudly, Jr. *Encyclopedia of American Architecture*. New York: McGraw-Hill, 1980.

Pickering, Ernest. *The Homes of America*. New York: Thomas Y. Crowell, 1951.

Poppeliers, John, S. Allen Chambers, and Nancy B. Schwartz. *What Style Is It?* rev. ed. Washington: Preservation Press, 1983.

Roth, Leland M. *A Concise History of American Architecture*. New York: Harper & Row, 1979.

Saylor, Henry H. *Dictionary of Architecture*. New York: John Wiley & Sons, 1952.

Walker, Lester. *American Shelter*. Woodstock, New York: Overlook Press, 1981.

Whiffen, Marcus. *American Architecture Since 1780: A Guide to Styles.* Cambridge, Massachusetts: M.I.T. Press, 1969.

—————, and Frederick Koeper. *American Architecture, 1607–1976.* Cambridge, Massachusetts: M.I.T. Press, 1981.

Williams, Henry Lionel, and Ottalie K. Williams. *A Guide to Old American Houses, 1700–1900.* New York: A. S. Barnes and Company, 1962.

HOUSE FORM AND STRUCTURE

Allen, Edith Louise. *American Housing.* Peoria, Illinois: Manual Arts Press, 1930.

Anderson, L. O. *How to Build a Wood-Frame House.* New York: Dover, 1973.

Blackburn, Graham J. *Illustrated Housebuilding.* New York: Bonanza Books, 1974/1978.

—————. *The Parts of a House.* New York: Richard Marek, 1980.

DiDonno, Lupe, and Phyllis Sperling. *How to Design and Build Your Own House.* New York: Alfred A. Knopf, 1978.

Dietz, Albert G. H. *Dwelling House Construction,* 4th ed. Cambridge, Massachusetts: M.I.T. Press, 1974.

Kauffman, Henry J. *The American Fireplace.* New York: Galahad Books, 1972.

McKee, Harley J. *Introduction to Early American Masonry: Stone, Brick, Mortar and Plaster.* Washington: Preservation Press. 1973.

Newcomb, Rexford, and William A. Foster. *Home Architecture.* New York: John Wiley & Sons, 1932.

Peterson, Charles E., ed. *Building Early America.* Radnor, Pennsylvania: Chilton, 1976.

Townsend, Gilbert, and J. Ralph Dalzell. *How to Plan a House.* Chicago: American Technical Society, 1942.

FOLK HOUSES

Brunskill, R. W. *Illustrated Handbook of* [British] *Vernacular Architecture,* 2nd ed. London: Faber and Faber, 1978.

—————. *Houses.* London, Collins, 1982.

Driver, Harold E., and William C. Massey. "Comparative Studies of North American Indians." *American Philosophical Society Transactions,* 47 (new series), pt. 2 (1957): 165–456.

Finley, Robert, and E. M. Scott. "A Great Lakes-to-Gulf Profile of Dispersed Dwelling Types." *Geographical Review,* 30 (1940): 412–19.

Glassie, Henry. *Pattern in the Material Folk Culture of the Eastern United States.* Philadelphia: University of Pennsylvania Press, 1968.

Hutslar, Donald A. *The Log Architecture of Ohio.* Columbus: Ohio Historical Society, 1977.

Jett, Stephen C., and Virginia E. Spencer. *Navajo Architecture: Forms, History, Distributions.* Tucson, Arizona; University of Arizona Press, 1981.

Jordan, Terry G. *Texas Log Buildings.* Austin: University of Texas Press, 1978.

Kniffen, Fred. "Folk Housing: Key to Diffusion." *Association of American Geographers Annals,* 55 (1965): 549–77.

—————, and Henry Glassie. "Building in Wood in the Eastern United States: A Time-Place Perspective." *Geographical Review,* 56 (1966): 40–66.

Lewis, Peirce F. "Common Houses, Cultural Spoor." *Landscape,* 19 (1975): 1–22.

Marshall, Howard Wight. *Folk Architecture in Little Dixie.* Columbia: University of Missouri Press, 1981.

Montell, William L., and Michael L. Morse. *Kentucky Folk Architecture.* Lexington: University Press of Kentucky, 1976.

Pillsbury, Richard, and Andrew Kardos. *A Field Guide to the Folk Architecture of the Northeastern United States.* Hanover, New Hampshire: Geography Publications at Dartmouth [College], no. 8, 1970.

Shortridge, James R. "Some Relationships Between External Housing Characteristics and House Types." *Pioneer America,* 13/2 (1981): 1–28.

Swain, Doug, ed. *Carolina Dwelling.* North Carolina State University School of Design Student Publication, volume 26. Raleigh: North Carolina State University, 1978.

Waterman, T. T. "North American Indian Dwellings." *Geographical Review,* 14 (1924): 1–25.

Welsch, Roger L. *Sod Walls: The Story of the Nebraska Sod House.* Broken Bow, Nebraska: Purcells, 1968.

Weslager, C. A. *The Log Cabin in America.* New Brunswick, New Jersey: Rutgers University Press, 1969.

Wilson, Eugene M. *Alabama Folk Houses.* Montgomery: Alabama Historical Commission, 1975.

COLONIAL HOUSES

Architects' Emergency Committee. *Great Georgian Houses of America,* 2 vols. New York: Dover, 1933, 1937/1970.

Baer, Morley, and Augusta Fink. *Adobes in the Sun.* San Francisco: Chronicle Books, 1972.

Bailey, Rosalie Fellows. *Pre-Revolutionary Dutch Houses and Families in Northern New Jersey and Southern New York.* New York: Dover, 1936/1968.

Bunting, Bainbridge. *Early Architecture in New Mexico.* Albuquerque: University of New Mexico Press, 1976.

——————, Jean Lee Booth, and William R. Sims, Jr. *Taos Adobes: Spanish Colonial and Territorial Architecture of the Taos Valley.* Fort Burgwin Research Center Publication No. 2. Sante Fe: Museum of New Mexico Press, 1964.

Cummings, Abbott Lowell. *The Framed Houses of Massachusetts Bay, 1625–1725.* Cambridge, Massachusetts: Harvard University Press, 1979.

Forman, Henry Chandlee. *The Architecture of the Old South: The Medieval Style, 1585–1850.* Cambridge, Massachusetts: Harvard University Press, 1948.

——————. *Early Manor and Plantation Houses of Maryland,* 2nd ed. Baltimore: Bodine & Associates, 1982.

Garvan, Anthony N. B. *Architecture and Town Planning in Colonial Connecticut.* New Haven: Yale University Press, 1951.

Giffen, Helen S. *Casas and Courtyards: Historic Adobe Houses of California.* Oakland, California: Biobooks, 1955.

Guinness, Desmond, and Julius Trousdale Sadler, Jr. *Mr. Jefferson, Architect.* New York: Viking Press, 1973.

Hamlin, Talbot. *Benjamin Henry Latrobe.* New York: Oxford University Press, 1955.

Hannaford, Donald R. and Revel Edwards. *Spanish Colonial or Adobe Architecture of California, 1800–1850.* New York: Architectural Book Publishing Co., 1931.

Howells, John Mead. *The Architectural Heritage of the Piscataqua: Houses and Gardens of the Portsmouth District of Maine and New Hampshire.* New York: Architectural Book Publishing Co.,1937.

——————. *The Architectural Heritage of the Merrimack.* New York: Architectural Book Publishing Co., 1941.

Johnston, Frances Benjamin and Thomas Tileston Waterman. *The Early Architecture of North Carolina.* Chapel Hill: University of North Carolina Press, 1947.

Kelly, J. Frederick. *The Early Domestic Architecture of Connecticut.* New York: Dover, 1924/1963.

Kimball, Fiske. *Domestic Architecture of the American Colonies and of the Early Republic.* New York: Dover, 1922/1966.

Kirker, Harold. *The Architecture of Charles Bulfinch.* Cambridge, Massachusetts: Harvard University Press, 1969.

Lancaster, Clay. *The Architecture of Historic Nantucket.* New York: McGraw-Hill, 1972.

McCall, Elizabeth B. *Old Philadelphia Houses on Society Hill, 1750–1840.* New York: Architectural Book Publishing Co., 1966.

Millar, John Fitzhugh. *The Architects of The American Colonies.* Barre, Massachusetts: Barre Publishers, 1968.

Morrison, Hugh. *Early American Architecture.* New York: Oxford University Press, 1952.

Overdyke, W. Darrell. *Louisiana Plantation Homes.* New York: Architectural Book Publishing Co., 1965.

Pierson, William H., Jr. *American Buildings and Their Architects: The Colonial and Neoclassical Styles.* Garden City, New York: Doubleday and Co., 1970.

Porterfield, Neil H. "Ste. Genevieve, Missouri." John Francis McDermott, ed., *Frenchmen and French ways in the Mississippi Valley,* 141–77. Urbana, Illinois: University of Illinois Press, 1969.

Reynolds, Helen Wilkinson. *Dutch Houses in the Hudson Valley before 1776.* New York: Dover, 1929/1965.

Schuler, Stanley. *The Cape Cod House.* Exton, Pennsylvania: Schiffer, 1982.

Stoney, Samuel Gaillard. *Plantations of the Carolina Low Country.* Charleston, South Carolina: Carolina Art Association, 1938.

Tatum, George B. "Architecture." *The Arts in America: The Colonial Period,* 41–145. New York: Charles Scribner's Sons, 1966.

Toledano, Roulhac, Sally Kittredge Evans and Mary Louise Christovich. *New Orleans Architecture v. 4: The Creole Faubourgs.* Gretna, Louisiana: Pelican, 1974.

——————, and Mary Louise Christovich. *New Orleans Architecture v. 6: Faubourg Tremé and the Bayou Road.* Gretna, Louisiana: Pelican, 1980.

Waterman, Thomas Tileston. *The Mansions of Virginia, 1706–1776.* Chapel Hill: University of North Carolina Press, 1945.

——————. *The Dwellings of Colonial America.* Chapel Hill: University of North Carolina Press, 1950.

Whiffen, Marcus. *The Eighteenth-Century Houses of Williamsburg,* rev. ed. Charlottesville, Virginia: University Press of Virginia, 1984.

ROMANTIC AND VICTORIAN HOUSES

Andrews, Wayne. *American Gothic.* New York: Random House, 1975.

Brettell, Richard R. *Historic Denver, 1858–1893.* Denver: Historic Denver, 1973.

Cameron, Christina, and Janet Wright. *Second Empire Style in Canadian Architecture.* Canadian Historic Sites: Occasional Papers in Archaeology and History No. 24. Ottawa: National Historic Parks and Sites Branch, 1980.

Campen, Richard N. *Architecture of the Western Reserve, 1800–1900.* Cleveland: Case Western Reserve Universitty Press, 1971.

Cochran, Gifford A. *Grandeur in Tennessee: Classical Revival Architecture in a Pioneer State.* New York: J. J. Augustin, 1946.

Conover, Jewel Helen. *Nineteenth-Century Houses in Western New York.* Albany: State University of New York Press, 1966.

Cooper, J. Wesley. *Ante-Bellum Houses of Natchez.* Natchez, Mississippi: Southern Historical Publications, 1970.

Denison, Allen, and Wallace Huntington. *Victorian Architecture of Port Townsend, Washington.* Seattle: Books America, 1978.

Downing, A. J. *Cottage Residences, Rural Architecture & Landscape Gardening* [pattern book]. Watkins Glen, New York: American Life Foundation, 1842/1967.

——————. *The Architecture of Country Houses* [pattern book]. New York: Dover, 1850/1969.

Early, James. *Romanticism and American Architecture.* New York: A. S. Barnes'and Co., 1965.

Fowler, Orson S. *The Octagon House, A Home for All* [pattern book]. New York: Dover, 1853/1973.

Garvin, James L. "Mail-Order House Plans and American Victorian Architecture." *Winterthur Portfolio,* 16 (1981): 309–334.

Gillon, Edmund V., Jr., and Clay Lancaster. *Victorian Houses.* New York: Dover, 1973.

Hamlin, Talbot. *Greek Revival Architecture in America.* New York: Dover, 1944/1964.

Hammond, Ralph. *Ante-Bellum Mansions of Alabama.* New York: Architectural Book Publishing Co., 1951.

Hitchcock, Henry-Russell. *The Architecture of H. H. Richardson and His Times,* rev. ed. Cambridge, Massachusetts: M.I.T. Press, 1961/1966.

Hussey, E. C. *Victorian Home Building* [pattern book]. Watkins Glen, New York: American Life Foundation, 1875/1976.

Keyes, Margaret N. *Nineteenth Century Home Architecture of Iowa City.* Iowa City, Iowa: Universitty of Iowa Press, 1966.

Lancaster, Clay. *Architectural Follies in America.* Rutland, Vermont: Charles E. Tuttle, 1960.

Lewis, Arnold. *American Country Houses of the Gilded Age (Sheldon's "Artistic Country-Seats").* New York: Dover, 1886–87/1982.

——————, and Keith Morgan. *American Victorian Architecture.* New York: Dover, 1886/1975.

Loth, Calder, and Julius Trousdale Sadler, Jr. *The Only Proper Style: Gothic Architecture in America.* Boston: New York Graphic Society, 1975.

Maass, John. *The Victorian Home in America.* New York: Hawthorn, 1972.

Major, Howard. *The Domestic Architecture of the Early American Republic: The Greek Revival.* Philadelphia: J. B. Lippincott, 1926.

McArdle, Alma deC., and Deirdre Bartlett McArdle. *Carpenter Gothic: Nineteenth-Century Ornamented Houses of New England.* New York: Watson-Guptill, 1978.

Ochsner, Jeffrey Karl. *H. H. Richardson: Complete Architectural Works.* Cambridge, Massachusetts: M.I.T. Press, 1982.

Olwell, Carol, and Judith Lynch Waldhorn. *A Gift to the Street.* San Francisco: Antelope Island Press, 1976.

Palliser, George, and Charles Palliser. *The Palliser's Late Victorian Architecture* [3 pattern books]. Watkins Glen, New York: American Life Foundation, 1878, 1888/1978.

Peat, Wilbur D. *Indiana Houses of the Nineteenth Century.* Indianapolis: Indiana Historical Society, 1962.

Pierson, William H., Jr. *American Buildings and Their Architects: Technology and the Picturesque; The Corporate and the Early Gothic Styles.* Garden City, New York: Doubleday & Co., 1978.

Plymat, William, Jr. *The Victorian Architecture of Iowa.* Des Moines: Elephant's Eye, 1976.

Schmidt, Carl F. *The Octagon Fad.* Scottsville, New York: Author, 1958.

Schmitt, Peter J., and Balthazar Korab. *Kalamazoo: Nineteenth-Century Homes in a Midwestern Village.* Kalamazoo, Michigan: Kalamazoo City Historical Commission, 1976.

Scully, Vincent J., Jr. *The Shingle Style and the Stick Style,* rev. ed. New Haven, Connecticut: Yale University Press, 1971.

Skjelver, Mabel Cooper. *Nineteenth Century Homes of Marshall, Michigan.* Marshall, Michigan: Marshall Historical Society, 1971.

Thomas, George E., and Carl Doebley. *Cape May, Queen of the Seaside Resorts.* Philadelphia: Art Alliance Press, 1976.

Wilson, Samuel, Jr., and Bernard Lemann. *New Orleans Architecture v. 1: The Lower Garden District.* Gretna, Louisiana: Pelican, 1975.

ECLECTIC AND MODERN HOUSES

American Builder Publishing Corporation. *Modern Homes* [pattern book]. Chicago: Author, 1931.

Appelbaum, Stanley. *The Chicago World's Fair of 1893*. New York: Dover, 1980.

Architectural Forum. *The Book of Small Houses* [pattern book]. New York: Simon and Schuster, 1936.

Barnstone, Howard. *The Architecture of John F. Staub: Houston and the South*. Austin: University of Texas Press, 1979.

Brooks, H. Allen. *The Prairie School*. Toronto: University of Toronto Press, 1972.

Cardwell, Kenneth H. *Bernard Maybeck: Artisan, Architect, Artist*. Santa Barbara, California: Peregrine Smith, 1977.

Cerwinske, Laura. *Tropical Deco: The Architecture and Design of Old Miami Beach*. New York: Rizzoli International, 1981.

Current, William R., and Karen Current. *Greene & Greene: Architects in the Residential Style*. Dobbs Ferry, New York: Morgan & Morgan, 1974.

Edgell, G. H. *The American Architecture of To-day*. New York: AMS Press, 1928/1970.

Embury, Aymar, II. *The Dutch Colonial House*. New York: McBride, Nast & Company, 1913.

Etter, Don D. *Denver Going Modern*. Denver: Graphic Impressions, 1977.

Ford, James, and Katherine Morrow Ford. *The Modern House in America*. New York: Architectural Book Publishing Co., 1940.

Grady, James. *Architecture of Neel Reid in Georgia*. Athens, Georgia: University of Georgia Press, 1973.

Hitchcock, Henry-Russell. *In the Nature of Materials. 1887–1941: The Buildings of Frank Lloyd Wright*. New York: Da Capo Press, 1942–1975.

_____, and Philip Johnson. *The International Style*. New York: W. W. Norton, 1932/1966.

Hodgson, Fred T. *Practical Bungalows and Cottages for Town and Country* [pattern book]. Chicago: Frederick J. Drake, 1916.

Hoffstot, Barbara. *Landmark Architecture of Palm Beach*, rev. ed. Pittsburgh: Ober Park Associates, 1980.

Hunter, Paul Robinson, and Walter L. Reichardt, eds. *Residential Architecture in Southern California*. N. p.: American Institute of Architects, Southern California Chapter, 1939.

Jackson, Allen W. *The Half-Timber House*. New York: Robert M. McBride, 1912.

Johnson, Paul C., ed. *Western Ranch Houses by Cliff May*. Menlo Park, California: Lane Books, 1958.

Jordy, William H. *American Buildings and Their Architects: Progressive and Academic Ideals at the Turn of the Century*. Garden City, New York: Doubleday & Co., 1972.

Junior League of Tulsa. *Tulsa Art Deco: An Architectural Era, 1925–1942*. Tulsa, Oklahoma: Author, 1980.

Kidney, Walter C. *The Architecture of Choice: Eclecticism in America, 1880–1930*. New York: George Braziller, 1974.

Kohler, Sue A., and Jeffrey R. Carson. *Sixteenth Street Architecture, volume 1*. Washington, D.C.: Commission of Fine Arts, 1978.

Lancaster, Clay. *The American Bungalow, 1880s–1920s*. New York: Abbeville Press, 1983.

Makinson, Randell L. *Greene & Greene: Architecture as a Fine Art*. Salt Lake City, Utah: Peregrine Smith, 1977.

McCoy, Esther. *Five California Architects*. New York: Praeger Publishers, 1960/1975.

McKim, Mead & White. *A Monograph of the Works of McKim, Mead & White, 1879–1915*. New York: Arno Press, 1915/1977.

Newcomb, Rexford. *The Spanish House for America*. Philadelphia: J. B. Lippincott, 1927.

_____. *Mediterranean Domestic Architecture in the United States*. Cleveland: J. H. Jansen, 1928.

Platt, Frederick. *America's Gilded Age: Its Architecture and Decoration*. Cranbury, New Jersey: A. S. Barnes, 1976.

Radford Architectural Company. *Radford's Artistic Homes: 250 Designs* [pattern book]. Chicago: Author, 1908.

Saylor, Henry H., ed. *Architectural Styles for Country Houses*. New York: McBride, Nast & Company, 1912.

Sclare, Liisa, and Donald Sclare. *Beaux-Arts Estates: A Guide to the Architecture of Long Island*. New York: Viking Press, 1980.

Smith, Henry Atterbury. *The Books of a Thousand Homes, Volume 1: 500 Small House Plans* [pattern book]. New York: Home Owners Service Institute, 1923.

Sprague, Paul E. *Guide to Frank Lloyd Wright and Prairie School Architecture in Oak Park*. Oak Park, Illinois: Village of Oak Park, 1976.

Stickley, Gustav. *Craftsman Homes* [pattern book]. New York: Dover, 1909/1979.

Storrer, William Allin. *The Architecture of Frank Lloyd Wright: A Complete Catalog*, 2nd ed. Cambridge, Massachusetts: M.I.T. Press, 1978.

Underwood, Francis H. *The Colonial House Then and Now*. Rutland, Vermont: Charles E. Tuttle, 1977.

Von Holst, Hermann V. *Country and Suburban Homes of the Prairie School Period* [pattern book]. New York: Dover, 1913/1982.

Wilson, Henry L. *The Bungalow Book*, 5th ed. [pattern book]. Chicago: Author, 1910.

Wilson, Richard Guy. *McKim, Mead & White*. New York: Rizzoli International, 1983.

Wolfe, Tom. *From Bauhaus to Our House*. New York: Farrar Straus Giroux, 1981.

REGIONAL AND LOCAL GUIDES: NORTHEASTERN STATES

Andrews, Wayne. *Architecture in New England: A Photographic History.* Brattleboro, Vermont: Stephen Greene Press, 1973.

Bassett, William B. *Historic American Buildings Survey of New Jersey.* Newark: New Jersey Historical Society, 1977.

Brown, Elizabeth Mills. *New Haven: A Guide to Architecture and Urban Design.* New Haven, Connecticut: Yale University Press, 1976.

Buffalo Architectural Guidebook Corporation: *Buffalo Architecture: A Guide.* Cambridge, Massachusetts: M.I.T. Press, 1981.

Bunting, Bainbridge. *Houses of Boston's Back Bay: An Architectural History, 1840–1917.* Cambridge, Massachusetts: Harvard University Press, 1967.

Cambridge Historical Commission. *Survey of Architectural History in Cambridge, Reports 1–5* [in 5 volumes]. Cambridge, Massachusetts: Author, 1965–1977.

Dibner, Martin, ed. *Portland.* Portland, Maine: Greater Portland Landmarks, 1972.

Dorsey, John, and James D. Dilts. *A Guide to Baltimore Architecture,* 2nd ed. Centreville, Maryland: Tidewater Publishers, 1981.

Downing, Antoinette F., and Vincent J. Scully, Jr. *The Architectural Heritage of Newport Rhode Island, 1640–1915,* 2nd ed. New York: Clarkson N. Potter, 1967.

Eberlein, Harold Donaldson, and Cortlandt Van Dyke Hubbard. *Historic Houses of the Hudson Valley.* New York: Architectural Book Publishing Company, 1942.

—————. *Historic Houses and Buildings of Delaware.* Dover, Delaware: State Archives Department, 1962.

Foerster, Bernd. *Architecture Worth Saving in Rensselaer County, New York.* Troy, New York: Rensselaer Polytechnic Institute, 1965.

Forman, H. Chandlee. *Maryland Architecture: A Short History From 1634 Through the Civil War.* Cambridge, Maryland: Tidewater Publishers, 1968.

Goldberger, Paul. *The City Observed, New York: A Guide to the Architecture of Manhattan.* New York: Vintage Books, 1979.

Goldstone, Harmon H., and Martha Dalrymple. *History Preserved: A Guide to New York City Landmarks and Historic Districts.* New York: Schocken Books, 1974/1976.

Gowans, Alan. *Architecture in New Jersey.* New Jersey Historical Series, volume 6. Princeton, New Jersey: D. Van Nostrand, 1964.

Greiff, Constance M., Mary W. Gibbons, and Elizabeth G. C. Menzies. *Princeton Architecture.* Princeton, New Jersey: Princeton University Press, 1967.

Hartford Architecture Conservancy Survey. *Hartford Architecture, Volumes 1–3.* Hartford, Connecticut: Author, 1978–1980.

Historic American Buildings Survey. *Historic Buildings of Massachusetts.* New York: Charles Scribner's Sons, 1976.

Hitchcock, Henry-Russell. *Rhode Island Architecture.* Cambridge, Massachusetts: M.I.T. Press, 1939/1968.

Howland, Richard Hubbard, and Eleanor Patterson Spencer. *The Architecture of Baltimore.* Baltimore: Johns Hopkins Press, 1953.

Huxtable, Ada Louise. *The Architecture of New York: A History and Guide,* 3 vols. Garden City, New York: Doubleday & Company, 1964.

Jacobs, Stephen W. *Wayne County* [New York]: *The Aesthetic Heritage of a Rural Area.* New York: Publishing Center for Cultural Resources, 1979.

Junior League of Kingston. *Early Architecture in Ulster County,* [New York]. Kingston, New York: Author, 1974.

Lancaster, Clay. *Old Brooklyn Heights: New York's First Suburb,* 2nd ed. New York: Dover, 1979.

—————, Robert A. M. Stern, and Robert J. Hefner. *East Hampton's Heritage: An Illustrated Architectural Record.* New York: W. W. Norton, 1982.

Larew, Marilynn M. *Bel Air,* [Maryland]: *The Town Through Its Buildings.* Edgewood, Maryland: Northfield Press, 1981.

Lockwood, Charles. *Bricks & Brownstone: The New York Row House, 1783–1929.* New York: McGraw Hill, 1972.

Malo, Paul. *Landmarks of Rochester and Monroe County.* Syracuse, New York: Syracuse University Press, 1974.

Maryland Historical Trust. *Inventory of Historic Sites in Calvert County, Charles County, and St. Mary's County,* rev. ed. Annapolis, Maryland: Author, 1980.

McGowan, Robert Harold. *Architecture From the Adirondack Foothills: Folk and Designed Architecture of Franklin County, New York.* Malone, New York: Franklin County Historical and Museum Society, 1977.

Myers, Denys Peter. "The Historic Architecture of Maine." *Maine Catalog, Historic American Buildings Survey,* pp. 1–198. Augusta, Maine: Maine State Museum, 1974.

New York State Office of Planning Coordination. *Long Island Landmarks.* Albany, New York: Author, 1969.

Prokopoff, Stephen S., and Joan C. Siegfried. *The Nine-teenth-Century Architecture of Saratoga Springs.* New York: State Council on the Arts, 1970.

Raymond, Eleanor. *Early Domestic Architecture of Pennsylvania.* Exton, Pennsylvania: Schiffer, 1931/1977.

Reiff, Daniel D. *Architecture in Fredonia, 1811–1972.* Fredonia, New York: Michael C. Rockefeller Arts Center Gallery, State University College, 1972.

Rettig, Robert Bell. *Guide to Cambridge Architecture: Ten Walking Tours.* Cambridge, Massachusetts: M.I.T. Press, 1969.

Rifkind, Carole, and Carol Levine. *Mansions, Mills, and Main Streets: Buildings and Places to Explore Within Fifty Miles of New York City.* New York: Schocken Books, 1975.

Sanchis, Frank E. *American Architecture: Westchester County, New York.* Croton-on-Hudson, New York: North River Press, 1977.

Schiffer, Margaret Berwind. *Survey of Chester County, Pennsylvania, Architecture: 17th, 18th and 19th Centuries.* Exton, Pennsylvania: Schiffer, 1976.

Schull, Diantha Dow. *Landmarks of Otsego County* [New York]. Syracuse, New York: Syracuse University Press, 1980.

Schwartz, Helen. *The New Jersey House.* New Brunswick, New Jersey: Rutgers University Press, 1983.

Stotz, Charles Morse. *The Architectural Heritage of Early Western Pennsylvania: A Record of Building Before 1860.* Pittsburgh: University of Pittsburgh Press, 1936/1966.

Tatum, George Bishop. *Penn's Great Town; 250 Years of Philadelphia Architecture Illustrated in Prints and Drawings.* Philadelphia: University of Pennsylvania Press, 1961.

Teitelman, Edward, and Richard W. Longstreth. *Architecture in Philadelphia: A Guide.* Cambridge, Massachusetts: M.I.T. Press, 1974.

Thompson, Deborah, ed. *Maine Forms of American Architecture.* Camden, Maine: Downeast Magazine, 1976.

Tolles, Bryant F., Jr., and Carolyn K. Tolles. *New Hampshire Architecture: An Illustrated Guide.* Hanover, New Hampshire: University Press of New England, 1979.

Tucci, Douglass Shand. *Built in Boston: City and Suburb, 1800–1950.* Boston: New York Graphic Society, 1978.

University of Vermont Historic Preservation Program. *The Burlington Book: Architecture, History, Future.* Burlington, Vermont: Author, 1980.

Van Trump, James D., and Arthur P. Ziegler, Jr. *Landmark Architecture of Allegheny County, Pennsylvania.* Pittsburgh: Pittsburgh History and Landmarks Foundation, 1967.

Webster, Richard J. *Philadelphia Preserved: Catalog of the Historic American Buildings Survey.* Philadelphia: Temple University Press, 1976.

Weeks, Christopher. *The Building of Westminster in Maryland.* Annapolis, Maryland: Fishergate Publishing Company, 1978.

White, Norval, and Elliot Willensky. *AIA Guide to New York City*, rev. ed. New York: Macmillan, 1978.

REGIONAL AND LOCAL GUIDES: SOUTHERN STATES

American Institute of Architects, New Orleans Chapter. *A Guide to New Orleans Architecture.* New Orleans: Author, 1974.

American Institute of Architects, Winston-Salem Section. *Architectural Guide, Winston-Salem, Forsyth County.* Winston-Salem, North Carolina: Author, 1978.

Andrews, Wayne. *Pride of the South: A Social History of Southern Architecture.* New York: Atheneum, 1979.

Biloxi, City of. *The Buildings of Biloxi: An Architectural Survey.* Biloxi, Mississippi: Author, 1976.

Butchko, Tom. *An Inventory of Historic Architecture, Sampson County, North Carolina.* Clinton, North Carolina: City of Clinton, n.d.

Chambers, S. Allen, Jr. *Lynchburg,* [Virginia]: *An Architectural History.* Charlottesville, Virginia: University Press of Virginia, 1981.

Cox, Ethelyn. *Historic Alexandria, Virginia Street by Street: A Survey of Existing Early Buildings.* Alexandria, Virginia: Historic Alexandria Foundation, 1976.

Cox, Warren J., and others. *A Guide to the Architecture of Washington, D.C.,* 2nd ed. New York: McGraw-Hill, 1974.

Crocker, Mary Wallace. *Historic Architecture in Mississippi.* Jackson: University Press of Mississippi, 1973.

Dulaney, Paul S. *The Architecture of Historic Richmond,* [Virginia], 2nd ed. Charlottesville, Virginia: University Press of Virginia, 1976.

Eufaula Heritage Association. *Historic Eufaula: A Treasury of Southern Architecture, 1827–1910.* Eufaula, Alabama: Author, 1972.

Harris, Linda L. *An Architectural and Historical Inventory of Raleigh, North Carolina.* Raleigh, North Carolina: City of Raleigh, 1978.

Historic Beaufort Foundation. *Historic Beaufort,* 2nd ed. Beaufort, South Carolina: Author, 1973.

Jeane, D. Gregory, and Douglas Clare Purcell. *The Architectural Legacy of the Lower Chattahoochee Valley in Alabama and Georgia.* University, Alabama: University of Alabama Press, 1978.

Lancaster, Clay. *Eutaw: The Builders and Architecture of an Ante-Bellum Southern Town.* Eutaw, Alabama: Greene County Historical Society, 1979.

Linley, John. *Architecture of Middle Georgia: The Oconee Area.* Athens: University of Georgia Press, 1972.

_____. *The Georgia Catalog, Historic American Buildings Survey: A Guide to the Architecture of the State.* Athens, Georgia: University of Georgia Press, 1982.

Little-Stokes, Ruth, and Tony P. Wrenn. *An Inventory of Historic Architecture in Caswell County, North Carolina.* Yanceyville, North Carolina: Caswell County Historic Association, 1979.

Lyle, Royster, Jr., and Pamela Hemenway Simpson. *The Architecture of Historic Lexington,* [Virginia]. Charlottesville, Virginia: University Press of Virginia, 1977.

Maddex, Diane. *Historic Buildings of Washington, D.C.* Pittsburgh: Ober Park Associates, 1973.

Mobile, City of. *Nineteenth Century Mobile Architecture.* Mobile, Alabama: Author, 1974.

Morrison, Mary L., ed. *Historic Savannah,* 2nd ed. Savannah, Georgia: Historic Savannah Foundation, 1979.

Nichols, Frederick Doveton, and Frances Benjamin Johnston. *The Early Architecture of Georgia.* Chapel Hill, North Carolina: University of North Carolina Press, 1957.

_____, and others. *The Architecture of Georgia.* Savannah, Georgia: Beehive Press, 1976.

Overdyke, W. Darrell. *Louisiana Plantation Homes.* New York: Architectural Book Publishing, 1965.

Patrick, James. *Architecture in Tennessee, 1768–1897.* Knoxville, Tennessee: University of Tennessee Press, 1981.

Schwartz, Nancy B. *District of Columbia Catalog, 1974, Historic American Buildings Survey.* Charlottesville, Virginia: University Press of Virginia, 1976.

Severens, Kenneth. *Southern Architecture: 350 Years of Distinctive American Buildings.* New York: E. P. Dutton, 1981.

Simons, Albert, and Samuel Lapham, Jr. *The Early Architecture of Charleston* [S.C.]. Columbia, South Carolina: University of South Carolina Press, 1927/1970.

Stoney, Samuel Gaillard. *This Is Charleston: A Survey of the Architectural Heritage of a Unique American City,* rev. ed. Charleston, South Carolina: Carolina Art Association, 1976.

Virginia Historic Landmarks Commission. *Virginia Landmarks Register,* 2nd ed. Richmond: 1976.

_____. *Virginia Catalog, Historic American Buildings Survey.* Charlottesville, Virginia: University Press of Virginia, 1976.

Whitwell, W. L., and Lee W. Winborne. *The Architectural Heritage of the Roanoke Valley* [Virginia]. Charlottesville, Virginia: University Press of Virginia, 1982.

REGIONAL AND LOCAL GUIDES: MIDWESTERN STATES

American Institute of Architects, Kansas City Chapter. *Kansas City.* Kansas City, Missouri: Author, 1979.

Andrews, Wayne. *Architecture in Chicago and Mid-America.* New York: Harper and Row, 1968.

Bach, Ira J. *A Guide to Chicago's Historic Suburbs On Wheels and On Foot.* Athens, Ohio: Ohio University Press, 1981.

Block, Jean F. *Hyde Park* [Chicago] *Houses, An Informal History, 1856–1910.* Chicago: University of Chicago Press, 1978.

Bryan, John Albury. *Missouri's Contribution to American Architecture.* St. Louis: St. Louis Architectural Club, 1928.

Campen, Richard N. *Ohio; An Architectural Portrait.* Chagrin Falls, Ohio: West Summit Press, 1973.

Ehrlich, George. *Kansas City, Missouri: An Architectural History, 1826–1976.* Kansas City, Missouri: Historic Kansas City Foundation, 1979.

Ferry, W. Hawkins. *The Buildings of Detroit.* rev. ed. Detroit: Wayne State University Press, 1968.

Gebhard, David, and Tom Martinson. *A Guide to the Architecture of Minnesota.* Minneapolis: University of Minnesota Press, 1977.

Indiana Architectural Foundation. *Indianapolis Architecture.* Indianapolis: Author, 1975.

Johannesen, Eric. *Cleveland Architecture, 1876–1976.* Cleveland, Ohio: Western Reserve Historical Society, 1979.

Johnson, Carl H., Jr. *The Building of Galena: An Architectural Legacy.* Galena, Illinois: Author, 1977.

Jones, Elizabeth F., and Mary Jean Kinsman. *Jefferson County: Survey of Historic Sites in Kentucky.* Louisville: Jefferson County Office of Historic Preservation and Archives, 1981.

Junior League of Evansville. *Reflections Upon a Century of Architecture: Evansville, Indiana.* Evansville, Indiana: Author, 1977.

Kansas City, Missouri Landmarks Commission. *Kansas City: A Place in Time.* Kansas City, Missouri: Author, 1977.

Kennedy, Roger. *Minnesota Houses.* Minneapolis: Dillon Press, 1967.

Kentucky Heritage Commission. *Ballard County: Survey of Historic Sites in Kentucky.* Frankfort, Kentucky: Author, 1978.

_____. *Jessamine County: Survey of Historic Sites in Kentucky*. Frankfort, Kentucky: Author, 1979.

Kidney, Walter C. *Historic Buildings of Ohio: A Selection From the Records of the Historic American Buildings Survey*. Pittsburgh: Ober Park Associates, 1972.

Koeper, Frederick. *Illinois Architecture*. Chicago: University of Chicago Press, 1968.

Lancaster, Clay. *Vestiges of the Venerable City: A Chronicle of Lexington, Kentucky*. Lexington: Lexington-Fayette County Historic Commission, 1978.

Mason City, City of. *Mason City, Iowa: An Architectural Heritage*. Mason City, Iowa: Author, 1977.

McArthur, Shirley du Fresne. *North Point Historic Districts—Milwaukee*. Milwaukee, Wisconsin: North Point Historical Society, 1981.

McCue, George. *The Building Art in St. Louis: Two Centuries*, 3rd ed. St. Louis, Missouri: Knight Publishing Co., 1981.

Meyer, Katharine Mattingly, ed. *Detroit Architecture: A.I.A. Guide*, rev. ed. Detroit, Michigan: Wayne State University Press, 1980.

Newcomb, Rexford. *Architecture of the Old Northwest Territory*. Chicago: University of Chicago Press, 1950.

_____. *Architecture in Old Kentucky*. Urbana, Illinois: University of Illinois Press, 1953.

Perrin, Richard W. E. *Historic Wisconsin Architecture*, rev. ed. Milwaukee, Wisconsin: Wisconsin Society of Architects, 1976.

_____. *Historic Wisconsin Buildings: A Survey in Pioneer Architecture, 1835-1870,* 2nd ed. Milwaukee, Wisconsin: Milwaukee Public Museum, 1981.

Sandeen, Ernest R. *St. Paul's Historic Summit Avenue*. St. Paul, Minnesota: Macalester College Living Historical Museum, 1978.

Schofield, Mary-Peale. *Landmark Architecture of Cleveland*, [Ohio]. Pittsburgh: Ober Park Associates, 1976.

Scott, James Allen. *Duluth's Legacy, volume 1: Architecture*. Duluth, Minnesota: City of Duluth, 1974.

Shank, Wesley I. *Iowa Catalog: Historic American Buildings Survey*. Iowa City, Iowa: University of Iowa Press, 1979.

REGIONAL AND LOCAL GUIDES: WESTERN STATES

Alexander, Drury Blakeley, and Todd Webb. *Texas Homes of the Nineteenth Century*. Austin: University of Texas Press, 1966.

American Institute of Architects, Dallas Chapter. *Dallasights: An Anthology of Architecture and Open Spaces*. Dallas, Texas: Author, 1978.

Andree, Herb, and Noel Young. *Santa Barbara Architecture: From Spanish Colonial to Modern*, 2nd ed. Santa Barbara, California: Capra Press, 1980.

Barnstone, Howard. *The Galveston* [Texas] *That Was*. New York: Macmillan, 1966.

Bernhardi, Robert. *The Buildings of Berkeley* [California]. Oakland, California: Holmes Book Co., 1971.

Bracken, Dorothy Kendall, and Maurine Whorton Redway, *Early Texas Homes*. Dallas, Texas: Southern Methodist University Press, 1956.

Burkholder, Mary V. *The King William Area* [San Antonio]: *A History and Guide to the Houses*, 2nd ed. San Antonio, Texas: Outland Press, 1977.

Butler, Phyllis Filiberti, and Junior League of San Jose. *The Valley of Santa Clara* [California]: *Historic Buildings, 1792-1920*, 2nd ed. Novato, California: Presidio Press, 1981.

Chase, John. *The Sidewalk Companion to Santa Cruz Architecture*, rev. ed. Santa Cruz, California: Paper Vision Press, 1979.

Clark, Anne. *Historic Houses of San Augustine* [Texas]. Austin, Texas: Encino Press, 1972.

Fairfax, Geoffrey W. *The Architecture of Honolulu*. Sydney, Australia: Island Heritage, 1972.

Gleye, Paul. *The Architecture of Los Angeles*. Los Angeles, California: Rosebud Books, 1981.

Gebhard, David, and others. *A Guide to Architecture in San Francisco and Northern California*, 2nd ed. Santa Barbara, California: Peregrine Smith, 1976.

_____, and Robert Winter. *A Guide to Architecture in Los Angeles and Southern California*. Santa Barbara, California: Peregrine Smith, 1977.

Goeldner, Paul. *Utah Catalog: Historic American Buildings Survey*. Salt Lake City: Utah Heritage Foundation, 1969.

_____. *Texas Catalog: Historic American Buildings Survey*. San Antonio, Texas: Trinity University Press, 1974.

Goins, Charles R. and John W. Morris. *Oklahoma Homes, Past and Present*. Norman: University of Oklahoma Press, 1980.

Hart, Arthur A. *Historic Boise: An Introduction to the Architecture of Boise, Idaho, 1863-1938*. Boise: Historic Boise, 1980.

Kirker, Harold. *California's Architectural Frontier: Style and Tradition in the Nineteenth Century*, rev. ed. Santa Barbara, California: Peregrine Smith, 1973.

Lenggenhager, Werner, and Lucile McDonald. *Where the Washingtonians Lived*. Seattle, Washington: Superior Publishing Co., 1969.

McDonald, William L. *Dallas Rediscovered: A Photographic Chronicle of Urban Expansion, 1870-1925*. Dallas, Texas: Dallas Historical Society, 1978.

Neil, J. Meredith. *Saints and Oddfellows: A Bicentennial Sampler of Idaho Architecture*. Boise, Idaho: Boise Gallery of Art Association, 1976.

Noel, Thomas Jacob. *Richthofen's Montclair: A Pioneer Denver Suburb*, 2nd ed. Boulder, Colorado: Pruett Publishing Co., 1978.

Olmsted, Roger, and T. H. Watkins. *Here Today: San Francisco's Architectural Heritage*. San Francisco, California: Chronicle Books, 1968.

Regnery, Dorothy F. *An Enduring Heritage: Historic Buildings of the San Francisco Peninsula*. Stanford, California: Stanford University Press, 1976.

Stoehr, C. Eric. *Bonanza Victorian: Architecture and Society in Colorado Mining Towns*. Albuquerque: University of New Mexico Press, 1975.

University of Kansas Museum of Art. *Nineteenth Century Houses in Lawrence, Kansas*. Lawrence, Kansas: Author, 1968.

Vaughan, Thomas, and Virginia Guest Ferriday, eds. *Space, Style and Structure: Building in Northwest America*. 2 volumes. Portland: Oregon Historical Society, 1974.

Wiberg, Ruth Eloise. *Rediscovering Northwest Denver*. Boulder, Colorado: Pruett Publishing Co., 1976.

Williamson, Roxanne Kuter. *Austin, Texas: An American Architectural History*. San Antonio, Texas: Trinity University Press, 1973.

Woodbridge, Sally, B., ed. *Bay Area Houses*. New York: Oxford University Press, 1976.

——————, and Roger Montgomery. *A Guide to Architecture in Washington State*. Seattle: University of Washington Press, 1980.

——————, and John M. Woodbridge. *Architecture San Francisco: The Guide*. San Francisco, California: 101 Productions, 1982.

HOUSE PRESERVATION AND RESTORATION

Anderson Notter Associates. *The Salem Handbook: A Renovation Guide for Homeowners*. Salem, Massachusetts: Historic Salem, 1977.

Ferro, Maximilian L. *How to Love and Care for Your Old Building in New Bedford*. New Bedford, Massachusetts: City of New Bedford, 1977.

Harris, Kip. *Confronting the Older House: A Homeowner's Guide*. Salt Lake City: Utah Heritage Foundation, 1979.

Howard, Cynthia. *Your House in the Streetcar Suburb*. Medford, Massachusetts: City of Medford, 1979.

Hutchins, Nigel. *Restoring Old Houses*. Toronto: Van Nostrand Reinhold, 1980.

Labine, Clem, and Carolyn Flaherty, eds. *The Old-House Journal Compendium*. Woodstock, New York: Overlook Press, 1980.

Legner, Linda. *City House: A Guide to Renovating Older Chicago-Area Houses*. Chicago: City of Chicago, 1979.

Maddex, Diane, ed. *The Brown Book; A Directory of Preservation Information*. Washington, D.C.: Preservation Press, 1983.

Moss, Roger W. *Century of Color: Exterior Decoration for American Buildings, 1820–1920*. Watkins Glen, New York: American Life Foundation, 1981.

Oakland, City of. *Rehab Right: How to Rehabilitate Your Oakland House Without Sacrificing Architectural Assets*. Oakland, California: Author, 1978.

Phillips, Morgan W. *The Eight Most Common Mistakes in Restoring Houses (And How to Avoid Them)*. AASLH Technical Leaflet 118. Nashville: American Association for State and Local History, 1979.

Shopsin, William C., and Grania Bolton Marcus, eds. *Saving Large Estates*. Setauket, New York: Society for the Preservation of Long Island Antiquities, 1977.

Stanforth, Deirdre, and Martha Stamm. *Buying and Renovating a House in the City*. New York: Alfred A. Knopf, 1972.

Stephen, George. *Remodeling Old Houses, Without Destroying Their Character*. New York: Alfred A. Knopf, 1972.

U.S. National Park Service, Technical Preservation Services. *Respectful Rehabilitation: Answers to Your Questions About Old Buildings*. Washington, D.C.: Preservation Press, 1982.

Photo Credits

Allison Abraham, 437:1, 2, 3, 4, 5

State of Alabama Bureau of Publicity and Information, 346–7:4

Alabama Department of Archives and History, 384–5:4

Architektursammlung, Technische Universitat Munchen from *L'Architecture Americaine*, 209:5; 274:5; 282–3: 5, 7; 284–5:6, 7; 286–7:1; 375–7:4

Arkansas Historic Preservation Program, 349:3; 450–1:7. Bob Dunn, 216–19:14

Atlanta Historical Society, Peachtree-Cherokee Trust Collection, 330–1:8. Kenneth Kay, 339:5

City of Biloxi, 268–73:1; 274:1; 316–17:2

Biltmore House and Gardens, 375–7:9

Bentz-Thompson Architects, 485:4. Eric Sutherland, 472–3:9

Jean F. Block, *Hyde Park Houses* (Chicago: University of Chicago Press, 1978). Samuel W. Block Jr., 226–7:1; 275:1; 282–3:2; 370–1:2

Bowdoin College Library, Special Collections, 204:4

R. Bruhn (© 1978), 250–1:4

Buffalo and Erie County Historical Society, 328–9:4, 8; 334–5:1; 370–1:6; 448–9:8. Roy Nagle Collection, 350–1:1

Cambridge Historical Commission, 340–1:1, 4; 472–3:6. Richard Cheek, 244–5:3; 246–7:3; 275:5; 280:1; 338:1; 472–3:1, 4. Roger Gilman, 258–9:8. B. Orr, 244–5:4; 268–73:14; 326–7:1; 332–3:8; 340–1:2

Catskill Center for Conservation and Development, Arkville, New York. Mark Zeek, 268–73:12

John Chase, *The Sidewalk Companion to Santa Cruz Architecture* (Paper Vision Press), 268–73:15

Commission of Fine Arts. Jack E. Boucher, 384–5:2, 3, 7; 392–3:7

Connecticut Historical Commission. Susan Babbitt, 260:4. Brian Pfeiffer, 79:4; 226–7:7; 248–9:1. Ellen Rosebrock, 268–73:8; 296–7:2

Paul Crews, 312:3

Mary Wallace Crocker, *Historic Architecture in Mississippi* (1973). 204:3; 220–1:2

Cuyahoga County Archives, 276–9:5; 490:2. David M. Thum, 216–19:5

Dallas Historical Society, 276–9:4, 10

Dallas Public Library, Texas/Dallas History and Archives Division, 292:1

Detroit Public Library, Burton Historical Collection, 209:2

Dome Kits International, 498–9:5

State University College at Fredonia, New York, Jewel Conover Archives in the Reed Library, 349:1

Galveston Historical Foundation, 313–15:5; 328–9:1

David Gebhard, 412–13:8; 414–15:6, 8; 472–3:2

Robert C. Giebner, 136–7:2

Greene and Greene Library, 456–7:8

Julia Guice, editor, *The Buildings of Biloxi: An Architectural Survey*, 90–1:5

Thomas Hahn, 186–7:4, 6; 206–7:1; 216–19:2; 224–5:3; 226–7:6; 232–3:8; 248–9:4; 258–9:1; 274:2, 3; 275:3; 276–9:14; 281:1, 2; 284–5:4, 5; 286–7:5 292:2, 5; 311:4; 326–7:4; 346–7:7; 362–5:3, 9, 16

Historic American Buildings Survey Office. Jack E. Boucher, 151:3

Historic Landmarks Foundation of Indiana, 250–1:6

Indiana Historical Society Library, 13:3; 186–7:8; 244–5:2; 268–73:7, 11; 276–9:8

Iowa State Historical Department, Division of Historic Preservation. Robert Ryan, 268–73:13

Kansas City Landmarks Commission, 298–9:3

Kentucky Historical Society, 84–5:6

Margaret M. Keyes, *Nineteenth Century Home Architecture of Iowa City* (University of Iowa Press), 206–7:5; 226–7:8

The King William Association, San Antonio, Texas. Mary V. Burkholder, 316–7:3

Kirksville College of Osteopathy and Surgery, 276–9:13

Carleton Knight III, 150:3; 209:1; 220–1:4; 222–3:7; 226–7:4; 236–7:7; 248–9:3, 5; 248–9:5; 260:2; 281:3, 4; 306:4

Lexington-Fayette County Historic Commission, 94–5:9; 97:2; 222–3:2

511

Library of Congress, 190–1:3; 232–3:7. American Press Assn., 400–1:5. George S. Cook, 148–9:6. Francis B. Johnston Collection, 110–11:1–2; 126–7:5; 148–9:5; 166–7:5; 172–3:7; 175:1; 190–1:5; 194–5:7. National Photo Co., 463:2. W. H. Sutton, 250–1:8. Witteman Collection, 260:5; 369:5; 412–13:2. Marion Post Wolcott, 485:2

Library of Congress, Farm Security Administration Archives, 98–9:7. Walker Evans, 84–5:4; 311:3; 314–15:6. Lange, 134–5:5. Russell Lee, 84–5:7; 362–5:10; 424–5:1. Carl Mydans, 98–9:4. Arthur Rothstein, 87:1, 4; 90–1:7; 136–7:4. John Vachon, 98–11:5, 6. Marion Post Wolcott, 90–1:8; 96–7:1; 98–9:1; 100–1:2, 3; 366–7:1

Library of Congress, Historic American Buildings Survey, 100–1:1; 134–5:6; 144–6:9, 10, 11; 162:7; 164:1; 166–7:6; 174:2; 286–7:6; 306:3; 334–5:7; 339:4; 382–3:8; 444–5:7; 450–1:6. L. D. Andrew, 172–3:3. W. Harry Bagby, 110–11:4. Nelson E. Baldwin, 117:2; 118:1. John M. Beckstrom, 160–1:3. John O. Bostrup, 160–1:6. Jack E. Boucher, 81:2; 110–11:7; 117:1; 147:2, 3; 148–9:2, 4; 151:2; 166–7:8; 174:1; 186–7:5; 194–5:3; 206–7:2, 7; 258–9:7; 268–73:16; 294–5:3; 306:5; 307:4; 384–5:1; 426–7:6. Branzetti, 79:1, 2; 147:1; 150:1; 164:4. James Butters, 172–3:5; 188–9:7; 208:1. Richard Cheek, 108–9:6. Clinedinst, 412–13:6 C. O. Greene, 110–11:5, 8; 148–9:3, 7; 174:5. Arthur C. Haskell, 160–1:4, 5; 162–3:1. Cortlandt Hubbard, 150:2. John A. Huffman, 314–15:4. Lester Jones, 79:5; 126–7:4, 7. Kenneth Kay, 268–73:6. Richard Koch, 124–5:1, 6; 126–7:8. R. Merritt Lacey, 119:1, 2, 4, 5. Leslie, 125:3. Jane Lidz, 202–3:1; 268–73:2; 276–9:11; 402–3:6; 428:1–2; 458–9:2. E. P. MacFarland, 119:3; 194–5:6. Stanley P. Mixon, 118:2; 166–7:2. Eric Muller, 202–3:6. Mydans, 362–5:1. Frederick D. Nichols, 136–7:1, 6. Paul Piaget, 194–5:4. E. H. Pickering, 165:1, 3, 4; 166–7:1. James Rainey, 144–6:3. Cervin Robinson, 144–6:4; 162–3:6, 8; 188–9:8; 232–3:5; 236–7:5; 282–3:6; 294–5:8. Sirlin Studies, 216–19:9; 228–9:1; 258–915 Roger Sturtevant, 134–5:1. Robert Thall, 250–1:7; 444–5:8; 467:5. Laurence E. Tilley, 144–6:2; 160–1:1; 162–3:4, 5; 216–19:7. Josiah Tully, 162–3:2. Thomas Waterman, 110–11:3; 118:5; 144–6:7. Carl F. White, 193:1. Henry F. Withey, 134–5:2

Louisiana State Museum, 205:3

Louisiana State Parks Commission, 126–7:6

University of Louisville Photographic Archives. Brown-Doherty Collection, 307:2; 375–7:2. Caufield and Shook Collection, 15:5 (neg. 36593); 15:4 (neg. 41271); 90–1:6 (neg. 3909?); 175:5 (neg. 38025); 216–19:11 (neg. 40954); 294–5:1 (neg. 37097); 332–3:2 (neg. 72429); 332–3:3 (neg. 72425); 332–3:9 (neg. 41518); 336–7:1 (neg.

68196); 346–7:8 (neg. 79590); 352–3:1 (neg. 72648); 352–3:2 (neg. 5774A); 360–1:7 (neg. 41209); 360–1:7 (neg. 5613); 362–5:14 (neg. 41252); 366–7:3 (neg. 72638); 392–3:1 (neg. 72687); 412–13:7 (neg. 2614); 424–5:3 (neg. 89283); 444–5:2 (neg. 36378); 458–9:5 (neg. 41267); 460–2:4 (neg. 541259). Potter Collection, 339:2 (neg. 2523.5). A. B. Rue, 85:5. Standard Oil of New Jersey Collection, 84–5:2 (neg. 52483); 94–5:8 (neg. 48981); 98–9:3 (neg. 49832); 202–3:5 (neg. 51912); 202–3:7 (neg. 53953)

Louisville Landmarks Commission, 144–6:6; 220–1:6; 232–3:4; 304–5:8; 307:1; 382–3:1; 400–1:8; 404–5:4

Madison County Historical Society. Howard L. Colyer, 220–1:7

Maine Historic Preservation Commission, 250–1:5

Manufactured Housing Institute, 498–9:1, 2, 3

Marshall Historical Society, 186–7:3; 280:2

Van Jones Martin, 188–9:3; 188–9:6; 190–1:1, 4; 192:2; 216–19:6, 15

Tom Martinson, 202–3:8; 206–7:4; 467:4; 472–3:8; 484:3; 485:5

Maryland Historical Society, 244–5:6

Virginia and Lee McAlester, prints by Doug Tomlinson, 13:2, 4, 5; 15:1, 2; 17:2, 4, 5, 6; 18:1, 2, 3, 4, 5, 6, 7, 8, 9; 90–1:1, 2, 3; 92–3:2, 3, 4, 5; 94–5:5, 6; 96–7:4, 5; 98–9:2; 100–1:5, 6; 124–5:2, 4, 7; 126–7:2; 144–6:1; 147:4, 5; 160–1:2, 7; 165:2, 5; 166–7:4; 172–3:1, 6; 190:7; 193:3; 194–5:1, 2, 5; 202–3:2, 3; 204:1; 205:2, 4; 206–7:3, 8; 216–19:1, 3, 10; 220–1:1, 5; 222–3:1, 3, 4, 6; 224–5:1, 2, 4, 6; 226–7:2, 3, 5; 228–9:2, 4, 6; 232–3:1, 2, 6; 244–5:1; 246–7:5, 6; 248–9:2; 250–1:2; 252–3:1, 2, 4, 5, 6; 268–73:3, 10, 17; 274:4; 276–9:2, 3, 7, 9, 12, 15, 16; 282–3:1, 4; 284–5:1; 286–7:2; 293:1, 2, 3, 5; 294–5:4, 5, 6, 7; 296–7:1, 3, 6; 298–9:4, 5, 6, 7, 8; 304–5:2, 3, 6, 7; 306:2; 307:3; 311:1, 2; 312:1, 2; 314–15:1, 2; 326–7:3, 5, 6; 328–9:2, 5, 6; 330–1:1, 3, 5, 6; 332–3:1, 4, 6, 7; 334–5:2, 3, 5, 6, 8: 336–7:2, 3, 6, 8 9; 338:2, 3, 4; 339:3; 340–1:3, 6; 346–7:1, 2, 3, 5, 6; 348:2, 3, 4: 350–1:2, 3, 4, 5, 6, 7, 8; 352:3, 5, 6, 7, 8; 360–1:1, 2, 4, 5, 6; 362–5:2, 5, 6, 8, 11, 13, 15; 366–7:2, 4, 5, 6, 7; 368:1, 2, 3, 5; 369:1, 3, 4; 370:1, 3, 4, 5; 375–7:3, 6, 7, 8, 10; 382–3:2, 3, 4, 6; 384–5:5; 390–1:1, 2, 3, 4, 5, 6, 7; 392–3:2, 3, 4, 5, 6, 8; 394–5:1, 2, 3, 4, 5, 6, 7; 400–1:1, 2, 3, 4, 6, 7; 402–3:1, 2, 3, 4, 5, 7, 8; 404–5:2, 3, 5, 6, 8; 406–7:1, 2, 3, 4, 5, 6; 412–13:1, 3, 4, 5; 414–15:1, 2, 3, 4, 7; 422–3:1, 2, 3, 5, 6, 7; 424–5:4, 5, 6, 7, 8; 426–7:1, 2; 428:3, 4, 5; 429:3, 4, 5; 433:1, 3, 4, 5; 444–5:1, 2, 3, 4, 6; 446–7:1, 2, 3, 4; 448–9:1, 2, 3, 4, 5, 6; 450–1:1, 2, 3, 4, 5; 456–7:2, 3, 4, 5, 6, 7; 458–9:3, 4, 6; 460–2:1, 3, 5, 6, 7, 8, 9, 10, 12; 463:1, 3, 4; 467:1; 472–3:7; 478:1, 2, 3, 5; 479–80:8, 9; 482–3:7, 8, 9; 488:2, 3, 4, 5;

The Association for the Preservation of Tennessee Antiquities, Nashville Chapter, 190–1:8

Texas Historical Commission, 188–9:1, 2; 202–3:4; 224–5:8; 246–7:1; 268–73:9, 13; 313:1, 3; 316–17:6; 467:3

Transylvania University, Lexington, Kentucky, The J. Winston Coleman Kentuckiana Collection, Francis Carrick Thomas Library, 84–5:8; 166–7:3; 188–9:5; 193:4; 208:2

United States Department of Housing and Urban Development, 164:5; 192:3; 450–1:8; 479–80:1, 2, 6; 481:3; 482–3:2, 5; 490:5. Chauncey T. Hinman, 479–80:5. David Valdez, 84–5:3

Utah State Historical Society, Historic Preservation Office, 304–5:4

Virginia Historic Landmarks Commission, 162–3:3; 172–3:2; 174:3, 4; 175:2, 4; 208:3; 250–1:1

M. E. Warren, 144–6:8; 150:4

Westchester County Historic Society by permission of The North River Press, Inc. Frank Sanchis. 246–7:4; 414–15:5

Western Reserve Historical Society, 13:1; 15:3; 209:3; 296–7:5; 304–5:5

Wichita/Sedgwick County Historical Museum, Wichita, Kansas, 258–9:2; 460–2:11

State Historical Society of Wisconsin, 446–7:5. Jeff Dean, 332–3:4. E. C. Hamilton, 236–7:6. James A. Sewell, AIA, 216–19:12. Mary Ellen Young, 446–7:7

Index

A NOTE ABOUT THE AUTHORS

VIRGINIA MCALESTER is an honor graduate of Radcliffe College (Architectural Sciences) and attended Harvard Graduate School of Design. She is a founding member and past president of the Historic Preservation League, Inc. (Dallas), and for nine years, was Texas Advisor and a member of the Administrative Committee of the National Trust for Historic Preservation. She is co-author of *The Making of a Historic District: Swiss Avenue*.

LEE MCALESTER, a geologist by profession, is professor at Southern Methodist University and was formerly Dean of the School of Humanities and Sciences there. From 1960 to 1973 he was Professor of Geology at Yale University. He is the author of several widely used introductory textbooks as well as numerous scientific monographs and papers. He has an active hobby interest in architectural history and has been involved in historic preservation in New England, Georgia, and the Southwest.

A NOTE ON THE TYPE

The text of this book was set on the computer in Janson, a direct recutting of type cast from matrices long thought to have been made by the Dutchman Anton Janson, who was a practicing type founder in Leipzig during the years 1668–87. However, it has been conclusively demonstrated that these types are actually the work of Nicholas Kis (1650–1702), a Hungarian, who most probably learned his trade from the master Dutch type founder Dirk Voskens. The type is an excellent example of the influential and sturdy Dutch types that prevailed in England up to the time William Caslon developed his own incomparable designs from them.

Composed by American–Stratford Graphic Services, Inc., Brattleboro, Vermont.
Printed and Bound by The Murray Printing Company, Westford, Massachusetts.
Designed by Anthea Lingeman.